Critical Reading for
College and Beyond

Praise for *Critical Reading for College and Beyond*

"This text will be a great addition to the reading textbook market."

—MAUREEN CONNOLLY, Joliet Junior College

"I am very impressed with this text. Now for the first time [our developmental reading students] will have a 'tool box' to solve their reading problems. It gives them an entire new way to look at reading. It gives them a sense of control."

—LOIS HASSAN, Henry Ford College

"[Critical Reading] is perhaps the most complete freshman reading text I have read. Its strengths lie in the areas of concise and clear explanation of skills and meaning and multiple formats to show students how to apply those skills, [in addition to its] inclusion of technology and Internet resources. Your text will sell itself to any professor who knows his/her discipline well."

—BETH CHILDRESS, Armstrong Atlantic Community College

"This text has been thoughtfully prepared by reading professionals. It offers students a tremendous number of opportunities to engage the text. It offers many opportunities for collaborative learning. The readings are of sufficient range and length to be really useful…The thoroughness of the text, the quality readings, the many opportunities for students to engage the text—these things lead me to praise the text."

—BOB ROGERS, San Antonio College

"I love the interdisciplinary reading selections. I especially think that the longer reading selections will be an enormous benefit to our students."

—VIRGINIA GARRETT, Sinclair Community College

"The webliographies are great! They will be a valuable resource to students."

—DAWN SEDIK, Valencia Community College, West

"The chapter opening vignettes are very good. This is so relevant to students' thoughts and feelings. These are almost word for word what I have heard from my students."

—JUDY MITCHELL, Oklahoma State University

Critical Reading for College and Beyond

Deborah B. Daiek

Schoolcraft College

Nancy M. Anter

Macomb Community College

Boston   Burr Ridge, IL   Dubuque, IA   Madison, WI   New York
San Francisco   St. Louis   Bangkok   Bogotá   Caracas   Kuala Lumpur
Lisbon   London   Madrid   Mexico City   Milan   Montreal   New Delhi
Santiago   Seoul   Singapore   Sydney   Taipei   Toronto

CRITICAL READING FOR COLLEGE AND BEYOND

Published by McGraw-Hill, a business unit of The McGraw-Hill Companies, Inc., 1221 Avenue of the Americas, New York, NY 10020. Copyright © 2004 by The McGraw-Hill Companies, Inc. All rights reserved. No part of this publication may be reproduced or distributed in any form or by any means, or stored in a database or retrieval system, without the prior written consent of The McGraw-Hill Companies, Inc., including, but not limited to, in any network or other electronic storage or transmission, or broadcast for distance learning.

Some ancillaries, including electronic and print components, may not be available to customers outside the United States.

This book is printed on acid-free paper.

4 5 6 7 8 9 0 DOC/DOC 0 9 8 7 6

ISBN-13: 978-0-07-247376-6
ISBN-10: 0-07-247376-2 (student edition)
ISBN-13: 978-0-07-247377-3
ISBN-10: 0-07-247377-0 (annotated instructor's edition)

President of McGraw-Hill Humanities/Social Sciences: *Steve Debow*
Senior sponsoring editor: *Alexis Walker*
Developmental editor: *Gillian Cook*
Executive marketing manager: *David S. Patterson*
Project manager: *Jill Moline*
Production supervisor: *Janean A. Utley*
Designer: *Sharon C. Spurlock/Cassandra Chu*
Supplement producer: *Kathleen Boylan*
Associate photo research coordinator: *Natalia C. Peschiera*
Associate art editor: *Carin C. Yancey*
Art director: *Jeanne Schreiber*
Permissions: *Marty Granahan*
Cover design: *Claire Seng-Niemoeller*
Interior design: *Claire Seng-Niemoeller*
Typeface: *10/12.5 New Aster Roman*
Compositor: *Electronic Publishing Services Inc., NYC*
Printer: *R.R. Donnelley and Sons Inc.*

Library of Congress Cataloging-in-Publication Data

Daiek, Deborah B.
   Critical reading for college and beyond / Deborah B. Daiek, Nancy M. Anter.
    p. cm.
   Includes Bibliographical references and index.
    ISBN 0-07-247376-2 (student ed. : softcover : alk. paper) -- ISBN 0-07-247377-0 (annotated instructor's ed.)
    1. Reading (Higher education) 2. Reading comprehension. 3. College readers. I. Anter, Nancy M. II. Title.
LB2395.3.D35 2004
428.4'071'1--dc21   2003056206

www.mhhe.com

I would like to dedicate the book in memory of my father, Kenneth E. Brooks, who taught me how to think with my heart.

Deborah Daiek

I dedicate this book to Mary D. Pilat, the best teacher I ever had.

Nancy Anter

About the Authors

Deborah B. Daiek earned her B.S. in Education, and an M.A. in Adult Education in the Community College, from Western Michigan University, Kalamazoo, MI. She earned a Ph.D. in Instructional Technology from Wayne State University, Detroit, MI. She has been involved with developmental education and the design and teaching of reading courses for 20 years. She has been president of the Michigan Developmental Education Consortium and of the North Central Reading Association. She is the recipient of MDEC's Outstanding Developmental Educator Award; ACPA's Commission XVI's, Learning Centers in Higher Education, Service Award and Research Award; and received NADE's John Champaign Memorial Award for an Outstanding Developmental Education Program. She has published articles in ACPA's *Learning Assistance Digest, Crosswalks* for Educational Testing Services, and *The Community College Enterprise.* Currently she is serving as the Associate Dean of Academic and Assessment Services at Schoolcraft College, Livonia, Michigan, which provides a wide range of learning assistance services.

Nancy Anter earned her Bachelor of Arts degree in English from the University of Michigan. She earned two Master of Arts degrees from Wayne State University in Detroit, Michigan, one in English education and the other in English, with an emphasis on composition theory. For over 10 years, she has taught high school English, developmental reading and writing, and undergraduate composition, as well as national and local workshops and seminars on learning theory and composition. She has developed programs and taught test preparation for the writing portion of national, graduate-level exams, such as the Medical College Admission Test (MCAT) and the Law School Admission Test (LSAT). She created a test for spoken English proficiency for international employees at Detroit Police Headquarters, which now serves as a model test for other states. In addition, she has developed instructional aids for the Detroit Police Department regarding English proficiency and Detroit city geography. She has been an assistant editor for the University of Michigan Press, and published articles in *The Learning Assistance Digest, American College Personnel Association,* and *Academic Staff News,* Wayne State University. She currently teaches at Macomb Community College in Michigan.

To the Instructor

Critical Reading for College and Beyond is geared to developmental education students who read at the 10th grade-level and above. The text focuses on teaching students critical reading and thinking strategies and how to apply them to college textbooks. Once students have mastered these strategies, they become lifelong tools that can be used in many venues beyond college.

Approach

Critical Reading is written from the perspective of information processing theory, meaning that students are taught how to make sense of information and why specific steps are essential if they intend to remember what they have read. The text is designed to help students gain an awareness of, and control over, their reading and learning strategies by teaching them about relevant theory and processes. It also teaches students how to organize textbook information so that they can remember and access it effectively when needed.

In *Critical Reading* we focus on the importance of metacognition. Teaching students what they know and what they don't know, and how to monitor and adjust their learning, is essential for optimal learning. We believe that students benefit most from explicit critical thinking instruction *if* they are taught *how* critical thinking applies directly to their college textbooks. Research has shown that teaching students to attend to their reading and learning strategies helps them to become problem-solvers for their own reading deficits. They begin to understand why they need to consider using certain strategies rather than others, which strategies work best for them, and how to recognize when they need to try a new approach.

The primary vehicles used to teach metacognition are explicit explanations, modeling and journaling. We explain many reading strategies and show when and how they are useful. We also model the strategies so students can see them at work before trying them. Throughout the text we ask students to write in their learning journals using prompts that help them focus on what they are reading and how they learn. These entries require students to articulate what they have learned and what is still unclear to them in a reading assignment, and challenge them to analyze their study and reading strategies. Regular use of a learning journal can help students to become aware of how, when, and where they study, what areas of weakness they have, and how to develop strategies to address them.

Classroom Assessment Techniques (CATs) are incorporated throughout the text to ensure that learning is taking place and to provide students with prompt feedback when they need help. Instructors can use the Team Up! and Take One Minute CATs to quickly assess students' comprehension of, and ability to use, the reading strategies presented. Students can use the CATs as a self-assessment tool and, more importantly, as a self-monitoring tool. With regular use of the CATs, students begin to recognize and understand their own reading weaknesses and are encouraged to deal with them before continuing on to new strategies. The responsibility for mastery of the subject matter is thus shared between the instructor and student. A third CAT, Muddiest Point, is included in the Instructor's Manual and can be used to evaluate whether students have understood concepts being taught. It can also be used by instructors to assess whether they need to make adjustments in their teaching strategies, such as changing the pace of instruction, or providing additional quizzes.

Modeling and application are the predominant pedagogical teaching techniques we use to introduce new strategies and concepts. Each chapter introduces a more challenging reading strategy and more difficult exercises than the preceding one. This approach provides students with multiple opportunities to practice in-class exercises in groups, with partners and independently. We have found that providing students with the opportunity to work together is an excellent way for them to share their thinking, hear alternative points of view, assume leadership roles and gain confidence as they learn collaboratively.

Organization

Critical Reading has fourteen chapters, each with its own core objective and each overlapping with, and enhancing, the next. Each chapter opens with an advanced organizer in the form of a mind map, chapter goals, and a vocabulary list of important concepts introduced in the chapter. The body of each chapter consists of the following:

- a chapter introduction
- explicit reading instruction
- modeling
- numerous practice reading passages with exercises
- embedded CATs

- longer Practice with Reading passages
- a chapter summary
- a post test

Chapters 1–5, and 11 also include boxes containing test-taking strategies which precede the Practice with Reading passages.

Critical Reading is organized so that it can be covered in one semester and is divided into four parts:

- **Part One: Preparing to Read College Textbooks (Chapters 1–4)** teaches the basic reading strategies students need to become successful readers and covers learning styles, time management, vocabulary and concentration. We believe that concentration, use of time, and memory, often viewed as study skills, are in fact prerequisite reading strategies, and that their inclusion in the text provides less able and less confident students with crucial tools to help them assimilate the more difficult strategies of *Critical Reading*.

- **Part Two: Key Strategies for Reading Comprehension (Chapters 5–10)** builds on the preceding chapters, teaching students the more complex reading strategies they need to identify stated and implied main ideas and details. It also covers textbook methods of organization, how to preview and study material and how to effectively mark textbook information.

- **Part Three: Advanced Strategies for Critical Reading (Chapters 11–14)** teaches students the advanced strategies they need to read and create visual aids, identify and evaluate arguments, and critically assess reading material. The final chapter focuses on evaluating Internet information and provides students with clear guidelines for assessing the relevancy, reliability, credibility and accuracy of Internet sources.

- **Part Four: Application Selections**
  Two longer excerpts, taken from college level sociology and biology textbooks, are included in this section. Application questions for these selections, which allow students to practice, in combination, all the strategies they have learned in the preceding chapters, are available in the online Instructor's Manual.

Critical Reading offers numerous single- and multi-paragraph reading exercises and a variety of high interest academic and popular readings of different levels and lengths. All of the strategies are modeled and discussed, and exercises are designed so students can work independently, in groups, or as an entire class to answer them. The longer Practice with Reading Passages and Post Test selections include pre- and post-reading questions that test comprehension, vocabulary and use of the reading strategies taught in each chapter. They use a variety of objective, short answer and open-ended question types to test students' comprehension and critical thinking skills.

Readings

Because developmental students are often reluctant readers, we have included an array of interesting readings by many well-known authors in an effort to pique the interest of your students. Some authors your students will recognize are:

- Stephen King
- Dennis Miller
- The Dalai Lama
- Jay Leno
- John Grisham
- Christopher Darden

- Billy Graham
- Rush Limbaugh
- Anna Quindlen
- Mother Teresa
- Dr. Laura
- Sister Souljah

Some of the reading topics in this text are unconventional. The elation, anger, and sometimes shock that results from delving into these topics will release your students from the common misconception that developmental reading is boring and irrelevant to their lives. Although some of the readings are unabashedly direct, clearly biased, and include an occasional off-color word, all of them are well-written and thought-provoking. Topics sure to engage and challenge your students are:

- witchcraft
- shoplifting
- foot binding
- love
- talk shows
- homosexuality

- compassion
- religion
- prostitution
- bathrooms and wheelchairs
- lizards, ants, and other beasts

Sources for all the readings are listed with them, so when students find excerpts they enjoy, they can follow up and read more. Titles that will get your students' attention are:

- *That Takes Ovaries!*
- *The Highly Selective Dictionary for the Extraordinarily Literate*
- *The Life and Times of the Last Kid Picked*
- "Why the Young Kill"
- "It's a Bird, It's a Plane, It's Plagiarism Buster!"
- *Brothel: Mustang Ranch and Its Women*

- *Woe Is I: The Grammarphobe's Guide in Plain English*
- "Don't Subcontract bin Laden Hunt"
- "Lifting the Veil on Sex Slavery"
- *Hating Whitey and Other Progressive Causes*

Many of the reading selections in this text are from textbooks. We have used material from many disciplines so that a wide range of students can see how the reading strategies taught in this text can transfer to their specific coursework. Some of the different academic disciplines we have taken excerpts from are:

- history
- mathematics
- chemistry
- political science
- biology
- sociology

- psychology
- law
- medicine
- business
- English literature
- gerontology

Supplements to Critical Reading
Print Resources

Annotated Instructor's Edition (ISBN 0-07-247377-0)   The Annotated Instructor's Edition contains the full text of the student edition of the book, complete with answers and marginal notes that provide useful teaching tips, links to relevant material in the Instructor's Manual, and explanations of the goals of various features and specific activities.

Digital Resources

Critical Reading **Website (www.mhhe.com/daiek)**   For students, this website offers additional exercises, links for further research and to other supplemental resources for learning. For instructors,the website includes the full text of an **Instructor's Manual**, which offers sample syllabi, tips for classroom applications of text material, links to professional resources, and more. **Note:** Instructors will need a password in order to access instructor-specific material, including the Instructor's Manual. Please contact your McGraw-Hill sales representative for more information, or e-mail **english@mcgraw-hill.com.**

PageOut!   helps instructors create graphically pleasing and professional web pages for their courses, in addition to providing classroom management, collaborative learning, and content management tools. PageOut! is **FREE** to adopters of McGraw-Hill textbooks and learning materials. Learn more at **http:/www.mhhe.com/pageout/.**

AllWrite! 2.0   is an interactive, browser-based grammar and editing tutorial program that provides an online handbook,comprehensive diagnostic pretests and posttests, plus extensive practice exercises in every area. (User's Guide with Password for Online Access: 0-07-244992-6; also available on CD-ROM: 0-07-236207-3)

Please consult your local McGraw-Hill representative or consult McGraw-Hill's web site at **http://www.mhhe.com/catalogs/hss/english/** for more information on McGraw-Hill texts.

Acknowledgments

Thanks to Mr. Paul Moten, sales rep, who put the project in motion. We would like to thank our former editor, Sarah Touborg for believing in this project and working so hard to make it happen. We are deeply indebted to our Developmental Editor, Gill Cook, whose expertise, infinite patience, and wonderful sense of humor provided the energy that kept this project going. Special thanks go to Alexis Walker, Senior Sponsoring Editor, who readily added her talent during our desperate moments, and Marty Granahan, Permissions Editor, who gracefully handled the mountain of permission requests. We also want to express particular appreciation to Sharon Spurlock, Designer, and Claire Seng-Niemoeller, whose creative abilities helped make our vision of how the book should look a reality. Finally, Jill Moline, Project Manager, has our heartfelt appreciation for her indefatigable patience with our many changes to the project and her wonderful ideas for making those changes work.

We are so grateful for the support of our colleagues at Schoolcraft College and Macomb Community College, especially Donna Clack, Christine Rejniak, Linda Talbert, and to our NADE and MDEC colleagues and friends who have encouraged us along the way. We also owe a great deal to the students who helped shape and guide this text, especially Keith Binkowski, Alan Byrnes, Andrea Farmer, and Serja Goram.

We would like to thank our reviewers for their constructive criticism, perceptive and helpful suggestions, and supportive comments. We are grateful to:

Karin S. Alderfer	Miami-Dade Community College, FL
Elisabeth Bass	Camden County College, NJ
Beth Childress	Armstrong Atlantic State University, GA
Maureen Connolly	Joliet Junior College, IL
Gretchen M. Cupp	Yuba College, CA
Nancy Fallis	North Iowa Area Community College, IA
JoAnn Foriest	Prairie State College, IL

Virginia B. Garrett	Sinclair Community College, OK
Barbara Grossman	Essex County College, NJ
Lois Hassan	Henry Ford Community College, MI
Marian Helms	College of Southern Idaho, ID
Carol Helton	College of Southern Idaho, ID
Lesa Hildebrand	Triton College, IL
Susie Khirallah-Johnston	Tyler Junior College, TX
Janice McIntyre	Kansas City Community College, KS
Judith K. Mitchell	Oklahoma State University, OK
Bob Rogers	San Antonio College, TX
Dawn Sedik	Valencia Community College, FL
Lorrie Sheehy	Pima Community College, East Campus, AZ
Shirley Smart	Lake Superior State University, MI
Carol Snelson	University of Arkansas at Little Rock, AR
Jane Stilling	Guilford Technical Community College, NC
Pearl Williams	Estrella Mountain Community College, AZ

We would also like to thank our friends and families for their love, encouragement and confidence in us. Deborah Daiek would specifically like to thank: Karl Daiek, Dave Daiek, Andy Daiek, Ben Daiek, Jacqueline Brooks, Joe and Loretta Daiek, Susan and Landis Bryant, and Sifu Robert Brown who taught her the meaning of patience and perseverance. Nancy Anter would specifically like to thank: Mark Anter, in Tech Support; Thomas Anter and Julia Anter, for their love and teasing; Katherine Tombolesi; Clyde Manion; Thomas Manion; Mary O'Dowd; Laura Srinivasan; Clyde Manion, Sr.; Margaret and Peter Anter; Jesse Fuchs and his family; Mary Farmer; Kathleen Coleman and Elizabeth Masserang.

DEBORAH DAIEK AND NANCY ANTER

To The Student

"Passive learning is an oxymoron; there is no such thing."
PATRICIA CROSS

Never before in our society has reading and the ability to evaluate textual information been so important. Knowing how to read critically and effectively will improve your learning skills and prepare you for the world of work. This textbook has been designed to teach you the reading and comprehension strategies you need to be successful in college and beyond.

Many students are afraid to speak up in class because they feel as though they are the "only ones" not understanding a concept. As you will read, many students share the same concerns and frustrations as you do. We hope this textbook will provide you with the answers you need and the courage to share your voice in class. Learning is a process of asking questions. The only "foolish" question is the one not asked.

You will find that your academic success equals the amount of work you are willing to dedicate to it. The fact that you are in college indicates you are intelligent, but intelligence alone is not enough. Academic success boils down to using your time sensibly, hard work, and the application of effective learning strategies. Use this book and apply the strategies taught. Do the work, and you will benefit from the results of your efforts in class, in college and in your job.

Special Features of *Critical Reading*

Critical Reading for College and Beyond is divided into four parts. Each part will teach you specific reading strategies and prepare you for the more advanced strategies that follow it. Each new strategy is modeled, and there are ample exercises provided to allow you to learn and practice them individually, and as a member of a group. Throughout each chapter, you will monitor your understanding as you read and learn using journaling and the assessment techniques of Take One Minute and Team Up!

Part Four consists of two longer reading selections taken from sociology and biology textbooks. You can apply the reading strategies taught in this book to these selections and see how these strategies change the way you read and think.

Part One: Preparing to Read College Textbooks (Chapters 1–4)

This section teaches you the basic reading and learning strategies you need to become an effective reader:

- concentration strategies
- learning style preferences
- vocabulary development
- memory techniques
- time management skills

Part Two: Key Strategies for Reading Comprehension (Chapters 5–10)

Part Two builds on the skills you've learned in Part One by introducing more complex reading strategies to use in combination with them. This section will help you:

- identify main ideas
- differentiate between major and minor supporting details
- read inferentially to identify implied main ideas
- recognize textbook methods of organization
- use the Preview, Study-Read, Review method to read textbook material
- effectively mark textbook information

Part Three: Advanced Strategies for Critical Reading (Chapters 11–14)

In this part, you practice applying everything you have learned in Parts One and Two, and learn advanced reading strategies, which include:

- how to understand and create visual aids
- how to identify and evaluate arguments
- how to read critically at different levels of understanding
- how to evaluate Internet sources

Part Four: Application Selections

Part Four consists of two longer reading selections taken from sociology and biology textbooks. Your instructor will use these to provide you with practice in applying, in combination, all the reading strategies taught in this book.

Built-in Learning Aids

Chapter Introduction

These pages include a **mind map** that provides you with an overview of each chapter and prepares your brain for active learning, the first step toward improving your current learning and reading abilities.

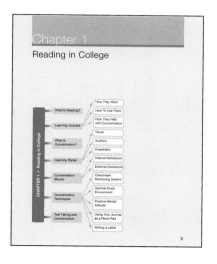

Chapter Table of Contents

These pages list the topics covered in the chapter and shows how they are organized. They also include a **Chapter Goals** section to show you what you will learn in each chapter, and a **Chapter Vocabulary** section which lists important terms highlighted and explained in the chapter.

Chapter Opening Page

Chapters open with **vignettes** describing reading problems faced by real students. Each chapter has major headings and subheadings to make the chapter's organization clear.

Learning Journals

Throughout this text you will be asked to write in your journal after you have been introduced to new concepts. Doing this will help you focus on how you learn, what you already know, what you have learned, and what is still unclear to you.

Take One Minute

These exercises allow you to reflect upon what you have just learned, and provide you and your instructor with instant feedback on whether or not you understand a concept.

Team Up!

These exercises provide opportunities for you to work with other students. They encourage you to think out loud, hear how and what other students think about a topic, and work as a productive and effective team member.

Test-Taking Tips

Chapters 1–5, and 11 include a box with test-taking tips relevant to the topics covered in the chapter.

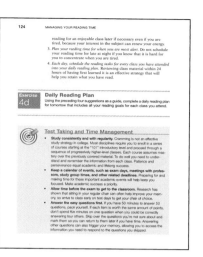

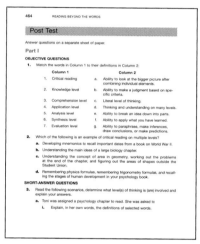

Post Tests

Post Tests are included at the end of each chapter. They are designed to test your understanding of what you have learned, your knowledge of chapter vocabulary, and your ability to apply new skills to longer reading selections. Questions include multiple-choice, true/false, fill-in-the-blank, and short answer and open-ended questions that require you to practice critical thinking skills.

Website Sources for Additional Practice

At the end of each chapter you will find a list of websites you can access to learn more about the topics you have been studying and to practice the reading strategies you have learned.

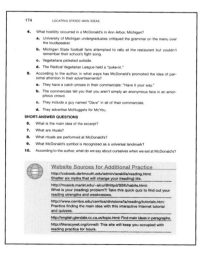

Reading Selections
for Chapters 1–13

Practice with Reading Passages

The longer reading selections in Chapters 1–13 represent a wide variety of the kind of introductory-level textbooks, news magazines, and novels you will be expected to read in college. They have been chosen because they are interesting, informative and will allow you to practice the skills you have learned, and will need, to be successful in your college career and beyond. Each reading selection is accompanied by the following exercises:

Prepare to Read

Introductory exercises designed to get you thinking about what you are going to read and how it connects to what you already know about the topic.

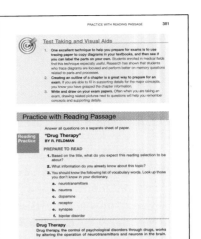

Check Your Understanding

Post-reading exercises designed to let you know whether you have correctly understood the reading selection, and can apply the concepts you just learned in combination with those you have learned in earlier chapters.

Application Selections

There are two, long textbook excerpts in Part Four. These selections allow you to practice, in combination, all the strategies you have learned in the preceding chapters. Questions for these selections will be provided by your instructor.

We wish you success and happiness, in college and beyond!

DEBORAH DAIEK AND NANCY ANTER

Brief Contents

Contents

Part Two
Key Strategies for Reading Comprehension   135

Part Four
Application Selections   491

Critical Reading for
College and Beyond

Part One

Preparing to Read College Textbooks

Chapter 1

Reading in College

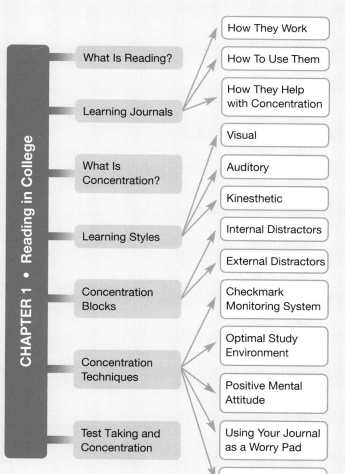

CHAPTER 1 • Reading in College

- What Is Reading?
- Learning Journals
  - How They Work
  - How To Use Them
  - How They Help with Concentration
- What Is Concentration?
- Learning Styles
  - Visual
  - Auditory
  - Kinesthetic
- Concentration Blocks
  - Internal Distractors
  - External Distractors
- Concentration Techniques
  - Checkmark Monitoring System
  - Optimal Study Environment
  - Positive Mental Attitude
- Test Taking and Concentration
  - Using Your Journal as a Worry Pad
  - Writing a Letter

Chapter Contents

Chapter Goals

In this chapter you will learn:

- What reading is.
- How effective journaling helps you read better.
- What concentration is.
- What is involved in active reading and learning.
- Techniques for improving your concentration while reading.

Chapter Vocabulary

As you read, note these words and phrases which represent important concepts from the chapter and will be in **boldface** type. Make sure you understand them before the post test at the end of the chapter.

reading	**learning style**	**external distracter**
learning journal	**internal distracter**	**checkmark monitoring**
concentration	**worry pad**	**system**

Several students were interviewed during their freshman orientation at Schoolcraft College in Michigan. They were asked to describe their reading strategies and to report how much they read while attending high school. Seventy percent said that they were not aware of using any particular reading strategy. Ninety-seven percent said they didn't even have to read their textbooks in high school; attending class was always enough.

What is Reading?

All of us read every day, but what exactly is reading? Take five minutes to write down *your* definition of reading.

Here are some of the things you may have written:

- Reading is a form of communication, using written language or symbols (text).
- Reading is two-way communication between an author and a reader.
- Reading is interpretation and understanding.
- Reading is a process (processes).
- Reading is thinking.

All of these responses are correct. Written words are meaningless if you do not understand, or think about, what an author is saying. You can look at the pages of books written in German, Chinese, Greek, or Russian, but you will not be able to read them unless you are familiar with and understand those languages. The same is true of college textbooks. **Reading** is an *active process* that depends on both an author's ability to convey meaning using words and your ability to create meaning from them. To read successfully, you need to constantly connect what you already know about the information to the words the author has written.

The average student who reads a book without using any learning strategies will remember only 10 percent of what she read two weeks later. However, if she actively works with the reading material, using the strategies presented in this textbook, she will be able to remember up to 90 percent of what she read after two weeks. Also, once she learns *how* to study and combines those skills with reading strategies, she will be able to achieve an almost 100 percent recall rate. The learning pyramid in Figure 1.1 illustrates how using many different strategies to learn information dramatically increases your ability to retain what you have learned.

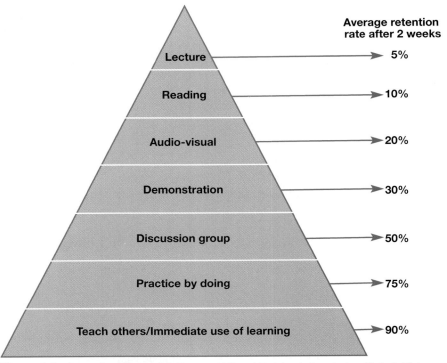

Figure 1.1 **Learning Pyramid** Source: National Training Laboratories, Bethel, Maine

Your ability to read college-level texts can be greatly enhanced if you learn, practice, and apply specific reading strategies. Not only will you notice that your college performance improves, but these techniques will help you *beyond* college in your chosen profession as the ability to read critically is rapidly becoming one of the top criteria for employment. To ensure that you understand and can use these reading strategies well, this book has built-in assessment techniques. Using them will immediately show what concepts you understand and which require further clarification. Each is identified by a specific symbol:

 Team Up! This technique requires you to work with one or more students in your class, sharing your thoughts regarding the concepts you are learning. This allows you to see how other students learn and think; more importantly, it lets you know if you adequately understand the concepts being presented.

 Take One Minute. This technique requires you to think about what you have just learned and quickly demonstrate that you understand it.

Learning Journal. This technique helps you analyze reading strategies and assess your learning. Using a learning journal helps you remember 80–90 percent of what you read.

Learning Journals

Writing in your **learning journal** helps you to think on paper about what you have read, to identify what you do (and do not) understand, and to explore how you think. As you write, use your journal to connect new material you have learned from your textbooks to information you already know about a subject. Learning journals also help you to apply, monitor, and amend your critical reading strategies. Knowing which strategies work for you—and which don't—is essential for college reading success.

Take One Minute

Take one minute to reflect on how you define reading and why using a learning journal could help you to become a better, more efficient reader.

How Learning Journals Work

Throughout this book you will be asked to write in your learning journal, using prompts that will help you focus on *what* you read. These prompts are free-writing exercises that you complete during and after reading assignments. Your entries will help you determine how well you have read your textbook material by requiring you to explain:

- What you have learned.
- What is still unclear to you.

In addition to writing about your reading, you will also be asked to write about *how* you learn. These journal prompts, free-writing exercises you complete after reading, will challenge you to analyze your study and reading strategies by asking you to explain:

- How you have learned from the reading.
- What else you know about the topic of the reading.
- What reading or study problems you still face.

For example, when one of your instructors returns a homework assignment to you, you can summarize his or her comments and use them to explore ways to improve your performance in the future. If you do well on an exam, you can make a short list of the reading and study strategies that you used to prepare for it. If you do not do well, you can assess why not and list the areas you need to work on.

When you use a journal regularly, you will find that you benefit in other ways too. You will have a greater interest in your textbooks because you are not just passively taking in what is on the page but are interacting with it. The journal will make you aware of how you study, when you study, and where you study. Changes you make, based on this information, will improve your concentration, which in turn, will help you better understand your textbook material.

Using Your Learning Journal

Purchase a divided spiral notebook to use as a learning journal. It should have enough divisions so that you can use one for each class. Begin each journal entry by writing the date on the top right side of the page. If your journal entry is in response to a reading assignment, write the title (or the chapter number) of the book you are reading and include page numbers in case you have to refer to them later. Use the journal prompts provided throughout this book to begin writing about what you have read and how you think about it. As you learn more about how you read and the reading and study challenges you face, you can start to create your own journal prompts that target your specific reading and study difficulties.

How a Learning Journal Helps You Develop Concentration

Your first journal entries will focus on concentration. Many college students complain that one of the reasons they are not performing to their full academic potential is that they are unable to concentrate as they read. Tony is one of them:

> I'm a good student. I get mostly Bs for my courses so I know I'm doing O.K. The problem is, it's really hard for me to concentrate on my textbooks. I read for hours and when I'm finished I can hardly remember anything I've read. I like my classes and I want to learn, but I just can't seem to concentrate. I know if I could concentrate better, I'd learn more and do better.

By practicing and using concentration strategies, Tony could control how he pays attention as he reads and perform better in college, and later in the workplace. Before you begin work with your journal, assess your current knowledge of concentration by completing the following survey. The results will tell how much you know about concentration as a reading strategy and what new information you would benefit from learning.

Exercise 1a

Concentration Survey

Read each of the following statements and respond to them based on your *current* reading habits. In the space provided, write **yes** if the statement correctly describes you, or **no** if it does not.

Concentration Survey

_____ **1.** I know that concentration is a skill that can be learned.

_____ **2.** I have a study area, complete with study supplies, and this area is used only for studying.

_____ **3.** I try to concentrate as I read, but my mind usually drifts to other things, such as bills I have to pay or people I have to call.

_____ **4.** If I get angry, I am unable to concentrate on my reading.

_____ **5.** I know how to minimize all distractions.

_____ **6.** I cannot read unless my house, or study environment, is immaculate.

_____ **7.** I have a system to let others know when I am reading and that I do not want to be disturbed.

_____ **8.** I lose concentration easily when I am bored with what I'm reading.

Team Up!

With one or two other classmates, discuss your responses to the concentration survey. Share what you currently do to improve your concentration.

What Is Concentration?

Just like a blossom, bright colored but scentless: a well-spoken word is fruitless when not carried out.—BUDDHIST SAYING

Concentration is not an accident of good fortune that happens to only some lucky students. It is a skill that can be learned with patience and perseverance. According to Sam Horn, an expert on the subject, concentrating is the ability to focus exclusively on a project and to ignore *all else*. Well-known for his ability to focus, Hindu Swami Sri Yuketeswar said that concentration is simply "making the mind behave." Peter Drucker, a prolific writer on subjects relating to society, economics, politics, and management, has been quoted as saying, "Concentration is having the courage to impose on time, people, and events your decision as to what is important and what must come first."

The concentration techniques described in this chapter will help you develop positive study strategies, which will make you a more effective reader. You will use your journal to apply these strategies, track their effectiveness, and make adjustments as needed. Like any reading strategy, concentration takes practice before it will kick in automatically every time you open a textbook. With hard work and determination, you can train yourself to concentrate, even when what you are reading seems boring or tedious.

The first step in this process is to recognize what blocks your concentration. When, where, and how you read affect how well you concentrate, so keep track of this information in your journal every time you read. Then, if you don't perform as well as you would have liked in a class, read your journal to see what you were doing. This will help you learn what times, places, and strategies work best for you. If you find that your current study habits are not working for you, *change them so they do.*

Learning with Purpose

Learning with purpose occurs when you actively engage with what you are reading. This is another important step in developing good concentration habits because the more actively involved you are in reading, the less you will be distracted. The reading strategies taught in this textbook focus on active learning and will be described in greater detail in future chapters. They include:

- Previewing your reading assignments to get an idea of what you will be reading about.
- Asking questions and trying to locate the answers to them as you read.
- Connecting previously learned information to new information.
- Outlining chapter or lecture notes to see how ideas are related.
- Creating diagrams to "map out" your understanding of information.
- Noting the headings and titles that provide the organization for each chapter.
- Reading other sources on the topic you are studying, especially if you are unfamiliar with it.

Exercise 1b

Active and Passive Learning Strategies

Indicate in the space provided whether you think each of the following activities is an active (A) or passive (P) learning strategy and explain why. The first one is modeled for you:

MODEL **1.** Copying down everything your professor says. _____*P*_____

Most professors don't want or expect you to write down everything they say. Active learners listen intently and choose carefully what to take notes on.

2. Revising lecture notes. _____

_____

_____

3. Reviewing sections of your textbook by summarizing and reciting information. _____

_____

_____

4. Reading each chapter straight through. _____

_____

_____

5. Always begin reading by previewing each chapter and developing questions to help you focus. _____

_____

_____

6. Testing yourself on the information in your notes. _____

_____

_____

Team Up!

Discuss your answers to Exercise 1b with the members of your group. If your group decides that a listed activity is a passive learning strategy, change it so that it becomes an active learning strategy.

Now that you have a better understanding of active versus passive learning, discuss how you currently learn new information. Do you tend to rely on active or passive learning strategies?

Learning Styles

Another way to develop effective study habits and increase your concentration level is to learn about yourself and your preferred **learning style.** Most of us use all of the different learning styles to a greater or lesser extent, but we tend to prefer one of them. Most of what we learn comes from what we *hear* (*auditory learning*) in lectures or on audiotapes; *see* (*visual learning*) through reading or watching people, videotapes, or television; or *touch and do* (*kinesthetic learning*) by practicing techniques, drawing maps, creating outlines, or making models. Identifying your preferred learning style makes it easier for you to concentrate. For example, if you are primarily a visual learner, you might find it easier to understand and remember a Shakespearean play if you watch a performance of it. Knowing your preferred learning style allows you to identify and strengthen the learning styles you find more challenging. It is also the first step toward achieving your maximum reading potential, because your learning style remains the same no matter what subject area you are studying.

Learning Styles Inventory

To discover your preferred learning styles access the website **www. varklearn.com.** (If you do not have a computer, your instructor will provide you with a printed copy of this exercise.) Read the introduction on learning styles, and think about what your primary learning style is; then complete the "Questionnaire."

After you have determined your preferred learning style, read the following lists of useful learning strategies for different learning styles. You can use these aids to strengthen your preferred learning style or to improve weaker ones. Becoming proficient in all three styles will increase your learning capacity because you will be able to process information in many different ways. (Adapted from www.varklearn.com)

VISUAL	AUDITORY	KINESTHETIC
Use guided imagery.	Listen to tapes. Tape your notes.	Pace as you study.
Form pictures in your mind.	Watch documentaries.	Physically "do it"—hands on.
Use notebooks.	Speak about your subject.	Role play.
See parts of words.	Sound out words.	Pretend to teach the subject.

VISUAL	AUDITORY	KINESTHETIC
Watch movies on subjects.	Use rhymes	Write lists repeatedly.
Use color codes.	Have discussions.	Use notecards.
Use flow charts.	Explain your notes.	Projects.
Underline in color.		
Draw pictures.		Create pictures.
Use cue words.	Use word links.	Follow your reading with your finger.
Use study cards.	Tape-record your studying.	Practice by repeated motion.
Use charts, graphs, and maps.	Use oral directions.	Take notes and create pictures.
Draw on/use drawings.	Talk and listen with a partner.	Stretch and move in your chair.
Use exhibits.	Use rhythmic sounds.	Ride a stationary bike while reading.
Use photographs.	Listen carefully.	Put your feet in a tub of sand while reading.
Use mind maps and acrostics.	Talk to yourself.	Dance as you study.
Select courses that are reading-centered.	Read aloud.	Select project-driven courses.
	Select lecture-centered courses	

Learning Journal

Look at the strategies listed under your preferred learning style, and free-write about specific ways you could use five of them. Then pick one strategy from each of the other two lists and describe how you could use those.

Discovering Your Concentration Blocks

Another important way to improve your concentration is to recognize what distracts you when you are reading. There are two kinds of distracters: internal and external. **Internal distracters** come from inside you.

Preoccupation with your new girlfriend, worry about your rent and tuition bills for next semester, or excitement about an upcoming vacation can all break your concentration. **External distracters** come from your environment and can include television, loud music, constant phone calls, or unexpected visitors.

Before you can tackle the distractions that block your concentration, you need to know what they are. Exercise 1c will help you develop a list of the distracters you most often have trouble with.

Exercise 1c	**Distracters**

On a separate sheet of paper, make a list of your common distracters. Some possible internal distracters are: boredom, fatigue, mental disorganization, perfectionism, money problems, unclear goals, or family problems. Some possible external distracters are: the telephone, television, noise, conversation, beautiful weather, friends, or campus activity.

Five Techniques for Improving Your Concentration

Now that you know which distracters block your concentration, here are some techniques that will help you to combat them.

Technique #1: Using the Checkmark Monitoring System

This technique will help you as you read, especially if you are distracted by internal concerns such as anxiety, anticipation of an upcoming event, romance, or boredom.

The **checkmark monitoring system** helps you monitor how many times you lose your concentration as you read. Once you become aware of when you lose your concentration, you can make a conscious decision to refocus your attention back to your studies and reduce the number of times your mind wanders. For example, if you are reading a history textbook and find yourself thinking about an upcoming date, the checkmark system can help you purposely redirect your attention away from your weekend plans and back to your history text. You cannot attend to both your history text and your social life simultaneously.

Here is how you use the checkmark monitoring system:

1. Start reading a textbook assignment. Every time you lose your concentration, make a check on a piece of paper.

2. After you have finished 50 minutes of reading, count how many checks you have on the paper. This number will be your baseline.

3. As you practice the other concentration improvement techniques in this chapter, periodically use the checkmark monitoring system to assess how effective each technique is for you. As the number of checkmarks decreases, you will know that your concentration is improving.

By keeping track of your concentration behaviors in your journal, you will not only reduce the number of times you lose focus, but you will also learn your concentration limit—that is, when it is time to stop and take a break. Most students need to take a short break after about an hour, though some prefer to read in two-hour blocks and others for only 45 minutes at a time. Completing Exercise 1d will help you learn what works for you.

Exercise 1d	**Finding Your Concentration Baseline**

In this exercise you will use the checkmark monitoring system to find out how long you actually stay focused when you are reading. Write the results in your journal.

1. Pick a textbook that you are using this semester. Read the text for 50 minutes, monitoring your concentration, and then take a 10-minute break. Use this measurement as your baseline. For example, if you lose your concentration four times during the first 50-minute reading episode, aim for fewer than four times during the next one. By actively attending to your reading, you will lose your concentration less often.

2. Read the text for another 50 minutes, again monitoring your concentration, and compare the two reading episodes. Did your concentration improve during the second episode? Record your results in your journal.

Here is a journal entry from a community college student who is learning the checkmark technique:

> I read my chemistry chapter for 50 minutes and lost concentration a total of 17 times. I realize I daydream a lot while I read. And not only that, I daydream for minutes at a time before I notice that I'm turning pages that I don't remember reading. By using the checkmark technique, I was able to stop my daydreaming instantly because I had to put a checkmark in my journal

*each time I lost my concentration. I also wasted less time day-
dreaming because after I wrote my checkmark, I began reading
again. The second time I read I had only 10 checkmarks.*

Technique #2: Creating a Study Environment

This technique is especially helpful if you have difficulty with external distracters such as telephone calls, television, or family and friends. It is also
helpful for internal distracters like perfectionism or mental disorganization.

One way you can avoid these distracters is to create a study environment
that is conducive to concentration. Choose a space without a telephone,
where you can organize your study materials so they are easily accessible.
Ask family members and friends not to disturb you when you are studying. By taking these steps you can avoid many of the distracters you normally have to contend with. What makes a good study environment varies
from student to student, but here are some useful tips to keep in mind:

Seven Tips for Creating a Successful Study Environment

1. *Do not read homework for college in bed;* you will fall asleep quickly,
   even if you are not tired.
2. *Avoid reading in the social areas of your house or apartment,* such as
   the living room or family room. Instead, place your desk in another
   room in your house, or try studying at the library.
3. *Use a chair that is firm and not too comfortable.* You want to be
   alert, but not completely relaxed.
4. *Make sure you have enough light in your study area.* Reading in a
   dimly lit area can cause eyestrain and make you tire faster.
5. *Collect all the study materials you need,* such as paper, pens, books,
   and notebooks, *before* you begin to read. Having to break from
   reading to hunt down a calculator or an eraser can be distracting.
6. *Turn off the television.*
7. *Invest in an answering machine* so you do not have to answer the
   phone while you are studying.

Learning Journal

Describe your current study environment in your journal. Based on what you
have just read, explain how you could improve your concentration during reading by changing your study environment.

Technique #3: Creating a Positive Mental Attitude

This technique is especially helpful if you have difficulty with external distracters such as telephone calls; family and friends, and internal distracters such as romance, perfectionism, or mental disorganization.

In addition to creating the best physical environment for studying, you must also create a positive mental attitude toward studying to have the best chance of successful reading. You can create a positive mental state using these steps:

Five Steps for Creating a Positive Mental Attitude

1. *Discover your best study time.* Try reading at different times of the day and evening, and record the results in your journal. You will be amazed at the information you discover about yourself.

2. *Read the required material for your most difficult or least familiar subject first.* If you save the most difficult subject for last, you may never get to it because you are too tired and less able to concentrate.

3. *Wear a favorite sweatshirt, hat, or other item of clothing.* Wearing a favorite item and then studying serves two "concentration-friendly" purposes: You create a psychological set so every time you put on the item, your mind will know that it is time to concentrate on reading; when others see you wearing your "homework hat" or "study sweatshirt," they will know that you should not be disturbed.

4. *Preview your reading assignment before beginning to read it.* Read the title, headings, subheadings, any highlighted vocabulary words, and the summary (if one is provided). Previewing your reading assignment helps you mentally prepare for what you are about to read. After previewing, think about your reading; ask yourself what you already know about the subject. As you read, try to connect what you are learning with what you already know.

5. *Plan a study reward for a good study session.* You should make the reward positive and fun. Watch a favorite show on TV, call a friend on the phone, read a novel, or go out with friends and family— whatever gives you joy!

Here is a journal entry from a community college student that illustrates how she determined the best study environment and mind-set for her.

> I am reading a text from my biology class and using the checkmark monitoring system to see how well I concentrate. I set the timer for 50 minutes. When it went off I found I had lost my concentration 15 times. I started this at home around 3:30 p.m.

Between the kids playing, the dogs barking, and the telephone ringing, being able to concentrate was pretty much impossible.

Now I am reading the same text but it's nighttime. In a 50-minute period I had only three checkmarks, but I also fell asleep before I finished reading. I can remember only about a quarter of what I read.

Third try and I am at the library in one of the cubicles. When the timer went off this time I counted 10 checkmarks. I tried again but set the timer for 40 minutes and found I had only 5 checkmarks. After a 10-minute break I read for first 30 minutes and then 35 minutes. Both times I lost my concentration only twice. So I think my baseline for really understanding what I have read and not losing concentration is 30—35 minutes.

My current mental environment is quite cluttered. I have so many things to do and too little time to do them in. I have found I prefer to read in the early evenings, just before dusk, or early mornings, as the sun starts to rise. I think I can improve my current mental environment by making a schedule of things that need to get done and then prioritizing them so I am not always worrying about how to fit everything in.

Take One Minute

On a separate sheet of paper, describe a time when you were so focused on what you were doing that you forgot about the world around you and lost track of time. Explain why you think this happened. Then describe ways to improve your concentration and explain why that is important.

Learning Journal

Describe your current mental environment. When do you prefer to read? What do you usually read first? Do you reward yourself? If so, how? In your journal, explain how you could improve your concentration during reading by changing your current mental environment.

Technique #4: Using Your Journal as a Worry Pad

This technique is especially helpful if you are distracted by internal concerns such as personal problems, financial problems, or anxiety or the external distracter of household chores.

A **worry pad** is where you can write down your worries so you can focus on other things. For example, you may begin studying and quickly become distracted by stray thoughts like the due date on your credit card bill, the dishes piled up on the counter, or the argument you just had with your roommate. Rather than stopping to solve these problems immediately, write them down in your journal and postpone dealing with them until after you finish reading. You will then find it easier to keep your attention focused on your studies.

Technique #5: Writing a Letter

This technique is especially helpful if you are distracted by internal concerns such as romance, anger, excitement, personal problems, or anxiety.

Personal concerns often seem to become particularly noticeable right before a big exam or when you are overwhelmed with reading assignments. Another way to refocus your thoughts back to your studies is to write a letter. In this letter, include everything that distracts you; be as specific as possible. When you are done, throw it away and begin studying. The act of writing down your preoccupations and throwing the paper away creates the psychological effect of throwing your preoccupations away, at least temporarily. It will not remove the distractions forever, but it will allow you to concentrate on the task at hand.

Exercise 1e

Write a Letter

Write a letter about someone or something that is bothering you. Write down everything you want to say, then throw the letter away. Wait at least two hours and then write in your journal about whether this technique helped you to concentrate. As silly as it sounds, it is really quite effective.

Test Taking and Concentration

Give yourself the best possible chance to shine by following these basic guidelines on test days:

1. **Avoid cramming.** Cramming is the enemy of concentration. If you try to cram several weeks' worth of information into one day of studying, you will not be able to concentrate on each point long enough to thoroughly understand it. During a test, your confidence will be shaken as you

scramble to answer the questions correctly. Study every day for each subject that you had that day. (See Chapter 4 for developing a study schedule.)

2. **Get a good night's sleep.** A rested brain concentrates better.

3. **Stay hydrated.** Drink a glass of water before the test. Being well hydrated helps you think more clearly.

4. **Eat breakfast.** A cup of coffee and some candy do not constitute a good breakfast. What you really need on the morning of a test is a combination of complex carbohydrates and protein; peanut butter on whole wheat toast with a glass of orange juice is a good choice. Avoid large quantities of caffeine, sugar, and fat, and don't eat too much or you will feel sleepy.

Create a Positive Mental Environment

1. **Decide that you will get the most out of each class session and from your instructors.** Thinking this way increases your ability to concentrate in the classroom and do well in exams.

2. **Wear your "homework hat" or "study sweatshirt."** These items tell your mind its time to concentrate.

3. **Stay calm!** If you have prepared well for an exam, you can be confident that you will do well. Taking a few deep breaths right before the test starts helps you to relax and focus your concentration.

4. **Read all of the directions.** It is important to know exactly what you are being asked to do. Listen to any verbal test instructions very carefully and be sure that you understand any last-minute changes the instructor makes.

5. **Do the easy questions first.** This will help build your confidence. When tackling more difficult questions, don't panic if the answers don't immediately come to mind. Relax. Breathe. And silently talk yourself through the question and its solution.

6. **Don't change your answers unless you are absolutely sure they are wrong**. If you're unsure…leave them alone!

7. **Don't be concerned if other students finish before you do.** Set a pace that is comfortable for you.

8. **Don't take things too seriously.** A test is just a test. If you fail a test, it doesn't mean you are a failure. It just means that you need to try different approaches to how you study.

Create a Positive Physical Environment

1. **Arrive early on test days.** Research has shown that sitting in your regular seat can often help improve your memory and concentration.

2. **Avoid the same distracters during test time that you would during your study time.** Don't sit next to your friends or by windows or doors if at all possible. Try to sit as close to the front as you can in case your instructor writes important directions on the board; this will also decrease the distraction of other students' test behavior.

3. **Find out beforehand if the exam is open-book or open-notes.** If it is, remember to bring your books and notes with you.

4. **Make sure you bring all necessary supplies** such as calculators, pencils, sharpeners, and pens with you.

Practice with Reading Passage

Write all responses on a separate sheet of paper.

Reading Practice

Letting Justice Flow
BY ALISON KAFER

PREPARE TO READ

1. Based on the title, what do you expect the reading to be about?

2. What do you already know about the subject?

3. Here are several vocabulary words that might be unfamiliar to you. Look them up, if necessary, and refer to the definitions as you encounter these words in the article.

   a. Seminary

   b. Christening

   c. Emblazoned

   d. Irony

   e. Relevant

   f. Condescending

   g. Academia

4. Read the following article and make a checkmark in the left margin of the reading passage each time you lose your concentration.

Letting Justice Flow

I have no legs.

One night, six years ago, I fell asleep an active, able-bodied young woman. Months later I woke up, my arms, belly, and back covered in burn scars. The legs that had carried me for years were missing, amputated above the knees as a result of my burns. The last few years have been a continual process of learning how to move and understand myself in this new, and yet old, body.

Before my disability, I saw myself as a political activist only when involved in a demonstration or protest. Now, however, I understand my very body as a site of resistance. Every single time I leave my house, people stare. Their eyes linger on my scars, my half-legs, and my wheelchair as they try to understand what happened and why I look the way I do. Their stereotypes about disability are written in their expressions of confusion and fear as they watch me pass. I am powerfully aware that merely by living life in a wheelchair, I challenge their stereotypes about what bodies look like and what bodies do. I feel like an activist just by rolling out my front door.

Sometimes, however, simply rolling outdoors isn't enough of a statement. Sometimes you have to pee outdoors, too.

Three years ago, during my first semester of graduate school, I took an exchange class at a local seminary. A month into the course, I was assigned to give a presentation on the week's readings. Halfway through class we took a break, after which I was to give my talk. I desperately had to pee, and I rolled over to the library, sure I'd find accessible toilets there. I was met only with a wall of narrow stalls—too narrow to slide my wheels into.

I dashed about campus, rolling from one building to another, hoping to find a wide stall door, muttering to myself, "There *has* to be an accessible can somewhere on this damn campus." After checking every bathroom in every building, I realized I was wrong.

What the hell was I going to do?

Going home wasn't possible because I would never make it back to school in time to give my presentation. "Holding it" also wasn't possible because… well, when a girl's gotta go, a girl's gotta go. I exercised my only remaining option: I went outside, searched for a dark and secluded part of campus, hiked up my skirt, leaned my body over the edge of my wheelchair, and pissed in the grass.

It just so happened that the dark, secluded place I'd found was the Bible meditation garden.

I went back to class angry. With mild embarrassment, I told the professor what had happened. I felt validated when she stopped the class to tell everyone the seminary president's name so they could write letters demanding an accessible bathroom at the school.

The next day, I, too, wrote a letter to the president informing him of both my accessibility problem and my solution. "Odds are," I wrote, "I will need a bathroom again. And I am doubtful that my 'christening' of the Bible garden is a practice you would like me to continue." In closing, I mentioned the Bible verse I'd found emblazoned on the garden wall (the one I'd practically peed on), and hoped its irony would not escape him. "Let justice roll down like waters," the words proclaimed, "and righteousness like an everlasting stream." Never before had the Bible seemed so relevant to me!

Within forty-eight hours, I had an appointment with the school president. He ushered me into his office and sat down across from me. "Before we discuss possible construction," he said, "I just want to give you a moment to share your pain."

I paused, thinking his comment a rather condescending way to begin a meeting. "I'm not in any pain," I said curtly, "I just want a place to go to the bathroom."

Our conversation could only go downhill from there.

The president informed me that although he wanted to provide me with an accessible bathroom, the school could not currently afford such construction. When I suggested that removing a forty-year-old skanky couch from one of the women's rooms would free up space for an accessible stall, he responded with a sentiment as old as the couch: "Well, I'm reluctant to remove the sofa because some of the lady students like to rest there *during their time*."

Right. I'd forgotten how much we lady students, brains overtaxed by academia, liked to rest, bleeding, on musty couches in dank bathrooms. What a traitor to my sisters I must have been to suggest that my need to pee was more important than a couch that hadn't seen human contact since 1973.

Not surprisingly, that meeting did not result in an accessible toilet. So, as threatened, I continued to piss in the garden and complain in the halls. What had started out as a necessity became an interesting combination of necessity *and* protest—a pee protest. Word got around, and to my delight most students supported me. Petitions were signed in a number of classes. One student even proposed a documentary on *The Bathroom Debates* to her film class, showing them a short teaser clip she'd made. I became a bit of a celebrity, known in the halls as "the bathroom girl."

About a month after the first incident, I fired off another letter to the president informing him of my continued use of the Bible meditation site. This time I meant business. I told him I was ready to expose his total disregard of the needs of disabled Americans by going to the press with my story. Bingo. Construction began on the most beautiful accessible bathroom you ever did see.

Justice and righteousness were rolling down at last. They had just needed a little boost from a girl, her wheelchair, and a full bladder.

Alison Kafer is a graduate student in Women's Studies and Religion. In between battles with university administrators about inaccessible buildings, she kayaks, camps, and hikes. A relentless optimist, Alison insists that most people stare at her not because of her disability, but because of her Southern charm and dazzling physical grace.

Kafer, Alison. "Letting Justice Flow." *That Takes Ovaries*. Solomon Rivka (ed.). Three Rivers Press: New York, pp. 127–130.

CHECK YOUR UNDERSTANDING

OBJECTIVE QUESTIONS

Read each of the following multiple-choice questions and select the best possible answer from the four choices given.

1. What was the problem that the author had in the essay?

  a. She had a difficult time riding in her wheelchair.

b. She had to use the bathroom and could not find a bathroom stall on campus wide enough to accommodate her wheelchair.

c. She found her graduate-level classes difficult.

d. She wanted to be a political activist.

2. How did she solve her problem?

a. She waited until she went home.

b. She went to the library to find a bathroom.

c. She went to the student union.

d. She relieved herself outside in the meditation garden.

3. What did her professor do when she told her about her problem and what she had to do to solve her problem?

a. She told the students the school president's name so that they could write letters.

b. She urged everyone to write a letter of protest.

c. The professor wrote a letter of protest.

d. She gave the student a few minutes to talk so that she could share her pain.

4. What did the president of the school do when the author had a meeting with him to discuss the problem?

a. He suggested removing an old couch from one of the women's bathrooms to free up space for an accessible stall.

b. He said that building construction was not up to him and that she should contact the ombudsman of the school.

c. He said the school could not currently afford to build an accessible stall but that he would ask for money at the next budget meeting.

d. He said the school could not currently afford to build an accessible bathroom stall.

5. What did the author do to help resolve the problem?

a. She made a documentary on *The Bathroom Debates* for her film class.

b. She continued to relieve herself in the garden, complained in the halls, and wrote another letter to the president.

    c. She started passing petitions around and found that most students supported her.

    d. She called herself "the bathroom girl" and called the newspaper.

SHORT-ANSWER QUESTIONS.

6. Go back to the checkmarks you made in the left margin of the essay and try to remember why you lost your concentration at each of those spots.

7. Were you able to maintain your concentration throughout the entire passage? If you were, what factors do you think contributed to your ability to do so? If you did not, why do you think you lost your concentration?

8. Did you find the passage interesting? Do you think your ability to maintain your concentration was related to whether you found the passage interesting? Explain.

9. What concentration strategies did you use to stay focused on the reading? What other strategies could you have used?

10. Explain how you used your particular learning style to get the most from this reading.

Chapter Summary

Reading is an active process based on an author's ability to convey meaning through the written word and your ability to extract meaning from those words. One way to read actively is to connect what you already know to the new information you are learning. Active learners become involved in their learning experience by previewing their reading assignments, outlining chapter or lecture notes, creating visuals, and reading books, other than their textbooks, to learn more about the subject they are studying.

Keeping a learning journal is also an active learning task. It helps you identify what you understand in a reading assignment and what is still unclear. It can also help you to understand how you learn, which learning styles work best for you, and how you can improve those with which you have difficulty. Using a learning journal will help you to identify, analyze, and correct reading and learning difficulties.

Concentration involves purposely focusing your attention on a task while simultaneously blocking out distractions. The first step in achieving this is to learn what internal and external distracters block your concentration. The second step is to record your concentration habits in your reading journal. By using this information, you can learn to change your study environment and state of mind so that you can read and learn effectively.

Post Test

Answer questions on a separate sheet of paper.

Part I

OBJECTIVE QUESTIONS

1. Indicate whether the following statements are true or false?

_____ **a.** Reading is a process where the author conveys meaning and you receive it.

_____ **b.** Using a learning journal can help build concentration.

_____ **c.** Concentration is the ability to focus exclusively on a task.

_____ **d.** Internal distracters should be accepted because they happen to everybody.

_____ **e.** The checkmark monitoring system helps you to monitor your concentration.

_____ **f.** A worry pad is a letter that you write to someone who has made you angry.

_____ **g.** People learn new information only by using their preferred learning style.

2. Read each of the following multiple-choice questions and choose the best answer from the four choices provided.

a. What helps you mentally prepare to read a reading assignment?

  i. Drinking water.

  ii. Previewing.

  iii. Turning off the ringer on the phone.

  iv. Not reading in bed.

b. Why are learning journals helpful?

  i. They give you a chance to vent your frustrations.

  ii. They help you analyze your learning behavior.

  iii. Both i and ii.

  iv. Neither i nor ii.

   c. What is your preference for how you learn new information called?

      i. Kinesthetic appeal.

      ii. Learning style.

      iii. Preferred system.

      iv. Primary store.

   d. What is the key to concentrating well?

      i. Getting your friends not to bother you while you're studying.

      ii. Finding a quiet space to study.

      iii. Blocking out the things that bother you.

      iv. Purposely focusing on one task while ignoring all others.

   e. Which of the following is *not* an example of active reading?

      i. Reading the heading, subheadings, summary, and questions at the end of a chapter before reading the chapter thoroughly.

      ii. Copying the chapter into a notebook.

      iii. Analyze your reading by making an entry in your learning journal.

      iv. Drawing a diagram of the chapter contents after reading the chapter.

SHORT-ANSWER QUESTION

3. Explain why you think it is a good idea to make a journal entry if your reading assignment seems uninteresting, difficult, or unclear. How do you think your journal writing will improve your reading?

Part II

Reading Passage

The Perfect Picture
BY JAMES ALEXANDER THOM

1. Based on the title, what do you expect the reading to be about? What do you think the topic is?

2. What do you already know about the topic?

The Perfect Picture

James Alexander Thom (born 1933) is a native of Gosport, Indiana, where his parents were physicians, and a graduate of Butler University. Before becoming a freelance writer in 1973, he worked as an editor for the Indianapolis Star *and the* Saturday Evening Post *and as a lecturer at Indiana University. He has authored one volume of essays and several historical novels, one of which,*

Panther in the Sky, earned the Best Novel Award from the Western Writers of America. His latest novel, The Red Heart, *appeared in 1998. He is a contributor to many magazines.* "The Perfect Picture" *depicts an incident and an ethical dilemma that Thom experienced as a cub reporter.*

It was early in the spring about 15 years ago—a day of pale sunlight and trees just beginning to bud. I was a young police reporter, driving to a scene I didn't want to see. A man, the police dispatcher's broadcast said, had accidentally backed his pickup truck over his baby granddaughter in the driveway of the family home. It was a fatality.

As I parked among police cars and TV news cruisers, I saw a stocky white-haired man in cotton work clothes standing near a pickup. Cameras were trained on him, and reporters were sticking microphones in his face. Looking totally bewildered, he was trying to answer their questions. Mostly he was only moving his lips, blinking and choking up.

After a while the reporters gave up on him and followed the police into the small white house. I can still see in my mind's eye that devastated old man looking down at the place in the driveway where the child had been. Beside the house was a freshly spaded flower bed, and nearby a pile of dark, rich earth.

"I was just backing up there to spread that good dirt," he said to me, though I had not asked him anything. "I didn't even know she was outdoors."

He stretched his hand toward the flower bed, then let it flop to his side. He lapsed back into his thoughts, and I, like a good reporter, went into the house to find someone who could provide a recent photo of the toddler.

A few minutes later, with all the details in my notebook and a three-by-five studio portrait of the cherubic child tucked in my jacket pocket, I went toward the kitchen where the police had said the body was.

I had brought a camera in with me—the big, bulky Speed Graphic which used to be the newspaper reporter's trademark. Everybody had drifted back out of the house together—family, police, reporters, and photographers. Entering the kitchen, I came upon this scene:

On a Formica-topped table, backlighted by a frilly curtained window, lay the tiny body, wrapped in a clean white sheet. Somehow the grandfather had managed to stay away from the crowd. He was sitting on a chair beside the table, in profile to me and unaware of my presence, looking uncomprehendingly at the swaddled corpse.

The house was very quiet. A clock ticked. As I watched, the grandfather slowly leaned forward, curved his arms like parentheses around the head and feet of the little form, then pressed his face to the shroud and remained motionless.

In that hushed moment, I recognized the makings of a prize-winning news photograph. I appraised the light, adjusted the lens setting and distance, locked a bulb in the flashgun, raised the camera, and composed the scene in the viewfinder.

Every element of the picture was perfect: the grandfather in his plain work clothes, his white hair backlighted by sunshine, the child's form wrapped in the sheet, the atmosphere of the simple home suggested by black iron trivets and World's Fair souvenir plates on the walls flanking the window. Outside, the police could be seen inspecting the fatal rear wheel of the pickup while the child's mother and father leaned in each other's arms.

I don't know how many seconds I stood there, unable to snap that shutter. I was keenly aware of the powerful story-telling value that photo would have, and my professional conscience told me to take it. Yet I couldn't make my hand fire that flashbulb and intrude on the poor man's island of grief.

At length I lowered the camera and crept away, shaken with doubt about my suitability for the journalistic profession. Of course I never told the city editor or any fellow reporters about that missed opportunity for a perfect news picture.

Every day on the newscasts and in the papers, we see pictures of people in extreme conditions of grief and despair. Human suffering has become a spectator sport. And sometimes, as I'm watching news film, I remember that day.

I still feel right about what I did.

Reprinted with permission from August 1976 *Reader's Digest*. Copyright © 1976 by The Reader's Digest Assn., Inc.

OBJECTIVE QUESTIONS

Read the following multiple-choice questions and choose the *best* answer from the four choices provided.

1. Why was the author driving to the scene?

   a. To arrest someone.

   b. To take pictures for the *Enquirer.*

   c. To investigate a tragic scene.

   d. To interview a man about gardening.

2. What did the grandfather actually say happened?

   a. He was backing up to spread some dirt.

   b. He ran over the little girl.

   c. The little girl ran out of the house to greet him.

   d. The little girl was going to help him garden.

3. Why did the author not take the picture?

   a. He ran out of film.

   b. The grandfather asked him not to take the picture.

   c. He didn't want to intrude on the grandfather's sadness.

   d. He didn't feel it was a good shot.

4. Why was the scene in the kitchen described as a perfect picture?

   a. It was perfectly staged.

    b. The girl's whole family was around her.

    c. Every element of the picture—the grandfather, the child, the home—told the story.

    d. The grandfather agreed to the photo and so did the parents.

5. At the time the author was a_____.

    a. Police reporter.

    b. Magazine reporter.

    c. TV reporter.

    d. Freelance writer.

SHORT-ANSWER QUESTIONS

6. Describe how well you concentrated while reading the above essay.

7. Did you have any concentration problems as you read? Why or why not?

8. List the concentration techniques you used to overcome any concentration blocks.

9. How did you "actively read" this essay?

10. If you were taking a test on this essay tomorrow morning, what four things would you do to prepare your physical environment?

Website Sources for Additional Practice

http://www.ucc.vt.edu/stdysk/studydis.html:
Are you wasting time by studying in the wrong place? Take this quiz to find out.

http://www.utexas.edu/student/lsc/handouts/1442.html:
What does concentration have to do with your body? Look here.

http://www.swarthmore.edu/socsci/tburke1/professor.html#reading
"Professors assign more than you can possibly read in any normal fashion." Could it be true? And how do I cope with it? Read *Professor Burke Explains It All for You,* **and find the truth straight from a prof.**

http://gator1.brazosport.cc.tx.us/~lac/reading.htm:
Here it is ..."The Seven Habits of Highly Effective Readers."

http://www.berea.edu/cltcr/reading_app_test.htm:
Are you reading apprehensive? Take this test to find out.

Chapter 2

Developing Your College Vocabulary

Words are everything else in the world!
—Wallace Stevens

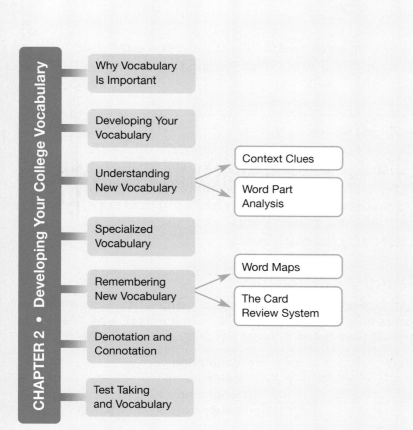

CHAPTER 2 • Developing Your College Vocabulary

- Why Vocabulary Is Important
- Developing Your Vocabulary
- Understanding New Vocabulary
  - Context Clues
  - Word Part Analysis
- Specialized Vocabulary
- Remembering New Vocabulary
  - Word Maps
  - The Card Review System
- Denotation and Connotation
- Test Taking and Vocabulary

Chapter Contents

Chapter Goals

In this chapter you will learn:

- Why developing your vocabulary is important.
- How to discover the meaning of a word using context clues and word analysis.
- How to remember new vocabulary words using word maps, the card review system, and journal writing.
- What test-taking vocabulary means.

Chapter Vocabulary

As you read, take note of these words and phrases, which represent important concepts from the chapter, and will be in **boldface type**. Make sure you understand them before the post test at the end of the chapter.

context clue	**denotation**
root	**connotation**
prefix	**word maps**
suffix	**card review system (CRS)**

Bryce encounters several unfamiliar words in his economics book. He skims over them because they are not signaled in boldface print as designated vocabulary words for the chapter. As a result, he doesn't understand key points in the chapter, and is unable to participate in class discussion. He doesn't want to appear unprepared, so he doesn't ask his instructor for clarification. He ends up not benefiting from either the text or the classroom discussion.

Why Vocabulary Is Important

Like Bryce, if you are reading a chapter in a textbook and skim across unfamiliar words, you will probably have difficulty understanding what the author is saying. Look up new vocabulary words in a dictionary as you read your textbooks: paragraphs that at first seemed confusing often become clear once you know what all the words mean. Ask your professors for help when you don't understand your reading material. Don't worry about appearing foolish. If you don't ask questions about key concepts and vocabulary, most instructors will assume that you know and understand them. Asking for help is a sign that you've done your homework and are actively seeking to understand your assignments.

Here is an example of a journal entry written by a freshman at a two-year college:

> Like I have time to look up every word I don't know! There are so many words I don't know. It gets real frustrating. I don't have a great system right now. I guess I get lazy. It seems like it's one more thing I have to do on top of all of my other work. But, my instructor says that learning new vocabulary will make a difference, so I'm going to try using the tips in this chapter. I'll start keeping track of the words I don't know and looking them up in my dictionary. I'll see if it makes any difference.

Learning Journal

In your journal, write down how you currently learn new words. Do you believe you have a good system for learning and remembering words? Do you write down words you don't know? Do you look them up in a dictionary? Do you believe that a better vocabulary will improve your reading and grades? Do you believe that a better vocabulary will ultimately help you land the job of your choice?

Developing Your Vocabulary

If you do not already own a dictionary, you should buy one as soon as possible. Increasing your vocabulary so that you know the meaning of more words, and how to use them, is an important reading strategy. *Understanding* a word's meaning is very different from just recognizing or knowing how to pronounce it. Knowing what a word means provides the key to understanding what you read. Not knowing what words mean accounts for a large percentage of all reading comprehension problems.

There are other benefits to developing a solid vocabulary. Both your reading and listening comprehension will improve if you know more words. As you will learn in Chapter 3, you can't remember what you don't understand. In college, all of your courses build upon one another, so it is important to understand and remember the basic concepts and language from your entry-level courses in order to do well in those that follow. Also, on at least one level of brain functioning, we think in words, so increasing your vocabulary will increase your ability to think critically about new information.

Learning Journal

In your journal, write down what you have just learned about the importance of learning textbook vocabulary.

Understanding New Vocabulary

You can use two important strategies to help you figure out the meaning of unfamiliar words: looking for context clues and word part analysis.

Context Clues

One way to work out the meaning of a new word is to relate it to familiar words in a sentence and use those words as **context clues**. For example, read the following sentence: "Although Cheryl is usually quite *polemical* (1) during class discussion, today she didn't *argue* (2) anyone's point." Clue one tells you that Cheryl is usually "quite *polemical* (new vocabulary word) during class discussion." Clue 2 helps explain what polemical means: "today she didn't *argue* anyone's point." Using the context in which you read the word *polemical*, you can work out that it means *argumentative*. Even if you are able to define new words using context clues, you should write them down in your journal as you are reading so that you can double-check your definition later using your dictionary.

Take One Minute

Read the following sentences: "The little girl was famished; she hadn't eaten anything in days. When she was given a sandwich, she began stuffing it into her mouth." What do you think famished means?

Types of Context Clues

Authors use several different types of context clues to convey the meaning of words:

1. DEFINITION: brief explanations of what a word means. When authors are using definitions as context clues, the following words and phrases are often used: "in other words," "is," "is known as," "also known as," "is the same as," "is called," and "means the same as."

    EXAMPLE: A **homestead** *is the home and adjoining land occupied by a family.*

2. EXAMPLE: items of information that illustrate what a word means. Examples are often introduced by clue words such as "for example," "such as," "for instance," "e.g.," "i.e.," "means the same as," "in other words," and "like."

    EXAMPLE: *In other words*, a witness can *lose all* **credibility** *after being caught in a lie.*

3. PUNCTUATION: used to set a word off from the rest of a sentence (through the use of commas, dashes, brackets, or parentheses) in order to define it. An author may also restate material in order to make the meaning of the word clearer.

    EXAMPLE: A **mala**, *Buddhist prayer beads*, are used for meditating. Many people in the United States refer to them as *power beads*.

4. PERSONAL EXPERIENCE, OPINION AND KNOWLEDGE: Authors often provide their readers with personal or additional information to enhance the point they are making and help define difficult words and concepts.

    EXAMPLE: *I never met* a more **apathetic** group of revolutionaries; they were *completely indifferent* and *unresponsive* to the suffering of those for whom they fought.

Context clues are helpful but not always definitive. Consider this sentence: "There is a dearth of useful information in this report." What do you think *dearth* means? Context is not very helpful in this case. You may confuse the word *dearth* with the more familiar word *girth,* which actually means "the measure around something" but is also used to refer to someone's waistline. This confusion of word meaning makes the message about the report unclear. *Dearth* means a scarcity of something. To say there is a "dearth of useful information" means that there is little useful information available. Guessing that *dearth* means "a fat belly" would be confusing, to say the least. So although it isn't always possible to look up new vocabulary words as you are reading, it is useful to write them in your journal so you can look them up later.

Once you have learned the meanings of new words you encounter in your reading, try adding them to your working vocabulary. The more you use them, the better you will remember what they mean.

Exercise **2a**	## Context Clues

Read the following sentences. Using the context clues, decide which of the answers provided for each comes closest in meaning to the word that is italicized, and circle the appropriate letter. Underline the context "clues." The first one is modeled for you:

MODEL   **1.** The child was able to *assuage* his irate father with <u>a smile</u> and <u>a small kiss</u> on his cheek. A <u>grin</u> slowly <u>replaced the father's angry frown</u>.

    a. Increase.

    (b.) Soothe.

    c. Lose.

    d. Handle.

2. She was so overcome with joy by the birth of her baby that she was able to say nothing other than that the whole experience was simply *ineffable*.

    a. Unhappy.

    b. Fair.

    c. Incapable of being expressed in words.

    d. Quickly forgotten.

3. Most of us eventually reach our goals, but life's path to success is often a *circuitous* one.

    a. Straight and certain.

    b. Jovial.

    c. Marked by roundabout or indirect procedures.

    d. Relating to a group.

4. The preacher took a *pedagogic* approach with his sermon, hoping that those attending would learn something meaningful from it.

  a. Instructional.

  b. Incomplete.

  c. Something that breaks the ice.

  d. To brighten or freshen up.

5. Although teaching is not a *lucrative* profession, I know that I wouldn't want to do anything else. Helping others learn is far more important to me than money.

  a. Very rewarding.

  b. Highly sensitive.

  c. Well paying.

  d. Highly exciting.

6. Buying a lottery ticket is a very *capricious* way to plan for your future. The chances of winning are 1 in 10,000,000.

  a. Lazy.

  b. Inventive.

  c. Unhappy.

  d. Unpredictable.

Exercise 2b

Context Clues in Textbooks

Read the following passages adapted from college textbooks. Using the authors' context clues, write down what you think the definition is for each italicized word. Then check the answers provided and circle the one closest in meaning to your definition.

1. Alcoholism *exacts* a horrible toll on the drinker and on the drinker's family, but the damage doesn't stop there. Drunk driving, workplace losses, and overburdened health care systems are only some of the larger-scale loss issues related to alcohol abuse. The search for effective methods of intervention has never been more intense.

Source: J. Halonen and J. Santrock, *Psychology: Contexts and Applications* (New York: McGraw-Hill, 1999).

Definition: _____

  a. Diminishes.

  b. Forces.

c. Feels.

d. Sizes.

2. The natural *circadian* rhythm of most animals, including humans, is 25 to 26 hours, but our internal clocks easily adapt to the 24-hour rhythms (light, sounds, warmth) of the turning earth. When we are isolated from environmental cues, our sleep/wake cycles continue to be rather constant but slightly longer than 24 hours.

Source: J. Halonen and J. Santrock, *Psychology: Contexts and Applications* (New York: McGraw-Hill, 1999).

Definition: _____

a. 24 hour cycle.

b. Daily behavioral cycle.

c. Seasonal cycles.

d. Insectlike.

3. When the Commissioner of Indian Affairs took office in 1933, he vowed to defend Indian rights. The *conciliatory* attitudes of the Commissioner and the Indian Office, regarding Indian rights, conformed with legal precedents established by state and federal courts.

Source: R. Nichols, *The American Indian* (New York: McGraw-Hill, 1999).

Definition: _____

a. Nervous and uncertain.

b. Agreeable, accommodating.

c. Unnecessary.

d. Disagreeable.

For the next two vocabulary words, create your own definition of the word, using the context clues provided.

4. Our own daily rhythms can become *desynchronized* when we take a cross-country or transoceanic flight. If you fly from Los Angeles to New York and then go to bed at 11 P.M. Eastern Standard Time, you may have trouble falling asleep because your body is still on West Coast time.

Source: J. Halonen and J. Santrock, *Psychology: Contexts and Applications* (New York: McGraw-Hill, 1999).

Definition: _____

5. If my argument so far has been sound, neither our distance from a preventable evil nor the number of other people who, in respect to that evil, are in the same situation as we are, lessens our obligation to *mitigate* or prevent that evil. I shall therefore take as established the principle I asserted earlier. As I have already said, I need to assert it only in its qualified form: if it is in our power to prevent something very bad from happening, without thereby sacrificing anything else morally significant, we ought, morally, to do it.

Source: J. Rachels, *The Right Thing to Do,* (New York: McGraw-Hill, 1999).

Definition: _____

Take One Minute

In your own words, explain what context clues are and how they can help you figure out the meaning of an unfamiliar word. Write your responses on a separate sheet of paper.

Word Part Analysis

To analyze words, you should break them up into smaller parts: roots, prefixes, and suffixes. These parts provide you with word clues, which you can use to decipher unfamiliar words.

Roots

A word's **root** is its most basic part, or building block. It is as fundamental to a word's meaning as a root is to a plant: you will not get a geranium from a tulip bulb, nor will you get a word that means "love" from the root *phobia*. Understanding the root of a word is key to understanding it. For instance, you might read in your local paper that a noted amateur *aquarist* has added two rare sea horses to his collection. Looking at the first part of the word, *aqua* (which means "water"), you could safely guess that his hobby has something to do with water. Since sea horses live in water, he would have to keep them in an aquarium, so it would be reasonable to conclude that an aquarist is someone who keeps or maintains aquariums.

Exercise 2c — Common Roots

Using a sheet of paper, cover the definitions and word examples for the list of roots and see how many you already know.

ROOT	DEFINITION	EXAMPLE	ROOT	DEFINITION	EXAMPLE
anthrop	man	anthropology	mit, mis	send	missile, transmit
aqua	water	aquarium			
audio	hear	audition	mort	death	mortal
bibl	book	Bible, bibliography	path	feeling	empathy
			philo	love	philanthropic
bio	life	biology	phobia	fear	acrophobia
cap	take, seize	capture	poli	city	metropolitan
capit	head	capital	rupt	break	erupt, disrupt
cede	to go	precede	scop	see	telescope
chron (o)	time	chronology	scrib/script	write	script, prescription
cred	believe	credible			
cur	run	current	sect	cut	section, intersection
dict	tell, say	dictate			
duc	lead	conduct, educate	sen/sent	feel	sentimental, sensitive
equ	equal	equivalent	spec/spic/spect	look	spectacle
fact	make	factory			
fid	trust	confident	tract	drag, draw	attract
geo	earth	geography	vac	empty	vacuum, vacant
graph	write	autograph			
gyn	woman	gynecologist	ver	true	verify
hemi	half	hemisphere	verb	word	verbose
ject	throw	trajectory, reject	vert	turn	convertible, revert
lith	stone	monolith	vis	see	vision
log/logo/logy	study, thought	anthropology	viv	live	vivid
man	hand	manual, manufacture			

Learning Journal

Look back at the word examples provided to illustrate the use of root word parts. Write down those you don't know in your journal, and look them up in your dictionary. Write down their definitions, and create sentences using each one.

Team Up!

Get together with three other students. Using the roots you have just learned, write down another word example for each one. If you can't think of a word, look one up in your dictionary.

Exercise 2d

Roots

Underline the root in each of the following words, and then write a definition of the word in the space provided.

1. equal _____
2. circumscribe _____
3. predict _____
4. untenable _____
5. current _____
6. extend _____
7. extensible _____
8. scribble _____
9. retentive _____
10. remit _____

Prefixes

Attaching a **prefix** to the front of a word changes its meaning. Different prefixes will change the meaning in different ways, as demonstrated when the prefixes *a, bi, homo* and *hetero* are attached to the word *sexual*.

Sexual: intimate; having or involving sex.

Asexual: not intimate; not having or involving sex.

Bisexual: intimate with both (two) sexes.

Homosexual: intimate with the same sex.

Heterosexual: intimate with the opposite (different) sex.

Although *sexual* is common to all the words, each prefix significantly changes its meaning. This is why knowing the meaning of prefixes will help you to figure out new vocabulary words.

Common Prefixes

Using a sheet of paper, cover up the following definitions and word examples for the list of prefixes and see how many you already know. Write down what you think the definitions are and then check your answers.

PREFIX	DEFINITION	EXAMPLE	PREFIX	DEFINITION	EXAMPLE
a	not, away from	asexual, atheist	ex	out of, from	exit
			extra	beyond	extraordinary
ab	away from	abhor	hetero	different, other	heterogeneous
ac	to, toward	accede	homo	same	homonym
ad	to, toward	adhere, advance	hyper	more than usual	hyperventilate
ambi	both	ambidextrous	hypo	below, under	hypodermic
amphi	around, on both sides	amphitheatre	il	not	illegitimate
			im	not, into	impossible
ante	before	antecedent	in	not, into, toward	instill
anti	against, opposed to	antidote	ir	not, into	irrigate
			kilo	thousand	kilometers
auto	self	autobiography	mal	wrong, bad	malnutrition
bene	well, good	benefactor	meta	after, change	metabolic
bi	two	biped	mis	wrong	misunderstand
bio	life	biography	mono	one, single	monologue
carn	flesh	carnivore	multi	many, much	multidimensional
circum	around	circumvent	neo	new	neophyte
co	with, together	coalesce	non	not	nonessential
com	with, together	combine	ob	against	object
con	together, with	consensus	omni	all	omnipotent
cor	with, together	correlate	op	against	opposed
corp	body	corpse	over	above, too much, beyond	overshadow
cred	believe	credible			
de	away, from, down	detach	pan	all, every	panacea
			para	beside, near	paraprofessional
dem	people	demographics			
derm	skin	dermatologist			
dis	apart, no longer, not	disconnect	ped	foot	pedestrian
			per	through	pervade
ec	out of, from	ecstasy	poly	many, several	polygon
ef	out of, from	effaced	port	carry	portable
em	make or cause to be	empower	post	after, behind, later	posthumous

PREFIX	DEFINITION	EXAMPLE	PREFIX	DEFINITION	EXAMPLE
pre	before, in front of	preface	super	above, beyond	superlative
pro	advancing forward	prominent	sym	with, together	symetrical
			syn	with, together	syntax
proto	first	prototype	techn	skill, art	technician
quadr	four	quadrant	trans	across, over	transportation
re	again, back	repeat	tri	three	triangle
retro	backward, behind	retroactive	ultra	very, beyond	ultramodern
se	apart, away from	separate	un	not	unbelievable
semi	half, partly	semicolon	under	beneath, lower	undermine
sub	under, below	submarine	uni	one	unicycle

Team Up!

Get together with three other students. Using the list of prefixes, write down another word example for each. If you can't think of a word, look one up in your dictionary.

Learning Journal

Go back and review the word examples provided for the list of prefixes. Write those you don't know in your journal, and look them up in a dictionary. Write the definition of each word you didn't understand, and create a sentence using it.

Exercise 2f

Prefix—Create a Word

Write the appropriate prefixes in the spaces here and then provide two words using each prefix. The first one is modeled for you:

MODEL **1.** A prefix that means "good" or "well" is _____*bene*_____

    1. _____*benefit*_____   2. _____*benediction*_____

2. A prefix that means "out" is _____

    1. _____   2. _____

3. A prefix that means "skill" is _____

    1. _____   2. _____

4. A prefix that means "bad" is _____

    1. _____   2. _____

5. A prefix that means "against" is _____

    1. _____   2. _____

6. A prefix that means "half" is _____

    1. _____   2. _____

7. A prefix that means "after" is _____

    1. _____   2. _____

8. A prefix that means "many" is _____

    1. _____   2. _____

9. A prefix that means "more than usual" is _____

    1. _____   2. _____

10. A prefix that means "before" is _____

    1. _____   2. _____

Suffixes

Suffixes are word parts that are added to the end of a word. They consist of one or more letters and usually don't change the meaning of a word as much as prefixes do, although they can change a word to the present, past, or future tense. For example, the verb *play* can be *play* now, *played* yesterday, or will be *playing* tomorrow.

Suffixes can also change the way a word can be used. For example, the verb *manage* can be changed to an adjective by adding the suffix *able*, which means "able to be": *manage + able = manageable* which means "able to be managed." Or the verb *manage* can be changed to a noun by adding the suffix *er*, which means "performer" or "one who does": *manage + er = manager*, which means "one who manages."

Exercise 2g

See What You Know

Using a sheet of paper, cover the definitions and word examples for the following list of suffixes and see how many you already know.

COMMON SUFFIXES

SUFFIX	DEFINITION	EXAMPLE	SUFFIX	DEFINITION	EXAMPLE
able/ible	able to be	legible	ive	tending toward	active
al/ic	like, suitable	angelic, comical	ize	to make	legalize
an/or/er	person who	musician, worker	less	without	penniless
ance	state of, action	resistance	ly	like	friendly
ant	causing, being	participant	ment	state of being	movement
ation	state, condition of	information	ness	state, quality	calmness
ful	full of	harmful, beautiful	or	performer	actor,
fy	to make	simplify, magnify		of action	instructor
hood	condition	brotherhood	ous	characterized	joyous
ible	capable	divisible		by	
ic	pertaining to	heroic	ship	condition, state	censorship
ion	state of being	vision	some	tending to	awesome
ious	characterized	auspicious	tion	act, process	election
	by		ty	state of,	loyalty
ism	system	symbolism		condition	
ist	agent, doer	biologist	ward	direction	homeward,
ity	condition,	community			toward
	degree		y	full of	milky

Learning Journal

Look back at the word examples provided to illustrate the use of suffixes.
Write those you don't know in your journal, and look them up. Write the definition of each word you didn't understand, and create a sentence using it.

Exercise 2h

Create Words with Suffixes

Write a word using one of the suffixes listed on the preceding pages. The first
one is modeled for you:

MODEL **1.** *One who professes knowledge*   *professor* _____

2. Able to mend   _____

3. Full of spite   _____

4. Like a mother   _____

5. Characterized by harmony   _____

6. A beginning; start, a graduation   _____

7. Sad at feeling alone   _____

8. A scientist who specializes in chemistry   _____

9. The act, practice, or profession of instructing   _____

10. Unable to manage by oneself; dependent   _____

Exercise 2i — Identify the Roots

Each of the following words contains one or more suffixes. Find the root word for each of the following and write it in the blank space. Do not include any of the suffixes in the base word you write. The first one is modeled for you:

MODEL **1.** *harmlessly*   harm

2. controversially   _____

3. commercialization   _____

4. talkatively   _____

5. mindlessness   _____

6. simplistically   _____

7. neighborliness   _____

8. wakefulness   _____

9. peacefully   _____

10. sinfulness   _____

Exercise 2j — Define the Following Words

Provide a definition for each of the following words, using your knowledge of word parts. You can refer back to the lists of word parts in this chapter, or use a dictionary, if you need assistance for this exercise. The first one is modeled for you.

MODEL **1.** *maltreat:*   to treat badly; to abuse

2. autonomous: _____

3. emit: _____

4. fidelity: _____

5. convey: _____

6. equivocal: _____

7. posthumous: _____

8. carnal: _____

9. misogynist: _____

10. synchronized: _____

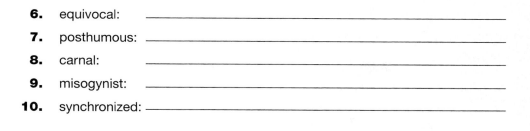

Exercise 2k	**Writing a Letter**

Using the new words you have learned while studying roots, prefixes, and suffixes, write a letter to a past or present workplace supervisor using six of them. The letter can be about anything you like—for example, working conditions, your ideas for increasing workplace efficiency, your need for a well-deserved pay raise, or your like or dislike of his or her management style.

Specialized Vocabulary

Every subject you study requires you to learn a lot of specialized vocabulary. Your instructors will expect you to remember these words, understand how they are used in the content area, and use them in class. Most of the words you will need to know for a specific discipline will be presented during your introductory courses. Before moving on to the next level of biology, chemistry, or psychology, it's a good idea to master the specialized vocabulary of your particular discipline in order to fully understand and remember what you read in your textbooks.

Below are some of the words used in the social sciences, math, science, literature, and history that are examples of specialized vocabulary. These are the kinds of words you will find used over and over again to convey specific, content-related information in your texts and in lectures.

LITERATURE VOCABULARY

aesthetic	infallible	protagonist	chronicle	trilogy
genre	juxtaposition	saga	surrealism	analogy
theme	satire	extemporize	melodrama	parody

SOCIAL SCIENCE VOCABULARY

authoritarian	demographic	fiduciary	phenomena
behaviorism	capitol	caucus	contribution margin
commodity	maximization	communism	deficit
descendant	reformist	liberalism	laissez-faire

HISTORY VOCABULARY

concomitant	covenant	expansionism	market
anthropology	decimated	epoch	monarchy
coup d'état	era	manifest destiny	infrastructure

SCIENCE VOCABULARY

aquatic	effusion	byte	reactant
atmosphere	endothermic	molecule	remnant
eon	energy	nebula	cyberspace

Exercise 21

Context Clues Using Specialized Vocabulary

Read the following paragraphs. Use your knowledge of context clues, prefixes, suffixes, and roots to define the italicized vocabulary words in the following selections.

Selection One

Profit analysis and *maximization(1)* are possible only when the *profitability(2)* of all product lines is known. The question is, which product or products contribute the most to company profitability in relation to the amount of capital assets or other scarce resources needed to produce the item(s)? To answer this question, the accountant must measure the *contribution margin(3)* of each product. The next step is to determine a set of ratios of contribution margin to the required capital equipment or other resources. Once this step is completed, management should request a marketing study to identify the upper limits of demand on the most profitable products. If product profitability can be computed and adequate market demand exists, management should shift production to the more profitable products. Many kinds of decisions can be related to the approach described here. *Sales mix analysis(4)* involves determining the most profitable combination of product sales when a company produces more than one product or offers more than one service.

Source: B. Needles, *Principle of Accounting,* 6th ed. (Boston: Houghton Mifflin, 1996), p. 1154.

1. _____

2. _____

3. _____

4. _____

Selection Two

So, in theory, affirmative action certainly has all the *moral symmetry(1)* that fairness requires—the injustice of historical and even contemporary white advantage is offset with black advantage; preference replaces prejudice, inclusion answers exclusion. It is *reformist(2)* and corrective, even *repentant(3)* and *redemptive(4)*. And I would never sneer at these good intentions...

Source: P. Andrews, *Voices of Diversity: Twentieth-Century Perspectives on History and Government*, 2nd ed. (New York: Dushkin/McGraw-Hill, 2000), p. 132.

1. _____

2. _____

3. _____

4. _____

Selection Three

The social theorists Karl Marx and Max Weber focused on the stratification systems associated with industrialization. From his observations in England and his analysis of 19th-century industrial capitalism, Marx (Marx and Engels 1848/1976) saw *socioeconomic stratification(1)* as a sharp and simple division between two opposed classes: the *bourgeoisie(2)* (capitalists) and the *proletariat(3)* (propertyless workers). The bourgeoisie traced its origins to overseas ventures and the world capitalist economy, which had transformed the social structure of northwestern Europe, creating a wealthy commercial class.

Source: Conrad Kottak, *Cultural Anthropology* (New York: McGraw-Hill, 2002), p. 364.

1. _____

2. _____

3. _____

Remembering New Vocabulary

Two useful strategies to help you remember new vocabulary are creating word maps and the card review system (CRS).

Word Maps

A **word map** is a picture that illustrates the various steps you should take in order to learn a new word. Creating word maps *ensures* that you don't forget any of the steps. The goal of creating and reviewing word maps is to be able to recognize new words when you see them in print, and to use them when you speak and write.

Six Steps for Creating Word Maps

1. In your journal, draw a circle and write a new vocabulary word in the center of it.

2. Write down the sentence in which you found your unfamiliar word (including the page number), place a large circle around the sentence, and connect it to the vocabulary word.

3. Predict what you think the word means, using the strategies discussed in this chapter. Write your prediction in the center of a circle, labeled "prediction," and connect it to the vocabulary word.

4. Look the word up in your dictionary, write its definition in the center of another circle, and connect it to the vocabulary word.

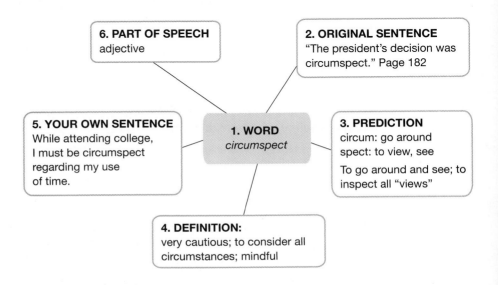

6. PART OF SPEECH
adjective

2. ORIGINAL SENTENCE
"The president's decision was circumspect." Page 182

5. YOUR OWN SENTENCE
While attending college, I must be circumspect regarding my use of time.

1. WORD
circumspect

3. PREDICTION
circum: go around
spect: to view, see

To go around and see; to inspect all "views"

4. DEFINITION:
very cautious; to consider all circumstances; mindful

5. Create your own sentence using the vocabulary word, and circle and connect it.

6. Identify the vocabulary word's part of speech—adjective, noun, verb, or adverb—and circle it and connect it to the vocabulary word. Some students find it helps to use different colors for each component of their word maps.

Exercise 2m	**Creating Word Maps**

Draw your own word maps for two of the following words:

1. concurrence   **3.** obdurate

_____   _____

2. gregarious   **4.** rapacious

_____   _____

Take One Minute

As you may have noticed, creating word maps is a particularly helpful exercise if you are a visual learner. Take some time to think about how the word map strategy could be altered so it would be more useful to auditory and kinesthetic learners. Write your ideas on a separate piece of paper.

Learning Journal

In your journal, write about your experience using the word mapping technique. How can you make the word map system work with your study habits, modifying it if necessary?

The Card Review System

The **card review system (CRS)** is a useful strategy for learning both general and specialized vocabulary. It also helps you to retain new information in your short- and long-term memory. Here's how it works:

1. Copy each new word that you encounter on the front of a 3 × 5 card.

2. Look up the word in your dictionary, and on the front of the card indicate how it should be pronounced and what part of speech it is (noun, verb, adverb or adjective).

3. On the back of the card write the definition(s) of the word, its origin, and one sentence you have created using it.

4. Organize the cards in chronological order to help you remember the source and context of each word and carry them with you at all times.

5. Some students find it convenient to punch a hole in the cards and place them on a ring.

6. Review the cards whenever you have a few free minutes each day—for example, standing in line.

7. When you can, review the words by saying them out loud. Tape-recording new words and playing them back can be especially useful because you are using several senses (seeing, speaking, hearing, and touching) to learn them. The more learning styles you use, the more successful you will be.

The CRS (see Figure 2.1) works as well with specialized vocabulary as it does with regular words, but there are a few additional details you should include on the cards:

1. For quick reference when studying, write the book title and the number of the page on which you first read the new word on the front right corner of the card.

2. Write the exact sentence in which the word was used on the back of the card.

3. Write down how the word functions within the discipline—for example, whether it describes a *process* such as photosynthesis or

Front	**Back**
ineffable in-ef-b'l adjective	Too overwhelming to be expressed or described in words My love for you is ineffable. Origin: France

Figure 2.1:   Card in CRS

plate tectonics or a *theory* such as psychoanalysis or quantum mechanics. Draw pictures on the cards to help you remember word meanings. If a word falls into a specific category, note this to remind yourself that the word is part of a special group, such as muscles in the face or events that occurred during World War II. Figure 2.2 provides an example of how technical words can be learned using the card review system.

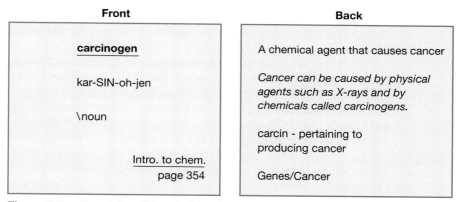

Front	Back
carcinogen kar-SIN-oh-jen \noun Intro. to chem. page 354	A chemical agent that causes cancer *Cancer can be caused by physical agents such as X-rays and by chemicals called carcinogens.* carcin - pertaining to producing cancer Genes/Cancer

Figure 2.2: Specialized Vocabulary Card

Reviewing your cards whenever you have a few free minutes will help you to "own" the words. It's a painless and effective way to learn specialized language as well as general vocabulary.

Team Up!

With one other student, discuss your three favorite vocabulary strategies for remembering new words. Provide examples for each strategy.

Exercise 2n ·· Application of the CRS

Read the following excerpt, identify all of the words that you are not familiar with, and practice using the CRS. Use one card for each unfamiliar word.

During the early years of space exploration, NASA scientist Wernher von Braun gave many speeches on the wonders and promises of rocketry and space flight.

After one of his luncheon talks, von Braun found himself clinking cocktail glasses with an adoring woman from the audience.

"Dr. von Braun," the woman gushed, "I just loved your speech, and I found it of absolutely infinitesimal value!"

"Well then," von Braun gulped, "I guess I'll have to publish the text posthumously."

"Oh yes!" the woman came right back. "And the sooner the better!"

Now there was someone who needed to gain greater control over her word choices. But, given the power that words confer on our lives, don't we all wish to acquire a richer vocabulary? Justice Oliver Wendell Homes once declared, "Language is the skin of living thought." Just as your skin encloses your body, so does your vocabulary bound your mental life.

It's a matter of simple mathematics: The more words you know, the more choices you can make; the more choices you can make, the more accurate, vivid, and varied your speaking and writing will be. "All words," observed Henry Ward Beecher, "are pegs to hang ideas on." Other things being equal, the larger your stock of word pegs, the closer you will come to finding the exact word that fits precisely the thought you want to express in speech or writing.

Ever since Adam assigned names to all the animals, we human beings have managed to come up with labels for almost everything on this planet—and beyond. The more of these names you acquire, ...the more concise will be your expression. Why should you wheeze through a dozen words—"the act of throwing a thing or person out of a window"—when you can capture the act in a single noun: *defenestration?* Why scrawl out "a place real or imaginary where living conditions are considered to be as bad as possible" when you can capture the concept with eight little letters: *dystopia?* Wouldn't it be convenient if our language possessed a *discrete* and *discreet* word to denote the excessive development of fat on the buttocks? It does: *steatopygia.* Doesn't your heart leap up when it beholds the *effulgent* word *lambent*, at your service to describe the soft radiance of light or flame playing on a surface?

English is the most cheerfully democratic and hospitable language in the history of humankind. English has acquired the most abundant of all word stocks—616,500 entries officially enshrined in the Oxford English Dictionary, our fattest unabridged lexicon. That's an extraordinary number, considering that German owns about 185,000, so our English language boasts almost four times the number of words as the second-place language. Then come Russian at 130,000 and French at 100,000.

While there are more English words, Horatio, than are dreamt of in your philosophy, relatively few are in actual circulation. The average English speaker possesses a vocabulary of 10,000 to 20,000 words but actively uses only a small fraction, the others being recognition or recall vocabulary. A literate adult may recognize 60,000 or more words, the most learned among us 100,000. Just as we human beings use only one-tenth of our brain power, the most articulate verbivore interacts with only one-sixth of our English word hoard and actually employs only one-sixth of that.

Sadly then, many of us miss out on the sheer euphony and sesquipedalian playfulness of thousands of English words....

One of the happiest features of possessing a capacious vocabulary is the opportunity to insult your enemies with impunity. While the madding crowd gets mad with exhausted epithets such as "You rotten pig" and "You dirty bum," you can *acerbate, deprecate, derogate,* and *excoriate* your *nemesis* with a battalion of laser-precise *pejoratives.*

Source: Richard Lederer, "Introduction" from Eugene Ehrlich, *The Highly Selective Dictionary for the Extraordinarily Literate* (New York: HarperCollins, 1997, excerpts from pp. xxi-xxiii).

Denotation and Connotation

Another important aspect of vocabulary building is recognizing the distinction between a word's denotation and connotation. **Denotation** is the dictionary definition of a word. It is what the word means, literally. It's easy to remember the difference in meaning between connotation and denotation if you remember that denotation starts with the letter *d* just as *dictionary* does; denotation is the dictionary definition.

Connotation is the dictionary definition *plus* any ideas suggested by, or associated with, that word. For example, the dictionary definition of the word *patriotism* is devoted love, support, and defense of one's country; but the word *patriotism* connotes much more to most Americans, especially since the tragedy of September 11, 2001. Many people think of outward displays of loyalty to the United States such as flying American flags at their homes or on their cars, or wearing T-shirts and pins with symbols of the United States on them. Others are reminded of the duties of Americans, such as voting, communicating regularly with politicians, and buying American-made products.

The key differences between denotation and connotation relate to content and emotional tone. The denotation of a word (its dictionary definition) is narrower in scope and often carries less emotional weight. Connotations, on the other hand, provide a subtle additive to the meaning of words, giving them greater depth and emotional substance. However, not all words have rich connotations, or even the same connotations, for everyone.

If you ignore the connotations of words, you can lose some of the meaning of what you are reading. The same is true when you are unaware of what a word denotes. For example, at one time, Chevrolet made and sold a car called a Nova. However, *no va* in Spanish literally means "no go." The car that "doesn't go" became a joke at Chevrolet's expense.

Exercise 2o

Denotation and Connotation

Read the following commentary taken from *Autoweek* magazine and answer the questions that follow it.

What, Was *Amistad** Already Taken?

Refusing to accommodate U.S. dealers who literally begged for a name change on VW's new sport/ute, company officials confirm they will forge ahead with the name *Touareg* (say TUR-ek, and spit when you do). Touareg is the French spelling for a sub-Saharan nomadic tribe known for dealing in the slave trade, along with other day-to-day activities. *Autoweek,* December 30, 2002, p.15

1. Define these words:

   a. sub-Saharan   _____

   b. nomadic   _____

2. Explain why U.S. car dealers object to the name *Touareg* for the new VW sport utility vehicle. Explain your answer using the words *connotation* and *denotation*.

   _____

   _____

   _____

   _____

Pronunciation

You will know you have mastered new words when you start using them in everyday speech. To do this successfully, you need to know how to pronounce them correctly, and this is where your dictionary comes in handy. All dictionaries contain pronunciation keys. Your instructor can also provide you with additional information, or you can access the websites **http://wordsmith.org** and **http://education.yahoo.com/reference/dictionary** on your computer to assist you with words you are having trouble pronouncing.

Exercise 2p

Pronunciation

Using the standard pronunciation key found in your dictionary, sound out the following phonetically spelled words and then write them in

Amistad was the name of a slave ship.

the spaces provided, using the regular English spelling. The first one is modeled for you:

MODEL	**1.**	`tə`māt-ō	tomato
	2.	ˌhal-ə-`tō-səs	_____
	3.	`rēd	_____
	4.	`tō-ˌnāl	_____
	5.	ˌkän-trə-`dikt	_____
	6.	`nīt-ˌkləb	_____
	7.	`täl-(ə-)rə-bəl	_____
	8.	`äk-tə-pəs	_____
	9.	`mäl-i-ˌkyül	_____
	10.	ˌhip-ə-`pät-ə-məs	_____

Team Up!

Compare your answers for Exercise 2p with one other student. If you missed more than three words, you should spend more time working with your dictionary to understand the pronunciation key. Improving your vocabulary includes understanding the correct pronunciation of words.

Test Taking and Vocabulary

Exam Terminology

In addition to learning the specific vocabulary words introduced in your classes, it is important to make sure you understand what exam terminology means before test time. The way questions are written can give you clues about how to answer them. If you don't understand exam terminology, you can perform poorly on tests.

Take the following quiz to see how much you already know about key terms for exams. Match the key word on the left with the correct definition on the right. The first one is modeled for you:

MODEL	___f___	1.	Evaluate	a. List and explain each point; list in concise form.

_____	2.	Analyze	b. State the meaning of a word or concept; place it in the class to which it belongs.
_____	3.	Prove	c. Bring out the points of similarity.
_____	4.	Describe	d. Use a chart, a word picture, a diagram, or a concrete example of something.
_____	5.	Explain	e. Bring out the points of difference.
_____	6.	Enumerate	f. Make a judgment based on specific criteria.
_____	7.	Define	g. Look at individual parts and examine each critically.
_____	8.	Summarize	h. Summarize by using a series of headings and sub-headings.
_____	9.	Contrast	i. Make clear, make plain, tell how to do, make clear by giving an example.
_____	10.	Illustrate	j. Tell about, give an account of or characteristics of something.
_____	11.	Compare	k. State your opinion—you can either support or not support an issue, but support your opinion by using examples.
_____	12.	Justify	l. Show good reasons for, give your evidence to support your position.
_____	13.	Outline	m. Provide a brief overview of the main points.
_____	14.	Criticize	n. Establish the truth by providing factual evidence or logical reasons.

Check with your instructor to see if your answers are correct. If you had difficulty with this terminology exercise, you can get additional test-taking assistance from your college's learning center.

Avoid Absolute Terms

Answers in multiple-choice or true/false tests that contain _absolute terms_, such as _all, every, entire, only, never, always, no, nobody, everyone_, and _forever_, are usually incorrect. Answers that contain words like _probably, few, might, may, commonly, some, frequently, could, often, should, usually, sometimes, nearly_, and _generally_ are more likely to be correct.

Practice with Reading Passage

Write all responses on a separate sheet of paper.

Reading Practice

"It's a Bird, It's a Plane, It's Plagiarism Buster!"
BY GILLIAN SILVERMAN

PREPARE TO READ

1. Based on the title and headings, what do expect this reading selection to be about?

2. What do you already know about the topic?

3. In order to get the most out of the reading selection, it's important that you understand the vocabulary. If you don't know any of the following words, use one or more of the vocabulary strategies you have learned in this chapter to figure out their meaning. Note the strategy (or strategies) you have applied and be prepared to discuss or submit your responses.

  a. Plagiarism

  b. Hackneyed

  c. Locution

  d. Paradoxical

  e. Purloining

  f. Deriving

  g. Scant

  h. Archives

  i. Salacious

  j. Pilfering

  k. Gaffe

  l. Inquiries

  m. Empathy

4. Create a question, using the title or topic of the reading selection, and look for the answer to it as you read the following essay.

"It's a Bird, It's a Plane, It's Plagiarism Buster!"

At around this time each year, I transform from mild-mannered English professor to take-no-prisoners literary sleuth. The beginnings are fairly undramatic. They usually involve myself, a starbucks, and a large stack of mediocre college-student papers. My mind numbs in response to the parade of hackneyed phrases ("And in conclusion, these books are both very similar and very different...") when suddenly something catches my eye—a turn of phrase or an extraliterary locution. "Paradoxically..." writes one, "In lieu of an example..." writes another. My breathing quickens, my heart skips, I reach for the red pen. And behold Plagiarism Buster, armed with a righteous sense of justice that would rival that of any superhero.

Plagiarism is the purloining of ideas or language from another source. It is literary theft, deriving from the Latin *plagiarius*, meaning kidnapper. Perhaps the dramatic derivation of the word is what attracts the academic set. We spend our days in libraries, classrooms, and archives. Given the scant opportunities for stimulation, a kidnapping, literary or otherwise, offers perhaps the only taste of salacious activity we may experience all year.

Maybe this is why the disappointment I feel upon discovering a suspected case of plagiarism is always mixed with a bit of excitement. A plagiarized paper presents itself as an act of aggression, a taunt behind a title page. To ignore the challenge would be worse than irresponsible; it would be cowardly. And so, I begin the chase.

The Web is always a productive place to start. With thousands of sites dedicated to armchair literary criticism, nothing has done more to accommodate paper pilfering. The thing my students don't seem to realize, however, is that as easily as they can steal language from the Web, I can bust them for it. All it takes is an advanced search on Google.com. Plug in any piece of questionable student writing and up pops the very paper from which the phrase originates. I've discovered papers plagiarized from collaborative high school projects and from essay services like screwschool.com. My personal favorite involved a paper cribbed from an Amazon.com reader's report for the Cliffs Notes of Herman Melville's *Bartleby the Scrivener*. Really, why take the trouble to cheat directly off the Cliffs Notes when you can simply crib from reviews?

It's not that my students are bad performers. Many of them do outstanding and original work. But on the whole, they are terrible cheaters. They will mooch just as readily from an adolescent chat room as they will from an online academic journal. And they can be sloppy in their deceptions: referencing page numbers to editions other than those we used in class or printing out essays without deleting underlined links. With gaffes like these, the job of Plagiarism Buster is often less than taxing.

This past semester, I discovered eight cases of plagiarism from the Internet, a new record. The confrontations that followed often verged on the comical. One student swore up and down that she had not cheated, and when I pointed to the proof on the computer screen, she looked genuinely perplexed and asked how her essay got there. "That's what I want to know," I told her. "Yeah," she said as if empathizing with my plight, "me too." Another student spent 10 minutes insisting that her brother wrote her paper for her and therefore it was *he* who was guilty of plagiarism.

Despite their efforts at defense, however, these students generally end up miserable. I fare little better. While I anticipate these confrontations will leave me victorious, they usually just make me depressed. The answer that I most frequently receive to my repeated inquiries of "why?" makes me think that plagiarism comes out of a misplaced effort to please. "You didn't like my last paper," one student told me. "I thought you'd be happier with this one." As if this weren't enough, I know that in the public university where I teach, it is largely my students' overtaxed lives that leave them so vulnerable to the temptations of cheating.

They're not off rowing crew instead of writing their literature paper. They're working 12-hour night shifts and caring for elderly parents. In the end, I'm forced to realize that my students are not bad guys; they're just guys trying to get by.

And yet, while empathy for my students is important, in cases of plagiarism it has little educational value. And so I fail them. With compassion, sure, but I fail them nonetheless. And then, feeling more villain than superhero, I head to the movies for some moral clarity.

Silverman is an assistant professor of English.

Source: *Newsweek,* July 15, 2002.

CHECK YOUR UNDERSTANDING

OBJECTIVE QUESTIONS

Read each of the following multiple-choice questions and select the best possible answer from the four choices given.

1. What is plagiarism?

   a. Using the Internet as a research tool.

   b. Quoting from the Internet too much.

   c. Taking someone else's words and/or ideas without giving proper credit to that source.

   d. Taking someone else's words and/or ideas but giving credit to the source.

2. What is it in a student's paper that makes Professor Silverman suspect that the student has plagiarized?

   a. When a student writes, "In conclusion, these books are both very similar and very different."

    b. When she reads something in a student's paper that doesn't sound like the student's real writing, something that sounds more polished and professional.

    c. When she reads something in a student's paper that she doesn't agree with.

    d. When she becomes tired of reading mediocre papers.

3. How does Professor Silverman prove that a student plagiarized material?

    a. She does an advanced search on the Internet that helps her locate the exact paper that the questionable piece of student writing came from.

    b. She does an advanced search on the Internet that helps her locate sites for English homework assistance.

    c. She confronts a student and the student usually admits it.

    d. She talks to the dean of the English department who handles the situation for her.

4. Why do students plagiarize, according to Professor Silverman?

    a. They don't really like to write English papers.

    b. They are off rowing crew instead of writing their English papers.

    c. They want to see if they can get away with it.

    d. They have overtaxed lives that leave them vulnerable to the temptations of cheating.

5. How does Professor Silverman react after she catches a student cheating?

    a. She feels more like a superhero than a villain.

    b. She fails them.

    c. She lacks empathy for them.

    d. She decides that her students can perform well enough on their own.

SHORT-ANSWER QUESTIONS.

6. How does the author describe her students who plagiarize?

7. Create word-maps using at least three vocabulary words from the reading selection.

Chapter Summary

Vocabulary building is one of the most important reading strategies you can learn. By increasing your vocabulary, you increase your understanding of textbook information. You also increase your ability to speak and write well—to communicate effectively. A rich vocabulary allows you access to many types of reading material, while a limited one prevents you from fully understanding what you read. Increasing your word power not only enhances your academic ability but also increases your chances of getting the job of your choice when you graduate.

Although no one knows every word, or interrupts reading to look up every unfamiliar word in the dictionary, using the simple strategies presented in this chapter will help you figure out and remember the meaning of new words. These strategies include using context clues, word analysis, writing in your textbook, creating word maps, understanding denotation and connotation, journal writing, and the card review system (CRS). Don't skim over words you don't know. It prevents you from really understanding what you read, makes it difficult for you to participate in class discussions, and can hurt you on exams.

An important way to make new words a part of your regular vocabulary is to use them in your everyday speech and writing. Writing in your journal daily will help.

Post Test

Answer all questions on a separate sheet of paper.

Part I

OBJECTIVE QUESTIONS

1. Three common word parts include _____, _____, and _____.

2. Match the prefixes and roots in Column A with their definitions in Column B.

Column A	Column B
1. a-	a. around
2. terr	b. life
3. circum-	c. not, away from
4. hypo-	d. beside, near
5. ver	e. true

6.	rupt	f.	believe
7.	post-	g.	against, opposed to
8.	bio	h.	land
9.	mis-	i.	after, behind, later
10.	para-	j.	wrong
11.	cred	k.	break
12.	anti-	l.	below, under

3. Which of the following is not a type of context clue:

   a. Definition

   b. Punctuation

   c. Duplication

   d. Example

4. When using the CRS (card review system), which of the following should *not* be written on the front of your index card?

   a. Part of speech

   b. Word

   c. Definition

   d. Pronunciation

5. In addition to context clues and word analysis, you can also _____ in your textbook.

SHORT-ANSWER QUESTIONS

6. You encounter a few unfamiliar words in your economics book. You skim over them because they are not signaled in boldface print as vocabulary words for the chapter. Why could this be a problem?

7. **a.** Define the following prefixes; for each one, provide a word that it is a part of.

Prefix:	**Definition**	
a-		mis-
anti-		photo-
circum-		post-
hyper-		

   b. Define the following suffixes; for each one, provide a word that it is a part of.

Suffix:	**Definition**	
-ant		-ive

-ly   -hood

-ic   -ship

-ness

Part II

Verbal Abuse: Words on the Endangered List
BY PATRICIA O'CONNOR

1. Based on the title and headings, what do you expect this reading selection to be about?

2. What do you already know about the topic?

"Verbal Abuse: Words on the Endangered List"

The give-and-take of language is something like warfare. A word bravely soldiers on for years, until one day it falls face-down in the trenches, its original meaning a casualty of misuse. *Unique* is a good example: a crisp and accurate word meaning "one of a kind," now frequently degraded to merely "unusual."

Then there are what I call mixed doubles: pairs of words and phrases that are routinely confused, like *affect* and *effect*. Finally, there are words that are mispronounced, misspelled, or so stretched out of shape that they aren't even words anymore—like that impostor *irregardless*. Keep in mind, though, that today's clumsy grotesquerie may be tomorrow's bon mot. The phrase *live audience* was a silly redundancy before sound and video recording came along.

Speaking of technology, a computer spelling checker is a wonderful resource—I don't know what I'd do without mine—but don't depend too much on it. For instance, my spell-check software tells me that *restauranteur* and *judgement* and *straightlaced* are spelled correctly, but I know better. And it doesn't care how I use *affect* and *effect*, as long as they're spelled right.

Here are some of the most commonly mauled words and phrases, and tips on how to rescue them. Bloodied but unbowed, an abused word shouldn't be given up for dead. Give it back its proper meaning, spelling, usage, and pronunciation, and it will live to fight another day.

What's the Meaning of This?

decimate. Who says grammar books don't have sex and violence? To *decimate* means literally "to slaughter every tenth one," although most people don't intend it literally. It can be used loosely to mean "to destroy in part" (*Gomez says the mushroom crop in the cellar has been decimated by rats*), but don't use it to mean "to destroy entirely." And definitely don't attach a figure to the damage: *The earthquake decimated seventy-five percent of Morticia's antiques.* Ouch!

dilemma. This is no ordinary problem; the *di* (from the Greek for "twice") is a clue that there's a *twoness* here. A *dilemma* is a situation involving two choices—both of them bad. (This idea is captured neatly in the old phrase about being caught on the *horns of a dilemma*.) *Richie faced a dilemma: he could wear the green checked suit with the gravy stain, or the blue one with the hole.*

eclectic. This word is mistakenly used to mean discriminating or sophisticated; in fact, it means "drawn from many sources." *Sherman has an eclectic assortment of mud-wrestling memorabilia.*

enervating. Energizing it's not. On the contrary: if something's *enervating*, it drains you of energy. *Frazier's date found his conversation enervating.*

fortuitous. No, this word doesn't mean fortunate or lucky. *Fortuitous* means accidental or by chance. *It was entirely fortuitous that Potsie washed his car just before it rained.*

hero. There was a time when this word was reserved for people who were… well…heroic. People who performed great acts of bravery or valor, often facing danger, even death. But lately, *hero* has started losing its luster. We hear it applied indiscriminately to professional athletes, lottery winners, and kids who clean up at spelling bees. There's no other word quite like *hero*, so let's not bestow it too freely. It would be a pity to lose it. *Achilles was a hero.*

hopefully. By now it's probably hopeless to resist the misuse of *hopefully*. Strictly speaking, there's only one way to use it correctly—as an adverb meaning "in a hopeful manner." (*I'm thinking of going to Spain," said Eddie. "Soon?" Mrs. Cleaver asked hopefully.*) In an ideal world, it wouldn't be used to replace a phrase like "It is hoped" or "I hope," as in: *"Hopefully the cuisine in Spain will be as delectable as your own," Eddie said.* But of course it *is* used that way. In the time it takes you to read this sentence, *hopefully* will be misused at least once by every man, woman, and child in the United States…. Whether we like it or not—and I don't—*hopefully* seems to be joining that class of introductory words (*happily, sadly, honestly, frankly, seriously,* and others) that we use not to describe a verb, which is what adverbs usually do, but to describe our own attitude toward the statement that follows. When I say, "Sadly, somebody else won the jackpot," I don't mean the other guy was sad about winning. I mean, "I'm sad to say that somebody else won the jackpot." And "Frankly, he disgusts me" doesn't mean the poor guy is disgusting in a frank way. It means, "I'm frank when I say that he disgusts me." So there you have it. Join the crowd and abuse *hopefully* if you want; I can't stop you. But maybe if enough of us preserve the original meaning it can be saved. One can only hope.

irony. I hope some TV news reporters are tuning in. A wonderful word for a wonderful idea, *irony* refers to a sly form of expression in which you say one thing and mean another. (*"You're wearing the green checked suit again, Richie! How fashionable of you," said Mrs. Cunningham, her voice full of irony.*) A situation is *ironic* if the result is the opposite—or pretty much so—of what was intended. It isn't merely coincidental or surprising, as when the newscaster thoughtlessly reports, "Ironically, the jewelry store was burglarized on the same date last year." If the burglars take great pains to steal what turns out to contain a homing device that leads the police to them, that's *ironic*. (And forget the correct but clunky *ironical*.)

literally. This means actually or to the letter. (*Martha Stewart sprayed a dried bouquet with metallic paint, literally gilding the lily.*) *Literally* is often confused with *figuratively*, which means metaphorically or imaginatively. No one says *figuratively*, of course, because it doesn't have enough oomph. I am reminded of a news story, early in my editing career in Iowa, about a Pioneer Days celebration, complete with covered wagons and costumed "settlers." Our reporter proposed to say that spectators "were literally turned inside out and shot backwards in time." Gee, we should have sent a photographer along....

livid. This isn't the colorful adjective you may think it is. *Livid* doesn't mean red or flushed (as in vivid or florid)—at least not yet. It means bluish, black-and-blue, or ashen. (*"The corpse is livid, Inspector," said Dr. Watson. "Obviously he's been dead for some time."*) Stay tuned, however. Dictionaries have started to notice that *livid* is sometimes taken to mean red, so change may be on the way.

unique. If it's *unique*, it's the one and only. It's unparalleled, without equal, incomparable, nonpareil, unrivaled, one of a kind. In other words, there's nothing like it—anywhere. There are no degrees of uniqueness, because the unique is absolute. Nothing can be more, less, sort of, rather, quite, very, slightly, or particularly *unique*. The word stands alone, like *dead, unanimous,* and *pregnant. The Great Wall of China is unique.*

via. This means "by way of," not "by means of." *Seiji drove to Tanglewood via Boston.* Not: *Seiji drove to Tanglewood via car.*

Source: Adapted from P. O'Connor, "Verbal Abuse: Words on the Endangered List," *Woe Is I: The Grammarphobe's Guide to Better English in Plain English* (New York: Putnam, 1996), pp. 81–87.

OBJECTIVE QUESTIONS

Read each of the following multiple-choice questions and select the best possible answer from the four choices given.

1. Which of the following sentences describes a *dilemma*?

   a. I didn't write my paper yet.

   b. It's Thursday night and I've finished my homework, so I can either go to the movies or go to the bar.

   c. I have to either tell him I'm cheating on him or risk that he will find out from someone else.

   d. I have two chances to win ice cream at TCBY because I entered the contest twice.

2. Which of the following sentences contains irony?

   a. He jumped in the river to save his dog from drowning, but ended up drowning himself.

   b. It did snow on Christmas after all.

   c. Surprisingly, I won the lottery.

   d. Three people in my class have the same birthday.

3. Which of the following sentences includes the correct use of unique?

   a. The painting was very unique.

   b. We had a pretty unique experience last summer when the red-winged blackbird attacked us in the memorial garden.

   c. I had the unique experience of belching in front of the queen.

   d. My situation is kind of unique; I was hit by a car but I got up and walked away.

4. Which of the following sentences includes the correct use of via?

   a. She transported her pot-bellied pig via a cat carrier, a *large* cat carrier.

   b. I went to Niagara Falls via Canada.

   c. Eminem rose to fame via 8 Mile Road in Detroit.

   d. He was taken to the penitentiary via a state police vehicle.

SHORT-ANSWER QUESTIONS

6. Create a word map for one word in "Verbal Abuse" that was unfamiliar to you.

7. Analyze the word parts of any two words presented in "Verbal Abuse".

8. Explain how you could use your learning journal to understand subtle differences between correct and incorrect uses of the word *unique*.

Website Sources for Additional Practice

Visit at least two of the following websites; enjoy!

http://www.wolinskyweb.com/word.htm

http://www.vocabulary.com/

http://www.ucc.vt.edu/stdysk/vocabula.html

http://www.word-dectective.com

http://home.earthlink.net/~ruthpett/safari/index.htm

http://webster.commnet.edu/grammar/vocabulary.htm

http://www.cln.org/int_expert.html

http://www.eslcafe.com

http://www.wordfocus.com

http://www.pobox.com/~verbivore

http://www.uri.edu/comm_service/cued_speech/1000

http://www.lexfiles.com/14-words.html
The 14 words that make all the difference.

Chapter 3

Remembering What You Read

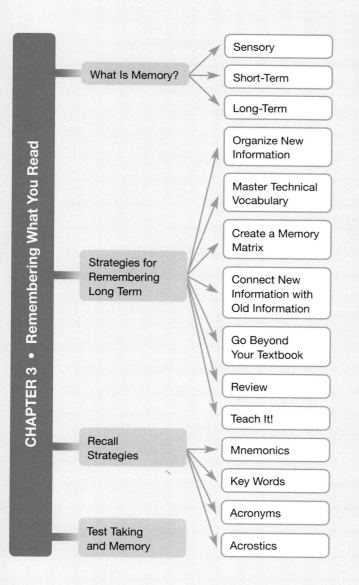

- What Is Memory?
  - Sensory
  - Short-Term
  - Long-Term
- Strategies for Remembering Long Term
  - Organize New Information
  - Master Technical Vocabulary
  - Create a Memory Matrix
  - Connect New Information with Old Information
  - Go Beyond Your Textbook
  - Review
  - Teach It!
- Recall Strategies
  - Mnemonics
  - Key Words
  - Acronyms
  - Acrostics
- Test Taking and Memory

Chapter Contents

Chapter Goals

In this chapter you will learn:

- The three stages of the memory process and how they work.
- Strategies to help you process information at each stage of the memory process.
- Why you can forget what you read or hear.
- Strategies that will help you remember what you read.

Chapter Vocabulary

As you read the chapter, take note of these words and phrases, which represent important concepts from the chapter and will be in **boldface type**. Make sure you understand them before the post test at the end of the chapter.

memory	**long-term memory**	**memory cue**
acronyms	**sensory memory**	**rote learning**
key words	**acrostics**	**short-term memory**
mnemonics	**chunking**	

Barb, an occupational therapy student, complained of having a poor memory in a journal entry. She believed that having a poor memory was a permanent condition; she thought that a person was born with either a good memory or a bad one and there was nothing she could do about it. She soon realized, after learning some basic memory strategies, that memory can be enhanced.

Have you ever flipped through a 500-page textbook and wondered how you would ever remember all the information in it? Perhaps you have noticed that other students seem to remember more than you do, or that you remember material from your psychology textbook more easily than from your physics text. We live in a very competitive, high-tech world in which we are bombarded with massive amounts of information daily. Those who can learn and retain information have an advantage, both in college and at work.

Learning Journal

In your journal, write about how you currently remember information. What are some techniques you use? Do you think you have a good memory? Why or why not? In what classes is it easier for you to remember information? Why do you think this is so? What do you think interferes with your memory?

Barb's Learning Journal Entry

I don't have a real technique to help me remember stuff. Right now, the only thing I do is read, reread, and reread my notes. There has to be a better way. I want to do well, but sometimes it scares me how much information I need to know for *my program. I want to become an occupational therapist. I didn't know that I'd have to memorize so much to be one! I've never had a good memory! I can't remember anything!!! I read a text-book chapter, and as soon as I'm done reading it, I've forgotten it. The easiest class for me to remember stuff in is biology. I seem to already know the information. I think it's because I really love it and I took biology courses in high school.*

There are reasons why people forget what they read, and you can learn a number of strategies to improve your memory.

Memory Survey

Before learning more about how your memory works, complete this survey. It will help you identify which memory skills you are already using and which ones you need to learn or practice more.

Exercise 3a	**Memory Survey**

Read each statement and respond to it based on your *current* reading habits. In the space provided, write **yes** if the statement correctly describes you or **no** if it does not.

_____ **1.** My use of concentration strategies affects how well I remember information.

_____ **2.** I relate previously learned information to the information I am currently learning.

_____ **3.** I really don't have to understand information in order to remember it.

_____ **4.** I review my textbooks only right before an exam; reviewing more frequently is unnecessary.

_____ **5.** I have trouble understanding and remembering information that contains technical vocabulary.

_____ **6.** I know why I sometimes forget what I read.

_____ **7.** I use mnemonic techniques to help me recall what I learned.

_____ **8.** Using mnemonic techniques is all you need to know about memorizing text-book material.

_____ **9.** When learning new and difficult information, I read out loud.

_____ **10.** I make a conscious effort to organize textbook information in my head, on paper, or with other students.

What Is Memory?

Memory is the process of storing information, and as in any process, successive steps or stages are *essential* for it to work. Imagine baking a chocolate cake. You need the right ingredients (baking chocolate, flour, sugar, eggs, butter, milk, salt, and baking soda), cooking utensils, and an oven. You have to follow specific steps in order: preheat the oven, prepare the pans, measure out the ingredients, mix the batter, pour it in a pan, and bake it for the correct time at the proper temperature. Unless you follow all these steps, your cake will end up undercooked, dry, or burned. In the same way, if you do not follow the steps in the memory process as you read your textbooks, you will not remember the information correctly or perform your best on exams.

The three stages in the memory process are *sensory memory*, *short-term memory*, and *long-term memory*.

Sensory Memory

Sensory memory is the first stage in the memory process. New information enters your brain via your senses of taste, smell, sight, touch, and hearing, but your sensory memory retains this information only for a fraction of a second. It has an extremely limited capacity and is easily erased unless you purposely *pay attention* to information, *intend* to remember it, and then *work* to transfer the information to your short-term memory.

Pay Attention while Reading

Karl is a first-year psychology student. He faithfully reads his child development assignments each week, but he feels overwhelmed by the number of theorists and the details of their theories. He can remember most of their names and the number of stages in each theory, but then his mind goes blank. He does not do well on multiple-choice tests, as he cannot remember the specific details of each theory. In his mind they all blend together. He performed poorly on his midterm exam, even though he had read all the material and regularly attended class.

Karl does not pay close enough attention to the details that distinguish one theory from another, which is why he has difficulty with multiple-choice tests. To perform well on them, Karl must pay close attention to details as he reads. The problem of not paying enough attention to textbook information is a sensory memory one. Although you recognize the words and the general topic as you read your textbooks, you may not pay enough attention to remember important details.

Attention

To illustrate how purposeful attention is necessary in order to remember specific details, think about a penny, a very common object you probably hold in your hand at least once every day. Test yourself now, and without looking, try to recall 10 details of a penny and write them here.

1. _____   2. _____

3. _____   4. _____

5. _____   6. _____

7. _____   8. _____

9. _____   10. _____

If you found it difficult to remember 10 details, it is probably because you have never paid close attention to pennies before, even though you see and use them every day. In the same way, if you do not pay close enough attention as you read, the details will not go through the necessary stages of the memory process, and you will not be able to remember them. *Seeing* the details does not guarantee perfect recall. You must purposely pay close attention in order for information to be stored in your sensory memory long enough for it to become part of your short-term memory.

Use All Your Senses

Your senses help you remember things even when you make no deliberate effort to do so. Certain songs can transport you back in time to where you were when you first heard them. The smell of cotton candy can trigger childhood memories of visits to the fair. So when you read new information, try to use as many of your senses as possible. The following strategies will help you increase your attention level and sharpen your sensory memory.

Six Strategies for Improving Sensory Memory

1. *Read your text aloud.* (Reading and hearing help visual and auditory learners.)

2. *Draw pictures of the information you are learning.* (Seeing and touching help visual and kinesthetic learners.)

3. *Act out a chapter in front of a mirror or an audience.* (Hearing, seeing and doing help all types of learners.)

4. *Visualize the information in your head.* (Seeing helps visual learners.)

5. *Touch the textbook pages and use your fingers to point to new words.* (Seeing and touching help visual and kinesthetic learners.)

6. *Read while riding an exercise bike.* (Seeing and doing help visual and kinesthetic learners.)

Learning Journal

In your journal, describe one additional way you could use your senses that is consistent with your preferred learning style.

Exercise 3c

Using Your Senses

Read the following textbook excerpt. On a sheet of paper, explain or demonstrate how you would purposely use at least one sensory memory strategy to help you remember the information. For example, you may draw a picture that represents *your* understanding of the excerpt. Whatever strategy you choose, be sure to explain how this technique will help you remember the information.

Excerpt from "Being Prey" by Val Plumwood

Escaping the crocodile was not the end of my struggle to survive. I was alone, severely injured, and many miles from help. During the attack, the pain from the injuries had not fully registered. As I took my first urgent steps, I knew something was wrong with my leg. I did not wait to inspect the damage but took off away from the crocodile toward the ranger station.

After putting more distance between me and the crocodile, I stopped and realized for the first time how serious my wounds were. I did not remove my clothing to see the damage to the groin area inflicted by the first hold. What I could see was bad enough. The left thigh hung open, with bits of fat, tendon, and muscle showing, and a sick, numb feeling suffused by entire body. I tore up some clothing to bind the wounds and made a tourniquet for my bleeding thigh, then staggered on, still elated by my escape. I went some distance before realizing with a sinking heart that I had crossed the swamp above the ranger station in the canoe and could not get back without it.

Source: Val Plumwood, "Being Prey." *The Best American Science and Nature Writing,* ed. E. Wilson and B. Bilger (City: Publisher, 2001), p. 190.

Short-Term or Working Memory

Short-term memory is the second stage in the memory process. Like sensory memory, it is temporary and limited in its capacity. Information stays in your sensory memory for about 20-30 seconds, but it can be stored in your short-term memory for several minutes if you *consciously* do something with it. Some information travels from sensory to short-term and even to long-term memory without a conscious effort on your part, such as when you have a traumatic experience like a car crash. When learning textbook material, however, you need to consciously apply strategies at each stage of the memory process to ensure that what you read will become part of your long-term memory.

There are many strategies you probably already use to retain sensory information in your short-term memory. You may ask for a phone number from an operator, for example, and recite it enough times to avoid having to write it down before you make your call. You may read your political science textbook and come across the words *Marxism* or *democracy* and pause a bit to ponder their meanings. Both these techniques achieve the goal of conveying sensory information into your short-term memory.

According to current brain research, the average short-term memory can hold between five and seven bits of information at a time (Miller's Theory of Chunking). For example, read the following set of numbers: 386205684. Now cover them up and continue reading. Think about all of the times you have looked up a number in the phone book, and when you were about to dial, someone said something, and you forgot the number and had to look it up again. Now, what were the numbers that you just read? Unless you gave the numbers your *attention* and *actively* did something with them, chances are you did not remember them.

Your difficulty in remembering them is partly due to the fact that there were more than seven. But more importantly, they did not stay in your mind because you did nothing to keep them in your short-term memory. Try the exercise again, but this time pretend the numbers are a social security number and organize them like this: 386-20-5684. Now, instead of memorizing nine *separate* "bits" of information, try to remember the three *groups* of numbers. Repeat the numbers to yourself using this format and then cover them up and see if you do better.

Were you able to remember the numbers this time? You probably were. The important thing to remember about short-term memory is that you must *do something*, use a memory strategy, to retain information. And, to remember information indefinitely, you must use additional strategies to transfer it from your short-term to your long-term memory where it will be permanently stored.

Chunking

The strategy you just used is called chunking. **Chunking** works by condensing the amount of information you have to learn. For example, suppose you have a change purse that can hold only seven coins. If you put in seven pennies, its capacity is going to be only seven cents. But if you place seven quarters, seven silver dollars, or even seven gold coins in it, its capacity will remain the same, but its value will increase significantly. Chunking works the same way; it increases the capacity of your short-term memory. It also assists in the transfer of information to your long-term memory.

There are many ways to chunk information. You can use time of occurrence, similar categories, alphabetical order, or similarities between items. Any grouping is good as long as it is meaningful to you. Grouping bits of information, using key ideas to help you organize them, will help you better remember what you have read.

Exercise 3d

Chunking

Study the following list of words for 60 seconds. Then cover them up and list as many as you can remember on a separate sheet of paper before turning to the next page.

accounting	forest	government	painting
animals	executive	river	nature
art	mountain	king	politics
beauty	corporation	market	rules
business	currency	museum	song

Were you able to remember them all? Probably not. An effective way to do so would be to chunk the words on the list. Instead of trying to remember 20 separate items, which will overload your short-term memory, you chunk the items by placing them into groups or categories. Look at the items again and try to determine how some of them are alike.

How many categories did you find? Most people find four: art, business, government, and nature. Instead of trying to remember 20 separate items, you can now chunk the words into four groups using these categories, a manageable number of items for your short-term memory. If you ever want to recall the words again, the four key categories will serve as cues to help you do so.

Learning Journal

Based on your understanding of chunking, use your journal to write about how you would use this technique to organize the information from the following biology passage. Chunk the information into categories that make sense to you.

A muscle is a contractile organ consisting of many cells. The human body contains three types of muscle tissue: skeletal muscle, cardiac muscle, and smooth muscle.

Skeletal muscle is attached to the periosteum of bone, either directly or by a tough connective tissue called a tendon. Skeletal muscles have striations, dark bands located at right angles to the long axis of the muscle. Because their contractions can usually be controlled, skeletal muscles are referred to as voluntary muscles.

Cardiac muscle, which makes up the walls of the heart, is also striated. Cardiac muscle is controlled by a special nerve center called the sinoatrial node, which sends electrical signals through the cells. Because its movements cannot be controlled, cardiac muscle is called involuntary muscle.

Smooth muscle, which is found in the walls of the stomach, intestines, and blood vessels, does not have striations. It is made up of long spindle-shaped cells that contain a single nucleus. Smooth muscles are involuntary muscles.

Source: Albert Towle, *Modern Biology* (Austin: Holt, Rinehart and Wilson, 1989).

Long-Term Memory

Long-term memory is the third and final stage in the memory process. Information cannot be permanently stored there until it has passed through both the sensory and short-term memory stages. If you try to memorize information you don't really understand, you will have difficulty remembering it later. Memorizing textbook material without understanding it is called **rote learning** and is similar to the way a parrot repeats words that are meaningless to it. Your college instructors expect you to demonstrate your *understanding* of textbook information on exams, so rote memorization is not an effective memory strategy.

Strategies for Remembering Information Long-Term

You can use a number of strategies to embed information in your long-term memory so that you can access it efficiently when you need it.

Organize Newly Learned Information

> *Joyce wants to be a history major. She reads history books in her spare time and is very good at answering history-related questions. However, in her class on the American Civil War, she does poorly on essay questions. She cannot understand why her extensive factual knowledge is not enough to help her perform well on essay tests.*

Joyce may love history and have a penchant for detail, but in order to understand and remember information about the American Civil War, which is unfamiliar to her, she has to correlate the details with what she already knows about American history. Remembering isolated facts is not enough to do well on essay tests because essay tests are designed to test your complete understanding of a topic. Knowing that General Robert E. Lee surrendered on April 9, 1865, is not enough for Joyce to do well. Her instructor wants her to comprehend the broader picture, such as what economic and political issues led to the secession of the Southern states, and what events contributed to the success of the Federal army. Joyce needs to combine the new pieces of information from her course with what she already knows in order to really remember and understand it.

Even if you pay attention to what you are studying long enough for it to stay in your sensory memory, and understand it well enough to transfer it into your short-term memory, you won't be able to find it later unless you connect it to information already in your long-term memory. To illustrate how the organization of information affects how well you recall it, complete the following exercise.

Organization for Retrieval

Set 1

Write in the requested items using the letters on the right at the *beginning* of each word. The first one is modeled for you.

MODEL   Name a bird beginning with the letter   B bluejay _____

Name an animal beginning with the letter   C _____

Name a fruit beginning with the letter   P _____

Name a metal beginning with the letter   I _____

Name a country beginning with the letter   G _____

Name a boy's name beginning with the letter   M _____

Name a girl's name beginning with the letter   J _____

Name a weapon beginning with the letter   S _____

Name a vegetable beginning with the letter   P _____

Name a classic fairytale beginning with the letter   C _____

Name a flower beginning with the letter   P _____

Set 2

Write in the requested items using the letters on the right at the *end* of each word. The first one is modeled for you.

MODEL   Name a bird ending with the letter   W sparrow _____

Name an animal ending with the letter   G _____

Name a fruit ending with the letter   H _____

Name a metal ending with the letter   R _____

Name a country ending with the letter   Y _____

Name a boy's name ending with the letter   N _____

Name a girl's name ending with the letter   E _____

Name a weapon ending with the letter   W _____

Name a vegetable ending with the letter   T _____

Name a classic fairytale ending with the letter   E _____

Name a flower ending with the letter   T _____

Team Up!

Compare your answers for Exercise 3e with those of two other students. Was Set 2 more challenging? If so, discuss why you think it was more difficult.

Here is another example of how important good organization is for effective retrieval of information. Suppose an instructor has 300 students enrolled in four classes during a fall term. She creates a folder for each, in which she stores their completed work for the semester. Annie wants to see her folder to retrieve an old assignment. However, all 300 folders are piled haphazardly on the floor. Annie's folder is there, but it will require a lot of time and effort to find it. This isn't an effective or efficient system. The instructor would have been wiser to alphabetize or number the files and store them in a file cabinet so they would be easy to retrieve when needed. During an exam, you don't have the luxury of unlimited time to retrieve the information you want. You need immediate access. The way you organize and study your information will determine how easily you retrieve it.

Take One Minute

Explain why the way you organize information is important if you intend to remember it.

Master Technical Vocabulary

Annette is taking Chem 132 this year, and each chapter of the required textbook is at least 40 pages long. She can barely get through one page without encountering at least five technical

words, most of which she can neither pronounce nor understand.
Even though she reads each chapter page by page, she rarely
remembers enough about what she reads to do well in chem lab.

To remember something, you have to make sense of it first. Annette needs to make sense of the technical vocabulary in chemistry before she can understand the textbook chapters. The next two exercises illustrate the need to master technical vocabulary in order to remember and comprehend reading material.

Exercise
3f

Nonsense

Read the following paragraph and try to remember the information in it long enough to answer the questions that follow:

The Poxitation of Zraxquif

Each day, it has become more important that you bractoliote about Zraxquif. Zraxquif is a new griebe of zionter. It is poxitated each month in Arizantanna. The Arizantannians gristerlate large frialtonda of fevon and then bracter it to quasel Zraxquif. Zraxquif may well be one of our most precious snezlaus in the next 50 years because of our zionter lescelidge and lack of current poxitated fevons. It could save millions of lives.

---

1. Why is it important to know about Zraxquif?

_____

_____

2. Where is Zraxquif poxitated?

_____

3. How is Zraxquif quaseled?

_____

_____

4. What is Zraxquif?

_____

Were you able to answer the questions? What is zionter? What is a griebe? What does gristerlate mean? Do your answers make sense to you? What course could you use the information in? Biology? Sociology? History? Even though you may have answered all the questions from the Zraxquif passage using context clues, it really didn't make sense. There have probably been times when you have experienced the same confusion reading excerpts from specialized textbooks, as Exercise 3g will demonstrate.

Exercise 3g	**Apparent Nonsense**
	Read the following passage from a geology text, and try drawing a picture to illustrate the information in it.

A cactolith is a quasihorizontal chronolith composed of anastomosing ductoliths, whose distal ends curl up like a harpolith, thin like a sphenolith, or bulge discordantly like an akomlith or ethmolith.

Source: J. McPhee, *Basin and Range* (NY: Farra, Strauss, Giroux Inc., 1981), p. 27.

If the words in the geology passage weren't familiar to you, you probably felt exactly the way you did when you read the nonsense paragraph. And if you didn't understand the paragraph, you would not have been able to draw a picture of what it was about either. (In fact, although the words used here refer to specific rock formations, the USGS geologist who wrote the passage did so as a joke; he was making fun of all the specialized terminology used by geologists!) If, as you read your textbooks, you find that the content does not make sense, use the strategies from Chapter 2 to help you work out the meaning of the words you don't know. For example, many of the words in the geology paragraph end with the word part "lith," which, if you refer to the list of roots in Chapter 2, means a stone. Using this information, you can work out that cactolith, chronolith, ductolith, harpolith, sphenolith, akomlith, and ethmolith are all types of stones—in this case types of stone or rock formations.

Create a Memory Matrix

A matrix is an excellent way to learn and remember large amounts of information. Creating and completing a memory matrix requires you to understand the material you are working on, actively think about what it means, and organize the information in a useful format. Creating and completing a matrix is also an excellent study tool. Table 3.1 is an example of a memory matrix you could create if you had to remember a number of different minerals for a geology exam.

Table 3.1	Mineral Matrix							
MINERALS CLASS	**CHEMICAL COMPO-SITION**	**COLOR**	**HARD-NESS**	**SPECIFIC GRAVITY**	**FRACTURE**	**CLEAVAGE**	**CRYSTAL STRUCTURE**	
Acanthite (sulfides)	Ag2S	Lead-gray to black-metallic	2–2.5	7.2–7.4	Hacky	Indistinct	Isometric cubes, rare; octahedrons in parallel groups	
Cassiterite (oxides/ hydroxides)	SnO2	Brown to black, rarely reddish, yellow, gray, colorless	7	6.8–7.1	Conchoidal	Uneven	Tetragonal (short columnar or acicular common)	

Exercise 3h

Memory Matrix

Using the information you have learned in this chapter, complete the matrix in Table 3.2 on the memory process. You will have to know and understand the information about the memory process in order to complete it successfully.

Table 3.2	Memory Matrix		
STAGES OF MEMORY	**EXPLANATION OF STAGE**	**HOW TO "PROCESS" INFORMATION TO STAGE**	**STRATEGIES FOR PROCESSING INFORMATION**
Sensory memory			
Short-term memory (working memory)			
Long-term memory			

Drawing the Memory Process

Using only the information from your memory matrix, draw a picture of the three stages of the memory process on a piece of paper. Be creative with your drawing and make it as complete as possible. Be prepared to explain your picture to other students. Figure 3.1 shows an example.

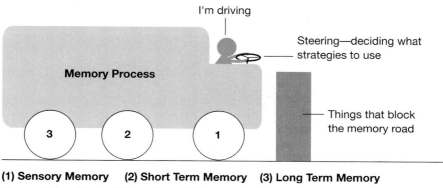

(1) Sensory Memory   (2) Short Term Memory   (3) Long Term Memory

Figure 3-1:   Student Drawing of Memory Process

Connect New Information to Information You Already Know

According to leading brain and learning specialist Janet Zadina, different types of information activate different pathways in the brain, and the brain stores new information according to how it relates to what we already know and have "on file." For example, everything related to color is stored (filed) in one part of the brain, while remembering faces is stored in another—just as you store information related to sociology, American literature, and biology in different files in your computer. The more you can relate new information to what you have already learned, the better you will understand and remember it. It's analogous to building onto your home. The foundation consists of your prior knowledge, and the new information is the addition. It fits snugly into the foundation and so becomes easy to locate. It has a place and an address. You know how to get there. By connecting new information to old you make both more meaningful, as the spatial memory test in Exercise 3j illustrates.

Spatial Memory Test

Take no more than 60 seconds to memorize the shapes in Figure 3.2 associated with each letter. Then cover them up and draw as many as you can remember on a sheet of paper.

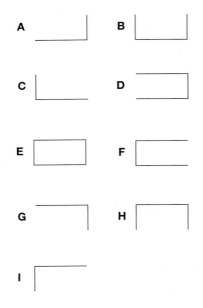

Figure 3-2:   Letter/Shape Combination Source: Janet Zadina

How many shapes were you able to remember? Drawing pictures to illustrate information you are learning is another useful technique for establishing connections between old and new information. It forces you to think about what you already know of a topic, and to connect newly learned information to it. (You also benefit from using the additional learning style of touch.)

Exercise 3k

Establishing Connections

Apply what you have just learned about making connections between old and new information to the following excerpt, and see how many and what kinds of relationships you can make. As you read the excerpt, think about what you already know about the topic. Be creative and enjoy yourself. Draw pictures, create lists, create a timeline; use whatever strategy works for you. This type of thinking takes practice. You will find that some of your responses are more effective than others because you made stronger connections to information already very familiar to you.

Geologic Time

The earth was formed about 4.7 billion years ago. When we think of a person who lives to be 100 years old as having had a long life, it becomes clear that the earth is incredibly old indeed. Because our usual concept of time is dwarfed when we speak of billions of years, it is useful to compare the age of the earth with something more familiar.

Imagine that the height of the Sears Tower represents the age of the earth. The tower is 110 stories or 412 meters (1,353 ft) tall. In relative terms, even the thickness of a piece of paper laid on the roof would be too great to represent an average person's lifetime. Of the total building height, only 4.7 stories represent the 200 million years that have elapsed since the present ocean basins began to form. The first hominids, or humanlike creatures, made their appearance on earth about 15 million years ago, or the height equivalent of one-third of a story. Earth history is so long, and involves so many geologic events, that scientists have divided it into a series of recognizable, distinctive stages.

At this moment, the landforms on which we live are ever so slightly being created and destroyed. The processes involved have been in operation for so long that any given location most likely was the site of ocean and land at a number of different times in its past. Many of the landscape features on earth today can be traced back several hundred million years. The processes responsible for building up and tearing down those features are occurring simultaneously, but usually at different rates.

In the last 40 years, scientists have developed a useful framework within which one can best study our constantly changing physical environment. Their work is based on the early 20th century geological studies of Alfred Wegener, who proposed the theory of continental drift. He believed that all landmasses were once united in one super continent and that over many millions of years the continents broke away from each other, slowly drifting to their current positions. Although Wegener's theory was initially rejected outright, new evidence and new ways of rethinking old knowledge have led to wide acceptance in recent years by earth scientists of the idea of moving continents. Wegener's ideas were a forerunner of the broader plate tectonics theory, which encompasses continental drift, seafloor spreading, the movement of lithospheric plates, and the deformation of the earth's crust. The word *tectonics* comes from the Greek word for builder, *tekton*.

Source: A. Getis, J. Getis, and J. Fellmann, "Geologic Time." *Introduction to Geography,* 8th ed. (Boston: McGraw-Hill, 2002), p. 60.

Team Up!

With four other classmates, share your responses to Exercise 3k. Compare your associations. Select one to represent your team, and be prepared to explain to the class what made it the team's choice.

Strategies for Connecting Information

The importance of purposely relating new information to what you already know cannot be overemphasized. Here are three more strategies you can use:

Strategy 1, comparison: *Note the similarities between what you are studying and information you already know.* For example, if you are learning about the process of photosynthesis in biology class, you can remember it by noting its similarities to the *digestive process* in human beings. You can connect the details of the photosynthesis process—plants need light to grow (newly learned information)—to the corresponding details of the food consumption process—humans need food to grow (familiar information). When you need to recall how photosynthesis works for a paper or an exam, you can easily locate the information in your memory with the cue, "It's similar to the human process of food consumption."

Strategy 2, addition: *Add new information to more familiar information.* For example, plants need light (new information) *and* they also need water (familiar information).

Strategy 3, exemplification: Provide concrete, familiar examples to illustrate the new information. For example, a tulip (concrete example) is a plant that needs light to bloom (new information).

Exercise 3|

Connecting New Information to Information You Already Know

Look at the following sentences and try to relate each one to something you already know using any one of these connecting techniques: comparison, addition, or exemplification. Write your responses in the spaces provided. The first one is modeled for you.

MODEL   **1.**   The acronym *RAM* stands for *random access memory,* which is the main memory the computer uses to write, store, and retrieve information while the computer is running.

RAM is like your desktop. It is a place to put everything while you're

working. When you are done working, you put everything away and

your working materials—pens, calculator, address book—are no longer

immediately accessible (comparison: RAM = unfamiliar, desk = familiar).

_____

2.   A trapezoid is a four-sided figure with two parallel sides.

_____

_____

3.   An atom is the smallest particle of a chemical element that can exist alone.

_____

_____

4.   "Because a given weight of fat provides about twice as many calories as the same weight of carbohydrate or protein, energy is stored most compactly in the form of fat."

Arms, _Biology: A Journey into Life_ (Saunders College Publishing, 1994), p. 488.

_____

_____

_____

5.   "In East Africa a common name for the supreme being is Mulungu, a word of unknown origin but indicating the almighty and ever-present creator. The thunder is said to be his voice and the lightning his power; he rewards the good and punishes the wicked."

Parrinder (ed.), _World Religions: From Ancient History to the Present_ (The Hamlyn Publishing Group Limited, 1983), p. 62.

_____

_____

_____

Go beyond Textbook Information

You can make stronger connections between newly learned information and prior knowledge by doing additional research on a new topic. If you are learning about polynomials in algebra, for example, look up the word _polynomials_ in your dictionary. Seek out a high school algebra textbook for an alternate, perhaps less complicated explanation of polynomials. Talk to people in your math class and have them explain to you how polynomials work.

Review

One of the most effective ways to embed new information into your long-term memory is to read and review it aloud. Verbalizing helps you attend to the new information better because you are using more of your senses as you read (seeing, hearing, and touching). Reading aloud also helps you to block out external distracters like background noise and inner ones such as worries about how you will do in an upcoming exam.

An important aspect of reviewing your textbooks involves timing. *When you review newly learned textbook information is almost as important as the review process itself.* Over 50 percent of what you read or heard in a lecture today will be forgotten 24 hours from now if you do nothing to transfer the information from sensory memory to long-term memory. It is actually easier for your brain to forget information than to learn it, so just reading your assignments is not enough. Schedule regular review sessions shortly after having read textbook assignments. A few minutes of consistent, daily review are far more effective than having to relearn everything several weeks later.

Teach It!

Another review technique that works well is to lecture aloud on the material you are studying. Explaining something is an excellent way to find out how well you know and understand it. Try giving a lecture (using a topic from a textbook chapter you are currently studying) in the privacy of your own home in front of the mirror, or to someone who knows little about the subject. Someone with little background in the topic is likely to be an excellent judge of how well you explain yourself. To them, the success of your lecture will depend on the clarity of your explanations and your choice and use of words. Getting together with a group of classmates who are familiar with what you are discussing is even better because they can also let you know how accurate you are.

Strategies for Recalling Information

Mnemonics

Mnemonics are tricks you can use to help you recall information *after you have understood and learned it.* By associating a mnemonic device with information stored in your memory, you create a *cue* to that specific topic. **A memory cue** helps you locate information in a similar way to a telephone hotline. It calls up the required information by giving you direct access to where it is stored in your long-term memory.

Key Words

Key words represent the topic or main ideas of the material you are reading. Instead of trying to remember an entire chapter word-for-word, you can use them as memory cues by attaching related information to them. For example, if you were studying endangered species, key words could be *pollution* (attach information on manufacturing, agricultural runoff, and sewage), *commercialization* (connect information on the commercial use of turtle shells, elephant tusks, and rhinoceros horns), and *habitat* (include information on the cutting of old-growth forests and strip mining). Key words can also cue you to details if you chunk them using the same technique.

Acronyms

Acronyms are words created by using the first letters of each word or phrase that you intend to remember. One of the more famous acronyms is HOMES, which people use to help them remember the names of the Great Lakes: Huron, Ontario, Michigan, Erie, and Superior. Another acronym is FACE, used by beginning music students to remember the musical notes written in the spaces of the treble clef: F, A, C, E. Both HOMES and FACE are easy to remember because they are familiar words.

Read the following excerpt from a sociology textbook and create an acronym that will help you to remember the characteristics of adults considered at high risk for heart disease.

Risk Factors*
Heredity—people with two relatives under age 60 who have heart disease.
Age—people who are 51—65 years old.
Tobacco Usage—people who smoke 30 cigarettes, or more, per day.
Lbs.—people who are 36 to 50 pounds, or more, over their optimal body weight.
Exercise—people who do sedentary work and get only light recreational exercise.
Habits of eating food—people who eat 40 percent or more of animal or solid fat.

Your acronym: _____

---

*Adapted from J. Greenberg and G. Dintiman, *Exploring Health: Expanding the Boundaries of Wellness* (Boston: Allyn & Bacon, 1991).

There are no wrong answers for this activity. However, you want to create an acronym that is easy to remember, relates to the topic, and provides cues for all the significant details.

Acrostics

Acrostics are created by using the first letter of each item you need to remember to make a phrase or sentence. For example, suppose you had to remember the order of classifications in the animal kingdom for a biology test: kingdom, phylum, class, order, family, genus, and species. Using the first letter of each word, K, P, C, O, F, G, S, you could create a variety of sentence using all seven letters in their correct order, for example "**K**ing **P**eter **C**alls **O**ften **F**or **G**reat **S**paghetti" or "**K**ing **P**eter **C**ries **O**ut **F**or **G**round **S**ausage." The acrostic sentences you create are purely for your use. The stranger they are, the more likely you will be to remember them. (No one said learning shouldn't be fun!)

Team Up!

On your own, go to the website **http://www.demon.co.uk/mindtool/ mnemeffc.html**. Read the information under "Using Mnemonics to Learn Effectively," and develop a mnemonic technique to help you recall the nine tips listed at this site. (The tips are the bulleted items.) With one other classmate, share your mnemonic technique, and give a specific example of how you could use two of the tips with a class you are taking right now.

Putting It All Together

The following extended analogy illustrates the process by which you take information in through your senses, transfer it to your short-term memory, and ultimately store it in your permanent, long-term memory. You will recognize many of the strategies discussed in this chapter to help you remember and retain information at each stage of the process.

You are walking beside a stream and see a bright yellow flower that catches your attention. You want to see the flower (*desire to learn*) so you lean over to examine it. The flower has three large backward–curving yellow petals, three smaller ones that stand up, and leaves that are long, stiff, and swordlike (*attention — sensory memory*). You continue to stare at it as you resume your walk, reciting the physical properties of the flower to yourself as you go—its color, height, and the shape of its leaves—so you can look it up later (*reciting and intending to remember—short-term memory*).

When you get home, you look the flower up in the *Field Guide to North American Wildflowers* (*going beyond information provided*). You learn a number of details about it, including its name, Yellow Flag, and that it is a perennial that grows in marshes and stream margins. At this point you realize that it is similar to some flowers you have seen in your neighbor's back-yard (*connect the flower to previously learned information*). The next day, talking to your neighbor about the flower, she tells you it was originally introduced from Europe and escaped cultivation (*another connection to something familiar—more details to help you learn about the flower and store it in your long-term memory*).

Two weeks later you read an article in the newspaper on landscape gardening, a particular hobby of yours, and the flower is described there (*connect the flower, new information, to prior knowledge*). As you read the article, you recall the flower in detail and decide you would like to include it in your water garden. Later that day you create a matrix of flowers that you intend to plant the following year, including the Yellow Flag. In your matrix you list the names, features, and characteristics of the flowers you are going to use, and when and where to plant them (*review, long-term memory*).

Four years later, someone describes a wedding to you where she saw the most beautiful yellow flowers used in the floral decorations. Her description triggers your memory. You think of the flower and remember its name, yellow flag, and what it looks like, because the flower and the information related to it are now permanently stored in your long-term memory.

Test Taking and Memory

Even if you have studied well, you may still experience some memory blocks while taking an exam. This is normal and usually temporary. If it happens to you, *remain calm* and continue to work on the exam, focusing on the easy questions first. Oftentimes, reading other easier questions will trigger your memory, which will help you find answers for the questions on which you are blocked. You will do better on exams when you consistently use memory strategies while studying because they help you to store and efficiently recall what you have learned. Here are some other tips to aid your memory during an exam:

- **Drink lots of water the night *before* an exam.** Your brain doesn't function well if it's dehydrated. Avoid excessive caffeine and sugar before an exam.
- **Think positively.** Sometimes the answers will come if you keep a clear head and don't panic. Answer easy questions first.
- **When taking an objective test, think big.** Focus on generalizations—the big picture. Often you will be able to plug in the minor details if you understand the bigger picture.
- **Attempt to answer multiple-choice questions without looking at the answer choices.** This will boost your memory and increase your confidence when your answer matches one of the options.
- **No matter what kind of answer pattern you think has been established in an objective test, don't assume anything.** It is possible to have all of the answers be false or to have "c" be the correct choice four times in a row.
- **Write on your exam paper!**
- **In multiple-choice questions, cross off the answer options you have eliminated.**
- **Underline key terms in essay questions so you know exactly how to answer.**
- **Draw pictures to help you remember what you have learned.**
- **Place checkmarks by questions you want to return to.**

Practice With Reading Passage

Write all responses on a separate sheet of paper.

Reading Practice

How to Really Start Your Own Business
BY D. GUMPERT

PREPARE TO READ

1. Based on the title of the reading passage, what do you expect it to be about?

2. What do you already know about the topic?

3. In order to get the most out of the reading, it's important that you understand the vocabulary. If you don't know the following terms, you will need to look them up in your dictionary before you begin reading.

a. Entrepreneur

b. Proprietorship

A Sole Proprietorship

In a sole proprietorship, a business and its owner are essentially one and the same. Sole proprietorships are generally service businesses that can be handled by one person, such as a plumbing, copywriting, or consulting business. While sole proprietorships tend to be limited to one person, they can hire employees.

Sole proprietorships comprise the bulk of all businesses; approximately 70 percent of the nation's more than 20 million businesses consist of sole proprietorships. Of course, in many cases these sole proprietorships are part-time businesses established as much for tax write-off purposes as for their money-earning potential.

The Advantages

The main advantage of a sole proprietorship is its simplicity to establish and operate. Because there's no need for a company charter or special papers, you don't need an attorney's help to set it up.

Taxes are similarly straightforward. You report your business income and expenses on Schedule C of your personal income tax return. Your profit or loss is then combined with your other income.

The inclusion of your business income on your personal taxes can lead to lower tax rates than if your business were incorporated, because personal rates tend to be lower than corporate rates and you avoid local corporate taxes required by many states.

The Disadvantages

The main disadvantage of being a sole proprietorship is a potential legal one. Because you and the business are one and the same, you are personally liable for its debts and other problems that may arise.

Therefore, if the business runs into financial problems, creditors can come after your personal assets, including your house, to obtain payment. Similarly, if your business injures someone or otherwise harms that person so that they sue you, any financial obligations that result and aren't covered by insurance can be yours personally.

If a sole proprietorship begins to grow and hire employees, the potential legal problems only multiply. If an employee is injured working for you or causes injury to a customer, as the owner you could be personally responsible, depending on the situation.

Sole proprietorships also tend to find financing difficult to come by, either for start-up or expansion. Banks and professional investors prefer the legal protection afforded by a corporation and tend to avoid sole proprietorships.

The tax benefits of not having to pay corporate taxes can be at least partially outweighed by the fact that you can't deduct all your payments for health insurance and other benefits you may provide yourself.

Getting Started

While the federal government has no special requirements for establishing a sole proprietorship, state and local governments often do. You may need to obtain certain local licenses. If you are preparing food products, for instance, you may need a license from the local board of health. If you are an employment or education counselor, you may need to fulfill certification requirements to receive a license and open a practice.

If your business will be started out of your home, you may have to register with county or town officials. This can lead into the tricky area of zoning regulations, which determine how neighborhoods and buildings can be used. For example, some localities allow businesses to be operated from the home, provided no signs are posted. So if you plan to name your business something other than your name, you wouldn't be able to hang a sign outside. But if the business is Smith Associates, you can at least hang a sign that says Smith.

Another matter that needs tending to is that of insurance. You should insure any equipment against damage or theft. You should also have liability insurance to protect you if someone is injured using your product or while doing business on your property. In certain professions, it may be advisable to have specialized liability insurance, such as medical malpractice insurance for doctors and libel insurance for writers. Other insurance areas to investigate are coverage for medical care if someone is injured while visiting your business and for lost business in the event a fire or storm shuts your business down for an extended period.

Clearly, a good insurance agent can help steer you toward the types and amounts of coverage that best suit your needs and your budget.

Partnership

I discussed the matter of partners to some extent in the previous chapter but more in the generic sense. It's possible, for instance, for two or three people to form a business together and incorporate it. Thus, while they are working as partners, they do not have a partnership in a legal or tax sense.

Two or more people may also establish a partnership for legal and tax purposes. A partnership agreement should be drawn up to define the obligations of each partner. Such a partnership files a tax return that computes partnership income and loss. Each partner's share of the income or loss, however, is reported on his or her personal tax return.

The Advantages

A partnership allows a group of owners to get tax benefits similar to those of a sole proprietorship. As noted earlier, individual tax rates tend to be lower than corporate rates.

A partnership also allows for much flexibility in distribution of ownership and income. It may be that there are senior partners who get a larger stake in the business and share of profits than junior partners. Or it could be that income is tied to the amount of business each partner brings in.

The flexibility also allows new partners to be added over time as they prove their ability to contribute to the business. Partnership income in this situation is constantly being redistributed.

The possibility of becoming a partner in a thriving business becomes an important incentive to new employees. The flexibility and motivational aspects of the partnership arrangement have been exploited most effectively by professional service firms—principally law and accounting firms.

The Disadvantages

The main drawbacks of a partnership are the same as those associated with a sole proprietorship. The partners are each personally liable for any debts if the business fails or insurance fails to cover obligations from an accident or lawsuit. In addition, bankers and investors are usually reluctant to make funds available to a partnership because of the potential legal complications that can result.

A partnership can also be subject to serious tensions if the business situation goes less favorably than the partners anticipated. As described in the previous chapter, these interpersonal tensions can be quite intense. But they can carry over to the legal aspect of the partnership as well.

Even assuming the partnership has a well-conceived written agreement, there can be disputes if one partner wants to leave the business or several partners want one partner to leave. These disputes may be over the value of the departing partner's share in the business or the timing of those payments.

What to Do

A key to a successful legal partnership is the quality of the written agreement that sets out the partnership's terms. The more clearly and realistically this agreement anticipates possible future occurrences, the more likely the partnership will be able to weather adversity.

One of the most important sections of any partnership agreement is the buy–sell agreement. This provides terms covering the departure of one or more partners from death, disability, retirement, or resignation. A partnership will usually want to carry life insurance on each partner so that if one partner dies, the partnership will be able to pay that partner's estate for the value of his or her interest in the business.

Other eventualities, though, are less clear-cut and need to be negotiated. There should be a way to value the business if one partner resigns and wants to sell his or her interest. There also needs to be a way to set the length of the payout terms so that the business isn't burdened with suddenly having to make such a huge payment to one partner that the business's viability is jeopardized.

It certainly simplifies the process if a single attorney prepares the partnership agreement and is available to advise the business as it implements the agreement. But each partner should still have his or her own personal attorney review the agreement to make sure each partner's individual interests are protected.

As noted earlier in this section, partnership agreements seem to work best for professional service firms. They don't work as well for companies that make products because of the personal legal exposure for each partner and the need for financing that usually arises as the company expands.

Source: D. Gumpert, *How to Really Start Your Own Business* (Boston: Goldhirsh Group, 1994) pp. 114–20.

CHECK YOUR UNDERSTANDING

OBJECTIVE QUESTIONS

Read the following multiple-choice questions and select the best possible answer from the four choices given.

1. The main advantage of a sole proprietorship is

   a. It's easy to establish and operate.

   b. It allows new partners to be added over time.

   c. The taxes are straightforward.

   d. You avoid local corporate taxes.

2. Which of the following choices is an advantage of having a partnership?

   a. You and your partner are not personally responsible for debts and other problems.

   b. Banks welcome a partnership and lend money to it relatively easily.

   c. Partners get tax benefits similar to those who are in business for themselves.

   d. Partnerships are susceptible to internal tensions.

3. How do taxes differ for a sole proprietorship and a partnership?

   a. Business income is reported on Schedule D of your personal income tax return for a sole proprietorship and on Schedule E for a partnership.

   b. Your profit or loss is combined with your other income for a partnership but not with a sole proprietorship.

    c. Lower tax rates are a benefit for a sole proprietorship but not for a partnership.

    d. In a sole proprietorship, one person benefits from a potentially lower tax rate for business; in a partnership, more than one person benefits.

4. What type of insurance is *not* mentioned in the excerpt for sole proprietors?

    a. Insurance for injuries.

    b. Car insurance.

    c. Insurance for lost business in the event of a fire or storm.

    d. Liability insurance.

5. Which of the following is not a requirement mentioned in the excerpt for starting a sole proprietorship?

    a. Town or county registration requirements.

    b. License requirements.

    c. Business plan requirements.

    d. Federal government zone requirements.

SHORT-ANSWER QUESTIONS.

6. In one sentence, explain what the reading selection was about.

7. What key words would you remember to help you recall what is involved in starting a sole proprietorship? Explain why you would choose those words or phrases as key.

8. Describe the "buy–sell" agreement.

9. What needs to be negotiated in a partnership?

10. What are the advantages and disadvantages of the two ways described to structure a business? Complete a matrix to organize your answer.

Chapter Summary

Memory is the process of storing and retrieving information. You will have difficulty remembering what you read if you do not know the stages in the memory process, and purposely use strategies at each stage to ensure that newly learned information becomes permanently stored. The single most important aspect of memory is understanding what you are trying to remember. It is difficult, if not impossible, to remember concepts you do not understand.

The three primary stages in the memory process are sensory memory, short-term memory, and long-term memory. Specific strategies you can use to enhance your sensory memory include the following: reading your text aloud, drawing pictures of the information you are learning, acting out a chapter in front of a mirror or an audience, visualizing information in your head, using your fingers to point to new words, and reading while riding an exercise bike. Chunking is an effective strategy for organizing and remembering new information so that it remains in your short-term memory long enough to transfer into your long-term memory. In order to permanently store new information you can use strategies such as organizing newly learned information, mastering difficult vocabulary, creating a memory matrix, connecting new information with information you already know, going beyond the textbook, reviewing, and teaching the new information to someone else. Recall techniques called mnemonics can help you retrieve information once it has been learned and stored properly. Some mnemonics introduced in this chapter are key words, acrostics, and acronyms.

Post Test

Answer the following on a separate sheet of paper.

Part I

OBJECTIVE QUESTIONS

1. Match each word in Column A to its correct meaning in Column B.

	Column A		**Column B**	
1.	Memory	a.	Organizing information into 5–7 similar groups	_____
2.	Sensory memory	b.	Memory tricks	_____
3.	Short-term memory	c.	First stage of memory process	_____
4.	Long-term memory	d.	Represent topic or main ideas	_____

5.	Rote learning	e.	Memorizing without understanding	_____
6.	Mnemonics	f.	Final stage of memory process	_____
7.	Memory cue	g.	Helps to call up information	_____
8.	Key words	h.	Process of storing information in your brain	_____
9.	Chunking	i.	Second stage of memory process	_____

2. Which of the following is not an example of a mnemonic strategy:

   a. Chunking

   b. CRS

   c. Acrostic

   d. Acronym

3. If you found it difficult to remember 10 details of a penny, it is probably because you really have never _____ to the details.

4. How you store information does not have a long-term effect on your memory. T or F

5. Which of the following best explains long-term memory?

   a. Having a good memory for things that happened a long time ago.

   b. The first and easiest stage of the memory process.

   c. The third stage of the memory process where information can be permanently stored.

   d. The transition stage between sensory memory and permanent recall.

SHORT-ANSWER QUESTIONS

6. Picture yourself in this scenario: You are taking a biology course for the first time. You are unfamiliar with the terminology and concepts. List three memory strategies you could use to help you effectively learn and recall the new terms and main concepts.

7. What is the difference between processing information into your short-term memory and processing it into your long-term memory? Why is processing information into just your short-term memory not considered effective learning?

8. Explain how you can use concentration and memory skills together to help you read a difficult textbook chapter.

9. Read the following list of items. If you had to remember all of them, which mnemonic technique(s) would you use to recall them?

gold	chicken	rivers	table	crates
potatoes	lakes	beef	silver	lead
meadows	cucumbers	televisions	valleys	iron

10. Why wouldn't it be an effective memory technique to organize the items in Question 9 alphabetically?

Part II

Reading Passage

Kick Florida, or at Least *South* Florida, Out of the Union
BY DAVE BARRY

1. Based on the title of the reading passage, what do you expect it to be about?

2. What do you already know about the topic?

Kick Florida, or at Least *South* Florida, Out of the Union
—DAVE BARRY

I don't say this lightly. I personally live in South Florida, and if we got kicked out of the union, I would no longer enjoy the many benefits of United States citizenship, such as...

OK, here's one: When I purchase a food item at the supermarket, I can be confident that the label will state how much riboflavin is in it. The United States government requires this, and for a good reason, which is: I have no idea. I don't even know what riboflavin is. I do know I eat a lot of it. For example, I often start the day with a hearty Kellogg's strawberry Pop-Tart, which has, according to the label, a riboflavin rating of 10 percent. I assume this means that 10 percent of the Pop-Tart is riboflavin. Maybe it's the red stuff in the middle. Anyway, I'm hoping riboflavin is a good thing; if it turns out that it's a *bad* thing, like "riboflavin" is the Latin word for "cockroach pus," then I am definitely in trouble.

But the point is that I would not have this helpful nutritional information if I lived in some lawless foreign country that does not have strict food-labeling laws, or carelessly allows dried plums to be marketed under the name "dried plums." And that is only *one* advantage of living in the United States. There are many more, but I am not going to go into them, because I have already almost forgotten my topic here, which is: If we want to avoid having another weird presidential election, we should kick Florida out of the union.

As long as South Florida is part of the United States, weird things are going to happen to the nation. Because South Florida is a nuclear generator of weirdness. For one thing, it's a swamp. The entire lower end of the state is about the same height above sea level as Dustin Hoffman. All the people are squeezed onto the coast lines on either side; in the middle is the Everglades, a vast expanse of oozing muck populated by a small tribe of casino-dwelling Native Americans and at least 300 billion mosquitoes, many with the wingspan of a mature osprey.

This means that if you move to South Florida, you are settling down smack-dab in the ancient stomping grounds of a teeming mass of swamp and marine life, which apparently was never notified that this area is now supposed to be zoned for humans.

The first thing I noticed when I moved to the Miami area in 1986 was that I had crabs on my lawn. At my previous residence, in Pennsylvania, I had dealt with crab *grass,* but in Miami, when I went outside in the morning to pick up the newspaper I was confronted by actual *crabs*, dozens of them, scuttling around. And these crabs were *hostile*. It was crab mating season, when the male crabs defend the females fiercely. I'd be half asleep, stumbling back into the house with the paper in my hand, and my path would suddenly be blocked by an irate male crab, lunging at my bare toes with his pincers to keep me from having sex with his woman.

"I don't want to have sex with your woman!" I'd yell at him, leaping backward. "Your woman is a *crab!*" But that only made him angrier, because deep in his heart[1] he knew it was true.

My neighborhood was also the world convention headquarters for the International Association of Big Hairy Spiders. They looked like severely mutated Yorkshire terriers that had developed extra legs and eyeballs, and they were all over the place, in every tree and bush, spinning trampoline-size webs that could stop an NFL fullback. It goes without saying that South Florida also had active populations of ticks, gnats, psychotic fire ants, and these scary huge mutant grasshoppers that could, without any special effects, be cast as major villains in *Jurassic Park II.*

On the amphibian and reptile front, South Florida is semi infested with large, hideous toads that secrete a deadly venom, which means they feel free to saunter onto your patio and sit there for hours, looking insolent, as if they expect you to make them a cheeseburger. And everywhere you look, indoors and out, you see lizards, scampering around and engaging in acts of wanton lizard sex. Many a morning I've awakened to the sight of a lizard on the bedroom ceiling, hanging casually upside down via his suction feet, looking at me with an expression that says: "Perhaps, while you were snoring, I pooped in your mouth."

I personally have encountered only a few smallish alligators, but there are plenty around; Florida's alligator population is currently estimated at over a million.[2] Every

---

[1] Or possibly hearts, depending on how crabs work.
[2] I think they have their own member of Congress.

now and then the newspapers carry stories about alligators chomping on people's dogs, or, on occasion, actual people. It is not at all unusual for a Floridian in a nice suburban neighborhood to walk out onto the patio and discover an alligator in the swimming pool.

Or a major snake. People down here routinely find huge members of the constrictor family in their pools, or lounging on their patios. These are, believe it or not, escaped pets. That's right: As if there weren't already enough local snakes, some Florida residents[3] choose to import, both legally and illegally,[4] immense carnivorous snakes,[5] which are always getting out of their cages, causing the owners to become very worried about what might happen…to the snakes.

"Her name is Midge," they'll tell reporters, referring to a 17-foot escaped python capable of consuming a water buffalo whole. "She hasn't eaten in days! She must be terrified!"

Some of these escaped snakes are later found, wrapped around a tree, or a lamppost, or a slow-moving citizen. But many of them are never found, which means they're still out there somewhere, slithering around and feeding on God knows what. Perhaps cougars. You may think I'm kidding, but a surprising number of Floridians keep large, predatory, extremely nonvegetarian jungle cats as pets. A while back, the commissioners of Pompano Beach were forced to consider an ordinance requiring residents to keep their pets on their property after, in the words of *The Miami Herald*, "a cougar escaped from a private home and briefly chased a small boy."

So you do not want to randomly wander onto a residential Florida property. A painting contractor once told me that one of his men, while attempting to do a job, got chased out of a backyard by an extremely angry emu.

"He was on the radio, scared to death," the contractor said. "He was shouting 'THERE'S A GIANT CHICKEN IN THERE!'"

Did I mention the monkeys?

Source: Dave Barry, *Dave Barry Hits below the Beltway* (New York: Random House, 2001), pp. 128–32.

---

[3]Not to name names, but one of these residents is my good friend Carl Hiaasen, the legendary South Florida columnist and novelist, who keeps pet snakes. He feeds them rats, which he buys at the pet store (rat sales are big down here). "I have to stop on the way home and get some rats" is something you will actually hear Carl say.

[4]Reptile smuggling is a big business down here. In 1999, a man arriving from Barbados was detained at the Miami airport when officials noticed that his pants had some suspicious, wriggling bulges; he turned out to have fifty-five turtles in there. *The Miami Herald* account of this does not say whether the man was wearing a protective cup, but let us hope to God he was.

[5]True story from *The Miami Herald:* A Hollywood, Florida, firefighter was searching through a burning house when he found a 10-foot boa constrictor in distress. He bravely grabbed its head, and the snake coiled around his body. He walked briskly outside and returned the snake to its owner, who said: "Thanks, man, but there's two more in there."

OBJECTIVE QUESTIONS

Read each of the following multiple-choice questions and choose the best answer from the four choices provided.

1. What benefits of living in the United States does Barry mention in this excerpt?

    a. Being able to buy Pop-Tarts.

    b. Having nutrition labels on food items.

    c. Having presidential elections.

    d. Eating riboflavin.

2. According to Barry, why is South Florida so strange?

    a. The mosquitoes aren't big enough.

    b. Everyone lives in the middle of the state.

    c. Dustin Hoffman lives there.

    d. It's a swamp.

3. What problem did Barry have with crabs?

    a. The crabs were hostile.

    b. The male crabs were not loyal to their females.

    c. Barry kept stepping on them.

    d. The crabs bit him.

4. What was Barry's complaint about the reptiles and amphibians in South Florida?

    a. The toads chase him.

    b. The toads are scarce.

    c. The snakes are insolent and expect you to feed them.

    d. Lizards are having lizard sex everywhere.

5. What happens when snakes escape in South Florida?

    a. They attack people.

    b. They consume water buffalo.

    c. Some are never found.

    d. They run loose in Wal-Mart's parking lot.

SHORT-ANSWER QUESTIONS

6. Barry jokes that as long as South Florida is part of the United States, weird things will happen. What weird things does he describe?

7. Explain how you would process the list you have created into your sensory memory, short-term memory, and long-term memory.

8. As a result of what you have learned in this chapter, what changes will you make to improve your learning?

9. What do the terms *saunter* and *insolent* mean as Barry uses them in the following sentence: "On the amphibian and reptile front, South Florida is semi-infested with large, hideous toads that secrete a deadly venom, which means they feel free to *saunter* onto your patio and sit there for hours, looking *insolent*, as if they expect you to make them a cheeseburger" (9th paragraph in the excerpt). What clues did you use to help you figure out the meanings?

10. What is riboflavin?

Website Sources for Additional Practice

http://gator1.brazosport.cc.tx.us/~lac/memory1.htm (interactive quiz to learn more about memory).

http://braindance.com/frambdi1.htm (exercises for memory).

http://www.psychwww.com/mtsite/memory.html (methods for memory improvement).

Chapter 4

Managing Your Reading Time

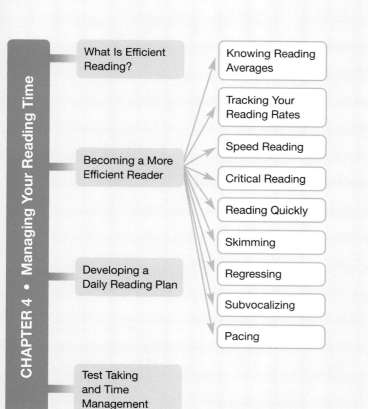

CHAPTER 4 • Managing Your Reading Time

- What Is Efficient Reading?
- Becoming a More Efficient Reader
  - Knowing Reading Averages
  - Tracking Your Reading Rates
  - Speed Reading
  - Critical Reading
  - Reading Quickly
  - Skimming
  - Regressing
  - Subvocalizing
  - Pacing
- Developing a Daily Reading Plan
- Test Taking and Time Management

Chapter Contents

Chapter Goals

After reading this chapter you will know:

- What efficient reading is.
- How to track your reading rate and compute your reading rate averages in different subjects.
- How to develop a daily reading plan.
- Several strategies, including skimming, regressing, subvocalizing, and pacing, that will increase your reading efficiency.

Chapter Vocabulary

As you read, take note of these words and phrases, which represent important concepts from the chapter and will be in **boldface** type. Make sure you understand them before the post test at the end of the chapter.

efficient reading	**speed-reading**	**critical reading**
skimming	**regressing**	**subvocalizing**
pacing		

Do you know how long it really takes you to read a psychology chapter? Should you study biology or psychology first? At what time during the day should you study physics? Every day students intend to read the chapters assigned to them, but only some have a concrete plan for making sure they do. Having a written plan—I will read 21 pages of Chapter 9 at 7 P.M.—is more of a commitment than thinking, I have to read that chemistry chapter tonight sometime. The more specific a reading plan you develop, the better the chance you will complete your reading assignments on time.

Time Survey

Test your present knowledge of time management by completing this survey. Read each statement and respond based on your *current* reading habits. In the space provided, write in the word **yes** if the statement correctly describes you or **no** if it does not.

_____ 1. I complete the reading for my easiest classes first.

_____ 2. I currently use a reading plan.

_____ 3. I use different reading strategies to help me read more efficiently.

_____ 4. I know what my best study times are.

_____ 5. Each day I complete the reading for my favorite classes first and fit reading time for my other classes in later.

_____ 6. Each day I make a list of reading tasks that I need to do.

_____ 7. I save time by taking regular breaks when I read.

_____ 8. It takes me too long to read a chapter.

_____ 9. Sticking to a schedule seems too rigid for me; I'm too spontaneous to stick to a regular reading plan.

_____ 10. Speed-reading is the best strategy for reading efficiently.

What Is Efficient Reading?

Martin can read 22 pages of his political science textbook in an hour, while it takes Vanessa the same time to read only 14 pages of the same book. Who is the more efficient reader? If time is the only criterion, then clearly Martin is. However, time is not the only criterion used in judging reading efficiency in college. It is not even the most important one. **Efficient reading** can be defined as being able to read and comprehend textbook material in an appropriate amount of time *for you*.

Deciding what an appropriate amount of time is for you depends on many factors. It is related to how much time you actually have available to read for each course, the level of difficulty of the textbook material, and the grade you want to earn in a course. Martin works two days a week, so he has little time to read his textbooks. However, he finds the textbook content easy and is comfortable earning a B– in political science. Vanessa, on the other hand, has chosen not to take a job during the semester so she can devote all her time to her studies. She finds the textbook material moderately challenging but still wants an A in the course. Given their goals, they are both reading for an appropriate amount of time to meet their needs.

How you manage your reading time is more important than learning how to read rapidly. Always make comprehension your primary goal: reading efficiently the first time through is often faster. If you make speed your priority, you may finish more quickly, but understand less. As a result, you may have to reread material before a test in order to understand and remember it, which is time-consuming. You will also find that if you make comprehension your primary reading goal, your speed will automatically improve over time.

Learning Journal

Think about your current approach to reading efficiently. What strategies do you use? Do your current strategies work for you? Are you having difficulty completing and understanding reading assignments? Do you have a goal for your grade in each class you take?

Becoming a More Efficient Reader

Everyone wants to know how long it takes their classmates to read an assignment. What's important, though, is to judge your reading rate against *your* prior reading experience and to use other students' reading rates only to help you set appropriate reading goals for yourself. Given the variability of college courses, the wide variety of texts in use, and the extreme diversity of the student population, it is not useful to compare yourself to other people. Someone with a strong interest in British literature, for example, will probably find it easier and quicker to read a novel by Charles Dickens than a student who finds literature boring and considers studying it time wasted that could be better spent on the intricacies of quantum mechanics.

Knowing Reading Averages

The average college student reads about 300 words per minute when reading for pleasure. Table 4.1 details the *average* reading rates for students reading in specific disciplines.

Table 4.1 Reading Rates by Subject Matter	
COURSES	**APPROXIMATE NUMBER OF PAGES PER HOUR**
History, English, political science (lower level)	20–25
Psychology, biology, economics, geography, sociology, math, reading (lower level), accounting	15–20
Chemistry, physics, anatomy, microbiology, physiology, cost accounting	10–15
Difficult, upper-level courses, such as bio-chemistry physics, electrical engineering	8–10

Source: J. Kollaritsch, *Reading and Study Organization Methods for Higher Learning,* 4th ed. (Belmont, CA: Wadsworth, 1990).

If your reading rate in a specific subject is dramatically lower than the average rate in Table 4.1, you may have a reading problem. However, before deciding that your reading is not up to par, find your actual average rate. To do this, you will need to track how fast you read for each of your content courses.

Tracking Your Reading Rates

For two weeks record how many pages of reading you complete per hour for each of your subjects. Then analyze your numbers and, if necessary, adjust your reading behavior. For example, if you find you can read 10 pages per hour for Physics 202 on Mondays and Wednesdays, but only five pages per hour on Fridays, you could decide that Friday is not a good day and study earlier in the week when you are less tired. However, the day may not be the problem. You also need to look at the reading assignment. Friday's reading material could have been more difficult than the other two assignments. If this is the case, calculate your average reading rate for physics as being somewhere between five and 10 pages per hour, depending on the complexity of the material.

After two weeks of record keeping, begin setting reading goals for yourself. If you know that your physics class covers one 42-page chapter per week, and you read seven pages of physics per hour, then you should schedule six hours of reading time per week into your semester study schedule. Seven pages per hour is below the average on the reading chart for physics, but if you are earning As and Bs in the course, you are doing fine. If you read only four pages per hour of physics and are barely holding a D average, then you may have a problem. Visit your academic counseling center on campus; the staff will help you determine if you have a reading problem or if the content of what you are reading is the issue. You might find you would benefit from tutoring. Get help if you need it. Having difficulty with college reading is not a sign of academic failure.

Tracking Your Reading Rates

Pick one subject you are studying this semester. Plan to read the subject material for one hour on each of 14 days (the days need not be consecutive). Use Table 4.2 to record the number of pages you read per hour for each one. Remember to focus on comprehension as you read, not speed.

You can compute your average page per hour reading rate for the subject you chose by adding up the number of pages read in 14 days and dividing the total by 14. For example, if you read a total of 322 pages of history, your average page per hour rate would be 322 ÷ 14 = 23 pages per hour.

Table 4.2 Number of Pages Read

SUBJECT:														
Session Number	1	2	3	4	5	6	7	8	9	10	11	12	13	14
Date														
Number of Pages Read														

Learning Journal

Track your reading rates for all your subjects using copies of Table 4.2. Compute your average page per hour reading rate for each subject.

Analyzing Your Current Reading Rates

Using the results from your learning journal exercise, answer the following questions in the space provided:

1. Was there a difference among reading rates for each of your subjects? For example, were the average pages per hour greater for your biology course than for your history course?

_____

_____

2. If there was a difference, for which course did you have the highest reading rate?

_____

_____

3. Why do you think you read the textbook for this course the fastest?

_____

_____

4. For which course did you have the lowest reading rate?

_____

_____

5. Why do you think you read the textbook for this course more slowly than you did the other textbooks?

_____

_____

_____

6. How do your reading rates compare with the averages in Table 4.1?

_____

_____

Team Up!

Discuss, with one other classmate, how (or if) you currently use any speed-reading techniques. If so, what techniques do you use? If you do not use any such techniques, discuss why you don't.

Take One Minute

On a sheet of paper, write about whether you think you read efficiently.

Speed-Reading

Speed-reading consists of visually grouping words together, reading them in chunks instead of separately. Students in speed-reading classes learn to do this by practicing eye exercises that allow them to read word groups very quickly. In some courses students are advised to skip words like prepositions or avoid subvocalizing, reading words aloud, regressing, rereading, or using their hands to pace themselves. Many speed-reading courses boast that using such strategies can result in 1,000-word-per-minute reading rates.

Critical Reading

Regardless of the claim or the method, speed-reading your college textbooks will not help you understand the material better. The goal of speed-reading is to hurry up, get to the main point, and finish the reading assignment as soon as possible. The goal of **critical reading** is to slow down, take time to digest an author's points (perhaps even disagree with them), relate the newly learned information to previous knowledge on the subject, and think about what you are reading. Critical reading is thinking, and thinking takes time. Speed-reading is not a critical reading strategy.

Take One Minute

On a separate sheet of paper, explain why speed-reading and critical reading are conflicting activities.

Reading Quickly

Reading groups of words can be a useful strategy. Pacing yourself with your hand as you read is okay. But your aim as you read should not be to finish as quickly as possible using any means necessary. You should read, and sometimes reread textbook assignments with the goal of thoroughly understanding them.

Skimming

Reading only some of the words on a page is called **skimming**. Skimming is helpful when you are doing research and want to know if a book or article is going to be useful to your studies. By skimming all or parts of a text, you can see whether the information it contains is pertinent to your project. Skimming is also a good strategy to use before you read an assignment in depth. It tells you how long a selection is so you can estimate how much time you will need to read it, as well as giving you an idea of its content. Knowing what you are going to read about helps you mentally prepare.

Rereading or Regressing

If you don't understand a word, it helps to *reread* the sentence it is in and try to figure out its meaning using context clues. If this does not work, you can look it up in your dictionary and then reread the sentence. When you do not understand a point an author is making, **regressing**, or rereading the paragraphs preceding the one you are having trouble with, will give you another chance to piece together what is being said. Putting what you remember from the later paragraphs together with the information you understood from earlier in the reading, *as you reread* the material, can help you get back on the author's track. It is not useful to skip over the difficult parts of a reading assignment because you will not fully understand them if you do so.

Subvocalizing

Subvocalizing, or reading aloud, is helpful because you use both your eyes and your voice to read. This combination of learning styles improves your understanding of the material and helps you remember it better. But you should not subvocalize if you find the sound of your own voice distracting because it will impair your ability to concentrate.

Pacing

Pacing your reading by using your fingertips to follow each word, or group of words, can improve your reading speed because you become more physically involved in the process, which heightens your ability to concentrate. Another way to pace your reading is to use a bookmark placed horizontally on the page to cover the lines that you have just read. Using a bookmark prevents you from becoming distracted by the sentences you have already read; it also helps you keep your place if you are interrupted or start to daydream.

Learning Journal

How can you read efficiently without sacrificing comprehension? Which of the strategies just described would best fit your study habits?

Practicing with Reading Rates

Exercise 4c

You will need a watch or timer for this exercise. Read the following three passages, timing each one separately. Read for comprehension, not speed. Refer to Table 4.3 to determine how many words you read per minute. For example, if it took you two minutes to read a passage, your reading rate is 200 words a minute.

Table 4.3 Reading Speed	
READING TIME	**WORDS PER MINUTE**
:10	2400
:20	1200
:30	800
:40	600
:50	480
1:00	400
1:10	345
1:20	300
1:30	265
1:40	240
1:50	220
2:00	200
2:10	185
2:20	170
2:30	160
2:40	150
2:50	140
3:00	135
3:10	125
3:20	120
3:30	115
3:40	110
3:50	105

Source: Reading speed formula based on Spargo and Williston, *Timed Readings* (Providence: Jamestown Pub., 1980).

Selection One

"Overcoming Intellectual Blocks"

Intellectual blocks involve obstacles to knowledge. You may find yourself unable to solve a problem because you lack information or because you have incorrect or partial information. When buying a car, for example, you can be blocked by being unaware of various cars' performance ratings, repair records, or safety features. Or you may be blocked because you have one-sided information that was presented by sales representatives for each of the auto models you are considering. Or, possibly, you may simply not know enough about cars to purchase one with confidence.

Perhaps you know quite a bit about a particular subject but still lack the skill to express your ideas effectively. How many times have you said to yourself, "I really knew more than I wrote on that essay test, or paper. I just couldn't get it down on paper. I couldn't organize my ideas clearly."

To break through an intellectual block, you need either to acquire additional information or to deepen your understanding of the information you have. For example, if you are working on a paper about dreams and you find that you are stuck on a point, it may be time to do some more reading or to talk with someone about the subject. Sometimes getting past an intellectual block may be less a matter of acquiring more or better information than of gaining a new perspective on that information. If you are basing your paper on one theory about dreams, you may need to consider introducing alternative theories. Or, if you have been relying on traditional psychological explanations, perhaps you should look at some medical studies. In any case, you may need to look at the information you cull from your reading in more than one way. You may need to question it and analyze it to understand its significance on a deeper level.

The way to overcome intellectual blocks, then, is first to identify whether your block is caused by a lack of information, by too much information, or by an inadequate perspective on the information. You may then need to review, study, or read more to prepare yourself better before you continue writing.

Emotional blocks, on the other hand, occur when feelings inhibit thinking. Such blocks include fears and anxieties. Perhaps the biggest emotional block to thought is the fear of being wrong.

Source: R. DiYanni and P. Hoy, *The Scribner Handbook for Writers* (Needham Heights, MA: Allyn & Bacon, 1995), pp. 147–148.

Reading rate _____

Selection Two

"More on Graphs of Functions"

In calculus the solution of a problem often depends on one's ability to sketch the graph of a function quickly and accurately. The algebraic techniques considered in this section, when combined with the powerful calculus methods of Chapter 3, provide a means for obtaining the graphs of functions without the drudgery of plotting many points.

INTERCEPTS

To graph a straight line we need to plot only two points. If a line with nonzero slope does not pass through the origin, we can find its x- and y-intercepts and draw the line through the corresponding points on the coordinates axes. The y-intercept for a linear function $f(x) = ax + b$, a does not $= 0$ and b does not $= 0$, is $f(0) = b$, and the x-intercept is the solution of $ax + b = 0$; that is, $x = -b/a$. When graphing any function, it is recommended that you look first for the intercepts of its graph. The y-coordinate of the point at which the graph of a function $y = f(x)$ crosses the y-axis is its y-intercept. This y-coordinate is the value $f(0)$. Note that the graph of a function can have at most one y-intercept. Moreover, if 0 is not in the domain of f, then $f(0)$ is not defined and the graph does not cross the y-axis. The x-intercepts of the graph of f are the x-coordinates of the points where the graph crosses the x-axis. Since $y = 0$ along the x-axis, the x-intercepts of the graph of f are the real solutions of the equation $f(x) = 0$. The values for which $f(x) = 0$ are the zeros of the function f; if f has no real zeros, then its graph has no x-intercepts. We have illustrated a function f whose graph has a y-intercept and three x-intercepts, x_1, x_2, and x_3.

SYMMETRY

Of three symmetries of graphs (symmetry with respect to the y-axis, symmetry with respect to the x-axis, and symmetry with respect to the origin) we note that the graph of a nonzero function cannot be symmetric with respect to the x-axis. This is because, in view of our definition, both points (x, y) and $(x, -y)$ cannot be on the graph of a function. A function whose graph is symmetric with respect to the y-axis is called an *even* function, whereas a function whose graph possesses symmetry with respect to the origin is called an *odd* function.

Source: D. Zill, *Calculus*, 3rd ed. (Boston: PWS Publishing, 1992), pp. 15–16.

Reading rate _____

Selection Three

"The Man in the Black Suit" by Stephen King

"Your mother is dead."

"No!" I cried. I thought of her making bread, of the curl lying across her forehead and just touching her eyebrow, standing there in the strong morning sunlight, and the terror swept over me again . . . but not for myself this time. Then I thought of how she'd looked when I set off with my fishing pole, standing in the kitchen doorway with her hand shading her eyes, and how she had looked to me in that moment like a photograph of someone you expected to see again but never did. "No, you lie!" I screamed.

He smiled—the sadly patient smile of a man who has often been accused falsely. "I'm afraid not," he said. "It was the same thing that happened to your brother, Gary. It was a bee."

"No, that's not true," I said, and now I did begin to cry. "She's old, she's thirty-five, if a bee sting could kill her the way it did Gary she would have died a long time ago and you're a lying bastard!"

I had called the Devil a lying bastard. On some level I was aware of this, but the entire front of my mind was taken up by the enormity of what he'd said. My mother dead? He might as well have told me that there was a new ocean where the Rockies had been. But I believed him. On some level I believed him completely, as we always believe, on some level, the worst thing our hearts can imagine.

"I understand your grief, little fisherboy, but that particular argument just doesn't hold water, I'm afraid." He spoke in a tone of bogus comfort that was horrible, maddening, without remorse or pity. "A man can go his whole life without seeing a mockingbird, you know, but does that mean mockingbirds don't exist? Your mother—"

A fish jumped below us. The man in the black suit frowned, then pointed a finger at it. The trout convulsed in the air, its body bending so strenuously that for a split second it appeared to be snapping at its own tail, and when it fell back into Castle Stream it was floating lifelessly, dead. It struck the big gray rock where the waters divided, spun around twice in the whirlpool eddy that formed there, and then floated off in the direction of Castle Rock. Meanwhile, the terrible stranger turned his burning eyes on me again, his thin lips pulled back from tiny rows of sharp teeth in a cannibal smile.

Source: Stephen King, *Everything's Eventual: 14 Dark Tales* (New York: Scribner, 2002), pp. 55–56.

Reading rate _____

Learning Journal

Compare your reading rates for the passages you read in Exercise 4c. Was your reading rate the same for each passage or was there a difference? Based on what you know of reading rates, should there be a difference in your rates?

Developing a Daily Reading Plan

A **daily reading plan** is a prioritized list of reading tasks for all your classes on any given day (see Table 4.4 for an example). Directions for completing reading tasks—such as reading textbooks, reviewing vocabulary, or

Table 4.4 Daily Reading Plan		
Date: Monday Sept 10		
TASK	**PRIORITY (A, B, C)**	**COMPLETED**
Read chemistry lab assignment pp. 56–73 at 5:30 P.M.	A	✓
Read sociology ch. 6 at 7:00 P.M.	A	✓
Construct study chart for sociology ch. 6 at 10:00 P.M.	C	
Review Spanish verbs, ch. 8 right before bed	B	

Source: J. Kollaritsch, *Reading and Study Organization Methods for Higher Learning,* 4th ed. (Belmont, CA: Wadsworth, 1990).

even drawing maps and charts as study aids—should be written into it using specific language. This means writing down the exact time you will read an assignment, the page numbers you expect to read, the name of the course you are reading for, the date of the lecture notes you plan to read, and the course and chapter vocabulary you plan to review. You have a much better chance of meeting your reading goals when the directions on your daily reading plan are clear. Vague directions like "read chem tonight" allow for procrastination; "tonight" could be any time between 7:00 P.M. and when you go to bed at midnight. Writing down that you will read pages 56–73 of chemistry at 5:30 P.M. is an exact direction and helps you make more of a commitment to getting your reading done.

Your daily reading plans should be incorporated into your **general study schedule**, a chart that includes information on class times, regularly scheduled study periods and leisure activities (see Table 4.5 for an example). If you do not have a general study schedule yet, seek help from your reading instructor or visit your college or university's learning lab and find out how to develop one.

Tips for Developing a Daily Reading Plan

1. *Keep a record of your pages per hour reading rate for each of your classes.* Knowing your specific reading rates will help you organize both your general study schedule and your daily reading plans so that they are realistic. As there will be variations in your reading rates depending on which classes you are reading for and how complex a particular assignment is, you will need to take into account

| Table 4.5 | General Study Schedule |

Date _September_   thru _December_   **Semester Schedule**

Times	Monday	Tuesday	Wednesday	Thursday	Friday	Saturday	Sunday
6:00–7:00							
7:00–8:00							
8:00–9:00		work		read/prepare for chem lab		work	leisure time
9:00–10:00	sociology 101		sociology 101		sociology 101		
10:00–11:00	chem 108		chem 108	chem lab	chem 108		
11:00–12:00							
12:00–1:00							
1:00–2:00	lunch	lunch	lunch	lunch	lunch	lunch	lunch
2:00–3:00		history 132		history 132	history 132		leisure
3:00–4:00	Span 101	Span 101	Span 101	Span 101	study history	study chemistry	
4:00–5:00	study Span	study Span	study Span	study Span			
5:00–6:00							
6:00–7:00	dinner	dinner	dinner	dinner	dinner	dinner	dinner
7:00–8:00	study chemistry	study history	study chemistry	study history	study chemistry	study sociology	study sociology
8:00–9:00							study Span
9:00–10:00	study sociology		study sociology		study sociology	study Spanish	
10:00–11:00							
11:00–12:00							
Class Time	3 hours	2 hours	3 hours	4 hours	3 hours		
Study Time	4 hours	3 hours	4 hours	5 hours	5 hours	6 hours	3 hours
Work Time		5 hours				5 hours	
Leisure Time							9 hours

what you will actually be reading in any given week when writing your daily reading plans.

2. *When reading for more than one class in a single study session, complete the reading for your most difficult or least favorite class first.* When you begin reading, you are usually more focused and energetic. As you read your eyes tire and your enthusiasm wanes. Beginning to read for a difficult class when you are already tired makes it hard to concentrate, and you may end up not completing an assignment or putting it off for another time. It is better to schedule

reading for an enjoyable class later if necessary even if you are tired, because your interest in the subject can renew your energy.

3. *Plan your reading time for when you are most alert.* Do not schedule your reading time for late at night if you know that it is hard for you to concentrate when you are tired.

4. *Each day, schedule the reading tasks for every class you have attended into your daily reading plan.* Reviewing class material within 24 hours of having first learned it is an effective strategy that will help you retain what you have read.

Exercise 4d — Daily Reading Plan

Using the preceding four suggestions as a guide, complete a daily reading plan for tomorrow that includes all your reading goals for each class you attend.

Test Taking and Time Management

- **Study consistently and with regularity.** Cramming is not an effective study strategy in college. Most disciplines require you to enroll in a series of courses starting at the "101" introductory level and proceed through a sequence of progressively higher-level classes. Each course assumes mastery over the previously covered material. To do well you need to understand and remember the information from each class. Patience and perseverance equal academic and lifelong success.

- **Keep a calendar of events, such as exam days, meetings with professors, study group times, and other related deadlines.** Preparing for and making time for these important academic events will help keep you focused. Make academic success a priority.

- **Allow time before the exam to get to the classroom.** Research has shown that sitting in your regular chair can often help improve your memory, so arrive to class early on test days to get your chair of choice.

- **Answer the easy questions first.** If you have 50 minutes to answer 50 questions, pace yourself. If each item is worth the same amount of points, don't spend five minutes on one question when you could be correctly answering four others. Skip over the questions you're not sure about and mark them so you can return to them later if you have time. Answering other questions can also trigger your memory, allowing you to access the information you need to respond to the questions you skipped.

Practice with Reading Passage

Answer all questions on a separate sheet of paper.

Read the following passage and time yourself. Then use Table 4.6 on page 128 to determine your reading rate. Complete the preview questions before starting to time yourself, and answer the comprehension questions after you have finished timing your reading.

Reading Practice

Excerpt from *Brothel: Mustang Ranch and Its Women*

BY A. ALBERT

PREPARE TO READ

1. Based on the title, what do you expect the reading to be about?

2. What do you already know about the subject?

3. Here are some vocabulary words that might be unfamiliar to you. Look them up, if necessary, and refer to the definitions as you encounter these vocabulary words in the reading.

   a. Evoke

   b. Empathy

   c. Pathologize

   d. Causative

   e. Respite

   f. Meager

   g. Contended

   h. Profound

4. Create a question to ask yourself, using the title or subject of the reading.

Brothel: Mustang Ranch and Its Women

Prostitutes have been cast as victimizers and victims, as dead to the pleasure of sex and as too alive to it. Whatever else, they have always been Other, sufficiently unlike the rest of us as to evoke sympathy, not empathy. Usually with the best of intentions, psychologists pathologize prostitutes by suggesting sweeping causative associations between prostitution and disadvantaged situations, physical limitations (e.g., substance abuse), and previous traumatic experiences, especially sexual abuse. And knee-jerk moralists speak of prostitutes as flawed characters lacking in values.

But no easy formula fit the women I met in Nevada's brothels. Several were black and Latino; a few were Asian and Native American; fully two-thirds of Mustang's prostitutes were white. Almost nine out of 10 had either graduated from high school or earned their general equivalency diplomas. While some of the prostitutes I met came from lower-income families, many grew up well-to-do. Some of the women came from broken homes with absent fathers, and some had mothers who had prostituted themselves, but many grew up in intact, functional two-parent households. Although some women admitted to drug and alcohol misuse, the brothel seemed to weed out women with profound addictions. Fewer than half of the women spoke to me of childhood sexual abuse, a prevalence that wasn't so much higher than national estimates that at least 20 percent of American women have experienced some form of sexual abuse as children. And two-thirds of Mustang's prostitutes considered themselves religiously observant and professed membership in traditional organized faith communities, almost exclusively Protestant, Catholic, or Jewish.

It was clear that the women working in Nevada's brothels represented a distinct group. Fewer than half of Mustang's prostitutes had sold sex outside the brothels, whether "on the track" (the street) or through escort or outcall services. Although it wasn't unusual for streetwalkers to give Nevada's brothels a try as a respite from the streets, George Flint figured that under 10 percent of the brothels' regular prostitutes were former streetwalkers. He speculated that the reason was the brothels' extensive rules and obligatory confinement: "True street girls can't make the adjustment. Every one of them fails. Maybe they're too accustomed to their independence. Or the fact that they choose their customers, their customers don't choose them."

One trait common to most of Mustang's women was financial hardship. Since Donna's husband was unemployable, or claimed to be, someone needed to earn a living for the family; she had only a high school education and meager work experience, and he convinced her she had few options. This was a pattern I saw frequently—women who had ended up at Mustang Ranch to provide for loved ones. Instead of lacking family values, as moralists contended, most of the women I came to know there possessed a profound sense of personal responsibility and an unwavering commitment to their families that ultimately drove them to do this "immoral" work.

Source: A. Albert, *Brothel: Mustang Ranch and Its Women.* (New York: Random House, 2001), pp. 71–73.

Rate _____ (Refer to Table 4.6 on pg. 128)

CHECK YOUR UNDERSTANDING

OBJECTIVE QUESTIONS
Do not refer back to the passage when answering these comprehension questions.

1. Which of the following statements is *not* accurate according to the excerpt?

   a. Prostitutes come from disadvantaged situations.

   b. Prostitutes have flawed characters lacking in values.

   c. Prostitutes have physical limitations (like substance abuse).

   d. Previous traumatic experiences, especially sexual abuse, are associated with most prostitutes' choice of employment.

2. Which of the following statements is *true*, according to the excerpt?

   a. Almost all the Ranch prostitutes came from lower-income families.

   b. All the Ranch prostitutes had drug or alcohol abuse problems.

   c. Most of the Ranch prostitutes had mothers who had prostituted themselves.

   d. Almost nine out of 10 Ranch prostitutes had earned their general equivalency diplomas or had graduated from high school.

3. According to the excerpt, what is one reason why streetwalkers rarely become regular brothel prostitutes?

   a. Many streetwalkers used drugs.

   b. Streetwalkers do not know where prostitution is legal.

   c. Brothels have lots of rules and mandatory confinement.

   d. Streetwalkers usually don't look for a break from street work.

4. According to the author, the prostitutes she investigated at the Mustang ranch were

   a. Immoral.

   b. Women who were very committed to their families.

   c. Religious.

   d. All abused as children.

5. In your opinion, the author's attitude toward the prostitutes at Mustang Ranch is

   a. Negative.

   b. Accepting.

   c. Sorrowful.

   d. Hateful.

   Support your opinion with an explanation, using evidence from the reading.

Table 4.6 Reading Rates for Reading Passages		
READING TIME	**READING PASSAGE 1 WORDS PER MINUTE**	**READING PASSAGE 2 WORDS PER MINUTE**
:10	2244	2820
:20	1122	1410
:30	748	940
:40	562	705
:50	449	564
1:00	374	470
1:10	323	405
1:20	280	353
1:30	248	311
1:40	224	282
1:50	206	259
2:00	187	235
2:10	173	217
2:20	159	199
2:30	150	188
2:40	140	176
2:50	131	165
3:00	126	159
3:10	117	149
3:20	112	141
3:30	108	135
3:40	103	129
3:50	98	123

Source: Reading speed formula based on Spargo and Williston, *Timed Readings* (Providence: Jamestown Pub., 1980).

Chapter Summary

Comprehension should be your main reading goal, not how fast you read. Develop a general study schedule that shows specifically when you plan to study for each class and for how long. Choose the times you study based on when you are most alert, and determine the length of each study session using your reading averages for the subjects you are taking. Some classes will require more hours of study than others, and the amounts of time you need to set aside can vary from week to week depending on the complexity of the material for a specific course.

Track your reading rates so you can create daily reading plans that set realistic goals for your classes each week. After using a study schedule and daily reading plans for several weeks, you will find that you begin to complete your reading assignments on time. Your reading comprehension will also improve, and you may even read a little faster. The reading tips suggested in this chapter that will contribute to your becoming a more efficient reader are: reading quickly when appropriate, skimming, regressing or rereading, subvocalizing, pacing.

Post Test

Answer all questions on a separate sheet of paper.

Part I

OBJECTIVE QUESTIONS

1. Match each vocabulary word in Column A with its correct definition in Column B.

Column A		Column B	
1.	Efficient reading	a.	Thinking about what you are reading
2.	Speed-reading	b.	Rereading
3.	Critical reading	c.	Using your finger to guide your reading
4.	Skimming	d.	Comprehending text at an appropriate reading rate
5.	Regressing	e.	Reading aloud
6.	Subvocalizing	f.	Reading groups of words instead of individual words
7.	Pacing	g.	Reading only some of the words

2. Which of the following best answers the question "What is an efficient reader?"

a. Someone who is able to read quickly and methodically.

b. Someone who understands what he or she is reading.

c. Someone who reads at the appropriate speed for him or her and understands the information.

d. Someone who always finishes his or her reading assignments within one hour each night.

3. The reading rate for an accounting book is approximately

    a. 15–20 pages per hour.

    b. 20–25 pages per hour.

    c. 10–15 pages per hour.

    d. 30–35 pages per hour.

4. The ability to read faster always improves your ability to comprehend what you are reading. T F

5. Reading faster can sometimes improve concentration and comprehension. T F

SHORT-ANSWER QUESTIONS

6. Based on your understanding of Chapter 1, explain what effect your study environment can have on your goal of reading efficiently.

7. Explain the benefit of knowing your reading rates when reading different types of materials, such as history, biology, or science fiction.

8. Review the following reading plan, and make three suggestions for how it could be improved:

    Daily Reading Plan
    Date: May 29

Task	Completed?
Read biology tonight	✔
Study French verbs before breakfast or before lunch	✔
Read library text to begin English research project	✔
Read two chapters in biology before Friday to catch-up	

9. Explain why speed-reading is not the same as critical reading.

Part II

Reading Passage

Excerpt from *Angela's Ashes*
BY FRANK McCOURT

The following excerpt is taken from *Angela's Ashes,* a memoir by Frank McCourt, who grew up very poor in Ireland. Some of the words in it reflect the way some people spoke in Ireland, at that time. For example, "aisy" is "easy" in standard American English. The Collection, which you will read about in the excerpt, refers to when children who had just made their First Communion celebrated by visiting people in their area and "collecting" presents of money from them.

1.   Based on reading the first and last sentences of the excerpt, what do you expect the reading to be about?

2.   What do you already know about the subject?

3.   Create a question to ask yourself, using the subject of the reading.

4.   Read the following excerpt and time yourself.

First Communion day is the happiest day of your life because of The Collection and James Cagney at the Lyric Cinema. The night before I was so excited I couldn't sleep till dawn. I'd still be sleeping if my grandmother hadn't come banging at the door.

Get up! Get up! Get that child outa the bed. Happiest day of his life an' him snorin' above in the bed.

I ran to the kitchen. Take off that shirt, she said. I took off the shirt and she pushed me into a tin tub of icy cold water. My mother scrubbed me, my grandmother scrubbed me. I was raw, I was red.

They dried me. They dressed me in my black velvet First Communion suit with the white frilly shirt, the short pants, the white stockings, the black patent leather shoes. Around my arm they tied a white satin bow and on my lapel they pinned the Sacred Heart of Jesus, a picture of the Sacred Heart, with blood dripping from it, flames erupting all around it and on top a nasty-looking crown of thorns.

Come here till I comb your hair, said Grandma. Look at that mop, it won't lie down. You didn't get that hair from my side of the family. That's that North of Ireland hair you got from your father. That's the kind of hair you see on Presbyterians. If your mother had married a proper decent Limerickman you wouldn't have this standing up, North of Ireland, Presbyterian hair.

She spat twice on my head.

Grandma, will you please stop spitting on my head.

If you have anything to say, shut up. A little spit won't kill you. Come on, we'll be late for the Mass.

We ran to the church. My mother panted along behind with Michael in her arms. We arrived at the church just in time to see the last of the boys leaving the altar rail where the priest stood with the chalice and the host, glaring at me. Then he placed on my tongue the wafer, the body and blood of Jesus. At last, at last.

It's on my tongue. I draw it back.

It stuck.

I had God glued to the roof of my mouth. I could hear the master's voice, Don't let that host touch your teeth for if you bite God in two you'll roast in hell for eternity.

I tried to get God down with my tongue but the priest hissed at me, Stop that clucking and get back to your seat.

God was good. He melted and I swallowed Him and now, at last, I was a member of the True Church, an official sinner.

When the Mass ended there they were at the door of the church, my mother with Michael in her arms, my grandmother. They each hugged me to their bosoms. They each told me it was the happiest day of my life. They each cried all over my head and after my grandmother's contribution that morning my head was a swamp.

Mam, can I go now and make The Collection?

She said, After you have a little breakfast.

No, said Grandma. You're not making no collection till you've had a proper First Communion breakfast at my house. Come on.

We followed her. She banged pots and rattled pans and complained that the whole world expected her to be at their beck and call. I ate the egg, I ate the sausage, and when I reached for more sugar for my tea she slapped my hand away.

Go aisy with that sugar. Is it a millionaire you think I am? An American? Is it bedecked in glitterin' jewelry you think I am? Smothered in fancy furs?

The food churned in my stomach. I gagged. I ran to her backyard and threw it all up. Out she came.

Look at what he did. Thrun up his First Communion breakfast. Thrun up the body and blood of Jesus. I have God in me backyard. What am I goin' to do? I'll take him to the Jesuits for they know the sins of the Pope himself.

She dragged me through the streets of Limerick. She told the neighbors and passing strangers about God in her backyard. She pushed me into the confession box.

In the name of the Father, the Son, the Holy Ghost. Bless me, Father, for I have sinned. It's a day since my last confession.

A day? And what sins have you committed in a day, my child?

I overslept. I nearly missed my First Communion. My grandmother said I have standing up, North of Ireland, Presbyterian hair. I threw up my First Communion breakfast. Now Grandma says she has God in her backyard and what should she do.

The priest is like the First Confession priest. He has the heavy breathing and the choking sounds.

Ah...ah...tell your grandmother to wash God away with a little water and for your penance say one Hail Mary and one Our Father. Say a prayer for me and God bless you, my child.

Grandma and Mam were waiting close to the confession box. Grandma said, Were you telling jokes to that priest in the confession box? If 'tis a thing I ever find out you were telling jokes to Jesuits I'll tear the bloody kidneys outa you. Now what did he say about God in me backyard?

He said wash Him away with a little water, Grandma.

Holy water or ordinary water?

He didn't say, Grandma.

Well, go back and ask him.

But, Grandma...

She pushed me back into the confessional.

Bless me, father, for I have sinned, it's a minute since my last confession.

A minute! Are you the boy that was just here?

I am, Father.

What is it now?

My grandma says, Holy water or ordinary water?

Ordinary water, and tell your grandmother not to be bothering me again.

I told her, Ordinary water, Grandma, and he said don't be bothering him again.

Don't be bothering him again. That bloody ignorant bogtrotter.

I asked Mam, Can I go now and make The Collection? I want to see James Cagney.

Grandma said, You can forget about The Collection and James Cagney because you're not a proper Catholic the way you left God on the ground. Come on, go home.

Mam said, Wait a minute. That's my son. That's my son on his First Communion day. He's going to see James Cagney.

No he's not.

Yes he is.

Grandma said, Take him then to James Cagney and see if that will save his Presbyterian North of Ireland American soul. Go ahead.

She pulled her shawl around her and walked away.

Mam said, God, it's getting very late for The Collection and you'll never see James Cagney. We'll go to the Lyric Cinema and see if they'll let you in anyway in your First Communion suit.

We met Mikey Molloy on Barrington Street. He asked if I was going to the Lyric and I said I was trying. Trying? he said. You don't have money?

I was ashamed to say no but I had to and he said, That's all right. I'll get you in. I'll create a diversion.

What's a diversion?

I have the money to go and when I get in I'll pretend to have the fit and the ticket man will be out of his mind and you can slip in when I let out the big scream. I'll be watching the door and when I see you in I'll have a miraculous recovery. That's a diversion. That's what I do to get my brothers in all the time.

Mam said, Oh, I don't know about that, Mikey. Wouldn't that be a sin and surely you wouldn't want Frank to commit a sin on his First Communion day.

Mikey said if there was a sin it would be on his soul and he wasn't a proper Catholic anyway so it didn't matter. He let out his scream and I slipped in and sat next to Question Quigley and the ticket man, Frank Goggin, was so worried over Mikey he never noticed. It was a thrilling film but sad in the end because James Cagney was a public enemy and when they shot him they wrapped him in bandages and threw him in the door, shocking his poor old Irish mother, and that was the end of my First Communion day.

Source: Frank McCourt, *Angela's Ashes* (New York: Simon & Schuster, 1996), pp. 127–31.

SHORT-ANSWER QUESTIONS

1. What was the boy most excited about on his First Communion Day?

2. Why do you think the grandmother was so insistent on the boy having breakfast before he "made The Collection"?

3. Why did the priest laugh at the boy in the confessional?

4. Why did the grandmother leave angry?

5. What do you think the boy remembers as the best thing from his First Communion? Why?

Website Sources for Additional Practice

http://efn.hud.ac.uk/studyskills/time.html

http://www.mindtools.com/page5.html

http://www.pvc.maricopa.edu

http://www.ucc.vt.edu/stdysk/priority.html

http://www.pvc.maricopa.edu/ISC/Services studyskills.html

http://www.coun.uvic.ca/learn/program/hndouts/studylog.html

http://cobweb.dartmouth.edu/admin/acskills/harvard.html

http://www.clarkson.edu/~pichergr/procrast.html

http://www.ncf.carleton.ce/ran588/time_man.html

http://www.readingsoft.com/quiz.html

Part Two

Key Strategies for Reading Comprehension

Chapter 5

Locating Stated Main Ideas

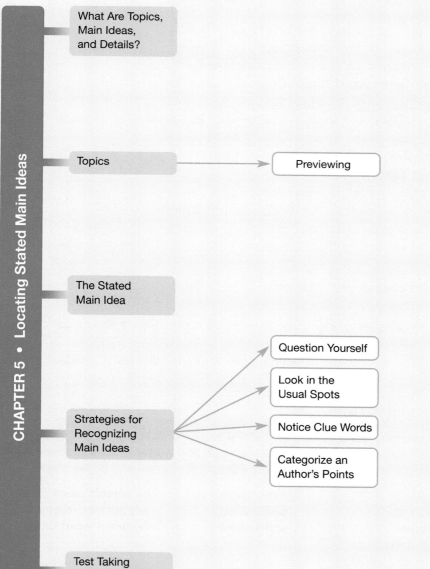

What Are Topics, Main Ideas, and Details?

Topics

Previewing

The Stated Main Idea

Strategies for Recognizing Main Ideas

Question Yourself

Look in the Usual Spots

Notice Clue Words

Categorize an Author's Points

Test Taking and Main Ideas

Chapter Contents

Chapter Goals

In this chapter you will learn:

- What main ideas are.
- Strategies for identifying main ideas in paragraphs and longer readings.
- How to check whether you have correctly identified main ideas.

Chapter Vocabulary

As you read the chapter, take note of these words and phrases, which represent important concepts from the chapter and will be in **boldface type**. Make sure you understand them before the post test at the end of the chapter.

topic	**mind maps**	**emphasis word clues**
main idea	**previewing**	**support word clues**
details	**word clues**	**contrast word clues**
categorization		

After three weeks of attending class, Jody, a single parent and a returning student, found her way to her college's reading department. She told the counselor about a concern that had bothered her since her senior year in high school. She had trouble identifying the main points in her textbooks. She could read and understand the words, but everything seemed equally important—everything blurred together. "Every time I read an assignment," she said, "it feels like I'm in a sea of words...and I'm drowning."

Being able to identify the main idea of the article or chapter you are reading is a major step toward understanding college-level material. Once you can pick out the main ideas in reading assignments, you can prioritize information and concentrate on understanding and remembering what is most important. If you can't distinguish between the main idea and less significant ideas, you can wrongly assume that all the information is of equal importance and feel you have to memorize a whole chapter in order to do well on your exams. Attempting to memorize an entire chapter is not usually successful, and fortunately it's also not necessary.

Learning Journal

Without reading ahead, write down your definitions of the terms *main idea, topic, details, major supporting details,* and *minor supporting details* in your journal.

What Are Topics, Main Ideas, and Details?

In order to be able to identify main ideas, you need to know the difference between topics, main ideas, and details. A **topic** is a word or short phrase that summarizes the general ideas presented on a page or in a chapter, book, or journal article. Identifying the topic of a reading helps you identify the main idea. But a topic and a main idea are not the same thing. The topic is general in scope and is the subject of a reading. Usually the title of an article or chapter will offer a hint about what the topic is; for example, the title of this chapter, "Locating Stated Main Ideas," is also its topic.

The **main idea** is the major point the author makes *about* the topic. It is usually stated in the form of a sentence and is narrower in scope than the topic. It serves as the controlling idea under which other ideas stack as support. These pieces, or supporting ideas, are called **details**. Details, which will be discussed in Chapter 6, are more specific than the main idea. They prove, clarify, justify, or otherwise support the main idea.

Remember the story of the "Three Little Pigs"? The topic of the story is, of course, pigs. The main idea of the story is *Pigs with well-built homes live longer.* The facts that the pigs were little, built their houses of different materials, and lived or died are all details that help support the main idea.

To demonstrate the general-to-specific relationship between topics, main ideas, and major supporting details, examine the mind map in Figure 5.1. **Mind maps** are line drawings that show the relationships between ideas. They begin with the most general idea at the top, or in the center, and then visually separate out the topic, main ideas, and major and minor supporting details.

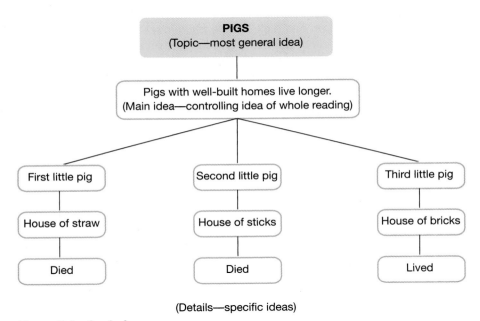

Figure 5.1   A mind map.

Topics

As topics are the most general ideas of readings, they are not complete sentences, but words or phrases that sum up the subject you are reading about. A chapter can have any subject as its topic. For example, an astronomy text might have a chapter on the topic of black holes; a book on American politics could include a chapter on the topic of the Republican Party; and a cookbook might devote a chapter to the topic of baking bread. Every sentence in these chapters would relate to its topic, either directly or indirectly. Consider the following excerpt from a novel about vampires by author Anne Rice:

"Here now, Bianca, drink, for I have more blood to give," I said against her ear, my cut wrist on her tongue once more. This time the blood flowed from it, scarce a deluge but what she must have, and her mouth closed over the fount and she began to pull against my heart.

"Yes, drink, my Bianca, my sweet Bianca," I said, and she in her sighs answered me.

The blood had imprisoned her tender heart. The night's dark journey had only begun.

Source: Anne Rice, *Blood and Gold: The Vampire Chronicles* (New York: Random House, 2001), p. 355.

The topic, creepy as it is, is *blood*. Or if you looked at the title from which this excerpt was taken, you might say the topic is *vampires and blood*, or just *vampires*. Each of these words or phrases is general enough, and accurate enough, to be the topic of the excerpt, every sentence of which has something to do with vampires and blood.

A key to recognizing topics is being able to distinguish between which ideas are general (topics) and which ideas are more specific (main ideas or details.)

Exercise 5a

General and Specific Ideas

Circle the most general item in each list. The first one is modeled for you.

MODEL

1. Saab
Audi
Mustang
(cars)

2. genetics
DNA
RNA

3. English
history
majors

4. gas
matter
solid
liquid

5. Buddhism
Sikhism
religions
Islam

6. control group
variables
research
(data)

Now that you have singled out the most general items in Exercise 5a, practice identifying topics in the next exercise.

Exercise 5b

Identifying Topics

For each list, think about what the separate items have in common and ask yourself, What is the general subject, or topic, of this list? The first one is modeled for you.

MODEL

1. Topic: _holidays_

Labor Day

Fourth of July

Memorial Day

Christmas

2. Topic: _Poets_

Langston Hughes

Emily Dickinson

T. S. Eliot

Walt Whitman

3. Topic: _Games_

crossword

riddles

jigsaw

conundrum

4. Topic: _Diet_

calories

carbohydrates

fat

protein

5. Topic: _resume_

name

education

employment experience

references

6. Topic: _Dental_

gingivitis

tartar

periodontal disease

plaque

Take a few moments to reflect on this exercise. What may have prevented you from answering the questions correctly? Did unfamiliar words make it difficult? If you did not know what a *conundrum* was, you could have had difficulty identifying the topic for the words in that list. Always look up words you don't know in a dictionary, and keep a list of new vocabulary words in your journal.

Identifying Topics in Paragraphs

Read the following excerpts and identify the topic (subject), or most general idea, in each. Make sure every sentence in the excerpt relates to the topic you have chosen.

1. The basic problem is that with so many parents justifying their [children's] stupid and destructive behaviors by permitting drinking, there's no longer a clear consensus about what our values are. It is increasingly difficult for those who hold traditional values to talk about them in a public way without being discounted or attacked as ignorant. When values are not clear, there are infinite choices and many more repercussions and risks.

Source: Laura Schlessinger, *Parenthood by Proxy: Don't Have Them If You Won't Raise Them* (New York: HarperCollins, 2000), p. 232.

Topic: VALUES

2. Perhaps it had something to do with living in a dark cupboard, but Harry had always been small and skinny for his age. He looked even smaller and skinnier than he really was because all he had to wear were old clothes of Dudley's, and Dudley was about four times bigger than he was. Harry had a thin face, knobby knees, black hair, and bright green eyes. He wore round glasses held together with a lot of Scotch tape because of all the times Dudley had punched him on the nose. The only thing Harry liked about his own appearance was a very thin scar on his forehead that was shaped like a bolt of lightning. He had had it as long as he could remember, and the first question he could ever remember asking his Aunt Petunia was how he had gotten it.

Source: J.K. Rowling, *Harry Potter and The Sorcerer's Stone* (New York: Scholastic Press, 1997), p. 20.

Topic: Harry

3. Television offers many advantages to national advertisers, but it's expensive. For example, the cost of 30 seconds of advertising during the Super Bowl telecast has risen to over $2 million. How many bottles of beer or bags of dog food must a company sell to pay for such commercials? The answer may seem to be a lot, but in the past, few other media besides television allowed advertisers to reach so many people with such impact. Marketers must now choose which media can best be used to reach the audience they desire.

Radio advertising, for example, is less expensive then TV advertising and often reaches people when they have few other distractions, such as driving in their cars. Radio is especially good, therefore, for selling services that people don't usually read about in print media—services such as banking, mortgages, continuing education, brokerage services, and the like.

Source: William Nickels, *Understanding Business* (New York: McGraw-Hill, 2002), p. 493.

Topic: Advertising cost

4. There are twelve pairs of ribs. All twelve pairs connect directly to the thoracic vertebrae in the back. A rib articulates with the body and transverse process of its corresponding thoracic vertebra. Each rib curves outward and then forward and downward.

The upper seven pairs of ribs connect directly to the sternum by means of costal cartilages. These are called the "true ribs." The next three pairs of ribs do not connect directly to the sternum, and they are called the "false ribs." They attach to the sternum by means of a common cartilage. The last two pairs are called "floating ribs" because they do not attach to the sternum at all.

Source: Sylvia Mader, *Human Biology* (New York: McGraw-Hill, 2002), p. 215.

Topic: _____ *ribs* _____

5. No matter what your personal style or how beautiful your furnishings may be, every room needs a fixed point around which everything else will revolve. The area should be the most defined, striking, eye-catching spot in the room.

Whether it's the most obvious architectural feature in the room, such as a fireplace or French doors that lead to a garden or terrace, or a significant piece of furniture, such as a wall unit, the focal point provides a visual anchor that helps hold the room together. In some situations you may create a focal point with the right combination of furnishings and accessories—the sofa against the wall with a large painting above it—but simply grouping furniture together in one place will not give you that anchor. Neither will even the most elaborate moldings or a gorgeous chandelier. (As beautiful and eye-catching as these elements are, they generally draw the eye away from the central feature of the room.) Whatever elements or furnishings help to establish your focal point, to be truly effective, they must be positioned on or against a wall facing your conversation area.

Source: Laurie Ward, *Use What You Have Decorating* (New York: Putnam, 1998), p. 97.

Topic: _____ ~~personal~~ visual anchor _____

Team Up!

Discuss your responses with another classmate. Do you disagree with any of their responses? Was the exercise easy or confusing? If there were any confusing parts, discuss them with each other.

Previewing

Previewing is a strategy that helps you mentally prepare for reading new material and involves reading the title of an assignment, the introduction, any headings, and, if there is one, the summary. Once you have done this, you should be able to predict the topic. Based on your more thorough reading of the assignment, determine whether your topic prediction is accurate or needs revising.

Previewing a reading is similar to the process you go through when finding out about a movie. Suppose a friend suggests you rent the movie *Devil's Advocate*. You go to a video store, find the movie, look at the picture on the front, check the names of the actors, and read the movie summary and other printed material on the back. Previewing this movie prepares you to see an R-rated drama with good actors. You think it might be about the devil, and you can tell there are bad guys in it. You rent the movie. It isn't until after you have watched it that you understand and appreciate all the twists and turns of the plot and get the main point, which is that the movie *Devil's Advocate* isn't really as much about the devil (although the devil is in it), but about human weakness.

Stated Main Idea

The main idea of a reading is the controlling point that an author makes about a topic. It is what the author believes and emphasizes as the central point of his or her writing. Some main ideas are implied, not directly stated, and they will be discussed in Chapter 7. Others are stated directly in the text, usually in a sentence or two in the opening paragraphs of each textbook chapter. (You might also find a main idea restated at the end of a chapter.) For example, if you were to state the main idea of this chapter, you might say that *locating stated main ideas involves specifically, but not exclusively, prioritizing ideas and determining the controlling idea of a reading assignment.*

Take One Minute

Brainstorm the strategies you already use to recognize the main idea of a reading.

Strategies for Recognizing Main Ideas

You can use several strategies to detect the main idea of the material you are reading.

Strategy 1: Question Yourself

The first step toward understanding an author's main point is to have in mind the question "What is this all about?" *before* you start reading. Then preview your reading assignment to get an idea of the topic. After reading the assignment thoroughly, question yourself again, this time asking "What is the most important point the author makes about the topic?" The answer to this second question should be the main idea, and it is useful to write it down in your own words. Using this questioning strategy will enable you to locate the main idea of a paragraph, journal article, or whole textbook chapter.

The following example shows the questioning strategy put into practice. Before reading the passage, ask yourself, "What is this all about?"

> **For a spell to work in the intended way, it must be properly directed. You can do this with words, naming your intent aloud. You can also use images, putting representations of the person or thing you want the spell to affect on the altar while you cast it. Old spells sometimes call for hair or fingernail clippings, but I've never used anything arcane like that. We have cameras now.**
>
> **Source:** Eileen Holland, *The Wicca Handbook* (York Beach, ME: Samuel Weiser, 2000), p.55.

The answer to the question "What is this all about?" is *casting spells—* the topic of the paragraph. The answer to the second question, "What is the most important point the author makes about casting spells?" is in the first sentence: *For a spell to work in the intended way, it must be properly directed.* This sentence is the controlling idea of the whole paragraph; all of the other sentences in the paragraph provide details that explain how to properly direct spells.

Questioning Yourself

For each reading selection, first ask: "What is this all about?" and read the title of the book the passage comes from. Then, read the passage and write the answer to your question, the *topic* of the passage, in the space provided. Then ask yourself the more specific question "What is the most important point the author makes about the topic?" Underline the sentence in the paragraph that best answers this question. The first selection is modeled for you.

MODEL   **1.**   Well, let me tell you: as the child of Italian immigrants, I happen to think that America is the most open, dynamic, creative nation on God's green earth. As a scholar, I also know that it is capitalist America that produced the modern independent woman. Never in history have women had more freedom of choice in regard to dress, behavior, career, and sexual orientation.

   Source: C. Paglia, *Sex, Art, and American Culture* (New York: Vintage Books, 1992).

   Topic: __America and women__

   2.   For centuries, philosophers and scientists have been searching for a central mechanism that causes aging. Most scientists now agree that aging probably does not have a single cause. The aging process occurs in part because of environmental factors and in part because of some genetically programmed purposeful process in which vulnerability to the environment increases over time as the body advances through a natural developmental process from adulthood to death. In this section, we focus first on the environmental theories of aging and then turn to a discussion of the developmental and genetic theories of aging.

Source: J. Quadagno, *Aging and the Life Course* (New York: McGraw-Hill, 1999), p. 125.

Topic: _Aging Bred cpste_

3. Geology is the science of the earth, and what particularly characterizes it is the sense of the length of time the earth has existed. Geologists think of the long history of the earth in terms of millions of years (units of 10^6 years), just as astronomers think of immense interstellar distances in terms of light years (units of 10^{13} kilometers), and they find it convenient to divide that history into broad divisions called eras. Indeed the divisions they use are curiously like those used by the historians to describe European history and can reasonably be translated as Modern, Medieval, and Ancient times, plus Prehistory.

Source: W. Zinsser, *Writing to Learn* (New York: Harper & Row, 1988), p. 82.

Topic: _Geology And science_

4. To be honest, I still wasn't sure how I felt about legalized prostitution. At the time, my head was spinning. I had long believed that prostitution represented "badness" on multiple levels. Practically, it disturbed me because of the dangers to the women who practiced it. Politically, I thought prostitution degraded all women. But Nevada's legal brothels were far less repugnant than I had expected. They appeared to be clean, legitimate workplaces, and the women were not shackled hostages but self-aware professionals there of their own free will.

Source: Alexa Albert, *Brothel: Mustang Ranch and Its Women* (New York: Random House, 2001), p. 32.

Topic: _prostituoo_

5. Doug Gaffka, the exterior designer for the 1996 Taurus, saw a car as having one of three primal faces: aggressive, friendly, or sad. To his way of thinking, a good front-end design could be aggressive or friendly, but not sad. Sad could be seen in the hangdog expression about the grilles of certain aging GM models—cars that had seen better days from a company that had seen better years. Sad was for losers.

Source: M. Walton, *Car* (New York: W.W. Norton & Company, 1997), p. 21.

Topic: _Cars_

6. Magic is very powerful, but to look to it for power over others is to miss the point entirely. Magic isn't for compelling love or obedience, it isn't for destroying your enemies. Magic is about empowerment. This is why I teach people how to cast spells rather than doing spells for them. Magic is for transformation, healing, and betterment. It brings self-improvement and self-determination. Power over yourself and your own life is real power. Use magic to change your life. Battle your demons with it: fears, addictions, diseases, negative patterns.

Source: Eileen Holland, *The Wicca Handbook* (York Beach, ME: Samuel Weiser, 2000), p. 29.

Topic: _____Magic_____

Take One Minute

Think about how the *topic* of a reading is different from the *main idea*. Write down your response.

Learning Journal

Think of a topic or subject you recently learned about in one of your classes. (You could use a chapter title from a textbook to help you come up with one.) In your journal, write down as much specific information as you can remember about the topic, enough to fill one page. When you are done, identify the main idea of the topic and write it down as a main idea sentence at the end of your journal entry.

Strategy 2: Look in the Usual Spots

Authors want to make their ideas clear. To achieve this goal, they usually put their main ideas, if they intend to state them directly, in predictable places. The main idea of a paragraph, also called a *topic sentence*, is usually placed at the beginning, in the first or second sentence, or at the end, of the paragraph. Less frequently, an author will put a main idea in the middle of a paragraph. Review Exercise 5d for examples of how main idea sentences can be found in different places in a paragraph.

In a journal article, editorial, or short essay consisting of more than one paragraph, an author is likely to put the main idea at the beginning, somewhere in the introductory paragraphs. Authors also frequently restate the main idea at the end of a reading in the concluding paragraph. In textbooks, authors normally state the main idea of a chapter in the beginning, during the introduction to the chapter, and usually in very direct language: *In this chapter we will focus on the two most treatable causes of obesity.* It is also common for textbook authors to restate the main idea in their conclusion, and again in the chapter summary.

Learning Journal

Keep track of the main ideas of the textbook chapters you read this semester in your journal. Keeping a list will help you when you study for exams. If you have difficulty identifying an author's main idea, make a note of the fact and discuss problem areas with your instructor during class or during office hours.

Strategy 3: Notice Word Clues

To ensure that you are following their thoughts, authors frequently use **word clues,** words and phrases that signal what is most important in the material you are reading. Just as recipes and road signs guide cooks and travelers, word clues provide you with directions when reading new and unfamiliar information. They indicate changes in the course of an author's thinking, and by using them, you can follow an author's thought path, no matter how winding it is.

Emphasis word clues are used to get your attention and indicate which ideas are especially important to remember. Table 5.1 contains a partial list of the kinds of words and phrases authors use to emphasize their main points. When you encounter these words in your reading, pause to ask yourself if what is being said is the most important point the author is making about the topic.

TABLE 5.1   EMPHASIS WORD CLUES

in conclusion	many reasons	therefore	hence
most importantly	thus	in summary	

Authors also use **support word clues** to let you know when they are presenting details that support their main idea or argument. Table 5.2 contains a partial list of the words and phrases that authors often use to do this. When you come across these words, or similar ones (this list is not exhaustive), pause and ask yourself what larger point do the details being discussed support.

TABLE 5.2 SUPPORT WORD CLUES			
for example	for instance	because	as a result
one of the reasons	first of all	second of all	finally
to illustrate the point	a case in point	also	

Although authors use many different word clues to help you see a main point more clearly or to understand how details support a main idea, some words and phrases serve both purposes. The words in Table 5.3 are examples of commonly used contrast words. **Contrast word clues** tell you that an author has stopped discussing one point and is moving on to discuss its opposite. Whenever you encounter these words, pay careful attention to the new direction the author is taking. Authors often place main ideas or important details right next to these phrases, so when you see them, *stop and look.*

TABLE 5.3 CONTRAST WORD CLUES			
however	but	on the other hand	on the contrary

Here is a guided example of how word clues can be used to identify the topic and main idea of a reading.

Water molecules cling together because of hydrogen bonding, and yet, water flows freely. This property allows dissolved and suspended molecules to be evenly distributed throughout a system. Therefore, water is an excellent transport medium. Within our bodies, the blood that fills our arteries and veins is 92% water. Blood transports oxygen and nutrients to the cells and removes wastes such as carbon dioxide.

Source: Sylvia Mader, *Human Biology* (New York: McGraw-Hill, 2002), p. 21.

The topic of the excerpt is *water* and the main idea is in the middle of the paragraph: *Therefore, water is an excellent transport medium.* The emphasis word clue *therefore* helps you see the most important point of the excerpt.

Now here is a longer excerpt. Prepare yourself by asking "What is this all about?" As you read, notice the word clues in italics. At the end ask yourself, "What is the most important point the author makes about the topic?" and underline the sentence that best answers the question.

What is compassion? Compassion is the wish that others be free of suffering. It is by means of compassion that we aspire to attain enlightenment. It is compassion that inspires us to engage in the virtuous practices that lead to Buddhahood. We must *therefore* devote ourselves to developing compassion.

In the *first step* toward a compassionate heart, we must develop our empathy or closeness to others. We must also recognize the gravity of their misery. The closer we are to a person, the more unbearable we find that person's suffering. The closeness I speak of is not a physical proximity, nor need it be an emotional one. It is a feeling of responsibility, of concern for a person. In order to develop such closeness, we must reflect upon the virtues of cherishing the well-being of others. We must come to see how this brings one an inner happiness and peace of mind. We must come to recognize how others respect and like us as a result of such an attitude toward them. We must contemplate the short-comings of self-centeredness, seeing how it causes us to act in unvirtuous ways and how our own present fortune takes advantage of those less fortunate.

It is *also important* that we reflect upon the kindness of others. This realization is also a fruit of cultivating empathy. We must recognize how our fortune is really dependent upon the cooperation and contributions of others. Every aspect of our present well-being is due to hard work on the part of others. As we look around us at the buildings we live and work in, the roads we travel, the clothes we wear, or the food we eat, we must acknowledge that all are provided by others. None of these would exist for us to enjoy and make use of were it not for the kindness of so many people unknown to us. As we contemplate in this manner, our appreciation for others grows, as does our empathy and closeness to them.

Source: The Dalai Lama, *An Open Heart: Practicing Compassion in Everyday Life* (New York: Little, Brown and Company, 2001), pp. 91–92.

If you paused at the word *therefore,* asked yourself if the sentence it is in is the most important point the author is making, and then read the rest of the excerpt with that question in mind, you would find the sentence *We must therefore devote ourselves to developing compassion* is the main idea of the passage. The rest of the sentences in the excerpt provide details about how to develop compassion. The word clues *first step* and *also important* let you know where the details for how to develop compassion are being stated. Details such as these typically answer questions about the main idea, such as "Who did it?" "What for?" "In what manner?" "How?" and "Why?"

One way to test whether you have correctly distinguished the main idea from the details is to ask a question about what you *think* the main idea is, and see if the details answer it. For example, using the main idea, *We must therefore devote ourselves to developing compassion,* you could ask yourself, "How do we develop compassion?" You would then find that the rest of the excerpt answers this question by telling you the steps you need to follow.

Finding Main Ideas Using Word Clues

Before reading each of the following excerpts, ask the question "What is this all about?" Then read each excerpt, circle clue words, and question yourself to find the main idea. Once you've found the main idea, underline it.

1. If you don't know how to use a computer, like me, one day, and that day is very soon, you are going to find yourself at the complete mercy of your children. Because while you've been blustering and bumbling through the computer age with all the technical proficiency of Tennessee Tuxedo's assistant Chumley, your Mr. Whoopee-like seven-year-old can reroute the space shuttle to land on the 405, crash the Belgian stock market, and convince complete strangers to donate their balls to a comet. When it comes to computers, your kids are MacGyver and you are a Hasidic Amish guy. And when your complete lack of computer knowledge becomes painfully obvious to your children, they will take the same condescending tone with you that Alex Trebek takes when he corrects somebody on *Jeopardy!* "Oh, I'm sorry, Dad. The correct answer was 'the on-off switch.' That's the on-off switch. Mom, you were the last correct questioner, please select again."

Source: Dennis Miller, *Ranting Again* (New York: Doubleday, 1998), p. 62.

2. Humans Threaten the Biosphere

Human populations tend to modify existing ecosystems for their own purposes. For example, humans clear forests or grasslands in order to grow crops; later, they build houses on what was once farmland; and, finally, they convert small towns into cities. Human populations ever increase in size and require greater amounts of material goods and energy input each year.... With each step, fewer and fewer original organisms remain, until at last ecosystems are completely altered. If this continues, only humans and their domesticated plants and animals will largely exist where once there were many diverse populations.

More and more ecosystems are threatened as the human population increases in size. As discussed in the Ecology Focus on pages 6 and 7, presently there is great concern among scientists and laypersons about the destruction of the world's rain forests due to logging and the large numbers of persons who are starting to live and to farm there. We are beginning to realize how dependent we are on intact ecosystems and the services they perform for us. For example. the tropical rain forests act like a giant sponge, which absorbs carbon dioxide, a pollutant that pours into the atmosphere from the burning of fossil fuels like oil and coal. An increased amount of carbon dioxide in the atmosphere is expected to have many adverse effects, such as an increase in the average daily temperature.

An ever-increasing human population size is a threat to the continued existence of our species when it means that the dynamic balance of the biosphere is upset. The recognition that the workings of the biosphere need to be preserved is one of the most important developments of our new ecological awareness.

Source: Sylvia Mader, *Human Biology* (New York: McGraw-Hill, 2002), pp. 4–5.

3. It happened that the inauguration coincided with the nationwide celebration of the birthday of Martin Luther King, Jr., and Clinton invoked King's name several times in his address. The two men, however, represented very different social philosophies.

By the time King was assassinated in 1968, he had come to believe that our economic system was fundamentally unjust and needed radical transformation. He spoke of the "evils of capitalism" and asked for "a radical redistribution of economic and political power."

On the other hand. as major corporations gave money to the Democratic Party on an unprecedented scale, Clinton demonstrated clearly, in the four years of his first term in office, his total confidence in "the market system" and "private enterprise." During the 1992 campaign, the chief executive officer of Martin Marietta Corporation noted: "I think the Democrats are moving more toward business and business is moving more toward the Democrats."

Martin Luther King's reaction to the buildup of military power had been the same as his reaction to the Vietnam War. "This madness must cease." And "…the evils of racism, economic exploitation, and militarism are all tied together…."

Clinton was willing to recall King's "dream" of racial equality, but not his dream of a society rejecting violence. Even though the Soviet Union was no longer a military threat, he insisted that the United States must keep its armed forces dispersed around the globe, prepare for "two regional wars," and continue the military budget at cold war levels.

Source: Howard Zinn, *A People's History of the United States 1492–Present* (New York: HarperCollins, 1999), pp. 631–632.

Using the three strategies described for identifying main ideas gets you to examine your reading material closely, and that's why they work. They teach you to think in a systematic way. With practice you'll find yourself reading an article or textbook chapter and automatically understanding the main ideas without purposely applying each strategy as a separate step. It's like the first time you drove a car with a manual transmission. Your first efforts at trying to use the clutch, stick shift, and accelerator simultaneously were probably clumsy; but as you practiced, your movements became more fluid, and eventually you were driving without consciously thinking about each step in the process.

Strategy 4: Categorize an Author's Points

As you use the strategies of asking questions, looking in the usual spots, and noticing word clues, you will begin to see that not all ideas are created equal; some are more important than others. You can use a fourth strategy, **categorization**, to help you decide which are main ideas and which are details. You do this by deciding how specific an idea is and looking at how it functions in a reading. General sentences are most likely to be main ideas, while very specific ones are usually the details that support them.

General and Specific Statements

Read each of the following pairs of sentences and decide which one is a general statement and which one is more specific. Circle the sentence that is more specific. The first one is modeled for you.

MODEL   **1.**   **a.**   There are many different religions practiced in the United States.

       (b.)   The Catholic and Jewish religions have many followers.

Notice that sentence *b* is circled as the more specific statement. *Religion* is mentioned in sentence *a* in a general way, but *specific kinds of religions* (Catholicism and Judaism) are mentioned in sentence *b*.

   2.   **a.**   Several poisonous spiders are indigenous to Michigan.

       (b.)   The black widow is a venomous spider with an hourglass-shaped red mark on the underside of its abdomen.

   3.   **(a.)**   The first two years of a child's life are known as the period of sensori-motor intelligence.

       b.   Piaget theorized that all children go through similar stages of cognitive development, each stage predicted by the child's age.

   4.   **a.**   Fat is critical to the human body.

       (b.)   The fatty tissue in our body supports organs, pads them from injury, and helps the body to retain heat.

   5.   **a.**   A fallacy is an error in reasoning.

       (b.)   A hasty generalization occurs when a conclusion is reached based on a very limited sample of evidence.

   6.   **a.**   Children of all ages like video games.

       (b.)   "Spiderman" is a video game that can be played on Game Cube.

Read the following excerpt and look at the mind map that follows it. When you are trying to sort out ideas, especially in a complicated piece of reading material, it helps to draw a mind map to clarify the difference between the topic, the main idea, and details. Mind maps let you literally see the relationships between ideas. (See Chapter 11 for more details on creating mind maps.)

For some unimaginable reason a handful of my teachers didn't give up on me as a hopeless moron. Mr. Robicheaud, my history teacher, never doubted that I had a brain that was actually functional. He always made me want to rise to any challenge. Same with Ms. Samara, my homeroom teacher. And my English teacher, Mrs. Hawkes, urged me to take her creative writing class. I figured, "What the hell, sounds easy!" But it wasn't—at first, anyway. One day, after class, she took me aside and said, "You know, I always hear you telling funny stories to your friends in class. You should write down some of those stories and we can make that your homework assignment." Hey, it sounded better than poetry!

So I gave it a try and—amazingly—it turned out to be the first time I ever did homework where I wasn't waiting for Ricky Nelson to come on TV. I actually enjoyed it. I'd spend hours writing a story (usually about something stupid that happened at school), reading it to myself, crossing out things that weren't funny. I'd do four or five drafts, then hand it in. Suddenly, it was fun to go to class and stand up to read my funny story—and, best of all, to get some laughs. I was always grateful to Mrs. Hawkes for that.

Another teacher who made a huge impression was Mr. Walsh. For whatever reason, he was always assigned to oversee detention duty in the library. And since I was always in detention, we'd sit together almost every day. Mr. Walsh was one of those guys who would laugh at anything. Tell him the simplest joke and he'd break up. Everything was hilarious to this man. So I'd have new stories for him all the time. One day he said to me, "Why don't you think about going into show business?"

This was a revelation. The idea never even occurred to me. I didn't know anybody in show business. The closest thing was an eighth-grade teacher named Mr. Duncan, who did magic tricks at student assemblies. And that was unbelievable! Someone we knew who could actually entertain people! When you grow up in a small town like Andover, show business is the furthest thing from being a career option.

Source: Jay Leno, *Leading with my Chin* (New York: HarperCollins, 1996), pp. 55–56.

The following mind map shows you how the ideas in the excerpt are related to each other. The topic (a phrase) is at the top, the main idea (a complete sentence) is immediately below it, and the details that support the main idea branch off it. The further an idea is from the topic and main idea, the less important it is to the overall meaning of the excerpt. So, although more details from the excerpt could have been added to the map, you really need to know only the topic, main idea, and major and minor supporting details.

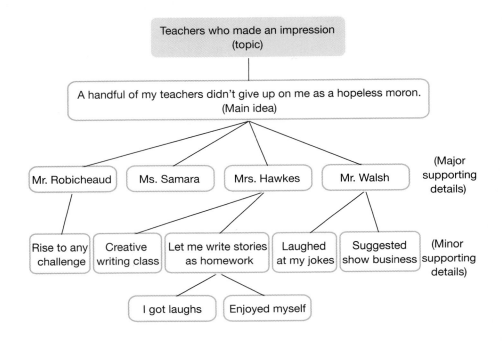

Using Main Idea Strategies

Exercise

5g

Read the following excerpts and use the four strategies presented in this chapter to locate the main ideas. Decide which sentence from each excerpt is the main idea and which sentences contain the supporting details. Also describe how each sentence functions in the excerpt. The first one is modeled for you.

MODEL **1.** #1Capital to finance the railroad boom came from many sources. #2Private American investors provided part of the necessary funding, and railroad companies borrowed large sums from abroad. #3But local governments—states, counties, cities, towns—also often contributed capital, because they were eager to have railroads serve them. #4This support came in the form of loans, stock subscriptions, subsidies, and donations of land for rights-of-way. #5The railroads obtained substantial additional assistance from the federal government in the form of public grants.

Source: A. Brinkley, *American History: A Survey* (New York: McGraw-Hill, 1999), p. 340.

#1: Main idea: This sentence answers the question "What is the author saying about money and railroads?" All the other ideas support this sentence.

#2: Detail: The author explains how railroads gained financial support (one source).

#3: Detail: The author explains how railroads gained financial support (another source).

#4: Detail: The author provides more detail for sentence #3.

#5: Detail: The author explains how railroads gained financial support (another source).

As you can see from this exercise, sentence #1 functions as the overall controlling idea of the paragraph. The other sentences are related in that they serve as support (details) for that idea.

2. #1The new American empire was small by the standards of the great imperial powers of Europe. #2But it created large challenges. #3It embroiled the United States in the politics of both Europe and the Far East in ways the nation had always tried to avoid in the past. #4It also drew Americans into a brutal war in the Philippines.

Source: A. Brinkley, *American History: A Survey* (New York: McGraw-Hill, 1999), p. 707.

#1 Detail: _____

_____

#2 Main idea: _____

_____

_____

#3 Detail: _____

#4 Detail: _____

3. #1To Freud, conscious experience is just the tip of the psychological iceberg. #2Like the unseen mass of a floating iceberg, the material in the unconscious far surpasses in quantity the information about which we are aware. #3Much of people's everyday behavior is viewed as being motivated by unconscious forces. #4For example, a child's concern over being unable to please her strict and demanding parents may lead her to have low self-esteem as an adult, even though she may be highly accomplished. #5Moreover, on a conscious level she may recall her childhood with great pleasure; it is her unconscious, holding her painful memories, that provokes the low self-evaluation.

Source: R. Feldman, *Understanding Psychology* (New York: McGraw-Hill, 1999), p. 473.

#1 Detail: _____

#2 Main idea: _____

_____

#3 Detail: _____

#4 Detail: _____

#5 Detail: _____

4. #1He'd given up sleeping in his bed. #2The memories of Rosie were overpowering there. #3He was unable to function when he walked into their room. #4All her clothes, the smell of her perfume—he'd just grabbed what he needed and put it in the guest room. #5But even that didn't help much. #6Every time he closed his eyes to sleep, he'd dream. #7In those dreams, he'd replay that night over and over again. #8And wake up screaming in terror. #9Worst of all were the dreams where he saved her, where he got them all out, only to wake up and have to face that terrible truth all over again.

Source: Tom Clancy, *Politika* (New York: Berkley Publishing Group, 1997), p. 308.

#1 Detail: _____

#2 Main idea: _____

_____

#3 Detail: _____

#4 Detail: _____

#5 Detail: _____

#6 Detail: _____

#7 Detail: _____

#8 Detail: _____

#9 Detail: _____

Exercise 5h

Practice on the Internet

Go to the website **http://literacynet.org/cnnsf/**. Select "current story" from the menu. Read it and take the multiple-choice test. Remember to use the strategies in this chapter to help you read more carefully. When you are done with the current story, you can go to the story archives for more practice.

Test Taking and Main Ideas

There are two basic types of comprehension questions: literal and inferential. Literal questions require answers related to *stated* main ideas, facts, and opinions. The following strategies will help you answer test questions that demand literal answers:

- **Skim the whole exam first to get an overview of what to expect.**
- **Read each question and identify its purpose.** Ask yourself, "What information is this question asking me to provide?" Circle key words to help you focus on the question's purpose.
- **Read carefully.** Make certain you understand each question completely. Accuracy is more important than speed.
- **Don't skip over unfamiliar words and phrases.** Try to determine their meaning from the context of the question. Then translate the question into your own words.
- **Read the questions as they are, not as you'd like them to be.** Don't add more to the question so that it fits the response you want to make rather than the one being asked for.
- **Make sure that the answer option you select for a multiple-choice question answers the question asked.** Just because an option is "true" doesn't mean that it answers the question correctly. If you are asked to pick the *best* answer, read *all* of the options and then decide which one answers exactly what's being asked.
- **If you are unable to select an answer for a multiple-choice question, skip it and return to it later.** Usually questions are interrelated, and other questions can give you a clue to the one you are having difficulty answering.
- **Note the grammar used in multiple-choice questions and answers.** If you choose an answer that does not fit grammatically within the question stem, you've probably chosen the wrong answer.
- **Remember that most multiple-choice tests include a main idea question or questions.** Make sure you understand the main idea of everything you read.

Practice with Reading Passages

Answer all questions on a separate sheet of paper.

Reading Practice 1

Excerpt from "The Spider and the Wasp"
BY ALEXANDER PETRUNKEVITCH

▄▄▄▄▄▄ PREPARE TO READ

1. Based on the title, what do you expect the following excerpt to be about?

2. What do you think the topic is?

3. What do you already know about the topic?

4. Here are some vocabulary words that might be unfamiliar to you. Look them up, if necessary, and refer to the definitions as you encounter them in the reading.
   a. Chitinous
   b. Girth
   c. Exasperated
   d. Secretion
   e. Qualitatively
   f. Chasm

5. Develop a question, using the title of this essay, to ask yourself before you read.

6. As you read the excerpt, circle all the word clues you find.

In the adult stage the [pepsis] wasp lives only a few months. The female produces but a few eggs, one at a time at intervals of two or three days. For each egg the mother must provide one adult tarantula, alive but paralyzed. The mother wasp attaches the egg to the paralyzed spider's abdomen. Upon hatching from the egg, the larva is many hundreds of times smaller than its living but helpless victim. It eats no other food and drinks no water. By the time it has finished its single gargantuan meal and become ready for wasphood, nothing remains of the tarantula but its indigestible chitinous skeleton.

The mother wasp goes tarantula hunting when the egg in her ovary is almost ready to be laid. Flying low over the ground late on a sunny afternoon, the wasp looks for its victim or for the mouth of a tarantula burrow, a round hole edged by a bit of silk. The sex of the spider makes no difference, but the mother is highly discriminating as to species. Each species of pepsis requires a certain species of tarantula, and the wasp will not attack the wrong species. In a cage with a tarantula, which is not its normal prey, the wasp avoids the spider and is usually killed by it in the night.

Yet when a wasp finds the correct species, it is the other way about. To identify the species the wasp apparently must explore the spider with her antennae. The tarantula shows an amazing tolerance to this exploration. The wasp crawls under it and walks over it without evoking any hostile response. The molestation is so great and persistent that the tarantula often rises on all eight legs, as if it were on stilts. It may stand this way for several minutes. Meanwhile the wasp, having satisfied itself that the victim is of the right species, moves off a few inches to dig the spider's grave. Working vigorously with legs and jaws, it excavates—like a machine—a hole 8 to 10 inches deep with a diameter slightly larger than the spider's girth. Now and again the wasp pops out of the hole to make sure that the spider is still there.

When the grave is finished, the wasp returns to the tarantula to complete her ghastly enterprise. First she feels it all over once more with her antennae. Then her behavior becomes more aggressive. She bends her abdomen, protruding her sting, and searches for the soft membrane at the point where the spider's legs join its body—the only spot where she can penetrate the horny skeleton. From time to time, as the exasperated spider slowly shifts ground, the wasp turns on her back and slides along with the aid of her wings, trying to get under the tarantula for a shot at the vital spot. During all this maneuvering, which can last for several minutes, the tarantula makes no move to save itself. Finally the wasp corners it against some obstruction and grasps one of its legs in her powerful jaws. Now at last the harassed spider tries a desperate but vain defense. The two contestants roll over and over on the ground. It is a terrifying sight and the outcome is always the same. The wasp finally manages to thrust her sting into the soft spot and holds it there for a few seconds while she pumps in the poison. Almost immediately the tarantula falls paralyzed on its back. Its legs stop twitching; its heart stops beating. Yet it is not dead, as is shown by the fact that if taken from the wasp it can be restored to some sensitivity by being kept in a moist chamber for several months.

After paralyzing the tarantula, the wasp cleans herself by dragging her body around the ground and rubbing her feet, sucks the drop of blood oozing from the wound in the spider's abdomen, then grabs a leg of the flabby, helpless animal in her jaws and drags it down to the bottom of the grave. She stays there for many minutes, sometimes for several hours, and what she does all that time in the dark we do not know. Eventually she lays her egg and attaches it to the side of the spider's abdomen with a sticky secretion. Then she emerges, fills the grave with soil carried bit by bit in her jaws, and finally tramples the ground all around to hide any trace of the grave from prowlers. Then she flies away, leaving her descendant safely started in life.

In all this the behavior of the wasp evidently is qualitatively different from that of the spider. The wasp acts like an intelligent animal. This is not to say that instinct plays no part or that she reasons as man does. But her actions are to the point; they are not automatic and can be modified to fit the situation. We do not know for certain how she identifies the tarantula—probably it is by some olfactory or chemo–tactile sense—but she does it purposefully and does not blindly tackle a wrong species.

On the other hand, the tarantula's behavior shows only confusion. Evidently the wasp's pawing gives it no pleasure, for it tries to move away. That the wasp is not simulating sexual stimulation is certain because male and female tarantulas react in the same way to its advances. That the spider is not anesthetized by some odorless secretion is easily shown by blowing lightly at the tarantula and making it jump suddenly. What, then, makes the tarantula behave as stupidly as it does?

No clear, simple answer is available. Possibly the stimulation by the wasp's antennae is masked by a heavier pressure on the spider's body so that it reacts when prodded by a pencil. But the explanation may be much more complex. Initiative in attack is not the nature of tarantulas; most species fight only when cornered so that escape is impossible. Their inherited patterns of behavior apparently prompt them to avoid problems rather than attack them. For example, spiders always weave their webs in three dimensions, and when a spider finds that there is insufficient space to attach certain threads in the third dimension, it leaves the place and seeks another, instead of finishing the web in a single plane. This urge to escape seems to arise under all circumstances, in all phases of life, and to take the place of reasoning. For a spider to change the pattern of its web is as impossible as for an inexperienced man to build a bridge across a chasm obstructing his way.

In a way the instinctive urge to escape is not only easier but often more efficient than reasoning. The tarantula does exactly what is most efficient in all cases except in an encounter with a ruthless and determined attacker dependent for the existence of her own species on killing as many tarantulas as she can lay eggs. Perhaps in this case the spider follows its usual pattern of trying to escape, instead of seizing and killing the wasp, because it is not aware of its danger. In any case, the survival of the tarantula species as a whole is protected by the fact that the spider is much more fertile than the wasp.

Source: Alexander Petrunkevitch, excerpt from "The Spider and the Wasp," *Scientific American,* 1952.

CHECK YOUR UNDERSTANDING

OBJECTIVE QUESTIONS

Read each of the following multiple-choice questions and select the best possible answer from the four choices given.

1. The wasp has to provide her egg with

   a. A fresh, 3-dimensional web.

   b. A live tarantula.

   c. A male tarantula.

   d. An egg from the tarantula's nest.

2. Which of the following statements is true?

   a. The wasp seeks a male tarantula to attach its egg to.

   b. Each species of pepsis requires a certain species of tarantula, and the wasp will not attack the wrong species.

    c. To identify the species the wasp must taste its prey.

    d. When attempting to taste the spider, the wasp must be careful to avoid the spider's hostility.

3. What happens after the wasp digs a grave?

    a. The wasp grasps one of the spider's legs in her jaws.

    b. The spider fights the wasp.

    c. The tarantula becomes paralyzed.

    d. The wasp feels all over the spider once more with her antennae.

4. What happens after the wasp drops the spider into the grave?

    a. She stays by the grave.

    b. She leaves to lay her egg.

    c. She kills the spider.

    d. She buries the spider.

5. How does the tarantula species survive?

    a. The wasps usually cannot find the right species very easily.

    b. The tarantula can run faster than the wasp can fly.

    c. The wasps have more babies than the tarantulas.

    d. The tarantulas have more babies than the wasps.

SHORT-ANSWER QUESTIONS

6. What is the main idea of the excerpt?

7. What does the tarantula do when the wasp explores it?

8. How does the wasp attack the tarantula?

9. Why doesn't the wasp kill the tarantula completely?

10. What answer does the author give for the tarantula's unusually compliant behavior?

Reading Practice 2

The 'Thrill' of Theft
BY JERRY ADLER

PREPARE TO READ

1. Based on the title, what do you expect the reading to be about?

2. What do you already know about the subject?

3. Here are some vocabulary words that might be unfamiliar to you. Look them up, if necessary, and refer to the definitions as you encounter these words in the article.

a. Avarice

b. Bellwether

c. Postulate

d. Condone

e. Ubiquitous

4. Before you read the following passage, *The 'Thrill' of Theft*, develop a question from its title. As you read the passage, try to answer that question.

The 'Thrill' of Theft

If all you've ever done is pay for stuff, you'd never know how it felt. It was thrilling, she says, a heart-pounding rush of greed and fear as she stuffed the bathing suits into her bag, two identical sets of tops and bottoms, because she was going to a concert the next night with a friend and they wanted to wear the same thing. She was in eighth grade then, and she'd been stealing for a year, partly for the fun of getting away with something, but also partly because no way was she going to spend $70 on one of those suits. "I think, I could be spending my money on this, but I'm getting it for free," she told Newsweek. "Then I get to spend my money on things my parents don't know I'm buying— like beer, drugs, and cigarettes." But there's always danger. "Your heart starts to race, and all you can think about is getting out of the store. It's like, 'I've taken what I need to take, let's get out of here.' But I get really excited because I'm thinking 'I already got a bunch of stuff in my bag and I can get a whole lot more'." She moved on to the rack of Mudd jeans.

Some 800,000 times a day, this tableau of temptation, fear, and exhilaration plays out in the humdrum aisles of department stores and supermarkets, frequently over such unlikely objects of avarice as batteries and souvenir knickknacks. It's a window into our desires: retailers like Brandy Samson, who manages a jewelry and accessories store in the Sherman Oaks (Calif.) Fashion Square, uses shoplifting as a guide to taste. "We know what's hot among teens by seeing what they steal," she says. It can be a cry for help on the part of troubled celebrities like Bess Myerson, Hedy Lamarr, and maybe Winona Ryder, who was arrested in December on felony charges of taking $4,760 in clothes from the Beverly Hills branch of Saks Fifth Avenue. She pleaded not guilty and was freed on bail, although her fans continue to protest the injustice of the arrest with FREE WINONA T-shirts. And it's an economic bellwether: thrills and temptation won out over fear in 2000 to the tune of some $13 billion, according to Checkpoint, a top retail security company (which notes that employees steal the most by far). And in the current recession, the company is predicting a $1 billion jump in shoplifting losses, with more people out of a job, and fewer salesclerks to watch them as they nervously sidle down the aisles heaped with DVDs, lingerie, and balsamic vinegar.

Shoplifting was the first distinctly modern crime, a product of late-19th-century mass merchandising. "Consumer culture manipulates the senses of the shoppers, seduces them, weakening their ability to resist temptation," says Lisa Tiersten, a cultural historian at Barnard College in New York. Department stores, bursting with fans and muffs and bustles stocked conveniently out of sight of the distant shop clerks, proved an irresistible lure to otherwise respectable housewives. The spectacle of middle-class women stuffing their corsets with swag was so unnerving to the Victorian sensibility that in 1890 a new mental disorder was postulated to explain it, "kleptomania." Shrinks no longer believe, as they once did, that it originates in the uterus, but kleptomania is still a recognized condition, although rarely diagnosed these days. By far the largest category of habitual shoplifters, experts say, are suffering from nothing more exotic than addictive–compulsive disorder; the rest include professional criminals, drug addicts supporting their habits—and thrill seekers, who are often high school kids. By some estimates, a quarter of all shoplifters are teenagers.

She made only one mistake that day, but it was a costly one: She began her spree by taking an empty shopping bag from another store to hold the items she planned to steal. A clerk at the first store watched her go and alerted the manager of the boutique where she was headed. As she left with the bathing suits, the jeans, and a couple of beaded T-shirts stashed in her bag, she was stopped by a clerk. "They arrested me and walked me through the mall, they took me to the juvenile center and called my parents. I got grounded for probably like a month and a half, but it was the first month of summer vacation so it was really bad." She was not prosecuted, although she had to write a 25-page report on how shoplifting affects the economy.

A few decades after the invention of kleptomania, a 6-year-old named Gretchen Grimm began what may be one of the longest criminal careers in history, swiping a lipstick for her mother at a Woolworth's. The only daughter in a family with seven older sons, Grimm felt overlooked and began stealing, she believes, to win her mother's attention and affection. It ended last year when Grimm, at the age of 83, finally kicked the habit with the help of psychotherapy and the anti-anxiety drug Paxil. Over the intervening years, while she raised five children and worked as a nurse at the University of Iowa, she stole, by her own account, "clothes, jewelry, toilet paper, towels, pencils, pieces of stone—everything." At the moment of theft, she says, "you feel wonderful, elated, slick and cool and cunning." But immediately afterward, guilt would set in, and often she would actually sneak her loot back into the stores.

Grimm's story illustrates two important truths about shoplifting. The first is the powerful ego boost it can provide, especially to insecure young people. In that context, experts say, while stealing can never be condoned, a single episode—especially as part of a group—is not necessarily a cause for parents to panic. "As an isolated thing, most 12-year-old girls with a peppery personality do it once," says child psychiatrist Elizabeth Berger, author of *Raising Children with Character*. "It shows you're a real badass."

The other lesson is that a crime that can be perpetrated with equal ease by first-graders and old ladies is pretty hard to stop. Grimm had only one serious arrest, and hid her habit from her family for almost her entire life. She started getting caught more often in her 80s, and would call her psychiatrist, Dr. Donald Black. "She usually gets off because she's old," Black says. Technology has provided merchants with a new generation of sensor tags sewn inside clothes or hidden in packaging. Cameras now are ubiquitous in large retail stores, hidden in clocks, smoke alarms, even the pushbars on fire-exit doors. But most stores, as every shoplifter knows, are reluctant to pursue criminal cases against amateur crooks, reasoning that the cost in publicity—and possible liability for false arrest—isn't worth the gain.

She's 17 now, and she's learned her lesson, which is to be more careful and steal stuff only when she really needs it—like last week, when because her car insurance payment was due she was out of cash for a Valentine's Day present for her boyfriend. So she picked up a nice candle for him, and, while she was at it, a Bob Marley T-shirt for herself. "Anything free is cooler," she says. "And I still get a rush from it."

With Julie Scelfo and Gretel C. Kovach in New York, Karen Springen in Chicago, and Tara Weingarten in Los Angeles.

Source: *Newsweek*, February 25, 2002.

■ CHECK YOUR UNDERSTANDING

OBJECTIVE QUESTIONS
Read the following multiple-choice questions and select the best possible answer from the four choices given.

1. According to the article, which of the following four statements is *not* true?

   a. One store used shoplifting as a guide to know what items are desirable among teenagers.

   b. Shoplifters usually steal things that they really need but cannot afford.

   c. Winona Ryder was arrested on felony charges for taking $4,760 in clothes from a Saks Fifth Avenue store.

   d. Shoplifting was the first distinctly modern crime.

2. Which is the largest category of habitual shoplifters?

   a. Drug addicts supporting their habit.

   b. Professional criminals.

    c. Those suffering from addictive–compulsive disorder.

    d. Thrill seekers.

3. What are the two important truths about shoplifting that were mentioned in the essay?

    a. Shoplifting provides a powerful ego boost and is hard to prevent.

    b. Shoplifting provides a powerful ego boost and is usually committed by men.

    c. Shoplifters usually are not arrested and they are good at avoiding security cameras.

    d. Shoplifters usually steal batteries and they usually strike during the day, when stores are the busiest.

4. According to the essay, what is one measure retailers are taking to prevent shoplifting?

    a. They are installing cameras in the stores.

    b. They are profiling certain people and following them around stores.

    c. They are watching their employees more carefully as they are the biggest offenders in shoplifting.

    d. They place expensive things out of the view of the customers.

5. Why did Gretchen Grimm, the woman in the essay who confessed to shoplifting until the age of 83, believe she stole things?

    a. She shoplifted because she suffered no guilt from it.

    b. She shoplifted because she knew that even if she were caught, she would never be prosecuted.

    c. She shoplifted because she refused the anti-anxiety drug Paxil, even though she needed it.

    d. She shoplifted because she felt overlooked and wanted to win her mother's attention and affection.

SHORT-ANSWER QUESTIONS

6. Were you able to maintain your concentration throughout the entire passage? If you did, what factors do you think contributed to your ability to do so? If you did not, where in the passage did you become distracted and why?

7. What other information do you know on the topic of shoplifting and how could you use it to help you remember the categories of habitual shoplifters presented in the passage?

8. List two word clues from the passage and explain what they signal.

9. What is the main idea of the reading passage?

10. Why do you think the author included stories of shoplifters' experiences?

Chapter Summary

The ability to locate an author's main idea is key to understanding your reading. In order to see the relationship between the main idea and the details that support it, you must first distinguish between general ideas and more specific ones. The topic is the most general idea (for example, *unusual edibles*). The main idea is the more specific controlling idea of a piece of writing *(for example, eating unusual things can be scary and exciting)*. The details, which are the most specific, support and illustrate the main idea (for example, *types of unusual foods: tongue, ants, intestine, raw lamb, alligator, kangaroo*).

Questioning yourself, looking in the usual places, noticing clue words, and categorizing an author's points are four strategies you can use to think systematically about what you read. If you ask yourself the question "What is this all about?" you will actively look for the answer to your question as you read. Looking in the obvious spots helps you to find the main idea more efficiently. Noticing clue words and categorizing ideas helps you to separate examples and other supporting ideas from the larger, main points, so the relationships between ideas become clear.

Some main ideas are stated directly in a reading and are easy to identify. Others are implied, and you must infer their meaning from the reading and then restate them in your own words. Implied main ideas and strategies for detecting them will be explored in Chapter 7.

Post Test

Answer all questions on a separate sheet of paper.

Part I

OBJECTIVE QUESTIONS

1.   Match each word or phrase in Column A with its correct definition in Column B.

A		B	
1.	Topic	a.	Major point about a topic.
2.	Main idea	b.	Technique used to help identify main idea.

3.	Clue words		c.	Words that signal a change in an author's thought.
4.	Question yourself		d.	Supporting ideas.
5.	Details		e.	Word or short phrase that summarizes the general idea(s) presented in a chapter.
6.	Contrast word clues		f.	Markers of very important material.

Indicate whether each of the following statements is *true* or *false*.

2. Mind maps show how ideas are related to one another.

3. The main idea of a reading is what you get from the reading.

4. If several people read a textbook chapter, they should all identify the same main idea.

5. Topics are more general than details.

6. Topics should always be stated in complete sentences.

7. Authors frequently put main idea statements in the same places in an essay.

8. To identify the main idea of a reading, all you have to do is look for word clues.

Part II

Reading Passage

"McDonald's"
BY CONRAD KOTTAK

1. Based on the title, what do you expect the reading to be about?

2. What do you think the topic is?

3. What do you already know about the topic?

4. Develop a question, using the title of the textbook excerpt, to ask yourself before you begin reading.

5. Circle any word clues you find.

McDonald's

Each day, on the average, a new McDonald's restaurant opens somewhere in the world. The number of McDonald's outlets today far surpasses the total number of all fast-food restaurants in the United States in 1945. McDonald's has grown from a single hamburger stand in San Bernardino, California, into today's international web of thousands of outlets. Have factors less obvious to American natives than relatively low cost, fast service, and taste contributed to McDonald's success? Could it be that natives—in consuming the products and propaganda of McDonald's —are not just eating but experiencing something comparable in certain respects to participation in religious rituals? To answer this question, we must briefly review the nature of ritual.

Rituals, we know from the chapter on religion, are formal—stylized, repetitive, and stereotyped. They are performed in special places at set times. Rituals include liturgical orders—set sequences of words and actions laid down by someone other than the current performers. Rituals also convey information about participants and their cultural traditions. Performed year after year, generation after generation, rituals translate messages, values, and sentiments into action. Rituals are social acts. Inevitably, some participants are more strongly committed than others are to the beliefs on which the rituals are founded. However, just by taking part in a joint public act, people signal that they accept an order that transcends their status as mere individuals.

For many years, like millions of other Americans, I have occasionally eaten at McDonald's. Eventually I began to notice certain ritual-like aspects of Americans' behavior at these fast-food restaurants. Tell your fellow Americans that going to McDonalds is similar in some ways to going to church and their bias as natives will reveal itself in laughter, denial, or questions about your sanity. Just as football is a game and *Star Trek* is "entertainment," McDonald's, for natives, is just a place to eat. However, an analysis of what natives do at McDonald's will reveal a very high degree of formal, uniform behavior by staff members and customers alike. It is particularly interesting that this invariance in word and deed has developed without any theological doctrine. McDonald's ritual aspect is founded on 20th-century technology, particularly automobiles, television, work away from home, and the short lunch break. It is striking, nevertheless, that one commercial organization should be so much more successful than other businesses, the schools, the military, and even many religions in producing behavioral invariance. Factors other than low cost, fast service, and the taste of the food—all of which are approximated by other chains—have contributed to our acceptance of McDonald's and adherence to its rules.

Remarkably, when Americans travel abroad, even in countries noted for good food, many visit the local McDonald's outlet. The same factors that lead us to frequent McDonald's at home are responsible. Because Americans are thoroughly familiar with how to eat and more or less what they will pay at McDonald's in its outlets overseas, they have a home away from home. In Paris, whose people aren't known for making tourists, particularly Americans, feel at home, McDonald's offers sanctuary (along with relatively clean, free restrooms). It is, after all, an originally American institution, where natives, programmed by years of prior experience, can feel completely at home. Given its international spread, McDonald's is no longer merely an American institution—a fact that McDonald's advertising has not ignored. A TV commercial linked to the 1996 Olympics (of which McDonald's was an "official sponsor") portrayed an Asian athlete finding sanctuary from an alien American culture at a McDonald's restaurant in Atlanta. For her, the ad proclaimed, McDonald's was home-culture turf.

This devotion to McDonald's rests in part on uniformities associated with its outlets: food, setting, architecture, ambience, acts, and utterances. The McDonald's symbol, the golden arches, is an almost universal landmark, as familiar to Americans as Mickey Mouse, Mr. Rogers, and the flag. A McDonald's near my university (now closed) was a brick structure whose stained-glass windows had golden arches as their central theme. Sunlight flooded in through a skylight that was like the clerestory of a church.

Americans enter a McDonald's restaurant for an ordinary, secular act—eating. However, the surroundings tell us that we are somehow apart from the variability of the world outside. We know what we are going to see, what we are going to say, and what will be said to us. We know what we will eat, how it will taste, and how much it will cost. Behind the counter, agents wear similar attire. Permissible utterances by customer and worker are written above the counter. Throughout the United States, with only minor variation, the menu is in the same place, contains the same items, and has the same prices. The food, again with only minor regional variation, is prepared according to plan and varies little in taste. Obviously, customers are limited to what they can choose. Less obviously, they are limited in what they can say. Each item has its appropriate designation: "large fry," "quarter pounder with cheese." The novice who innocently asks, "What kind of hamburgers do you have?" or "What's a Big Mac?" is out of place.

Other ritual phrases are uttered by the person behind the counter. After the customer has completed an order, if no potatoes are requested, the agent ritually asks, "Any fries?" Once food is presented and picked up, the agent conventionally says, "Have a nice day." (McDonald's has surely played a strong role in the diffusion of this cliché into every corner of contemporary American life.) Nonverbal behavior also is programmed. As customers request food, agents look back to see if the desired sandwich item is available. If not, they tell you, "That'll be a few minutes," and prepare your drink. After this, a proper agent will take the order of the next customer in line. McDonald's lore and customs are even taught at a "seminary" called Hamburger University in Illinois. Managers who attend the program pass on what they learn to the people who work in their restaurants.

It isn't simply the formality and regularity of behavior at McDonald's but its total ambience that invites comparison with ritual settings. McDonald's image makers stress "clean living" and refer to a set of values that transcends McDonald's itself. Agents submit to dress codes. Kitchens, grills, and counters should sparkle. Understandably, as the world's number one fast-food chain, McDonald's also has evoked hostility. In 1975, the Ann Arbor campus McDonald's was the scene of a ritual rebellion—desecration by the Radical Vegetarian League, which held a "puke-in." Standing on the second-story balcony just below the clerestory, a dozen vegetarians gorged themselves on mustard and water and vomited down on the customer waiting area. McDonald's, defiled, lost many customers that day.

The formality and invariance of behavior in a demarcated setting suggest analogies between McDonald's and rituals. Furthermore, as in a ritual, participation in McDonald's occurs at specified times. In American culture, our daily food consumption is supposed to occur as three meals: breakfast, lunch, and dinner. Americans who have traveled abroad are aware that cultures differ in which meal they emphasize. In many countries, the midday meal is primary. Americans are away from home at lunchtime because of their jobs and usually take less than an hour for lunch. They view dinner as the main meal. Lunch is a lighter meal symbolized by the sandwich. McDonald's provides relatively hot and fresh sandwiches and a variety of subsidiary fare that many American palates can tolerate.

The ritual of eating at McDonald's is confined to ordinary, everyday life. Eating at McDonald's and religious feasts are in complementary distribution in American life. That is, when one occurs, the other doesn't. Most Americans would consider it inappropriate to eat at a fast-food restaurant on Christmas, Thanksgiving, Easter, or Passover. Our culture regards these as family days, occasions when relatives and close friends get together. However, although Americans neglect McDonald's on holidays, television reminds us that McDonald's still endures, that it will welcome us back once our holiday is over. The television presence of McDonald's is particularly evident on such occasions—whether through a float in the Macy's Thanksgiving Day parade or through sponsorship of special programs, particularly "family entertainment."

Although Burger King, Wendy's, and Arby's compete with McDonald's for the fast-food business, none has equaled McDonald's success. The explanation may lie in the particularly skillful ways in which McDonald's advertising plays up the features just discussed. For decades, its commercials have been varied to appeal to different audiences. On Saturday morning television, with its steady stream of cartoons, McDonald's has been a ubiquitous sponsor. The McDonald's commercials for children's shows usually differ from the ones adults see in the evening and on sports programs. Children are reminded of McDonalds' through fantasy characters, headed by clown Ronald McDonald. Children can meet "McDonaldland" characters again at outlets. Their pictures appear on cookie boxes and plastic cups. Children also have a chance to meet Ronald McDonald as actors scatter visits throughout the country. One can even rent a Ronald for a birthday party.

Adult advertising has different but equally effective themes. Breakfast at McDonald's has been promoted by a fresh-faced, sincere, happy, clean-cut young woman. Actors gambol on ski slopes or in mountain pastures. The single theme, however, that for years has run though the commercials is personalism. McDonald's, the commercials drone on, is something other than a fast-food restaurant. It's a warm, friendly place where you are graciously welcomed and feel at home, where your children won't get into trouble. McDonald's commercials tell you that you aren't simply an anonymous face in an amorphous crowd. You find respite from a hectic and impersonal society, the break you deserve. Your individuality and dignity are respected at McDonald's.

McDonald's advertising tries to deemphasize the fact that the chain is a commercial organization. One jingle proclaimed, "You, you're the one; we're fixin' breakfast for ya"—not "We're making millions off ya." Commercials make McDonald's seem like a charitable organization by stressing its program of community good works. "Family" television entertainment is often "brought to you by McDonald's." McDonald's commercials regularly tell us that it supports and works to maintain the values of American family life.

I am not at all arguing here that McDonald's has become a religion. I am merely suggesting that specific ways in which Americans participate in McDonald's bear analogies to religious systems involving myth, symbol, and ritual. Just as in rituals, participation in McDonald's requires temporary subordination of individual differences in a social and cultural collectivity. In a land of ethnic, social, economic, and religious diversity, we demonstrate that we share something with millions of others. Furthermore, as in rituals, participation in McDonald's is linked to a cultural system that transcends the chain itself. By eating there, we say something about ourselves as Americans, about our acceptance of certain collective values, customs, and ways of living.

Source: Conrad Kottak, "McDonald's," *Cultural Anthropology* (New York: McGraw-Hill, 2002), pp. 466–468.

OBJECTIVE QUESTIONS

Read the following multiple-choice questions and select the best possible answer from the choices given.

1. According to the author, why do people eat at McDonald's?

  a. The French fries are only $ .99.

  b. Americans are not really concerned with their health.

  c. They are familiar with how to eat and what they will pay at McDonald's.

  d. Americans do not like to pay a lot for lunch, since lunch is not considered the main meal of the day.

2. The author argues that people are devoted to McDonald's because

  a. They believe that Wendy's has greasy hamburgers.

  b. They like the uniformities associated with McDonald's outlets.

  c. Each McDonald's is different.

  d. McDonald's was an "official sponsor" of the 1996 Olympics.

3. According to the author, what nonverbal behavior is customary for McDonald's employees?

  a. As customers request food, employees look back to see if the desired sandwich item is available.

  b. If no potatoes are ordered with a meal, employees routinely ask, "Any fries?"

  c. If a food item is not available, employees will say, "That'll be a few minutes."

  d. Employees frequently stare off into space and yell, "Next in line!"

4. What hostility occurred in a McDonald's in Ann Arbor, Michigan?

   a. University of Michigan undergraduates critiqued the grammar on the menu over the loudspeaker.

   b. Michigan State football fans attempted to rally at the restaurant but couldn't remember their school's fight song.

   c. Vegetarians picketed outside.

   d. The Radical Vegetarian League held a "puke-in."

5. According to the author, in what ways has McDonald's promoted the idea of personal attention in their advertisements?

   a. They have a catch phrase in their commercials: "Have it your way."

   b. The commercials tell you that you aren't simply an anonymous face in an amorphous crowd.

   c. They include a guy named "Dave" in all of their commercials.

   d. They advertise McNuggets for McYou.

SHORT-ANSWER QUESTIONS

6. What is the main idea of the excerpt?

7. What are rituals?

8. What rituals are performed at McDonald's?

9. What McDonald's symbol is recognized as a universal landmark?

10. According to the author, what do we say about ourselves when we eat at McDonald's?

Website Sources for Additional Practice

http://cobweb.dartmouth.edu/admin/acskills/reading.html:
Shatter six myths that will change your (reading) life.

http://musicb.marist.edu/~alcu/@httpd/SSK/habits.html:
What is your (reading) problem?! Take this quick quiz to find out your reading strengths and weaknesses.

http://www.cerritos.edu/cerritos/divisions/la/reading/tutorials.htm:
Practice finding the main idea with this interactive Internet tutorial and quizzes.

http://english.glendale.cc.ca.us/topic.html: Find main ideas in paragraphs.

http://literacynet.org/cnnsf/: This site will keep you occupied with reading practice for hours.

Chapter 6

Finding Supporting Details

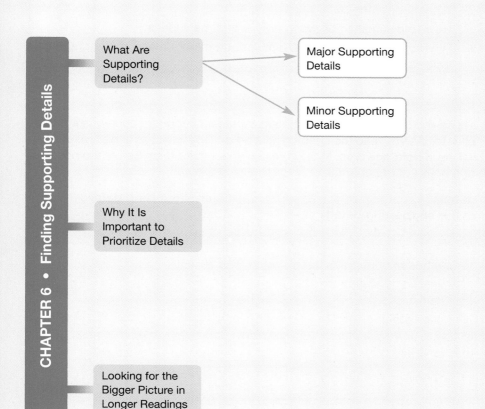

CHAPTER 6 • Finding Supporting Details

What Are Supporting Details?

Major Supporting Details

Minor Supporting Details

Why It Is Important to Prioritize Details

Looking for the Bigger Picture in Longer Readings

Chapter Contents

Chapter Goals

In this chapter you will learn:

- What supporting details are.
- How to distinguish between details and main ideas.
- How to identify and prioritize major and minor details in paragraphs, articles, and textbook chapters.

Chapter Vocabulary

These vocabulary words and phrases represent important concepts from this chapter. As you read the chapter, take note of these words and phrases; they will be in **boldface** type. Make sure you understand them before the post test at the end of the chapter.

details   **major supporting details**
minor supporting details

Sherrye's Journal Entry

When I read my textbooks I think everything is important. I get confused and don't know what I'm supposed to remember. I either overstudy or don't study the right information. It's frustrating. I quit using a highlighter because I underlined too many sentences with it. Looking for word clues helps, but different authors don't always use them the same way. At least the word clues help me stop and think as I'm reading. I've started using other reading strategies too, like asking questions, and I make sure I know what all the words in bold print mean. But I'm still not sure what's important and what isn't! If I don't study a piece of information, it seems that that's what turns up on the exam!

What Are Supporting Details?

Authors use **details** to illustrate and explain their main ideas. Unlike topics or main ideas, which are more general in nature, details consist of facts, examples, and other specific information. They are two types of details: major supporting details, which are the ideas and arguments an author uses to validate his or her main point or points; and minor supporting details, used to clarify and enhance the major details. Once you can recognize details, and distinguish major from minor ones, you will be able to follow an author's line of reasoning and see how all the ideas in a reading passage are related to each other.

Details are frequently introduced by word clues and phrases, such as *for example* and *one more reason*. (See Chapters 5 and 8 for more information on word clues.) They are usually organized within a paragraph or excerpt in a specific pattern, such as a list. (See Chapter 8 for more information on organizational methods.) The pattern used to organize major details shows how they are related to one another as well as how they support an author's main point or idea. Minor supporting details are not usually organized in a particular pattern but are directly related to the major details they support.

Here is an example that illustrates how topic, main idea, major supporting details and minor supporting details are connected. Read the following paragraph, first asking yourself, "What is this all about?" After reading it, ask yourself, "What is the most important point the author makes about the topic?"

> **Throughout the ages, poets have been waxing poetic about the beauties of white teeth. In the Old Testament's Song of Solomon, the beloved's teeth are compared to a flock of sheep, fresh-washed, evenly shorn, all twins.**

But how do you get white healthy teeth? It's a pursuit that dates back to the pharaohs and beyond. Egyptians used to rub their teeth with a chew stick coated with a paste made from granulated pumice stone and wine vinegar. In Europe in the Middle Ages and Renaissance, barber-surgeons filed the surface of the teeth and slathered on aqua fortis, a corrosive nitric acid. A dazzling smile would be followed in middle age by massive tooth decay because the filing and acid took all the protective enamel off the teeth.

Another early popular approach was human urine. In ancient Rome, women gargled and brushed with urine to help keep their teeth sparkling, and most prized was Portuguese urine, reputed to be the strongest. (Actually, the long delivery time might make that claim true.)

Source: Richard Zacks, *An Underground Education* (New York: Doubleday, 1997), p. 203.

The topic in this excerpt, the most general idea, is *white teeth*. The main idea, the main point about the topic, can be found in these two sentences: *But how do you get white healthy teeth? It's a pursuit that dates back to the pharaohs and beyond.* Since part of the main idea is stated as a question, you can use that question (*But how do you get white healthy teeth?*) to locate the major supporting details. These include the following facts: that Egyptians used a paste made from granulated pumice stone and wine vinegar to whiten teeth; barber-surgeons in the Middle Ages filed the surface of the teeth and applied a corrosive nitric acid; and many people used human urine. Word clues the author provides, such as *Another early popular approach was human urine,* provide hints that the author is about to list another example of teeth-whitening techniques.

The rest of the ideas in the excerpt, such as the comments about poets and the Old Testament, are minor supporting details. You wouldn't usually need to remember them unless, for some reason, your instructor emphasized them in a lecture. However, if these minor details help clarify the meaning of the passage for you, or help you to remember the main idea or major supporting details, then it would be useful to remember them.

Major Supporting Details

As previously stated, **major supporting details** provide support for the main idea of a reading. They are commonly presented in the form of examples, illustrations, explanations, definitions, facts, or opinions, and they typically answer *who? what? when? how?* or *why?* questions about the main idea.

The following topic sentence is taken from a paragraph in Roald Dahl's *Boy*, in which he writes about boyhood memories of a candy shop and its owner, Mrs. Pratchett: *But by far the most loathsome thing about Mrs. Pratchett was the filth that clung around her.* What kind of detailed information do you expect to follow this topic sentence? You probably expect a description of the most loathsome thing about Mrs. Pratchett, the filth. And that's what you get. Here's the entire paragraph:

> But by far the most loathsome thing about Mrs. Pratchett was the filth that clung around her. Her apron was grey and greasy. Her blouse had bits of breakfast all over it, toast-crumbs and tea stains and splotches of dried egg-yolk. It was her hands, however, that disturbed us most. They were disgusting. They were black with dirt and grime. They looked as though they had been putting lumps of coal on the fire all day long. And do not forget please that it was these very hands and fingers that she plunged into the sweet jars when we asked for a pennyworth of Treacle Toffee or Wine Gums or Nut Clusters or whatever. There were precious few health laws in those days, and nobody, least of all Mrs. Pratchett, ever thought of using a little shovel for getting out the sweets as they do today. The mere sight of her grimy right hand with its black fingernails digging an ounce of Chocolate Fudge out of a jar would have caused a starving tramp to go running from the shop. But not us. Sweets were our life-blood. We would have put up with far worse than that to get them. So we simply stood and watched in sullen silence while this disgusting old woman stirred around inside the jars with her foul fingers.
>
> **Source:** Roald Dahl, *Boy: Tales of Childhood* (New York: Penguin Books, 1984), pp. 31–32.

Notice how all the sentences directly (*Her apron was grey and greasy*) or indirectly *(We would have put up with far worse than that to get them)* describe what the filth was like. They provide the details that illustrate the main idea of the topic sentence. They also answer questions you might have asked yourself, such as "What was the filth like?" or "How did the author know Mrs. Pratchett was filthy?"

Now read the following excerpt from a history chapter on the hippie movement of the 1960s.

> Hippies represented the more exclusive focus on cultural revolution. Sporting unkempt hair, tie-dyed T-shirts, and necklaces of withering flowers, many young people rejected what they saw as the stultifying norms of bourgeois society: the nuclear family, corporate employment, and competitive consumerism. They wanted to replace the Cold War culture of the 1950s with peace and love. Seeking intense physical and spiritual experience as opposed to the deadening conformity they believed characteristic of the earlier decade, youth in the 1960s turned to hallucinogenic drugs, unfettered sex, and rock and roll. More young people participated at least tangentially in the cultural revolt of the 1960s than in organized political dissent.
>
> **Source:** Sonya Michel, *Engendering America: A Documentary History, 1865 to the Present* (New York: McGraw-Hill, 1999), p. 251.

The most general theme of this paragraph is the topic: hippies during the 1960s. The main idea is stated in the first, or topic sentence: *Hippies represented the more exclusive focus on cultural revolution.* The details that support the main idea answer the question "How did hippies participate in the cultural revolution?" and provide specific facts and explanations. Here is the excerpt again, this time with the major supporting details labeled:

> Hippies represented the more exclusive focus on cultural revolution. Sporting unkempt hair, tie-dyed T-shirts, and necklaces of withering flowers, many young people (1) rejected what they saw as the stultifying norms of bourgeois society (major detail): the nuclear family, corporate employment, and competitive consumerism. (2) They wanted to replace the Cold War culture of the 1950s with peace and love (major detail). (3) Seeking intense physical and spiritual experience as opposed to the deadening conformity they believed characteristic of the earlier decade (major detail), youth in the 1960s turned to hallucinogenic drugs, unfettered sex, and rock and roll. More young people participated at least tangentially in the cultural revolt of the 1960s than in organized political dissent.

Learning Journal

In your journal, explain how you currently determine which details in your textbook readings are important to remember and which are not.

Exercise 6a — Identifying Major Supporting Details

Read the following excerpts. For each one, underline the main idea and create a *who? what? when? how?* or *why?* question about it. Write your question in the space provided followed by the major supporting details that answer it. The first one is modeled for you.

MODEL   **1.** Anyone who has been properly beaten will tell you that the real pain does not come until about eight or ten seconds after the stroke. The stroke itself is merely a loud crack and a sort of blunt thud against your backside, numbing you completely (I'm told a bullet wound does the same). But later on, oh my heavens, it feels as if someone is laying a red hot poker right across your naked buttocks and it is absolutely impossible to prevent yourself from reaching back and clutching it with your fingers.

Source: Roald Dahl, "Galloping Foxley" from *Skin and Other Stories* (New York: Puffin Books, 2000), p. 82.

Your question: <u>How is it that the pain from a beating does not come</u>

<u>until about eight or ten seconds after the stroke?</u>

Major supporting detail: <u>The stroke itself is merely a loud crack and</u>

<u>a sort of blunt thud against your backside, numbing you completely.</u>

2.   You want to look like Dennis Rodman? Tattoos are a kind of label, but they don't say what the wearers think they say. They don't say, "I'm hip and cool and unique and pushing the envelope." No. They say, "Beneath these silly pictures and slogans on my skin, I'm a dunce." With a tattoo you are never going to make it in the white-collar world of America. That's your choice, of course. I leave you to it. But a tattoo is a bad thing if you care about your earning power.

Source: O'Reilly, Bill, *The O'Reilly Factor: The Good, the Bad, and the Completely Ridiculous in American Life* (New York: Broadway Books, a division of Random House, Inc., 2000), p. 197.

Your question: _____

Major supporting detail: _____

3.   Not that she approved very much of me. "Fat-and-Lazy" was the name she called me. After my midday dinner of baked cabbage and bread I would often nod off at my desk. "Wake up!" she would cry, cracking my head with a ruler, "you and your little red eyes!" She also took exception to my steady sniff, which to me came as natural as breathing. "Go out into the road and have a good blow, and don't come back till you're clear." But I wouldn't blow, not for anyone on earth, especially if ordered to do so: so I'd sit out on the wall, indignant and thunderous, and sniff away louder than ever. I wouldn't budge either, or come back in, till a boy was sent to fetch me. Miss Wardley would greet me with freezing brightness. "A little less beastly now? How about bringing a hanky tomorrow? I'm sure we'd all be grateful." I'd sit and scowl, then forget to scowl, and would soon be asleep again.

Source: Laurie Lee, *Cider with Rosie* (Middlesex, England: Penguin Books, 1959), p. 52.

Your question: _____

Major supporting details:

A. _____

B. _____

4.   Never looking at me, he slowly held up a knobby little hand. I took it—cool and quite oily—and inhaled the scent of the skin. It seemed human to me: a strong, sweet scent, untroubled by soap. For the first time in all these years, I was finally touching one of the visitors just as Raven had. His hand lay in mine like a cool little bird, absolutely still. I wanted to hug him. I was so glad. Apparently he detected this wish, because his hand shot out of mine as fast as a flash of light. I think that the thought of being enclosed in my arms was too much for him.

Source: W. Strieber, *Breakthrough: The Next Step* (New York : Harper Collins Publishers, 1995).

Your question: _____

_____

Major supporting detail: _____

5. The pointed arch, while seemingly not very different from the round one, offers many advantages. Because the sides arc up to a point, weight is channeled down to the ground at a steeper angle, and therefore the arch can be taller. The vault constructed from such an arch also can be much taller than a barrel vault. Architects of the Gothic period found they did not need heavy masses of material throughout the curve of the vault, as long as the major points of intersection were reinforced. These reinforcements, called ribs, are visible in the nave ceiling of Reims Cathedral.

    Source: Mark Getlein, *Gilbert's Living with Art* (New York: McGraw-Hill, 2002), p. 303.

    Your question: _____

    Major supporting details:

    A. _____

    B. _____

6. The Bacillus subtilis bacterium reproduces simply by splitting in two. It can do this every 20 minutes. Given perfect conditions, how many offspring do you think one organism could produce in eight hours?

    Source: R. Allen and J. Fulton, *Mensa: Mighty Brain Teasers* (Great Britain: Barnes & Noble, 1995), p.77—Puzzle 128.

    Your question: _____

    Major supporting details:

    A. _____

    B. _____

    (By the way, the answer to the question is over 16,000,000!)

Team Up!

Find one other classmate and review your answers to Exercise 6a together. Did you both agree on the answers? Did you write similar questions for each main idea? Discuss any differences.

Minor Supporting Details

Minor supporting details are intended to clarify and enhance the major supporting details and are not usually considered as important. However, some of them are significant and useful to remember. Here are two strategies you can use to identify which minor details you should remember when studying for a test:

- Note which ones help you better understand the main idea or its supporting details.
- Note those that are emphasized in lectures or classroom discussion.

Read the following short excerpt from a book on forensic science.

> In July 1982, human skeletal remains were found scattered across a 30-foot circle in a blackberry patch near Olville in Goochland County, a rural section of central Virginia. It was the height of summer and the finders were a group of berry pickers. Harvesters of natural crops have always played an important role in the science of anthropology, and in modern crime detection they are among the forensic scientist's best allies. Despite such scientific advances as ground-penetrating radar and magnetic resonance imaging systems that can define decayed bodies when they are almost invisible to the unaided eye, no machine has yet been made that surpasses the hunters and gatherers—along with man's ancient friend the dog—for the discovery of lost bodies.
>
> **Source:** (*Bones: A Forensic Detective's Casebook*, by Dr. Douglas Ubelaker and Henry Scammell. Harper Collins, NY, 1992, p.2)

The topic of the excerpt is *harvesters and their role in solving crimes*. The main idea is stated explicitly in the third sentence: *Harvesters of natural crops have always played an important role in the science of anthropology, and in modern crime detection they are among the forensic scientist's best allies.* and is the most important point the author makes about the topic. But what about the details? How do you decide which are major and which are minor supporting details? Major supporting details provide support for the main idea. So, if you ask a question about the main idea, the details that answer it will be the most significant ones. For example you could ask *What role do harvesters play in solving crimes?* The end of the last sentence in the excerpt answers this question: Despite such scientific advances as ground-penetrating radar and magnetic resonance imaging systems that can define decayed bodies when they are almost invisible to the unaided eye, no machine has yet been made that surpasses the hunters and gatherers—along with man's ancient friend the dog—for *the discovery of lost bodies*. It contains the only major detail. The rest of the information in the excerpt consists of minor supporting details such as the area in Virginia where the skeletal remains were found and that the finders were berry pickers.

If you had to take a test in a criminal justice course on how to solve crimes, what details from this excerpt should you remember? Definitely, the major supporting detail mentioned earlier, as well as any other minor details emphasized in a lecture. You might also ask yourself if any of the minor details in the excerpt would help you connect the new information you have learned to what you already know on the subject of solving crime.

Learning Journal

Write down any minor supporting details from the excerpt that would help you attach the new information on crime solving, to information you already know on the subject. Explain specifically how the minor supporting details you chose relate to the information you already know on the subject.

Exercise 6b

Identifying Minor Supporting Details

Read the following excerpts. For each one, circle the main idea, underline the major supporting details, and cross out the minor supporting details that do not provide vital support to the main idea. The first one is modeled for you.

MODEL 1. (1)I watched feng shui students in amazement as they completely abandoned their own sense of aesthetics and design in favor of the Eastern motifs expressed so frequently in Yun Lin's seminars. (2)During consultations in New York or London, I came across a number of cases in which "cures" employed to correct design imbalances directly conflicted with the culture and surroundings of the modern furniture; (3)bamboo flutes, placed at forty-five degree angles under heavy beams, contrasted with Chippendale tables. (4)Artifacts from Chinatown, purchased for less than ten dollars, were hung on doors next to walls holding paintings by Dutch masters worth millions. (5)Magic mirrors, red clothes, envelopes, and boxes were being carefully positioned under beds to attract money and improve health. (6)No wonder people were confused, and put off, by what was available on feng shui in print.

Source: William Spear, *Feng Shui Made Easy* (San Francisco: HarperSanFrancisco, 1995), p. 6.

Sentence #1 contains the main idea: *I watched feng shui students in amazement as they completely abandoned their own sense of aesthetics and design in favor of the Eastern motifs expressed so frequently in Yun Lin's seminars.*

Sentence #2 is a major detail. It supports sentence #1 by stating that the author witnessed actual cases of feng shui being used incorrectly.
Sentences #3, #4, and #5 are minor details that support sentence #2. They provide evidence that supports the author's statements in sentence #2. They could be crossed out because they don't directly support sentence #1; they directly support a major detail, sentence #2. Eliminating them won't change the main idea.

Sentence #6 is another major detail. People are confused about what is in print about feng shui because the people supposedly practicing it have "completely abandoned their own sense of aesthetics and design in favor of the Eastern motifs." This sentence directly supports the main idea stated in sentence #1.

2. And now, if we can, let's go on to the second part: "A fish can't whistle and neither can I." Coming from a wise man, such a statement would mean, "I have certain limitations, and I know what they are." Such a mind would act accordingly. There's nothing wrong with not being able to whistle, especially if you're a fish. But there can be lots of things wrong with blindly trying to do what you aren't designed for. Fish don't live in trees, and birds don't spend too much time underwater if they can help it. Unfortunately, some people—who always seem to think they're smarter than fish and birds, somehow—aren't so wise, and end up causing big trouble for themselves and others.

Source: Benjamin Hoff, *The Tao of Pooh* (New York: Penguin Books, 1983), p. 43.

3. The first step in improving critical thinking skills is motivation, not cognition. Critical thinking requires a willingness to engage in cognitive work. It simply takes more time and effort to think carefully and critically about a problem than to make the first decision that pops into your head. On the other hand, the amount of effort needed to dig your way out of the consequences of some poor decisions is much greater. So, we either work hard to make good decisions or we work hard to clean up the messes caused by our poor decisions—it's our choice.

Source: Adapted from Benjamin Lahey, *Essentials of Psychology* (Boston: McGraw Hill, 2002), p. 232.

4. In joy or sadness, flowers are our constant friends. We eat, drink, sing, dance, and flirt with them. We wed and christen with flowers. We dare not die without them. We have worshipped with the lily, we have meditated with the lotus, we have charged in battle array with the rose and the chrysanthemum. We have even attempted to speak in the language of flowers. How could we live without them? It frightens one to conceive of a world bereft of their presence. What solace do they not bring to the bedside of the sick, what a light of bliss to the darkness of weary spirits? Their serene tenderness restores to us our waning confidence in the universe even as the intent gaze of a beautiful child recalls our lost hopes. When we are laid low in the dust it is they who linger in sorrow over our graves.

Source: Okakura Kakuzo, *The Book of Tea* (Tuttle Publishing, 1956), p. 90.

5. Paul Slattery (UK) drew a caricature of soccer player Alan Shearer (UK) that measured 62 ft. × 30 ft. 4 in. on a giant canvas which is the largest caricature ever drawn. The drawing began with the subject's eye and was completed in three days. The caricature was hung off the Tyne Bridge, Newcastle, UK, and then auctioned to raise funds for the NSPCC (National Society for the Prevention of Cruelty to Children).

Source: Adapted from the *Guinness World of Records 2002* (London: Guinness World Records Ltd., 2002), p. 158.

Why It Is Important to Prioritize Details

Once you identify the main idea of a reading assignment, you can divide the rest of the material into two categories—major and minor supporting details. It is important to prioritize details because major ones are crucial to understanding a reading assignment, while minor ones, though interesting, are less helpful and take up valuable space in your memory.

Prioritizing Details

Follow the directions for each of the following excerpts. Each set of directions is different, so read them carefully. Although you are asked to identify the topic and main idea of each excerpt, the focus of this exercise is on the details.

1. Read the following excerpt. Underline the main idea statement. Number the major supporting details. Cross out all the minor supporting details.

Negative self-talk consists of irrational statements that must be recognized and changed. Keep track of your own negative self-talk. Write it down. Your journal is a great place to write it down. Examine what you say to yourself. Listen to the words you use. Learn to substitute neutral statements. For example, suppose a student thinks, "I'm never going to pass this test. I failed the last one, and I know the same thing will happen again." Negative self-talk can have a negative effect on a student's test performance.

Source: Adapted from Sembera and Hovis, *Math: A Four Letter Word!* (Wimberley, Texas: Wimberley Press, 1993), p. 23.

a. The phrase *for example* is a word clue. What do the authors indicate to you by using this phrase? Are they signaling a main idea, a major supporting detail, or a minor supporting detail?

_____

b. Why is the last sentence not the main idea?

_____

_____

_____

2. Read the following excerpt and answer the questions that follow it.

You know, there's 800,000 lawyers in our country, and many of their livelihoods depend on the fact that we have got no common sense. My theory is that intelligence, like every other resource on this planet, has a finite amount. And as the population increases, the intelligence resource is being stretched thinner than the elastic in Marge Schott's G-string.

For instance, some old lady burns herself on a cup of coffee at McDonald's and sues for three million dollars because it's not her fault. And she wins. She wins! We have trouble convicting people who actually confess to a murder, but this woman is able to take three mil off of McDonald's? If the judge had any common sense, the trial should have gone like this: "Will the plaintiff please rise? Yeah, it is your fault. You're stupid. Coffee is supposed to be hot. Why didn't you blow on it before you chugged it down like a pledge having his first beer? Get out of my courtroom, you stupid, stupid woman and take your pin-striped parasite lawyer with you. Next case."

Source: Dennis Miller, *Ranting Again* (New York: Doubleday, 1998), pp. 143–144.

a. What does the word clue *for instance* indicate to you? What purpose does the second paragraph in the passage serve?

_____

_____

b. What is the main idea of the excerpt?

_____

_____

3. Read the following passage and complete the mind map in Figure 6.1, making sure to include the topic, the main idea, and the major and minor supporting details.

Mind you, until recently my own family has never been much good at mourning. There is the case of my stepfather, who bade me get rid of my mother's clothes within a week of her death, sold the house they'd lived in for forty-nine years within the month, and promptly had his second, near-fatal heart attack. There is the case of my husband's aunt, eighty-six-year-old Rosalind, who, after the death of her second husband, committed suicide while staying at a summer hotel with her baby sister, my eighty-four-year-old mother-in-law. "Just send her ashes parcel post!" her sons bellowed on the telephone from New York when queried about funeral arrangements. And there is the case of my own father, the love of my early life, whose only daughter is as late a mourner as can be found.

Source: Francine Du Plessix Gray, "The Work of Mourning" from *The American Scholar* (New York: Houghton Mifflin Co., 2000), pp. 60–72.

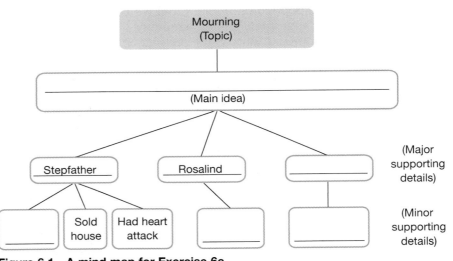

Figure 6.1   A mind map for Exercise 6c
Source: Mind map created from Joseph Dominick, *Dynamics of Mass Communication: Media in the Digital Age* (New York: McGraw-Hill, 2002), pp. 2–27.

4. Read the following textbook paragraph. Create a mind map on a separate piece of paper using the information in the paragraph, making sure that you include the topic, the main idea, all the major supporting details, and some minor supporting details. Label each part of your map.

Cherokee Women and the Trail of Tears

The Cherokees were not only matrilineal, they also were matrilocal. That is, a man lived with his wife in a house which belonged to her, or perhaps more accurately, to her family. According to the naturalist William Bartram, "Marriage gives no rights to the husband over the property of his wife; and when they part she keeps the children and the property belonging to them." The "property" that women kept included agricultural produce—corn, squash, beans, sunflowers, and pumpkins—stored in the household's crib. Produce belonged to women because they were the principal farmers. This economic role was ritualized at the Green Corn Ceremony every summer when an old woman presented the new corn crop. Furthermore, eighteenth-century travelers and traders normally purchased corn from women instead of men, and in the 1750s the garrison at Fort Loudoun, in present-day eastern Tennessee, actually employed a female purchasing agent to procure corn. Similarly, the fields belonged to the women who tended them, or rather to the women's lineages. Bartram observed that "their fields are divided by proper marks and their harvest is gathered separately." While the Cherokees technically held land in common and anyone could use unoccupied land, improved fields belonged to specific matrilineal households.

Source: R. Nichols, *The American Indian* (New York: McGraw-Hill, 1999), p. 111.

---

5. Now apply the strategies you have just practiced to a longer reading selection. Read the passage and underline the main idea and major supporting details.

The minute you walk through the door of the School of Chinese Martial Arts, you realize it is different than you imagined it would be. Here lies no hostile Van Damm wanna-be, kicking the life out of an unworthy opponent. This environment is peaceful, calming, as if beckoning you toward a greater sense of mindfulness.

Many adults find this a sanctuary from the outside world. In this environment, everyone is treated with respect, sincerity, and trust. "In our adult program, the workouts are not only difficult physically, but they challenge students mentally and spiritually as well," says owner and head instructor, Sifu Brown. "People discover how to discipline their minds and control their thoughts. They become masters over their own actions, rather than prisoners of their reactions. Make no mistake, they learn how to fight, but they also develop a greater sense of wisdom, patience, and personal control."

Looking at him today, you would never guess Sifu Brown's childhood difficulties and the reason he began a martial arts path. He was severely challenged as a child with both cerebral palsy and dyslexia. In the beginning, his goal was simply to walk without braces. By age 12 he was fully mobile, and by age 19 he had won many competitions. At this time, he had become interested in the deeper, more philosophical aspects of martial arts. He is a living example of the benefits of true martial arts.

Sifu Brown's search for knowledge has taken him to China, Japan, and India, where he has studied under some of the highest-ranking practitioners of the arts. He has also taught self-defense classes nationwide and is a well-respected leader throughout the industry. Using all of his experience, knowledge, and skills gained from almost thirty years of practice, he decided to open this school and share his many gifts. Although he teaches T'ai Chi and Kung Fu, his school's philosophy is founded in meditation as the key to success in techniques, life, and true happiness—not kicking and punching. After teaching classes all day, it is not unusual to see Sifu Brown engaged in philosophical discussions or meditation with his students for hours beyond. This is what separates the School of Chinese Martial Arts from other dojos and "gyms" in the martial arts industry.

Many area professionals and executives are in attendance. Like so many others, they come to this dojo in search of self-defense, powerful workouts, or maybe for relief from stress. During the process, they begin to realize incredible changes in their lives, both physically and mentally. Relationships at work and at home improve and the ability to concentrate is enhanced. Students find that these ancient techniques are invaluable in a busy modern world.

Women make up about half of those attending classes and can be found among the most skilled students. Many students find the peaceful, serene movements of T'ai Chi a good introduction to the martial arts. The practice provides men and women alike with a great physical work-out and a practical knowledge of self-defense, as well as a full scope of breathing and meditation exercises.

If T'ai Chi is the Yin of martial arts then Kung Fu, with its dynamic, powerful movements, is the Yang. The two disciplines complement each other, and usually most students enroll in both classes. These dynamic high-energy classes are not for everyone, but if your goals include phys-ical fitness, increased self-confidence, and living a happier, healthier, more successful life, the School of Chinese Martial Arts in Berkley, Michigan, is waiting for you.

Source: Metropolitan Detroit's Monthly Magazine, *HOUR Detroit* (Shelby Township, MI: Utica Enterprises, Inc., January 2002), p. 100.

Looking for the Big Picture in Longer Readings

When studying longer reading passages, especially entire textbook chap-ters, it's important to keep in mind the big picture in order to accurately prioritize the supporting details. Textbook chapters usually have more than one main idea, so it is useful to break them down into smaller parts, or sections, and then seek the main idea and supporting details for each part. A *part* of a chapter can be a paragraph, or group of paragraphs, that make a single, important point about the overall topic. Textbook chapters are often separated into these sections by headings, which makes it easy to identify them. Once you can see the main point of each part, you have the information you need to understand the whole chapter.

So when you read textbook chapters, instead of looking for one topic with one main idea, supported by several major and minor details, you should look at the bigger picture of one topic with a number of main points, each supported by a variety of major and minor supporting ideas (details).

A mind map is a useful way to organize information so that you can study and remember it. It's a great way to find out what you do and do not understand about a topic because a mind map is difficult to create if you are unsure about the main idea and supporting details of a passage. Mind maps also are effective study tools: you can literally see at a glance the rel-ative importance of different ideas and how they connect to each other. Look at the mind map in Figure 6.2, which is based on a chapter from a textbook titled *Dynamics of Mass Communication*. The mind map shows the topic, taken from the chapter's title, "Communication Mass and Other

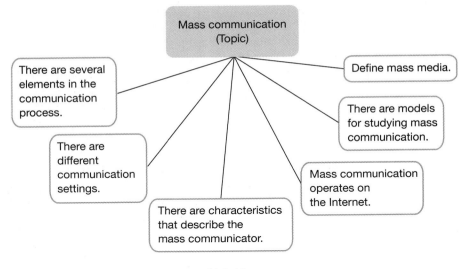

Main ideas

Figure 6.2   A textbook mind map
Source: Joseph Dominick, *Dynamics of Mass Communication: Media in the Digital Age* (New York: McGraw-Hill, 2002), pp. 2–27.

Forms," and six main ideas, which were suggested by the six headings within the chapter. The major supporting details you would need to remember could be found by asking a *who? what? when? how? or why?* question about each main idea.

Seeing the Bigger Picture

Exercise 6d

Complete the mind map in Figure 6.3 using information from the following outline. For each heading (main idea), write a question that would help you find the major details that support it.

Outline

Medicine	(chapter title)
Medical History: A Tradition of Incompetence	(heading)
Anatomy: Doctors and Body Snatchers	(heading)
Mistreating the Mentally Ill	(heading)
Research: Humans as Lab Rats	(heading)
Bizarre Breakthroughs	(heading)
Peering over the Shoulders of Early Gynecologists	(heading)
Malpractice Miscellany	(heading)
Dentistry before Novocaine	(heading)

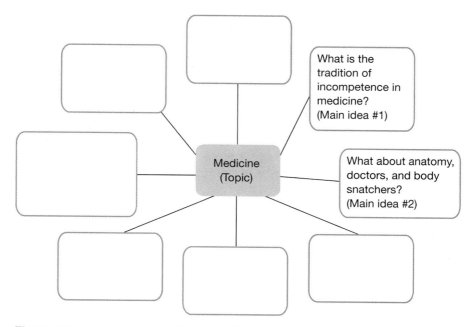

Figure 6.3   A mind map for Exercise 6d
Source: Adapted from Richard Zachs, *An Underground Education* (New York: Doubleday, 1997), pp. 175–208.

Exercise 6e

Seeing the Bigger Picture

Read the following excerpt which is taken from material under one of the headings listed in Exercise 6d. Under the appropriate main idea, use the information you learn to add the following items to the mind map you completed in Figure 6.3: the *one* major supporting idea (detail) in the passage, and only those minor supporting details that would help you to remember it.

Research: Humans as Lab Rats

Tuskegee Syphilis Experiment

The letter in a clean white envelope embossed with a government letterhead arrived at the run-down shacks of hundreds of sick black men in rural Alabama. It invited them to be examined by government doctors, and closed: REMEMBER THIS IS YOUR LAST CHANCE FOR SPECIAL FREE TREATMENT. BE SURE TO MEET THE NURSE.

Those words helped lure several hundred dirt-poor, uneducated black men in the middle of the Depression to participate in what would become the longest nontherapeutic experiment on human beings in medical history, according to *Bad Blood* by James H. Jones.

The U.S. Public Health Service (forerunner of the Centers for Disease Control), with the blessing of the various Surgeons General, from 1932 to 1972 studied the long-term effects of syphilis on 399 black men who were already infected. Government and local doctors periodically examined those men, routinely denying them any treatment for venereal disease, even when "miracle cure" penicillin became widely available in the 1950s. The families received a fifty-dollar burial allowance in exchange for allowing autopsies to be performed and the men, while alive, received minimal medical care for other ailments such as receiving pink aspirin tablets and red iron tonics. At least twenty-eight of the men died from syphilis-related complications.

The Tuskegee Syphilis Experiment arguably marks the ugliest stain on the public health record of the United States.

It took an outraged federal employee, Peter Buxtun, leaking details to the Associated Press to finally blow the whistle, and the U.S. government later settled a class action suit, paying $10 million to the victims.

In hindsight, it seems clearly unconscionable that an American government could authorize such a racist and cruel experiment.

How could it happen here?

Contrary to most reports, the Tuskegee Syphilis Experiment was not top secret. Doctors wrote numerous articles on it in medical journals, and the medical community at large never protested until Dr. Irwin Schatz wrote a scathing letter in 1965. "I am utterly astounded by the fact that physicians allow patients with a potentially fatal disease to remain untreated when effective therapy is available." Dr. Anne Yobs of the U.S. Public Health Service stapled a note onto it and filed it away: "This is the first letter of this type we have received. I do not plan to answer this letter."

The original rationale was to track long-term effects of untreated syphilis on black men, just as an earlier Oslo study had tracked the long-term effects on white European men. The enormous difference between the two studies: the Oslo researchers checked on untreated men who arrived at various clinics; the American study involved withholding treatment so as to study the men.

The experiment was facilitated by the collaboration of the prestigious Tuskegee Institute, a pioneer of African-American higher education.

Finally, once the plug was pulled, on March 3, 1973, Caspar Weinberger, secretary of Health, Education, and Welfare, authorized treatment for the survivors.

Jones states in his book that none of the white male doctors who founded and fought for the continuation of the experiment ever officially apologized.

Source: Richard Zachs, *An Underground Education* (New York: Doubleday, 1997), pp. 193–194.

Team Up!

Team up with two other students and compare your completed mind maps from Exercises 6d and 6e. Explain to each other the steps you took to complete the entire mind map.

Exercise 6f

Internet Exercise

Look up the words *ironic, solemn, fable, moral*. Then access the website **http://english.glendale.cc.ca.us/unicorn.intro.html**. Click on "Start the Reading" and read *The Unicorn in the Garden*. When you have completed it, take the quiz that follows.

Practice with Reading Passage

Answer all questions on a separate sheet of paper.

Reading Practice

Gawk Shows
BY NICOLS FOX

PREPARE TO READ

1. Based on the title, what do you expect this excerpt to be about?

2. What do you already know about the topic?

3. If you don't know the following words, look them up in your dictionary before you begin reading.

    a. Manifestations

    b. Gawk

    c. Wizened

    d. Hypocritical

    e. Demise

    f. Virtuosos

    g. Unbridled

    h. Paternalistic

    i. Interminably

    j. Titillated

    k. Managua

4. Use the title of this essay to create a question that you think this reading selection should answer.

Gawk Shows

I remember the dusty heat of late summer, the yellow and white tent, and the barker strutting on the platform. His voice rose above the sounds of the carnival, hinting of the wonders within the tent, wonders painted in cheap colors on the cracked backdrop: the two-headed baby, the world's fattest man, the bearded woman. I remember the sideshows. I thought they were long behind us.

I turn on the television and see an astonishing sight: a woman. Her soul is beautiful. It penetrates the atmosphere, even across airwaves. Her body is not. It is covered with the lumps and bumps of Elephant Man disease. Sally Jessy Raphael, wearing her trademark red spectacles, cocks her blond head and asks what the woman's life is like. A window is opened into pain. There are more victims of the disease sitting in the audience. We are treated to its various manifestations. We are horrified and amazed: We gawk.

Phil Donahue interviews tiny, wizened children. They have progeria, "the aging disease." With their outsize, hairless heads and huge eyes imparting solemnity and even wisdom, they offer us themselves as a sacrifice to our curiosity. We are compelled into silence, fascinated. We are back in the tent.

While I was living in Europe in the late sixties and early seventies, friends often asked me to tell them what to expect when they visited America. "Think of America as a carnival," I would tell them. "An unending carnival." This was the only way I knew to explain my country. Not just the quality of light and landscape but the excess, the enthusiasm, the love of excitement. We want no limitations on what we can have, on what we can do. We deny ourselves nothing—no objects, no sensations. "The pursuit of happiness": What other nation has made it an absolute right?

The carnival plays on, and we have returned to the sideshows—minus the honesty that made no pretense about what lay behind the curtain, the honesty that divided the world into those who were able to resist satisfying their curiosity at the expense of others and those who were not. Gawking is painted in shades of solicitude now. We justify much in the name of compassion, but we are in fact being entertained in the same ancient tradition. Gawk shows sell.

"I offer no apology," says Donahue. "These children have been unmercifully pressured by their very distinctive appearance." The purpose of the show? "To humanize people who have suffered. It becomes a vehicle for examining our prejudices. Just because it may be true that this kind of show draws a crowd does not condemn it," he says.

For Sally Jessy Raphael the rationale is the same: "Teaching the lessons of compassion. Man's triumph over adversity."

These are noble thoughts, and not entirely hypothetical. Compassion and understanding are always in short supply. There is an outside chance that some of each might be spread around in this exercise. We may also be witnessing exploitation. "These children are risking their lives to be here," says Sally, introducing children who will die if exposed to light. What may *she* be risking if they don't appear? As Donahue says, "If I don't draw a crowd, I could be parking cars for a living."

Donahue is open about the dilemma: "Americans are more interested in Madonna than Managua. The country suffers, in my opinion, from the diminished interest in serious news. Whichever way you look at it we have a culture of decay." It's tricky playing two sides at once. "It's like walking on eggs. I don't want to be a dead hero," he says.

We watch our cultural demise in living color.

Do you find yourself addicted to sex with prostitutes? Tell Oprah Winfrey and her audience all about it. Did you engage in an affair with your priest? Have your breast implants started slipping? Geraldo Rivera wants to know. Do you wish you could reverse your sex-change operation? Are you a celebrity subject to diarrhea at odd moments? Does your mother keep stealing your boyfriends? We care, we are interested. Whatever your problem, there's a television talk show that will accommodate you.

Donahue, Oprah, Sally, Geraldo: They are virtuosos of voyeurism, lifting the skirts of our culture, peering into the closets, airing the national soiled linen. Sally thinks of her program as a kind of updated town meeting—the modern version of something we no longer have. Electronic gossip, in other words—the national back fence. Wishful thinking.

As Americans we've been indulging in an orgy of self-analysis and self-revelation—coupled with a natural curiosity now totally unbridled. We've become a society hooked on the bizarre and the astonishing—living in a perpetual state of "Can you top this?" Transvestite men marry women on Sally's show, thus proving an important point, one we all needed to know: Sixty-five percent of all transvestites are not homosexual.

Nothing is sacred. There are no memories, no mysteries too precious to reveal. A woman discusses her husband's sexual addiction. Geraldo asks the husband for details—and gets them. There is nothing we won't share, or watch someone else share, with a million strangers.

We have invented a new social contract on the talk shows: Lay bare your body, your bed, your soul, your emotions, your worst fears, your innermost secrets, and we will give you a moment or two of fame. Every sacrifice can and should be made to the video god.

Are there topics too hot to talk about?

"How to blow up your local post office," says Donahue. He'd draw the line there.

There is no topic Sally wouldn't consider if it "concerns the human condition." She draws the line only at being boring. We have to want to watch it. So we set the agenda.

Donahue, a man obviously in conflict between his natural honesty and better instincts and his ambition, admits that his audience calls the shots. Devoting a recent show to strippers—both male and female—he says, "It must be ratings week. I don't want to do these shows…they make me." Sure they do. But who is making us watch?

Freedom of expression is not the issue here. Nobody's suggesting censorship or even paternalistic decisions based on what someone else thinks is good for us. The issue is honesty—honesty about why we watch. The talk shows are merely giving us what we want. The question is, Why do we want it?

In some cultures it was thought that illness or bad luck could be transferred from one person to another by magic. James G. Frazer, in his classic work *The Golden Bough,* told of one example: "To get rid of warts, take a string and make as many knots in it as you have warts. Then lay the string under a stone. Whoever treads upon the stone will get the warts, and you will be rid of them." Something like that draws us to the tent. We confirm our own normalcy because our worst fears have been manifested in someone else—the visual equivalent of burying the string. Or, if we see ourselves in someone who has survived our common plight, we are reassured; we are not alone.

There is no slouching into the tent today. We walk in shamelessly, casting off inhibitions in the name of openness.

The new openness has, in fact, turned out to be an empty promise. Are things any better than they were two decades ago? Has drug abuse or wife abuse or child abuse declined as we have learned more? Are we any happier thinking that a friend who takes a drink is a potential alcoholic, that every stranger is a child-snatcher?

How has this new compassion we are teaching been made evident? Ask the parents who have three HIV-positive sons and found their house burned down because of it. Ask the people who cluster over the grates of subways in our largest cities. If you were a trapped whale or a little girl down a well, solicitude would flow your way in great waves. It still helps to be cute or little or white or furry or totally nonthreatening when you're looking for compassion—or pretty, when you want a bone marrow transplant.

The potential is there on the TV talk shows for real entertainment—and for service. Oprah scored with a terrific show on female comics. Programs on health matters or economic questions are valuable. During the first days of the war in the Persian Gulf, Donahue aired shows that were serious and important contributions to our understanding of the conflict. "I do have a conscience," he says.

Geraldo, however, ever subject to the temptations of the flesh, spoiled what could have been a serious discussion of breast implants by having Jessica Hahn as the honored guest and by fondling examples of the implants interminably. Does he have it right? Are we a people who need to watch breast implants being fondled?

What happens when we set aside our last taboo? What happens when we've finally been titillated to a terminal numbness, incapable of shock, on the prowl for a new high? What manner of stimulation will we need next? Are we addicted? Talk show codependent?

Which topic affects us more: the discussion of the S & L crisis Donahue did last summer or the interviews with the strippers? Which do you think got the better ratings?

In a free society we get what we want. We shouldn't be surprised when we end up with what we deserve. But we can't transfer blame. It's not the hosts' fault—it's the viewers'.

Source: Nicols Fox, "Gawk Shows," *Lear's*, July 1991.

CHECK YOUR UNDERSTANDING

OBJECTIVE QUESTIONS

Read the following multiple-choice questions and choose the best answer from the choices provided.

1. The author describes the United States of America as what?

   a. A talk show.

   b. A circus tent.

   c. A carnival.

   d. *The Phil Donahue Show.*

2. Why does Donahue offer no apology about airing his show on children with progeria?

   a. He says he shows these disfigured children in order to humanize people who have suffered.

   b. He says he shows these children in order to humiliate those who have made fun of the handicapped.

   c. He says he shows these children in order to harm the people who have suffered.

   d. He says he shows these children in order to shelter the people who have suffered.

3. What does Sally Jessy Raphael say about her show?

   a. It demonstrates man's failure over adversity.

   b. It demonstrates man's triumph over adversity.

   c. It demonstrates man's prejudice.

   d. It is her right to pursuit of happiness.

4. What, according to the author, is contributing to our cultural demise?

   a. Not wanting to be a dead hero.

   b. Diminished interest in serious news.

   c. Madonna.

   d. Managua.

SHORT-ANSWER QUESTIONS

5. What is the overall main idea of the essay?

6. What, according to the author, made sideshows more acceptable than talk shows?

7. According to the author, whose fault is it that talk shows provide shockingly titillating stories?

8. What does the author consider as "real entertainment"?

9. According to the author, why do we watch talk shows?

Chapter Summary

Authors use details to help readers understand their ideas and arguments. Details are specific pieces of information that serve as the "arms and legs" of the main (body) idea. They are usually presented as facts, opinions, examples, illustrations, explanations, or definitions and are frequently discovered by asking questions such as *who? what? when? how?* or *why?* about the main idea. Major details provide support to the main idea in a reading. Minor details clarify major details.

If you are able to distinguish between the major and minor supporting details in a reading passage, it means you have understood what you read. If you have trouble doing so, it's an indication you need to get assistance. It is also a warning that you may have difficulty if you are tested on the textbook information, even though you have "read" the material.

Knowing how to locate the main idea and the major and minor supporting details in a reading assignment is the foundation of college reading. It isn't possible, or necessary, to remember every piece of information in your textbook chapters. Being able to identify the main ideas and supporting details will help you evaluate what is most important and determine what you need to remember for tests.

Post Test

Answer the following on a separate sheet of paper.

Part I

OBJECTIVE QUESTIONS
Read the following multiple-choice questions and choose the best answer from the choices provided.

1. Main ideas are

   a. More specific than details.

b. Less specific than details.

c. The same as a topic.

d. Stated in the form of a word or a phrase.

2. Minor supporting details

    a. Are always very important.

    b. Are not at all important.

    c. Usually support major supporting details.

    d. Are located at the beginning or end of a paragraph but never in the middle.

3. Textbook chapters

    a. Sometimes have no main idea.

    b. Usually have more than one main idea.

    c. Usually have only one main idea.

    d. Do not include minor supporting details.

4. To help organize textbook information, you can

    a. Create mind maps.

    b. Read your textbook aloud.

    c. Avoid looking up unfamiliar words so as not to lose concentration when you read.

    d. Avoid questioning yourself as you read in order to save time.

5. Mind maps are effective because

    a. They test your spelling skills.

    b. They are difficult to complete.

    c. They show others that you have understood the textbook material.

    d. They show relationships between ideas.

Part II

Reading Passage

Excerpt from *The Rainmaker*
BY JOHN GRISHAM

Read the following excerpt from John Grisham's *The Rainmaker*. This excerpt doesn't have a title and there are no headings. So read carefully, taking note of all the details. Picture what is going on in the excerpt in order to help store the details in your sensory memory. Try to answer the questions that follow without rereading the excerpt.

The narrator in this excerpt is a law student, who is preparing to take the state bar exam. He is in a hospital cafeteria.

It's almost eight before I drag myself through the maze of corridors deep in the heart of St. Peter's and find my favorite table occupied by a doctor and a nurse. I get coffee and sit nearby. The nurse is very attractive and quite distraught, and judging by their whispers, I'd say the affair is on the rocks. He's sixty with hair transplants and a new chin. She's thirty, and evidently will not be elevated to the position of wife. Just mistress for now. Serious whispers.

I'm in no mood to study. I've had enough for one day, but I'm motivated only by the fact that Booker is still in the office, working and preparing for the exam.

The lovers abruptly leave after a few minutes. She's in tears. He's cold and heartless. I ease into my chair at my table and spread my notes, try to study.

And I wait.

Kelly arrives a few minutes after ten, but she has a new guy pushing her wheelchair. She glances coldly at me, and points to a table in the center of the room. He parks her there. I look at him. He looks at me.

I assume it's Cliff. He's about my height, no more than six-one, with a stocky frame and the beginnings of a beer belly. His shoulders are wide, though, and his biceps bulge through a tee shirt that's much too tight and worn specifically to flaunt his arms. Tight jeans. Hair that's brown and curly and too long to be stylish. Lots of growth on his forearms and face. Cliff was the kid who was shaving in the eighth grade.

He has greenish eyes and a handsome face that looks much older than nineteen. He steps around the ankle that he broke with a softball bat, and walks to the counter for drinks. She knows I'm staring at her. She very deliberately glances around the room, then at the last moment gives me a quick wink. I almost spill my coffee.

It doesn't take much of an imagination to hear the words that have been passed between these two lately. Threats, apologies, pleas, more threats. It appears as though they're having a rough time of it tonight. Both faces are stern. They sip their drinks in silence. There's an occasional word or two, but they're like two puppy lovers in the midst of their weekly pouting session. A short sentence here, an even shorter reply there. They look at each other only when necessary, a lot of hard stares at the floor and the walls. I hide behind a book.

She's positioned herself so that she can glance at me without getting caught. His back is almost squarely to me. He looks around every now and then, but his movements are telegraphed. I can scratch my hair and pore over my studies long before he lays eyes on me.

After ten minutes of virtual silence, she says something that draws a hot response. I wish I could hear. He's suddenly shaking and snarling words at her. She dishes it right back. The volume increases and I quickly discern that they're discussing whether or not she'll testify against him in court. Seems she hasn't made up her mind. Seems this really bothers Cliff. He has a short fuse, no surprise for macho redneck, and she's telling him not to yell. He glances around, and tries to lower his voice. I can't hear what he says.

After provoking him, she calms him, though he's still very unhappy. He simmers as they ignore each other for a spell.

Then she does it again. She mumbles something and his back stiffens. His hands shake, his words are filled with foul language. They quarrel for a minute before she stops talking and ignores him. Cliff doesn't take to being ignored, so he gets louder. She tells him to be quiet, they're in public. He gets even louder, talking about what he'll do if she doesn't drop everything, and how he might go to jail, and on and on.

She says something I can't hear, and he suddenly slaps his tall cup and bolts to his feet. The soda flies across half the room, spraying carbonated foam on the other tables and the floor. It drenches her. She gasps, closes her eyes, and starts crying. He can be heard stomping and cursing down the hall.

I instinctively get to my feet, but she is quick to shake her head. I sit down. The cashier has watched this and arrives with a hand towel. She gives it to Kelly, who wipes Coke from her face and arms.

"I'm sorry," she says to the cashier.

Her gown is soaked. She fights back tears as she wipes her cast and legs. I'm nearby but I can't help. I assume she's afraid he might return and catch us talking.

There are many places in this hospital where one can sit and have a Coke or coffee, but she brought him here because she wanted me to see him. I'm almost certain she provoked him so I could witness his temper.

We look at each other for a long time as she methodically wipes her face and arms. Tears stream down her face, and she dabs at them. She possesses that inexplicable feminine ability to produce tears while appearing not to cry. She's not sobbing or bawling. Her lips are not quivering. Her hands are not shaking. She just sits there, in another world, staring at me with glazed eyes, touching her skin with a white towel.

Time passes, but I lose track of it. A crippled janitor arrives and mops around her. Three nurses rush in with loud talk and laughter until they see her, then they're suddenly quiet. They stare, whisper, and occasionally look at me.

He's been gone long enough to assume he's not coming back, and the idea of being a gentleman is exciting. The nurses leave, and Kelly slowly wiggles an index finger at me. It's now okay for me to approach.

"I'm sorry," she says as I crouch near her.

"It's okay."

And then she utters words I will never forget. "Will you take me to my room?"

In another setting, these words might have profound consequences, and for an instant my mind drifts away to an exotic beach where the two young lovers finally decide to have a go at it.

Her room, of course, is a semiprivate cubicle with a door that's subject to being opened by a multitude of people. Even lawyers can barge in.

I carefully weave Kelly and her wheelchair around the tables and into the hallway. "Fifth floor," she says over her shoulder. I'm in no hurry. I'm very proud of myself for being so chivalrous. I like the fact that men look twice at her as we roll along the corridor.

We're alone for a few seconds in the elevator. I kneel beside her. "Are you okay?" I ask.

She's not crying now. Her eyes are still moist and a shade red, but she's under control. She nods quickly and says, "Thanks." And then she takes my hand and squeezes it firmly. "Thanks so much."

The elevator jerks and stops. A doctor steps in and she quickly lets go of my hand. I stand behind the wheelchair, like a devoted husband. I want to hold hands again.

It's almost eleven, according to the clock on the wall at the fifth floor. Except for a few nurses and orderlies, the hallway is quiet and deserted. A nurse at the station looks twice at me as we roll by. Mrs. Riker left with one man, and now she's back with another.

We make a left turn and she points to her door. To my surprise and delight, she has a private room with her own window and bath. The lights are on.

I'm not sure how mobile she really is, but at this moment she's completely helpless. "You have to help me," she says. And she says it only once. I carefully bend over her, and she wraps her arms around my neck. She squeezes, and presses harder than necessary, but I'm not particularly concerned. She's a snug fit, up close to me, and I quickly discern that she's not wearing a bra. I squeeze her tighter to me.

I gently lift her from the chair, an easy task because she doesn't weigh more than a hundred and ten, cast and all. We maneuver up to the bed, taking as long as possible, making a fuss over her fragile leg, adjusting her just right as I very slowly ease her onto the bed. We reluctantly let go of each other. Our faces are just inches apart when the same nurse romps in, her rubber soles squishing on the tiled floor.

"What happened?" she exclaims, pointing at the stained gown.

We're still untangling and trying to separate. "Oh, that. Just an accident," Kelly explains.

The nurse never stops moving. She reaches into a drawer under the television and pulls out a folded gown. "Well, you need to change," she says, tossing it onto the bed beside Kelly. "And you need a sponge bath." She stops for a second, jerks her head toward me, and says, "Get him to help you."

I take a deep breath and feel faint.

"I can do it," Kelly says, placing the gown on the table next to the bed.

"Visiting hours are over, hon," she says to me. "You kids need to wrap it up." She squishes out of the room. I close the door and return to the side of her bed. We study each other.

"Where's the sponge?" I ask, and we both laugh. She has big dimples that form perfectly at the corners of her smile.

"Sit up here," she says, patting the edge of the bed. I sit next to her with my feet hanging off. We are not touching. She pulls a white sheet up to her armpits, as if to hide the stains.

I'm quite aware of how this looks. A battered wife is a married woman until she gets a divorce. Or until she kills the bastard.

"So what do you think of Cliff?" she asks.

"You wanted me to see him, didn't you?"

"I guess."

"He should be shot."

"That's rather severe for a little tantrum, isn't it?"

I pause for a moment and look away. I've decided that I will not play games with her. Since we're talking, then we're going to be honest.

What am I doing here?

"No, Kelly, it's not severe. Any man who beats his wife with an aluminum bat needs to be shot." I watch her closely as I say this, and she doesn't flinch.

"How do you know?" she asks.

"The paper trail. Police reports, ambulance reports, hospital records. How long do you wait before he decides to hit you in the head with his bat? That could kill you, you know. Coupla good shots to the skull—"

"Stop it! Don't tell me how it feels." She looks at the wall, and when she looks back at me the tears have started again. "You don't know what you're talking about."

"Then tell me."

"If I wanted to discuss it, I would've brought it up. You have no right to go digging around in my life."

"File for divorce. I'll bring the papers tomorrow. Do it now, while you're in the hospital being treated for the last beating. What better proof? It'll sail through. In three months, you'll be a free woman."

She shakes her head as if I'm a total fool. I probably am.

"You don't understand."

"I'm sure I don' t. But I can see the big picture. If you don't get rid of this jerk you might be dead in a month. I have the names and phone numbers of three support groups for abused women."

"Abused?"

"Right. Abused. You're abused, Kelly. Don't you know that? That pin in your ankle means you're abused. That purple spot on your cheek is clear evidence that your husband beats you. You can get help. File for divorce and get help."

She thinks about this for a second. The room is quiet. "Divorce won't work. I've already tried it."

"When?"

"A few months ago. You don't know? I'm sure there's a record of it in the courthouse. What happened to the paper trail?"

"What happened to the divorce?"

"I dismissed it."

"Why?"

"Because I got tired of getting slapped around. He was going to kill me if I didn't dismiss it. He says he loves me."

"That's very clear. Can I ask you something? Do you have a father or brother?"

"Why?"

"Because if my daughter got beat up by her husband, I'd break his neck."

"My father doesn't know. My parents are still seething over my pregnancy. They'll never get over it. They despised Cliff from the moment he set foot in our house, and when the scandal broke they went into seclusion. I haven't talked to them since I left home."

"No brother?"

"No. No one to watch over me. Until now."

This hits hard, and it takes a while for me to absorb it.

"I'll do whatever you want," I say. "But you have to file for divorce."

She wipes tears with her fingers, and I hand her a tissue from the table. "I can't file for divorce."

"Why not?"

"He'll kill me. He tells me so all the time. See, when I filed before, I had this really rotten lawyer, found him in the yellow pages or someplace like that. I figured they were all the same. And he thought it would be cute to get the deputy to serve the divorce on Cliff while he was at work, in front of his little gang, his drinking buddies and softball team. Cliff, of course, was humiliated. That was my first visit to the hospital. I dismissed the divorce a week later, and he still threatens me all the time. He'll kill me."

The fear and terror are plainly visible in her eyes. She shifts slightly, frowning as if a sharp pain has hit her ankle. She groans, and says, "Can you put a pillow under it?" I jump from the bed. "Sure." She points to two thick cushions in the chair.

"One of those," she says. This, of course, means that the sheet will be removed. I help with this.

She pauses for a second, looks around, says, "Hand me the gown too."

I take a jittery step to the table, and hand her the fresh gown. "Need some help?" I ask.

"No, just turn around." As she says this, she's already tugging at the old gown, pulling it over her head. I turn round very slowly.

She takes her time. Just for the hell of it, she tosses the stained gown onto the floor beside me. She's back there, less than five feet away, completely naked except for a pair of panties and a plaster cast. I honestly believe I could turn around and stare at her, and she wouldn't mind. I'm dizzy with this thought.

I close my eyes and ask myself, what am I doing here?

"Rudy, would you get me the sponge?" she coos. "It's in the bathroom. Run some warm water over it. And a towel, please."

I turn around. She's sitting in the middle of the bed clutching the thin sheet to her chest. The fresh gown has not been touched.

I can't help but stare. "In there," she nods. I take a few steps into the small bathroom, where I find the sponge. As I soak it in water, I watch her in the mirror above the sink. Through a crack in the door, I can see her back. All of it. The skin is smooth and tanned, but there's an ugly bruise between her shoulders.

I decide that I'll be in charge of this bath. She wants me to, I can tell. She's hurt and vulnerable. She likes to flirt, and she wants me to see her body. I'm all tingles and shakes.

Then, voices. The nurse is back. She's buzzing around the room when I reenter. She stops and grins at me, as if she almost caught us.

"Time's up," she says. "It's almost eleven-thirty. This isn't a hotel." She pulls the sponge from my hand. "I'll do this. Now you get out of here."

I just stand there, smiling at Kelly and dreaming of touching those legs. The nurse firmly grabs my elbow and ushers me to the door. "Now go on," she scolds in mock frustration.

At three in the morning I sneak down to the hammock, where I rock absently in the still night, watching the stars flicker through the limbs and leaves, recalling every delightful move she made, hearing her troubled voice, dreaming of those legs.

It has fallen upon me to protect her; there's no one else. She expects me to rescue her, then to put her back together. It's obvious to both of us what will happen then. I can feel her clutching my neck, pressing close to me for those few precious seconds. I can feel the featherweight of her entire body resting naturally in my arms.

She wants me to see her, to rub her flesh with a warm sponge. I know she wants this. And, tonight, I intend to do it.

I watch the sun rise through the trees, then fall asleep counting the hours until I see her again.

Source: John Grisham, *The Rainmaker* (New York: Bantam Doubleday Dell Publishing Group, 1995), pp. 214–223.

OBJECTIVE QUESTIONS

Read the following multiple-choice questions and choose the best answer from the choices provided.

1. What is the name of the woman in the wheelchair?

   a. Kirstin.

   b. Karen.

   c. Kelly.

   d. Karina.

2. Why is the woman in a wheelchair?

   a. Because the woman has polio.

   b. As a result of the abuse by her father.

   c. As a result of the abuse by her husband.

   d. As a result of an accident.

3. What is the woman's husband's name?

   a. Clyde.

   b. Clint.

   c. Charles.

   d. Cliff.

4.   What beverage was spilled on the woman?

  a. Coke.

  b. Beer.

  c. Water.

  d. Coffee.

5.   How does the narrator feel when he is asked to take the woman to her room?

  a. Sorrowful.

  b. Angry.

  c. Chivalrous.

  d. Scared.

SHORT-ANSWER QUESTIONS

6.   What does the narrator discover about the woman's clothing when he picks her up and puts her in her bed?

7.   What does the nurse say the woman has to do?

8.   What does the man say, after the nurse leaves, that makes both the man and the woman laugh?

9.   What does the woman ask the narrator to get in the bathroom?

10. What does the nurse do in the end?

11. What does the narrator fall asleep counting?

12. Draw a picture of the woman's husband Cliff, based on the description in the excerpt.

Website Sources for Additional Practice

Reading selections with self-scoring quizzes

http://english.glendale.cc.ca.us/bedfell.html: "The Night the Bed Fell"

http://english.glendale.cc.ca.us/carolan.intro.html: "Carolan the Harpist"

Chapter 7

Using Inference to Identify Implied Main Ideas

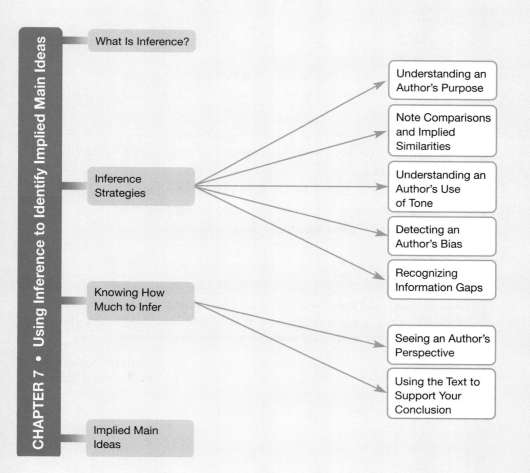

What Is Inference?

Inference Strategies

Understanding an Author's Purpose

Note Comparisons and Implied Similarities

Understanding an Author's Use of Tone

Detecting an Author's Bias

Recognizing Information Gaps

Knowing How Much to Infer

Seeing an Author's Perspective

Using the Text to Support Your Conclusion

Implied Main Ideas

Chapter Contents

Chapter Goals

In this chapter on advanced reading comprehension, you will learn:

- What inference is.
- Strategies you can use to infer an author's meaning as you read.
- What limits the amount of information you should infer.
- How to identify implied main ideas.

Chapter Vocabulary

As you read, note these words and phrases, which represent important concepts from the chapter and will be in **boldface** type. Make sure you understand them before the post test at the end of the chapter.

inference	**purpose**	**information gaps**
diction	**tone**	**implied main idea**
imply	**author's bias**	

Janet, a nursing student, is able to do well on most test questions that focus on literal information—that is, information directly stated in her textbooks. However, she finds it challenging to take exams that require her to go beyond what is written, to "read between the lines." Questions that ask her to interpret material, identify the bias and tone of a piece of writing, or state what the author is implying confuse her because the answers to those types of questions are not directly stated. She has to infer the answers from the evidence the author provides. Janet knows that if she is to complete her program and be successful in a job, she will be required to think and read more critically. She will need to learn how to read inferentially—to make assumptions—based on what the author says and does not say.

Learning Journal

In your journal, write down your definition of the term *inference*. What do you think it means when someone says they inferred an idea from a reading? What do you think it means when your instructor says that an author *implied* a certain idea in a textbook chapter?

What Is Inference?

When you read a textbook, you learn a certain amount of factual information, but in order to truly understand what it says you need to go beyond the literal level of comprehension. **Inference** is the process of making assumptions, and drawing conclusions about information when an author's opinions or ideas are *not directly stated*. If you have ever left an interview knowing, without being told, that you would be hired, you used the skill of inference to arrive at that conclusion. If you unexpectedly meet an old friend, who smiles and runs to greet you, you infer from her behavior and expression that she is happy to see you.

Authors assume a certain level of knowledge in their readers. They rely on them to connect what they already know about a topic to the new information they are reading. This chapter will teach you how to read textbooks and other material so you can "pull" more meaning from them. It focuses on strategies that will help you draw conclusions from your reading assignments by noting both what is said and what is *not* said, by an author, and combining this information with what you already know.

Whenever you read, you participate in a two-way conversation with an author. Sometimes in this conversation, the author will state the main idea and details explicitly. For example, most science books present literal information or facts: the number of bones in your body, the dates of major scientific discoveries, or the names of pioneering scientists. At other times, however, the author provides clues, much like two people flirting with one another do, to hint at or imply the main idea.

An author's **diction**, or choice of words, is significant when you are trying to work out exactly what he or she means. For example, suppose a newspaper editor wants to tell you indirectly whether he or she thinks a certain politician is honest or dishonest when reporting travel expenses. If the editor uses words such as *vague, indirect, concealed,* and *unclear* to describe the politician's financial reports, you could infer that something underhanded might have occurred. On the other hand, if the editor used words such as *frank, open, obvious,* and *transparent* it would probably suggest to you that the politician is accurate in reporting her expenses.

Learning Journal

Describe a time when you knew that someone was angry or upset with you, even though he or she didn't say a word. How did you know? What did he or she do that convinced you? Describe his or her body language.

Jennifer's Journal Entry

I can always tell when my mom is mad. She gets real quiet and slams things down a lot. She won't make eye contact with me and won't really talk to me either. She mumbles and pretends to be busy. It happened again, just in time for this journal exercise. Her nose gets red, too. She drives me nuts when she gets like this. I'd rather have her scream at me!

Exercise

7a

MODEL

Inferring an Author's Meaning

You have already had plenty of practice inferring meaning from what you read or hear, although you may not realize it. Read the following proverbs and try to infer what each one means. The first one is modeled for you.

1. A bird in the hand is worth two in the bush.
You are better off keeping what you have than risking losing it in

the hope of getting more.

2. A penny saved is a penny earned.

_____

3. Time heals all wounds.

_____

4. Give a man a fish and he'll eat for a day. Teach a man to fish, and he'll eat for a lifetime.

_____

_____

Inference Strategies

To establish a conversation with an author, you have to understand the meaning of what is being directly stated and indirectly **implied** in a reading passage. Understanding information that is not directly stated will help you remember it better. The following strategies will help you to effectively infer meaning when an author does not directly state his or her main points:

1. Understand an author's purpose.
2. Note comparisons and implied similarities.
3. Understand an author's use of tone.
4. Detect an author's bias.
5. Recognize information gaps.

Strategy 1: Understand an Author's Purpose

An author's **purpose** is an author's _reason_ for writing. Textbook authors want to inform you about specific subjects such as mathematics, biology, literature, sociology, or business. Authors of other types of college reading material such as essays, journal articles, and stories write for other purposes: to persuade you of the importance of addressing the issue of global warming, to document new scientific theories or discoveries, or to stimulate your imagination and entertain you. Successful readers understand that an author has a reason for writing, and that reason frames the author's main ideas even if he or she doesn't explicitly state them. To understand an author's purpose in writing about a topic, ask yourself, "What is the author's reason for writing?"

Exercise 7b

MODEL

Determining an Author's Purpose

For each of the following excerpts, decide what the author's purpose is in writing. The first one is modeled for you.

1. The ACT, like the SAT, is designed to test what a student has learned and demonstrate the application of ideas. It uses both multiple-choice and essay questions. The ACT is the most common college admission test in Michigan, and test administrators make slight adjustments to maintain the same degree of difficulty each year.

Source: Jodi Upton, *The Detroit News,* August 25, 2002.

The author's purpose in this excerpt is ___to inform.___

2. We finally have driven the fifth-generation Nissan Z-car, the new 350Z, and, like a chocolate souffle that takes an extra twenty minutes to emerge from the restaurant's kitchen, it was worth the wait. All of us who've been behind the wheel of the 350Z agree that to drive it is to love it.

Source: Joe Dematio, "Rising Son," *Automobile,* September 2002, p. 46.

The author's purpose in this excerpt is _____

3. God is not a jolly fellow like Santa Claus; He is a great bookkeeper. And He is keeping a book on you! I am a Western Union boy! I have a death message! I must tell you plainly—you are going to hell! You listen! Don't you trifle with God! Don't you think you can barter! You are a sinner! You have come short of God's requirements! Your punishment is sure!

Source: J. Lowe, *Billy Graham Speaks* (New York: John Wiley & Sons, 1999), p. 37, quoted from Martin, *A Prophet with Honor* (New York: Quill Books), p. 156.

The author's purpose in this excerpt is _____

4. I asked my mother, "What was Daddy like?"

"Crunchy, a bit salty, rich in fiber."

"Before you ate him, I mean."

"He was a little guy, insecure, anxious, neurotic—pretty much like all you baby boys."

I felt closer than ever to the parent I had never known, who'd been dissolved in Mom's stomach just as I was being conceived. From whom I had gotten not nurturing but nourishment. I thought, thank you Dad. I know what it means for a [praying] mantis to sacrifice himself for the family.

Source: Alessandro Boffa, "You're Losing Your Head, Viskovitz," in *You're an Animal Viskovitz!* (New York: Alfred A. Knopf, 2002), p. 27.

The author's purpose in this excerpt is _____

5. The terrorists who killed Danny stood at the other extreme of what Danny represents. They could only wield their knife and cowardice against Danny's intellectual courage and bold spirit. Danny died holding only a pen. They stole his life but were unable to seize his soul. By killing Danny, terrorists took my life as well but could not lay claim to my spirit. Dead and alive we will never let them win.

Source: Mariane Pearl, foreword in Helene Cooper, Ed. *At Home in the World: Collected Writings from* The Wall Street Journal (New York: Simon & Schuster, 2002), p. xv.

The author's purpose in this excerpt is _____

Strategy 2: Note Comparisons and Implied Similarities

In college texts, authors sometimes use comparisons to illustrate their points. For example, the author of a history text might use a familiar situation, that of parent and child, to illustrate and explain an unfamiliar situation, the relationship between Britain and the colonies before the American Revolution. A biology text author might liken the human circulatory system (unfamiliar) to a road map (familiar).

When an author draws a comparison between two items of information to illustrate a point, you may have to infer what the similarity is in order to understand the point he or she is making. Sometimes writers signal they are making comparisons by using words such as *like* or *as*. At other times they just present two apparently dissimilar pieces of information next to one another, without using any comparison words, and expect you to infer what they mean. Read the following comparison:

> Writers would soon learn to cultivate restraint if they were charged for every word used, *as* they are when they send a telegram.

Source: *The Little English Handbook*, Corbett, Scott, Foresman and Company, 1987.

The comparison here is between *writing a telegram* and *writing in general*. The implied similarity is that just *as* people writing telegrams choose words carefully to minimize the cost of sending them, writers would avoid using unnecessary or superfluous words if they were charged for using each one. The implication is that writers should choose words for their economy of expression; less can, in fact, be more.

Here are other examples of comparisons and implied similarities. Take note of the italicized words which help make the comparisons clearer.

EXAMPLE 1　Well, obviously no one's advocating that we kill all the *lawyers*. But it is time that we tighten the choke chain and make these *attack dogs* more accountable. I say we make law school four years—the last year spent learning how to vaguely resemble a human being.

Source: Dennis Miller, *Ranting Again* (New York: Doubleday Dell Publishing Group, 1996), p. 80.

The comparison here is between *lawyers* and *attack dogs*. The implied similarity is that lawyers, like attack dogs, need restraint: both should be taught how to behave appropriately.

EXAMPLE 2 Death can be something beautiful. It is *like* going home. He who dies in God goes home even though we naturally miss the person who has gone. But it is something beautiful. That person has gone to God.

Source: Mother Theresa, *No Greater Love* (CA: New World Library, 1989), p. 141.

The comparison here is between *death* and *going home*. The implied similarity is that just as people are usually happy to go home, death can bring happiness as the person returns to God.

Exercise 7C

Comparisons

Read the following textbook excerpts. For each one, identify what two items are being compared, and explain the similarity that is being implied.

1. After the long winter under the damp and chilly soil, that first sun-bath must have been like a drink of wine to the reptile. His legs were spread out from his shell, his neck extended as far as it could, his head resting on the ground; with eyes closed, the creature seemed to be absorbing sunshine through every bit of his body and shell.

Source: Gerald Durrell, *My Family and Other Animals* (New York: Penguin Books, 1956), p. 97.

Comparison between: a. _____ b. _____

Implied similarity: _____

_____

2. Mentally, Tiger simply loved the competition. "I like the feeling of trying my hardest under pressure," he said. "But it's so intense, it's hard to describe. It feels like a lion is tearing at my heart." Physically, Tiger had developed golf muscles that would allow him to drive the ball over 300 yards.

Source: Tim Rosaforte, *Tiger Woods: The Making of a Champion* (New York: St. Martin Press, 1997), pp. 27–28.

Comparison between: a. _____ b. _____

Implied similarity: _____

_____

3. Learn to do the drudgery of scientific work. Although a bird's wing is perfect, the bird could never soar if it did not lean upon air. Facts are the air on which the scientist leans.

Source: Hergenhahn, *An Introduction to Theories of Learning* (Englewood Cliffs, NJ: Prentice Hall, 1982).

Comparison between: a. _____ b. _____

Implied similarity: _____

_____

4. Viewing data as weapons and programs as their delivery system, the [computer] hacker considers himself a privateer of the modern era. He likens his computer to a vessel, a battleship for him to cruise the world's computer networks, assailing the weak and subverting the unsuspecting.

Source: Jonathan Ritter, "The World View of a Computer Hacker," reprinted with permission from the author. In M. Connelly, *The Sundance Reader,* 2nd ed. (New York: Harcourt Brace College Publishers, 2000), p. 187.

Comparison between: a. _____ b. _____

Implied similarity: _____

_____

5. On a molecular scale, liquids resemble the people in the stadium aisles, who move more freely than when sitting in their seats. A liquid is an example of a fluid, which is any substance that flows. Flowing occurs when molecules are free to slide past one another and continually change their relative positions. The molecules are in constant motion. They are free to flow under, over, and around their neighboring molecules.

Source: *Heath Chemistry* (New York: D.C. Heath and Company, 1987).

Comparison between: a. _____ b. _____

Implied similarity: _____

_____

6. Although I had been conceived in Africa, I had been started in urban England (like a delicate vegetable, started indoors, where it is safe—at a vulnerable age—from pests and too much sun). I had the constitution of a missionary.

Source: A. Fuller, *Don't Let's Go to the Dogs Tonight: An African Childhood* (New York: Random House, 2001), p. 39.

Comparison between: a. _____ b. _____

Implied similarity: _____

_____

Team Up!

With one or two other students, compare your responses to Exercise 7c. Make a note of the answers you disagreed on. Discuss your reasons for selecting the answers that you did.

Strategy #3: Understand an Author's Use of Tone

The **tone** authors use to discuss their subject matter can reveal their attitudes toward it. You can assess their tone by examining their choice of words, and taking the time to picture the images they create with their figurative language. An author's tone also serves to emphasize the author's purpose for writing. If the purpose is to entertain, the tone may be humorous; if the purpose is to persuade, the tone may be authoritative or even sarcastic; if the purpose is to inform, the tone may be formal and emotionless.

Tone is a subtle aspect of an author's writing. Identifying an author's tone, recognizing his or her purpose for writing, and noting the use of comparisons and implied similarities can help you piece together an author's main idea, particularly if it is implied.

Read the following excerpt from "Eat the Rich," the title essay in P.J. O'Rourke's book *Eat the Rich: A Treatise in Economics*. The notes in italics will prompt you to question how O'Rourke creates a certain tone to emphasize his point:

I had one fundamental question about economics: Why do some places prosper and thrive while others just suck? It's not a matter of brains. No part of the earth (with the exception of Brentwood) is dumber than Beverly Hills, and the residents are wading in gravy. *(What does the author imply about the wealthy people who live in Beverly Hills? How swift, mentally or physically, are people who wade in gravy?)* In Russia, meanwhile, where chess is a spectator sport, they're boiling stones for soup. *(If people in Russia rush to see a chess tournament, as opposed to a football game, what can be inferred about their intellect? What does the author imply about the economy in Russia when he says they boil stones for soup?)* Nor can education be the reason. Fourth graders in the American school system know what a condom is but aren't sure about 9 × 7. *(What does the author imply about the educational level of American students?)* Natural resources aren't the answer. Africa has diamonds, gold, uranium, you name it. Scandinavia has little and is frozen besides. *(What does the author imply about the economy of Africa? Of Scandinavia?)* Maybe culture is the key, but wealthy regions such as the local mall are famous for lacking it. *(How do you think the author feels about malls?)*

Perhaps the good life's secret lies in civilization. The Chinese had an ancient and sophisticated civilization when my relatives were hunkering naked in trees. (Admittedly that was last week, but they'd been drinking.) In 1000 B.C., when Europeans were barely using metal to hit each other over the head, the Zhou dynasty Chinese were casting ornate wine vessals big enough to take a bath in—something else no contemporary European had done. *(What does the author imply about Chinese civilization as compared to European civilization?)* Yet, today, China stinks. *(What "stinks" about China?)*

Source: P.J. O'Rourke, *Eat the Rich: A Treatise on Economics.* London: Picador, 1998.)

In this excerpt, it is obvious from the author's choice of language ("hunkering naked in trees") and the images he creates ("boiling stones for soup") that he intends to entertain his readers at the same time as he asks them to question certain puzzling realities of life. His humorous tone emphasizes his implied main idea that there are inequities in the distribution of global wealth and serves his purpose of encouraging his readers to think more deeply about the issue.

| Exercise 7d | ## Setting the Tone |

Read the following excerpts and circle the word in the list that follows each that you believe best matches the author's tone. Use the italicized words as guides in making your decisions. The first one is modeled for you.

MODEL **1.** The body of Richard Milhous Nixon was *scarcely* in the ground when the *struggle* for *control* of his legacy had begun. That day on the plane, the *dark* forces that *haunted* Nixon in life seemed to *reach beyond the grave*. Somewhere between the two coasts, Ed Cox, Tricia's New York attorney husband, brought up a plan to ensure the Nixon library would be *tightly controlled* by the family rather than by hired hands.

Source: Adapted from "Nixon Daughters Spar over Library," *The Detroit News*, April 28, 2002, p. 8a.

The tone of this excerpt can best be described as

a. Joyful.

b. Sarcastic.

c. Troubled.

d. Inspirational.

2. I used to *dread* coming home at night. I'd go around the side of the house, where there was a window that looked into the kitchen. I'd *stand in the dark* and look inside and try to judge what kind of night it was going to be. Mom had a *Jekyll-and-Hyde* personality. When she was sober, she was the sweetest, most sensitive, loving, and intelligent person you could ever meet. But when she was drunk she was a *holy terror*.

Source: General H. Norman Schwarzkopf and Peter Petre, *General H. Norman Schwarzkopf: The Autobiography: It Doesn't Take a Hero* (New York: Bantam Books, 1992), p. 19.

The tone of this excerpt can best be described as

a. Intense.

c. Angry.

b. Religious.

d. Sarcastic.

3. *Hassling innocent people* for class-trip money is a *cherished American student tradition*. The trip to Washington is considered to be the ultimate educational event—a chance for young people to visit their nation's capital and see, in person, how far they can *stick their tongues into one another's mouths. Because heavy petting in the back of the bus is a major element of every class trip*. I don't care if it's the senior class of the *Extremely Christian Academy for Unattractive Young People Wearing Chastity Belts*; I don't care if every single chaperone holds the rank of *ayatollah* or higher. Once those buses get rolling, there is going to be some *saliva exchanged*.

Source: Dave Barry, *Dave Barry Hits Below the Beltway* (New York: Random House, 2001), p. 67.

The tone of this excerpt can best be described as

a. Happy

c. Humorous.

b. Authoritative.

d. Angry.

4. I want a wife who is sensitive to my sexual needs, a wife who makes love passionately and eagerly when I feel like it, a wife who makes sure that I am satisfied. And, of course, I want a wife who will not demand sexual attention when I am not in the mood for it. I want a wife who assumes the complete responsibility for birth control, because I do not want more children. I want a wife who will remain sexually faithful to me so that I do not have to clutter up my intellectual life with jealousies. And I want a wife who understands that my sexual needs may entail more than a strict adherence to monogamy. I must, after all, be able to relate to people as fully as possible.

If, by chance, I find another person *more suitable* as a wife than the first wife I already have, I *want the liberty* to *replace* my present wife with another one. Naturally, I will *expect* a *fresh*, new life; my wife will take the children and be solely responsible for them *so that I am left free*. When I am through with school and have a job, I want my wife to *quit working* and remain at home so that my wife can more *fully* and *completely* take care of a *wife's duties*.

My God, *who wouldn't want a wife*.

Source: Judy Syfers, "I Want a Wife" from S. Barnet et al., *Literature for Composition* (New York: HarperCollins Customs Books, 1993), p. 776.

The tone of this excerpt can best be described as

a. Comforting.

c. Sarcastic.

b. Mysterious.

d. Religious.

Strategy #4: Detect an Author's Bias

To detect an **author's bias**, you must first picture the person with whom you are having a textbook conversation. All people have feelings, emotions, and opinions. As you read, remember the *human* aspect of the author; writers are people with biases or prejudices, just like you. For example, some people do not like dogs, so if they wrote about them, they might focus on their negative attributes and say *all* dogs bite, or *all* dogs are messy, mean, and inconvenient. Of course this is not true. Some dogs may bite, but not all dogs bite. Some dogs may be messy, but not all dogs are. Authors can be biased and sometimes don't present a balanced, accurate picture of an issue, either because they omit information that contradicts their own point of view, or they downplay and invalidate other viewpoints. Regardless of why an author may be biased, bias can exist even in textbook writing, and when it does, it is usually subtle. It is important to be able to detect bias so you can make an informed decision about whether to accept or challenge what an author says.

Detecting Bias by Noting Use of Emotive Language

One way to detect an author's bias is to notice use of emotive language. When a writer uses words that convey emotion, he or she is usually asserting an opinion. Opinions may or may not be founded on facts, but basing textbook material on opinions can promote bias. The following is an example of a biased textbook excerpt. The emotive words have been italicized:

> These *false* underlying assumptions about racism have led the general public, scholars, and activists all over the world to misread and *misunderstand* contemporary racism. The most notable of these well-intended misreadings in the United States is Wilson's *mistitled* book, *The Declining Significance of Race* (1978).
>
> **Source:** Benjamin Bowser, *Racism and Anti-Racism in World Perspective* (Sage Publications, 1995).

The italicized words are strong and evoke emotion as you read them. It is clear that the author has a bias toward the idea that racism is still a significant U.S. problem. Whether or not you agree with this point of view is up to you. But if you were to read this text, you would need to keep in mind that the material is influenced by the author's opinions about race relations.

Exercise

7e

MODEL

Detecting Bias in Paragraphs—Emotive Words

Read these passages and answer the questions that follow them. The emotive words have been italicized. The first answer is modeled for you.

1. Up to that time, the consensus had been that urban policy should attempt to bring jobs to the minority poor where they lived, that is, in the *ghetto*. My premise (which had been defined earlier by John F. Kain) was that such *"ghetto-gilding"* had little if any chance of success and should be replaced by a people-to-jobs strategy that would help *disadvantaged* people relocate to places with greater access to the economy's new job opportunities.

Source: Ebel, *Research in Urban Economics* (Jai Press, 1993).

How does the author feel about poor people?
This author is biased, or sympathetic, toward poor people and

believes that they have not been dealt with fairly in terms of equal

access to good jobs.

2. This brings us to another American characteristic: the work ethic. Captain John Smith's 1607 statement, "If you don't work, you won't eat," is the complete opposite of today's redistribution ethic that *subsidizes idleness*. Nothing would be *less traditionally American* than the modern welfare system.

Source: N. Gingrich, *To Renew America* (New York: HarperCollins Publishers, 1995), p. 39.

What is the author's opinion of the current welfare system?

_____

3. Although these kinds of studies have helped mental health professionals become more aware of the role that the sociocultural factors can play in psychological diagnosis, we *appear to have a way to go* before diagnosis is practiced in a culture-free way. Prejudice is a powerful force in the lives of all humans, and psychologists and psychiatrists *are only human, after all*. A *great deal* still needs to be done at all levels of the education of mental health professionals to reduce the *dangerous* effects of ethnic prejudice in diagnosis.

Source: Benjamin Lahey, *Essentials of Psychology* (Boston: McGraw-Hill, 2002). p. 388.

What is the author's opinion of the current state of mental health professionals regarding prejudice?

_____

_____

4. Just how many people are wealthy no one can say with any certainty, for nowhere do people *disguise* their lack of wealth so successfully. Argentines take great pride in *pretending* that they are more affluent than they really are; for them *faking prosperity* is not a sin, but a talent much admired. The *worst* examples of such *pretensions* have a *seedy, rather pathetic* quality to them, but the best are hardly distinguishable from the real thing.

Source: G. Wynia, *Argentina: Illusions & Realities* (New York: Holmes & Meier, 1992), p. 27.

How does the author feel about people who purposely try to appear wealthy when they are not?

_____

Exercise

7f

More Practice in Detecting Bias

Read the following editorial, "Don't Subcontract bin Laden Hunt," and respond to the questions that follow in the spaces provided. Take note of the emotive words the author uses and think about what the author's bias is. In the first paragraph, the emotionally charged words are italicized for you. Circle the rest of the emotionally charged words presented in the article.

Don't Subcontract bin Laden Hunt

Hopefully, the next time the American people see a videotape of Osama bin Laden, he will be *swinging from the end of a rope.* The tape of bin Laden released Thursday by the White House *erases any lingering doubt* that he was the mastermind of the September 11 terrorist attacks on the United States.

The al-Qaida leader is shown laughing and boasting that the death and destruction at the World Trade Center exceeded all his hopes. He also indicates detailed knowledge of how the attack would unfold, and acknowledges dispatching the terrorists to America. What's left now is to find bin Laden and bring him to justice. And that's a job for American soldiers.

With the Taliban vanquished in Afghanistan, the remaining fight is with bin Laden's al-Qaida network. U.S. commandos, supported by American air power, are working with Afghan opposition forces to rout the al-Qaida fighters. But it is still the native soldiers who are leading the fight.

The United States should take over and make sure the ultimate mission of this war—destroying bin Laden and his network—is accomplished. America cannot risk bin Laden slipping away to Somalia or Pakistan, nor can it allow itself to be placed in the position of having to negotiate for bin Laden if he is captured by others.

The chortling devil depicted on the videotape committed his crimes against America. America should not delegate the job of making him pay for those crimes.

Source: *Detroit News* editorial page, December 21, 2001, p. 7A.

---

1. How did this article make you feel? Provide examples from the passage to explain why you felt the way you did.

_____

_____

2. What was the author's purpose for writing the article?

_____

3. What is the main idea?

_____

_____

4. List five emotionally charged words that you found.

_____

_____

5. What word would you use to describe the tone of the article (angry, sarcastic, critical, joyful, anxious, encouraging, etc.)? Provide examples from the passage to support your response.

_____

_____

6. Locate all of the emotive words that you circled in the excerpt and, in the margin of the text, replace these words with more neutral/nonemotional words.

_____

_____

Team Up!

Get together with two other students and compare your answers to Exercise 7f.

Take One Minute

Now that you have completed Exercise 7f, explain why it's important to recognize and question the use of emotive language.

Strategy #5: Recognize Information Gaps

It is particularly difficult to draw inferences from reading material when limited information is presented or when information appears to be missing (**information gaps**). Sometimes, as you read you may find that an author leaps from one idea to the next, apparently skipping the information that should be in the middle. When writers do this, they assume that you have a certain amount of background knowledge and can fill in the gaps that are left on the page. Read the following paragraph:

> **Two years ago, as I was driving down a major street on my way home from work, I passed a young man hitting a teenage girl and throw-**

ing her to the ground. As I zipped by, I watched her repeatedly get up and try to run, only to have the guy push her down again and again. Now past them, I looked in my rearview mirror and saw him dragging her into the bushes. *My God, he's going to rape her!* Almost without thinking, I made an illegal U-turn on the busy road and pulled up alongside where he was slapping and dragging her.

Source: Mary Ann McCourt, "Not Minding My Own Business," from *That Takes Ovaries! Bold Females and Their Brazen Acts*, ed. Rivka Solomon (New York: Three Rivers, 2002), p. 101.

The author doesn't tell you why she made a U-turn and pulled up next to the couple, but you can infer why. She wanted to intervene in some way. Her intention is implied in the gap she leaves between the thought *My God, he's going to rape her!* and the action of making an illegal U-turn.

The concept of information gaps is brilliantly illustrated in cartoons. The information that is not specifically stated in the text is what makes them so funny. Your mind infers the punchline. Look at the following cartoon, "Rough Sketches," and answer the questions that follow. These are the types of questions you should ask yourself when reading a cartoon.

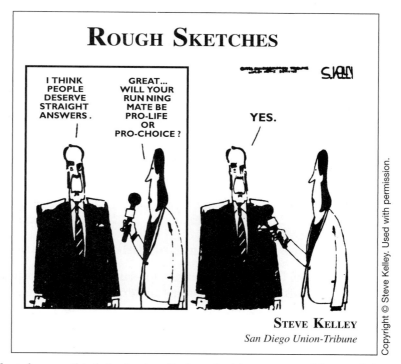

ROUGH SKETCHES

I THINK PEOPLE DESERVE STRAIGHT ANSWERS.

GREAT... WILL YOUR RUNNING MATE BE PRO-LIFE OR PRO-CHOICE?

YES.

STEVE KELLEY
San Diego Union-Tribune

1. What do you think is the implied main idea, or punchline, of this cartoon?

_____

2. What are some of the details the cartoonist uses to make his point?

_____

In textbooks authors also sometimes imply certain points by leaping from one idea to the next, and leaving information gaps in between. When they do this, they expect you to recognize their conversational pattern, mentally note the information gaps, and fill in the blanks.

Exercise 7g

Information Gaps and Cartoons

Read and enjoy the following cartoon. Then answer the following questions.

THE FAR SIDE®   **By GARY LARSON**

What is the main point that the cartoonist is making?

_____

Tips for Recognizing Information Gaps

The following tips can help you recognize information gaps in your textbooks and other reading materials:

1. In order to decide whether information is missing, read the entire textbook section and consider all the information presented.

2. Note the author's use of key words and phrases which represent the topic, or main ideas, of what you are reading.

3. Look for information gaps or leaps from one idea to the next following the use of key words. Pause to mentally fill in any information gaps.

To help clarify how you would use these strategies, read this excerpt from a political science textbook and the explanation that follows it:

> The original version of the Electoral College worked as the Framers intended only for as long as George Washington was willing to seek and hold the presidency. He was twice, and unanimously, elected President. That is, in 1789 and again in 1792, each elector cast one of his two ballots for the great Virginian.
>
> Flaws began to appear in the system in 1796, however. By then, political parties had begun to form. John Adams, the Federalist candidate, was elected to the presidency. Thomas Jefferson, an arch-rival and Democratic-Republican, who lost to Adams by just three votes in the electoral balloting, became his Vice President.
>
> **Source:** W. McClenaghan, *Magruder's American Government* (New York: Prentice-Hall, 1994).

In the first sentence of the second paragraph, the author says that "flaws began to appear in the system in 1796" and then in the next sentence leaps to the idea that political parties had already begun to form. As in cartoons, there is an information gap here. In this excerpt, the gap is signaled by the key words *flaws* and *political parties,* which are in close proximity to each other and suggest the reader should pause to draw an inference. The inference you should make here is that in governmental evolution, political party formation revealed a flaw in the system—candidates from opposing parties could be placed in office together as president and vice-president.

Exercise **7h**	**Information Gaps**

Read the following textbook excerpts and answer the inference questions that follow. Key words and phrases are in italics. The first one is modeled for you.

MODEL **1.** Some people take synthetic hormones called anabolic steroids to increase the size and strength of their muscles. The anabolic steroids are related to testosterone, a reproductive hormone secreted by the testes, except that they have been altered so that the reproductive effects of these compounds are minimized but their effect on skeletal muscles is maintained. *Testosterone* and *anabolic steroids* cause skeletal muscle tissue to hypertrophy.

Source: Seeley, *Anatomy & Physiology* (New York; Mosby-Year Book, 1992), p. 293.

Question: Which sex (male or female), can you infer, has the greater chance of skeletal muscle tissue hypertrophying (growing larger) after taking steroids? Explain how you arrived at your answer.

Answer: The male sex because testosterone and steroids affect the

growth of muscle tissue, and males naturally have more testosterone

than females.

2. We can see why there are no warm-blooded animals much smaller than the mouse. Fish and frogs and insects can be very much smaller because their *temperature is not higher than that of their surroundings*. In accord with the scaling laws of area and volume, small, *warm-blooded animals need relatively a great deal of food*; really small ones could not gather or even digest such an enormous amount.

Source: Serway, *College Physics* (New York: Harcourt Brace & Company, 1995).

Question: What does the author imply about the connection between the amount of food a warm-blooded animal consumes and its size?

Answer: _____

_____

3. Not only must any new or remodeled institutions pass the difficult test of keeping a united Germany committed to its integration in the democratic family of European nations, European strategists say; they must also minimize the continental aftershocks from the possible disintegration of an increasingly unstable Soviet Union. And they must maintain the *stabilizing presence* of the United States on the Continent against any temptation that Washington may entertain to withdraw in the *same way* it did after World War I.

Source: *Comparative Politics* (New York: The Dushkin Publishing Group, 1990).

Question: What can you infer happened to Germany as a result of the U.S. withdrawal after World War I?

Answer: _____

4. The practical conclusions that Protagoras and his fellow Sophists drew from this was that what counted was not so much the constitution or the laws but the people of the city. If they could be educated—or better, for the Sophists were not interested in the masses—if their *leaders could be educated*, the *laws* they made would be automatically good.

Source: D. Brendan, *The Ancient World: A Social and Cultural History* (New York: Prentice-Hall, 1989), p. 149.

Question: From this passage, one can infer that education affects what? Explain your answer.

Answer: _____

5. For thousands of years, human beings have fashioned natural materials into useful products. Modern chemistry certainly has its roots in this endeavor. After the discovery of fire, people began to notice changes in certain rocks and minerals exposed to high temperatures. From these observations came the development of ceramics, glass, and metals, which today are among our most useful materials. Dyes and medicines were other early products obtained from natural substances. For example, the ancient Phoenicians extracted a bright purple dye, known as Tyrian purple, from a species of sea snail. *One ounce of Tyrian purple* required over *200,000 snails*. Because of its brilliant hue and scarcity, the dye became the choice of royalty.

Source: Ebbing, *General Chemistry* (New York: Houghton Mifflin Company, 1943), p. 4.

Question: Why do you think the dye became the choice of royalty? What can you infer the author meant when he mentioned the brilliant hue and scarcity?

Answer: _____

_____

_____

_____

6. The Bean Eaters

They eat beans mostly, this old yellow pair.

Dinner is a casual affair.

Plain chipware on a plain and creaking wood,

Tin flatware.

Two who are Mostly Good.

Two who have lived their day,

But keep on putting on their clothes

And putting things away.

And remembering…

Remembering, with twinklings and twinges,

As they lean over the beans in their rented back room that is full of

beads and receipts and dolls and clothes, tobacco crumbs, vases

and fringes.

Source: Gwendolyn Brooks, *Blacks (The Bean Eaters)* (Chicago: The David Company, 1987).

Question: What can you infer about the couple?

Answer: _____

_____

Learning Journal

Describe the five strategies you can now use to infer meaning from an author's implied ideas.

Knowing How Much to Infer

One problem some students have with inference is that they infer too much. They quickly jump to a conclusion as they read without establishing sound reasons for it. Remember that reading is a two-way conversation; you cannot ignore the other person speaking, the author. Here are some strategies to ensure that your inferences are accurate.

Recognize an Author's Perspective

When you read, attend carefully to what an author is saying and try to see things from his or her perspective. For example, if the author of a cultural anthropology textbook writes "Many similarities between man and his closest primate relations, the great apes, have been described," (*Cultural Anthropology*, Melville Herskovits, 1960) you should not conclude from the words *man*, *closest relations*, and *apes* that the author implies that humans and apes are as closely related as human siblings. The words in the sentence do not support that conclusion; the inference that humans and apes are as closely related as siblings is an assumption that is not based on the actual content of the sentence. The author is a cultural anthropologist who defines the term *closest primate relations* in the context of thousands of years of history and the separate development of humans and ape; when he uses the word *closest* he is not talking in terms of the two to three years that commonly separate siblings.

Use the Text to Support Your Conclusion

When you infer something, you need to test your conclusion against the rest of the material in the text. Is there any information in the text that challenges your inference? If so, perhaps you are inferring too much. Are there details in the text that support your inference? If there are, your inference is probably accurate. Read the following excerpt from a business text:

> Time management specialists suggest it is important for a manager or business owner to *"do the important* and *delegate the urgent."* This principle is often *distorted* under the pressure of conflict, and

managers and owners are found ignoring many important business matters in an attempt to deal with the conflict.

Source: P. Pickering, *How to Manage Conflict* (Franklin Lakes, NJ: Career Press, 1993).

From these two sentences, what do you infer the author's message is about conflict? Is it important or is it urgent? A key word in these sentences is *distorted*: if the principal is distorted, you can infer that managers mistakenly consider conflicts to be important and try to solve them instead of seeing them as urgent and delegating someone else to deal with them while they attend to other, more important issues. As you read on in the text, you can test whether the idea of conflict being urgent is a fair inference by measuring it against other details provided by the author. Here are the next sentences:

Perspective is the key. In conflict, as with any management issue, the executive must know both the goals and direction in which the company is moving. Decisions and responses to conflict should match this overall direction. *But* sometimes *urgent needs interfere* with daily schedules. A time study should reveal that you have spent time managing the priorities and *not managing the conflict* unendingly.

Source: P. Pickering, *How to Manage Conflict* (Franklin Lakes, NJ: Career Press, 1993).

Nothing in the remaining sentences of this section of the text would challenge the inference that conflict is urgent but not of management-level importance. In fact, the key words *urgent needs interfere* and *not managing the conflict* support the inference that conflict in this section is considered urgent.

Exercise 7i

How Much to Infer

Read the following textbook excerpts. For each one, select from the list the most reasonable inference.

1. The day she would try to kill herself, she realised winter was coming again. She had been lying on her side, her knees drawn up; she'd sighed, and the heat of her breath had vaporized in the cold air of the bedroom. She pushed the air out of her lungs again, watching. Then she did it again, and again. Then she wrenched back the covers and got up. Alice hated winter.

Source: Maggie O'Farrell, *After You'd Gone* (New York: Penguin Books, 2000), pp. 3–4.

a. Alice hated winter.

b. Alice is depressed.

    c. Alice can't afford her heat bill.

    d. Alice has a bad cold.

2. The efficient learner, who will make connections easily, mentally files emotional, physical, and intellectual experiences in an orderly way. Language is the foundation and the tool.

Source: P. Vail, *Learning Styles* (Rosemont: Modern Learning Press, 1992).

    a. Language skills are necessary in order to be an efficient learner.

    b. College students who do not have highly developed language skills never will have them.

    c. Slang use makes students inefficient learners.

    d. Everyone who uses language is an efficient learner.

3. Learners have no need to accept anything which is not agreeable to their own intelligence—ideally they have a duty not to. And it is by the exercise of the teacher's intelligence, not by prestige, eloquence or tyranny, that the learners should be led to agree with their instructor. The teaching and learning of mathematics should thus be an interaction between intelligences, each respecting that of the other. Learners respect the greater knowledge of the teacher, and expect their own understanding to be enlarged.

Source: R. Skemp, *Psychology of Learning Mathematics* (Mahwah, NJ: Lawrence Erlbaum Associates, 1987).

    a. Learners will gain more math knowledge if they just agree that the teacher is always right, even if they do not understand why the teacher is right.

    b. Learners have some responsibilities when learning math.

    c. Math teachers are more intelligent than their students.

    d. Teachers have a lot of prestige.

4. The researchers found that 25 percent of the volunteers believed that genetic information had been used to deny them or members of their families life insurance; 22 percent believed the information had been similarly misused by health insurers; and 13 percent believed that the information had led to job discrimination.

Source: Steve Sternberg, "Genetic Discrimination: A Prejudice Is Born," *Science News*, October 26, 1996, p. 262.

    a. Forty percent of volunteers did not respond or didn't care about the survey.

    b Volunteers did not believe that personal genetic information affected their families' life insurance or job discrimination.

c. Health insurers cannot be trusted.

d. Many volunteers felt that sharing genetic information affected them in a negative way.

Learning Journal

In your journal, describe two strategies you can use to help determine how much to infer from a reading.

Implied Main Ideas

Implied main ideas are the main points of a paragraph, section, or chapter that are not stated explicitly. That means that you cannot look in the text and underline the sentence that contains the main idea. When main ideas are implied, you must use inference strategies and mentally construct the main idea for yourself. The following steps will guide you in how to do this:

1. *Read carefully.* Authors are asking you to infer meaning when they present seemingly dissimilar ideas without explaining their connection to each other, use emotive language, or leave information gaps.

2. *Identify the topic of the reading material.*

3. *Ask yourself what important point the author makes about the topic.*

4. *Combine the topic with the new information you have learned.* You can now write a main idea sentence that includes the topic of the reading material and states the main idea that supports it.

Now read the following excerpt. Italics and parenthetical information have been added to guide you in making appropriate inferences.

When I was fifteen years old *I saw the University of Chicago for the first time* and somehow sensed that *I had discovered my life.* [*What is the author's life? There is an information gap here.*] I had never before seen, or at least had not noticed, buildings that were *evidently dedicated to a higher purpose*, not to necessity or utility, not *merely* to shelter or manufacture or trade, [*What is his apparent bias? What emotive language suggests bias?*] but to something [*What? Another information gap.*] that *might be an end in itself*.

Source: A. Bloom, *The Closing of the American Mind* (New York: Simon & Schuster, 1987), p. 243.

What is the topic? Academia. What important point does the author make about academia? He implies that a university offers something more important than job training and practical skills; it offers a journey into the human intellect.

Implied Main Idea

Read the following textbook excerpts and write the main idea of each one. The first one is modeled for you.

MODEL   **1.**   When the ship veered into the Cape of Good Hope, Mum caught the spicy woody scent of Africa on the changing wind. She smelled the people: raw onions and salt, the smell of people who are not afraid to eat meat, and who smoke fish over fires on the beach and who pound maize into meal and who work out-of-doors. She held me up to face the earthy air, so that the fingers of warmth pushed back my black curls of hair, and her pale green eyes went clear-glassy.

"Smell that, " she whispered. "That's home."

Source: A. Fuller, *Don't Let's Go to the Dogs Tonight: An African Childhood* (New York: Random House, 2001), pp. 38–39.

Implied main idea: _____"Home" is a multisensory experience: it has strong_____ smells, earthy sights, raw tastes, bold people, and comforting warmth.

2.   It isn't just the selling of September 11 that offends me. There's also the aggression of our current patriotism, epitomized by the claim that alone among nations, the U.S. was entitled to make a political statement during the opening ceremony of the Olympics by displaying a flag from ground zero. In the immediate aftermath of the attacks, the courage and grace of ordinary Americans inspired millions around the world. But anyone who has traveled in the last month or who follows the foreign press knows that the store of international goodwill is fast being depleted—in part because we seem to think that others should recognize that our wounds, our needs, our flag exist on a higher plane that those of anyone else.

Source: Michael Elliott, "Don't Wear Out Old Glory," *Time*, February 18, 2002, p. 84.

Implied main idea: _____

3.   It was only first period at McKinley High School in Baton Rouge when 17-year-old Leslie-Claire Spillman sensed that something was wrong. The door to her classroom burst open; a girl jumped in and yelled, "It's time!" Spillman soon heard students murmuring and slamming lockers in the halls. As she edged her way outside, she realized what all the commotion was about—her. "No Gay Clubs!" the kids were chanting as the crowds began to grow thicker and meaner in the halls. Spillman is the openly bisexual cochairman of the Gay-Straight Alliance, a group she and her friend Martin Pfeiffer, also 17, had fought for six months to form.

Source: Marc Peyser and Donatella Lorch, *High School Controversial* (Boston: McGraw-Hill, 2002), p. 315.

Implied main idea: _____

_____

4. In many ways, Mr. Motsepe is indeed part of the family. He owns three gold mines and employs about 5,500 workers; five months ago his company, African Rainbow Minerals, became the first new gold company to be listed on the Johannesburg Stock Exchange in more than a decade. But these days, Mr. Motsepe often seems a lonely pinstriped figure in a sea of white faces.

Source: Rachel Swarns, "Rarity of Black-Run Businesses Worries South Africa's Leaders," *The New York Times,* November 13, 2002, p. 301.

Implied main idea: _____

_____

Practice with Reading Passage

Answer all questions on a separate sheet of paper.

Reading Practice

An Excerpt from *In Contempt*
BY CHRISTOPHER DARDEN

PREPARE TO READ

1. Based on the title, what do you expect this reading to be about?

2. What do you already know about Christopher Darden?

3. You should know the following list of vocabulary words. If not, you should look them up in a dictionary:

   a. Codified

   b. Hierarchy

   c. Indelibly

    d. Nomadic

    e. Hypocrisy

4. Using the title of the excerpt, create a question you would expect this reading selection to answer.

There was this white kid with a crooked leg who lived near where my father grew up in Gilmer, a dusty farming town on the eastern side of Texas, near the city of Tyler. This kid had a little tree house, and most days, when my father would walk past, the kid would pull himself up into his tree house, wait for that little nigger kid to walk past, and then spit on him.

As soon as that kid came down from his tree house, my father would beat his ass, but two weeks later, that white boy would drag his weak legs into his tree house and would proceed to spit on him again. My dad would wait for him to come down from his tree house and then beat his ass again. Didn't matter. The next day, that kid would be up in his tree house again.

It says something that, in America, a lame white boy would suffer a beating just for the chance to spit on a black kid. That's how important it has been, after slavery in this country, for whites to put blacks in their place, how important it has been to replace a codified social hierarchy with a lawless one, how important it has been for many white people to have someone beneath them.

Stokely Carmichael wrote in his book *Black Power* that it was important that we change from "Negroes" to "blacks" because of the deep need to define one's self. I've always believed that. To allow others to define us is to be shackled always to the past, to be chained to old stereotypes. To allow white people to define us is to be slaves forever, to be beneath whites on some artificial social order. I guess for a little white kid with birth defects, with warped and tired legs, well, for a kid like that, I guess that social order was invaluable. I guess having someone beneath him was worth a routine beating.

When he wasn't beating their asses, my dad played with white kids while growing up, and he especially liked a couple of children who lived between his house and the one-room general store. But one day, one of the children, a little girl about twelve, wouldn't come down from her porch to play with my father.

"I cain't play with you no more, Eddie."

"Why not?"

"I just cain't."

It wasn't until later that my father figured that the girl's parents didn't want their twelve-year-old girl having anything more to do with him. She was a young woman now. And in the South, white women didn't roll around in the dirt with niggers.

When you're a kid, you don't know anything about race. You don't think, I'm black and he's white and she's yellow. Not until someone decides that they must tell you. And when you're young and black, they might tell you from a tree house or from their front porch. They might even tell you with the word "nigger." It's an experience you can never forget. The details become a part of you, indelibly etched in your memory. And then you know your race and you know your place. When a white person decides it is time for you to know those things, when a white person looks you in the eye and calls you nigger, you're never able to forget.

I never met my father's father, Miles; never even saw a picture of him. He was a farmer initially, in that East Texas town of Gilmer. He was married at age thirteen, had ten children by the time he was twenty-five. One day, Miles said he had received his calling from God and he began farming less and preaching more until soon he stopped farming altogether and left his family to preach on the road. From that point on, he was something of a jack-legged preacher—a nomadic rookie preacher who moved from church to church, preaching one-Sunday stands and then moving on to the next community. Every month, he sent a little money to his family, but he never came home. My own father has always seen a certain hypocrisy in churches, and I believe that losing his own father hardened him to religion.

My dad said that it wasn't until he was a father himself that he understood his own father. He realized that Miles, married at thirteen, didn't figure his children needed him around once they reached age thirteen themselves. Grandpa Miles died in Monroe, Louisiana, in 1963, when I was just seven. But I got the feeling my father had given up on his dad long before that.

My father has worked as long as he can remember, since the time he was five years old, picking cotton in hot, East Texas fields. My father was a hard worker, but his sister was the best cotton picker in Texas, he would brag, a girl who could pick more than any man. Four hundred pounds a day, my father used to contend, which gives you an idea of the lack of shame with which my father will stretch a good story.

He also could tell you about the first nickel he ever earned, when he was five. He picked cucumbers all day and sold them a nickel a peck. He got that nickel, went home, and showed it to his mother, Viola, whom we called Big Mama. He asked her to keep his nickel for him and so she tied it into the corner of her apron. But that made my daddy nervous and so he went back and asked for it. He didn't want to lose that nickel and so he put it where it would always be safe, where he could always find it. He put the nickel in his mouth and was going to hold it there as long as he needed to.

Instead he swallowed it.

"Don't worry," Big Mama said. "You can get your nickel back when you go to the outhouse."

But Eddie was smart. He wasn't going to take any chances and he wasn't about to go digging around in someone else's shit. And so when the time came, he went to the bushes and squatted down there, dug around, and got his nickel back. My daddy can still pinch a nickel better than anyone I know.

When my father was twelve, Big Mama walked down a country road with him and talked about his future.

"Boy, when you get old enough, you leave the South," his mother said. "It ain't for you."

Daddy didn't say anything. He just kept walking, his head down, looking at the East Texas dirt. There was nothing to say. Big Mama was right. He was nobody's boy except hers. And on that day, he began thinking of a way out of Texas, a way out of the poverty that he associated with the South.

Source: Christopher Darden, *In Contempt* (New York: Harper Collins, 1996), pp. 13–16.

CHECK YOUR UNDERSTANDING

OBJECTIVE QUESTIONS

Read the following multiple-choice questions and select the best possible answer from the choices given.

1. Darden explains that when someone tells you your race, you never forget. What is he implying?

   a. They call you an unkind name.

   b. People cannot see their skin color unless someone points it out.

   c. Race matters in America.

   d. America should be colorblind.

2. What does Darden mean when he says his grandfather received his calling from God?

   a. The grandfather felt compelled by God to preach His Word more than to work on the farm.

   b. The grandfather died and went to heaven.

   c. The grandfather heard voices.

   d. The grandfather spoke in tongues.

3. What effect on the family does Darden imply occurred when his grandfather became a preacher?

   a. The whole family became more religious.

   b. The grandfather moved from church to church.

   c. The family flourished.

   d. The family struggled financially and emotionally.

4. What does Darden imply when he says "which gives you an idea of the lack of shame with which my father will stretch a good story"?

   a. His father told accurate stories.

   b. His father was not embarrassed to embellish stories.

    c. His father lied all of the time.

    d. His father told good stories.

5. What does Darden imply when he says "He (his father) was nobody's boy except hers"?

    a. Big Mama was not his real mother.

    b. His father was adopted.

    c. His father always listened to Big Mama.

    d. Big Mama knew his father's personality and temperament better than anyone.

SHORT-ANSWER QUESTIONS

6. What does Darden imply about a name when he says "it was important that we change from 'Negroes' to 'blacks' because of the deep need to define one's self"?

7. There is an information gap in the story about the author's father earning his first nickel. What did the author mean when he said "when the time came"?

8. What does the author mean when he says his father "can still pinch a nickel"?

9. What are the author's tone and purpose in this excerpt? Explain your answer.

10. Do you think that Darden's father ever got out of the poverty he associated with the South?

11. What point is Darden making by telling you about his father's life? What do you think he learned from his father's life experiences?

Chapter Summary

College instructors require you not only to read and understand what is explicitly stated on the page, but also to detect ideas that are implied or indirectly stated. In order to fully understand a reading assignment, you need to read the material and combine what is stated with the additional information you generate using inference as a tool. While inference is a skill you practice every day, inferring meaning from textbooks and other college reading material requires you to use specific strategies such as detecting an author's bias, noting comparisons, and recognizing information gaps. You also need to understand how an author's purpose, tone, and use of key words and emotive language can be used as clues to his or her implied main idea. There are limits to what you can infer, and you should use other information in a reading to check if your conclusions are accurate.

Post Test

Answer the following on a separate sheet of paper.

Part I

OBJECTIVE QUESTIONS

Match the words in Column A to their correct meanings in Column B.

	A		B
1.	Inference	a.	Choice of words or images that indicate an author's attitude.
2.	Diction	b.	Main idea that is not stated explicitly.
3.	Imply	c.	Author's preferences and opinions.
4.	Purpose	d.	Tool that allows a reader to make assumptions and to draw conclusions.
5.	Tone	e.	Author's reason for writing, which frames the main idea.
6.	Author's bias	f.	Limited information—information appears to be missing.
7.	Information gap	g.	To indicate without stating openly.
8.	Implied main idea	h.	Author's choice of words.

Read the following multiple-choice questions and select the best possible answer from the choices given.

2. Which of the following statements does not contain emotive language?

   a. The dogs were comfortable lying on the grass.

   b. The dogs were urinating on the grass.

   c. The dogs trampled the delicate grass so much that it might not continue to grow.

   d. The dogs tromped happily on the grass.

3. Information gaps are

    a. Examples of poor writing.

    b. Places where biased language was omitted.

    c. Places where an author omits information to save space.

    d. Places where an author omits information and expects the reader to infer it.

4. Implied main ideas are

    a. Main ideas that are not explicitly stated.

    b. Main ideas that are explicitly stated.

    c. Ideas that you have about the piece of writing.

    d. Ideas that can be found right in the text.

5. To find an implied main idea, you must

    a. Identify the topic and question yourself about it.

    b. Make inferences as you read, identify the topic, and then question yourself.

    c. Fill in the information gaps and then question yourself.

    d. Follow the same procedure for identifying stated main ideas.

SHORT-ANSWER QUESTIONS

6. How does recognizing an author's tone help you infer his or her main idea?

7. How do you know how much to infer when reading?

8. If you detect bias in someone's writing, should you reject the writer's ideas?

9. When inferring a main idea from a reading assignment, is it necessary that all the students in your class agree on what the implied main idea is?

Part II

Reading Passage

"A Victim"
BY BRUNO BETTELHEIM

1. Read the title and skim over the paragraphs. What do you expect this reading selection to be about?

2. What do you already know about the topic?

3. Using the title of this essay, create one question that you would expect this reading selection to answer.

Many students of discrimination are aware that the victim often reacts in ways as undesirable as the action of the aggressor. Less attention is paid to this because it is easier to excuse a defendant than an offender, and because they assume that once the aggression stops the victim's reactions will stop too. But I doubt if this is of real service to the persecuted, in which victim and persecutor are inseparably interlocked.

Let me illustrate with the following example: in the winter of 1938 a Polish Jew murdered the German attaché in Paris, von Rath. The Gestapo used the event to step up anti-Semitic actions, and in the camp new hardships were inflicted on Jewish prisoners. One of these was an order barring them from the medical clinic unless the need for treatment had originated in work accidents.

Nearly all prisoners suffered from frostbite, which often led to gangrene and then amputation. Whether or not a Jewish prisoner was admitted to the clinic to prevent such a fate depended on the whim of an SS private. On reaching the clinic entrance, the prisoner explained the nature of his ailment to the SS man, who then decided if he should get treatment or not.

I too suffered from frostbite. At first I was discouraged from trying to get medical care by the fate of Jewish prisoners whose attempts had ended up in no treatment, only abuse. Finally things got worse and I was afraid that waiting longer would mean amputation. So I decided to make the effort.

When I got to the clinic, there were many prisoners lined up as usual, a score of them Jews suffering from severe frostbite. The main topic of discussion was one's chances of being admitted to the clinic. Most Jews had planned their procedure in detail. Some thought it best to stress their service in the German army during World War I: wounds received or decorations won. Others planned to stress the severity of their frostbite. A few decided it was best to tell some "tall story," such as that an SS officer had ordered them to report at the clinic.

Most of them seemed convinced that the SS man on duty would not see through their schemes. Eventually they asked me about my plans. Having no definite ones, I said I would go by the way the SS man dealt with other Jewish prisoners who had frostbite like me, and proceed accordingly. I doubted how wise it was to follow a preconceived plan, because it was hard to anticipate the reactions of a person you didn't know.

The prisoners reacted as they had at other times when I had voiced similar ideas on how to deal with the SS. They insisted that one SS man was like another, all equally vicious and stupid. As usual, any frustration was immediately discharged against the person who caused it, or was nearest at hand. So, in abusive terms they accused me of not wanting to share my plan with them, or of intending to use one of theirs; it angered them that I was ready to meet the enemy unprepared.

No Jewish prisoner ahead of me in the line was admitted to the clinic. The more a prisoner pleaded, the more annoyed and violent the SS became. Expressions of pain amused him; stories of previous services rendered to Germany outraged him. He proudly remarked that he could not be taken in by Jews, that fortunately the time had passed when Jews could reach their goal by lamentations.

When my turn came he asked me in a screeching voice if I knew that work accidents were the only reason for admitting Jews to the clinic, and if I came because of such an accident. I replied that I knew the rules, but that I couldn't work unless my hands were freed of the dead flesh. Since prisoners were not allowed to have knives, I asked to have the dead flesh cut away. I tried to be matter-of-fact, avoiding pleading, deference, or arrogance. He replied, "If that's all you want, I'll tear the flesh off myself." And he started to pull at the festering skin. Because it did not come off as easily as he may have expected, or for some other reason, he waved me into the clinic.

Inside, he gave me a malevolent look and pushed me into the treatment room. There he told the prisoner orderly to attend to the wound. While this was being done, the guard watched me closely for signs of pain but I was able to suppress them. As soon as the cutting was over, I started to leave. He showed surprise and asked why I didn't wait for further treatment. I said I had gotten the service I asked for, at which he told the orderly to make an exception and treat my hand. After I had left the room, he called me back and gave me a card entitling me to further treatment, and admittance to the clinic without inspection at the entrance.

Because my behavior did not correspond to what he expected of Jewish prisoners on the basis of his projection, he could not use his prepared defense against being touched by a prisoner's plight. Since I did not act as the dangerous Jew was expected to, I did not activate the anxieties that went with his stereotype. Still, he did not altogether trust me, so he continued to watch while I received treatment.

Throughout these dealings, the SS felt uneasy with me, though he did not unload on me the annoyance his uneasiness aroused. Perhaps he watched me closely because he expected that sooner or later I would slip up and behave the way his projected image of the Jew was expected to act. This would have meant his delusional creation had become real.

Source: Bruno Bettelheim, "A Victim," *The Informed Heart* (New York: The Free Press, a division of Macmillan, Inc., 1960), pp. 220–225.

OBJECTIVE QUESTIONS

Read the following multiple-choice questions and select the best possible answer from the choices given.

1.　Why did other Jewish prisoners discourage Bettelheim from going to the clinic at first?

   a. They felt his wounds were not serious enough.

   b. They were jealous.

   c. They assumed he would listen to them.

   d. They assumed he would not be treated.

2. When asked about his plan to get into the clinic, what does Bettelheim mean when he says he'd "proceed accordingly"?

    a. He didn't have a plan and decided to use the plan of another prisoner.

    b. Standing in line would give him time to think of something.

    c. He would develop his plan but not tell anyone about it.

    d. He would develop his plan after he witnessed the SS man's behavior.

3. When Bettelheim says, "They insisted that one SS man was like another," what does he imply that he believes?

    a. There is a difference among SS men.

    b. There is no difference among SS men.

    c. The SS men would treat him differently.

    d. All SS men were vicious.

4. How was Bettelheim's attempt to get into the clinic different from the other prisoners' attempts to get in?

    a. He said he didn't know the rules and apologized.

    b. He said he knew the rules but that they were unjust.

    c. He was matter-of-fact, avoiding pleading, deference, or arrogance.

    d. He pleaded and deferred to the SS men's judgment.

5. Which of the following sentences supports this statement in the essay: "Because my behavior did not correspond to what he expected of Jewish prisoners on the basis of his projection, he could not use his prepared defenses against being touched by a prisoner's plight."

    a. A Polish Jew murdered the German attaché in Paris, von Rath.

    b. He showed surprise and asked why I didn't wait for further treatment.

    c. Less attention is paid to this because it is easier to excuse a defendant than an offender.

    d. The SS man felt compassion for the prisoner.

SHORT-ANSWER QUESTIONS

6. In paragraph eight, Bettelheim says, "The more a prisoner pleaded, the more annoyed and violent the SS became." According to Bettelheim's argument, why did this happen?

7. Why did Bettelheim get admitted into the clinic when all the other Jews before him were denied?

8. Why did Bettelheim suppress his feeling of pain when the orderly was cutting Bettelheim's flesh?

9. What does Bettelheim mean when he says, "This would have meant that his [the SS man's] delusional creation had become real"?

10. What is the implied main idea of the essay? What does Bettelheim mean by, "The victim and the persecutor are inseparably interlocked"?

Website Sources for Additional Practice

http://www.fno.org/mar97/deep.html:
"Deep Thinking and Deep Reading," an interesting series of articles on evaluating sources.

http://www.netsurf.com/nsd/index.html:
Here is a "netsurfer digest"—links to articles you can sink your teeth into.

http://www.southampton.liunet.edu/library/evaluate.htm:
Here's your guide to evaluating and citing Internet sources.

http://www2.widener.edu/Wolfgram-Memorial-Library/webeval.htm:
Lots of resources here, even PowerPoint presentations!

http://www.to.utwente.nl/user/ism/lanzinglom_home.htm

http://web.new.ufl.edu/~sullivan/4456.crit.read.html

Chapter 8

Textbook Methods of Organization

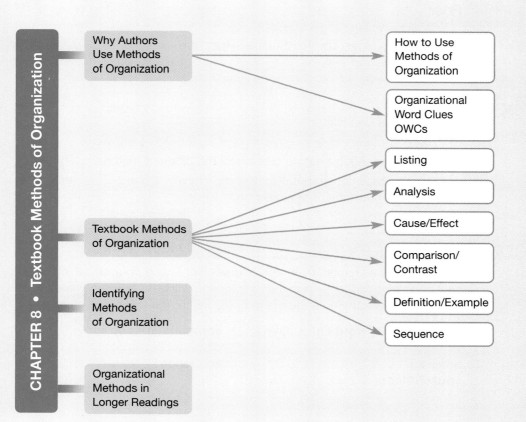

Textbook Methods of Organization

- Why Authors Use Methods of Organization
  - How to Use Methods of Organization
  - Organizational Word Clues OWCs
- Textbook Methods of Organization
  - Listing
  - Analysis
  - Cause/Effect
  - Comparison/Contrast
  - Definition/Example
  - Sequence
- Identifying Methods of Organization
- Organizational Methods in Longer Readings

Chapter Contents

Chapter Goals

In this chapter you will:

- Learn about the different methods of textbook organization.
- Learn to recognize words that signal the different methods.
- Practice techniques that will help you identify, organize, and remember textbook methods of organization.

Chapter Vocabulary

As you read the chapter, take note of these words and phrases, which represent important concepts from the chapter and will be in **boldface** type. Make sure you understand them before the post test at the end of the chapter.

organizational word clues (OWCs)   **comparison/contrast**
listing   **definition/example**
analysis   **sequence**
cause/effect

Amber's Journal Entry

I make good grades, but I have to work very hard. When I finish a chapter, I often forget what I read, and I never have a clear idea of what I should remember. I know there must be some way to figure out how it's organized, but what is it? I can find the main ideas and details pretty well now, but I still don't know how authors organize information, or how knowing the organization they use can possibly make a difference in remembering what I read.

Learning Journal

In your journal, write down what you know about the methods of organization authors use. Do you look for words that signal which method an author is using? If yes, how do you use these words as tools to help prepare you for exams?

Why Authors Use Methods of Organization

Authors use different methods of organization in order to present information in a logical format that suits the subject matter and goals of their books. For example, when discussing World War II, one author may compare and contrast it with other wars to highlight the reasons it became a global conflict. Another may describe the sequence of events leading up to the war to analyze its precursors. A third might detail the cause and effect of women's participation in the U.S. homefront war effort. At times authors will combine organizational methods, depending on the type and complexity of the topics they are discussing. Knowing the different patterns, or methods, of organization helps you make sense of what you are reading and remember the content more accurately. Authors use a number of classic organizational patterns:

- Listing.
- Analysis.
- Cause/Effect.
- Comparison/Contrast.
- Definition/Example.
- Sequence.

All the ideas in a textbook chapter relate to one another. If you try to remember them individually, outside of their relationship to each other, you are likely to miss the larger meaning of the chapter and fail to remember what you read. For example, a declaration of war against a country affects its economy, attitude toward other countries, feelings of nationalism, university enrollment, employment, social structure, and media. A textbook author can take all these ideas, and then compare, analyze, or list them depending on his or her purpose for writing. When you can identify these patterns of organization, you will more clearly understand what you read and how individual ideas are related to the larger main idea.

How to Use Methods of Organization

College instructors frequently develop test questions based on the methods of organization used by the authors of the textbooks they teach from. Once you recognize the patterns being used in a textbook chapter, you can use them as a blueprint for predicting the types of exam questions you might be asked. If the authors of a sociology text list and describe different kinds of interpersonal relationships, for example, you can recreate the list and use it to test yourself on the subject. If the author of a physics textbook explains the concept of motion using the cause/effect method of organization, you can write down the causes and then try to recall their effects as a way to prepare for an exam.

Organizational Word Clues: OWCs

In Chapter 5 you learned that word clues alert you to the twists and turns in the path of an author's thinking. They also help you determine the level of importance of an author's ideas. **Organizational word clues (OWCs)** are used to indicate the *overall organization* of a reading passage, journal article, or textbook chapter.

Textbook Methods of Organization

Listing

Authors use the **listing** method of organization to enumerate events, ideas, or other concepts. They organize their lists in a variety of ways: alphabetically, numerically, by order of importance, or by category. Unlike the sequence pattern of organization, listing is not used to illustrate the steps in a process or the order of chronological events. Although authors may use OWCs such as *first* and *second,* they are simply providing a list of items that will be discussed further. Table 8.1 provides examples of organizational words that signal an author is using the listing method.

TABLE 8.1   ORGANIZATIONAL WORD CLUES FOR LISTING METHOD

First...second...third	first of all... secondly...finally
the four levels of...	one way...another way...a third way...

Read the following textbook excerpt and note the italicized words and phrases—the listing OWCs—that let you know the author is using the listing method of organization.

> Elizabethan acting companies—each of which had approximately twenty-five members—were organized on a sharing plan. There were *three categories* of personnel in a company: shareholders, hirelings, and apprentices. Shareholders, the *first* category, were the elite members of the company, who received a percentage of the troupe's profits as payment. Hirelings, the *second* category, were actors contracted for a specific period of time and for a specific salary, and they usually played minor roles. And apprentices, the *third* category, were young performers training for the profession who were assigned to shareholders.
>
> **Source:** Adapted from Wilson and Goldfarb, *Theater: The Lively Art* (Boston: McGraw-Hill, 2002), p. 271.

Recognizing that chapters or paragraphs are organized using a listing pattern enables you to predict the format of many of the exam questions an instructor will ask about them. Here are some examples of the types of listing questions an instructor might ask based on the excerpt above, and therefore the kind you should ask yourself before a test:

- What are the three categories of personnel that comprised an Elizabethan acting company?
- Which category was comprised of young performers training for the profession?

After you have identified an author's method of organization as listing, you can visually represent the text information in your learning journal. See Figure 8.1 for a visual representation of the information in the excerpt.

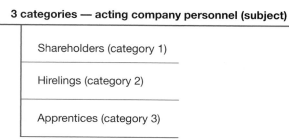

3 categories — acting company personnel (subject)

Shareholders (category 1)

Hirelings (category 2)

Apprentices (category 3)

Figure 8.1   Listing Diagram

Exercise 8a

Listing

Read the following excerpt and underline the listing OWCs. Identify the topic and main idea of the passage. Predict one question a professor might ask using listing OWCs in the question stem. Visually represent the information in the excerpt, using Figure 8.1 on p. 251 as a model.

There are four reasons to dump your doctor now. M.D.'s spill the scenarios that would make them ditch their docs faster than you can say "HMO." The reasons that they give include the following. The first good reason to dump your doctor is if she speaks medical mumbo jumbo. A good physician takes the time to explain your condition in lay language. Second, if he acts defensive. "If a doctor became belligerent while I was asking him questions, I'd walk out," says internist Hall. "You need a physician who listens to your concerns and is secure enough even to suggest you seek a second opinion." Third, if he runs a battery of tests without asking the right questions first. A careful taking of a patient's history and a physical give you 80 percent of what you need to know. And finally, the fourth reason is if she has a rude staff. Many believe that they can tell the kind of care they are getting the minute they step into a doctor's office. The attitude of the staff mirrors the attitude coming from the top. If the receptionist is obnoxious, it's a sign that the doctor is trying to get people in and out as quickly as possible.

Source: Adapted from H. Levine, "Advice Docs Give Their Own Families," *Redbook*, November 2002, p. 70.

Topic: _____

Main idea: _____

Question: _____

Visual representation:

Analysis

In the **analysis** method of organization authors break a concept down into its specific characteristics, properties, or basic elements. Their purpose might be to show the different parts or details of a complex issue in order to make it easier to understand. For example, a medical writer discussing diabetes could give readers information about its cause, symptoms, and treatment options. Table 8.2 provides examples of organizational words that signal an author's use of the analysis method.

TABLE 8.2   ANALYSIS OWCs

features	properties	characteristics	aspects
types	one sense or one part	one way	another way
is made up of	involves	categories	elements
setting	components	attributes	classes
factors	levels	findings	functions
in this case	analysis		

Read the following textbook excerpt and note the italicized words and phrases—the analysis OWCs—that let you know the author is using the analysis method of organization.

This paragraph will detail the *structure* and *functions* of leaf epidermis. The cells of leaf epidermis can have *different shapes* in *different types* of *leaves*. Some cells interlock like the pieces of a jigsaw puzzle, while others look more like bricks. A transparent coating—or cuticle—made of a waxy substance called cutin covers their outside surfaces. The cuticle helps to prevent the loss of water and allows light to reach the mesophyll below. In some plants, leaf epidermal cells develop hairlike growths on their outer surfaces. These growths give the leaves a fuzzy texture. The epidermal hairs on some leaves secrete a substance that makes the leaves feel sticky. This secretion can protect the plant because it can be poisonous to humans or grazing animals.

Source: I. Slesnick, L. Balzer, A. McCormack, and D. Newton, *Biology* (Teacher's Edition) (Glenview, IL.: Scott, Foresman, 1985), p. 352.

Here are some examples of the types of analysis questions an instructor might ask about the excerpt above, and therefore the kind you should ask yourself before a test:

- What are the characteristics of the structure of the leaf epidermis?
- What are the functions of the leaf epidermis?

- What conclusion did the author make regarding the main function of the epidermis?

After reading the textbook excerpt, and identifying the author's method of organization as analysis, you could visually represent the text information as shown in Figure 8.2

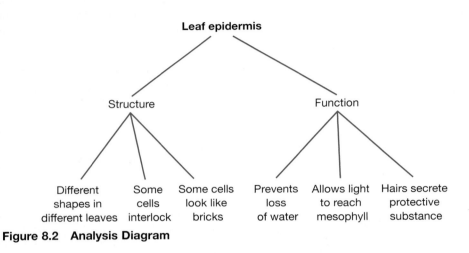

Figure 8.2   Analysis Diagram

Exercise

8b

Analysis

Read the following excerpt and underline the analysis OWCs. Identify the topic and main idea of the passage. Predict two questions a professor might ask using analysis OWCs in the question stems. Visually represent the information in the excerpt, using Figure 8.2 as a model.

What, have I explained countless times, is the whole purpose of the armed forces is that it is designed to kill people and break things. That's what the military does. It destroys. The best army in the world is the one that kills the most enemy soldiers and razes the most strategic targets. It's that simple. This is important to remember if we want to continue to be a great nation—the world's only superpower.

We have to look at the military as a separate and unique institution with separate and unique requirements. It's different from all other institutions in our society, and our only standard must be excellence—no matter whose feelings get hurt, including heterosexual men who can't meet the physical or mental requirements. Our only concern should be that the military does what it is supposed to do. That way the rest of us can be assured that our freedoms will have the best possible chance of being preserved.

Let's analyze these types of issues from that pragmatic perspective. Would an all-female combat force provide our nation with the best possible defense? Clearly, the answer to that question is no. With an all-female combat force, would there be a need for men? Clearly, yes.

Now, with an all-male combat force, do we have the best fighting machine we can assemble? Clearly, yes. We've proved it time and time again. No one has ever suggested that women are vitally needed on the line to improve our battlefield performance.

So, if there is no need for women in combat as it relates to our purpose and objective, why are we considering it? Obviously, the answer is, for political reasons. But do we want political considerations to interfere with our military preparedness and objectives? These same questions could be asked about the role of homosexuals in the military.

Source: R. Limbaugh, *See, I Told You So* (New York: Pocket Books, a division of Simon & Schuster, 1993), pp. 258–259.

Topic: _____

Main idea: _____

_____

Question #1: _____

_____

Question #2: _____

Visual representation:

Team Up!

With two other students, create a mind map, using the excerpt in Exercise 8b. As a group, try to come to consensus on the topic, main idea, and details.

Cause/Effect

When authors use the **cause/effect** method of organization, they show why something happened, the effects of something that occurred, or the outcome of an event. Table 8.3 provides examples of organizational words that signal an author's use of the cause/effect method.

TABLE 8.3   CAUSE/EFFECT OWCs

since	because	consequently
reasons	results	effects
happens because	may be due to	it is evident
as a result of	thus	impacts
affect	then	causes
therefore	for this reason	so that
the outcome	becomes	if…then

Read the following textbook excerpt and note the italicized words and phrases—the cause/effect OWCs—that let you know the author is using this method of organization.

So, as we go about our daily toil, the Bonn cesium-beam clock keeps the time. It is, so to speak, a custodian of Earth time. The trouble is, the Earth itself doesn't always keep good time. *Consequently,* our clocks, all supposedly linked to the master system in France like a retinue of obedient slaves, must occasionally be adjusted by a second to track changes in the Earth's rotation rate. *For this reason,* the last such "leap second" was added on 30 June, 1994. The Earth's spin, accurate enough to serve as a perfectly suitable clock for a thousand generations, *is now* defunct as a reliable chronometer. In this age of high-precision timekeeping, poor old Earth doesn't make the grade. *As a result,* the invention of an atomic clock, man-made and mysterious, *now* serves to deliver those all-important tick-tocks with the precision demanded by navigators, astronomers, and airline pilots. *Therefore,* one second is no longer 1/86,400 of a day: it is 9,192,631,770 beats of a cesium atom.

Source: Adapted from Paul Davies, *About Time: Einstein's Unfinished Revolution* (New York: Simon and Schuster, 1995), p. 22.

Here are some examples of the types of cause/effect questions an instructor might ask about the excerpt above, and therefore the kind you should ask yourself before a test, based on the excerpt you just read:

- What were the three primary effects of the invention of the atomic clock?

- What causes the need for the occasional adjuctment to the Bonn cesium-beam clock?

After reading the textbook excerpt and identifying the author's method of organization as cause/effect, you could visually represent the text information as shown in Figure 8.3.

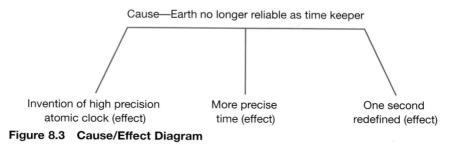

Figure 8.3   Cause/Effect Diagram

Exercise 8c	**Cause/Effect**

Read the following excerpt and underline the cause/effect OWCs. Identify the topic and main idea of the passage. Predict two questions a professor might ask using cause/effect OWCs in the question stems. Create a visual representation of the excerpt using Figure 8.3 as a model.

In 1928, Fred Griffith injected a mixture of heat-killed, smooth cells and living, rough cells into healthy mice. Griffith expected the mice to remain healthy because rough cells do not cause pneumonia and because the smooth cells were dead. On examining the blood in the dead mice, Griffith made an unexpected observation—living, smooth Pneumococcus cells were present. The reason was that the dead, smooth cells must have directed the rough cells to become smooth. An inherited trait of the rough cells must have changed.

Source: Raymond F. Oram, *Biology* (Columbus, OH: Merrill Publishing, 1989), p. 172.

Topic: _____

Main idea: _____

_____

Question #1: _____

Question #2: _____

_____

Visual representation:

Comparison/Contrast

When authors use the **comparison/contrast** method of organization, they examine the similarities or differences between two or more ideas, people, objects, events, or other things. For example, a political science author might explore the similarities and differences between a monarchy and a democracy. Table 8.4 provides examples of organizational words that signal an author's use of the comparison/contrast method.

TABLE 8.4   COMPARISON/CONTRAST OWCs

however	on the other hand	but	yet	although
on the contrary	like	as	compared with	in the same way
although	contrasted with	different from	similar to	in other words

Read the following excerpt and note that the italicized words and phrases are comparison/contrast OWCs.

> Change is a *double-edged* sword. Its relentless pace these days runs us off our feet. *Yet* when things are unsettled, we can find new ways to move ahead and to create breakthroughs not possible in stagnant societies. If you ask people to brainstorm words to describe change, they come up with a mixture of *negative and positive* terms. *On the one side*, fear, anxiety, loss, danger, panic; *on the other*, exhilaration, risk-taking, excitement, improvements, energy.
>
> **Source:** Michael Fullan, *Leading in a Culture of Change* (San Francisco: Jossey Bass, 2001), p. 1.

Here are some examples of the types of comparison/contrast questions an instructor might ask about the excerpt above, and therefore the kind you should ask yourself before a test:

- What is the negative side of change?
- How can change be described as being both positive and negative?

After reading the textbook excerpt about change and identifying the author's method of organization as comparison/contrast, you could visually represent the information as shown in Figure 8.4.

Change	
Negative	**Positive**
Pace runs us off our feet	New ways to move ahead
Fear, anxiety, loss, danger, panic	Creates breakthroughs
	Exhilaration, risk-taking, excitement
	Improvements, energizing

Figure 8.4   Comparison/Contrast Diagram

Exercise 8d

Comparison/Contrast

Read the following excerpt and underline the comparison/contrast OWCs. Identify the topic and main idea of the reading. Predict two questions a professor might ask using comparison/contrast OWCs in the question stems. Create a visual representation, using Figure 8.4 as an example.

With contracts to buy something, it's usually the consumer who makes the first move. It's the consumer who walks into the store, or makes a phone inquiry, or answers a "for sale" ad. Of course, sometimes consumers may be talked into buying things they don't really want. But usually they have had a chance to think about what they want beforehand.

Door-to-door sales are different. Here it's the salesman who makes the first move. The customer has not had a chance to think about the purchase beforehand. And door-to-door salesmen have a big advantage, because people are used to treating visitors in their homes as guests. So, it's not surprising that quite a lot of customers have second thoughts about at-home sales contracts.

Source: Susan McKay, *Civil Justice*, 3rd ed. (New York: Scholastic, 1988), p. 81.

Topic: ———————————————————————

Main idea: ———————————————————————

———————————————————————

Question #1: ———————————————————————

———————————————————————

Question #2: _____

Visual representation:

Definition/Example

Authors use the **definition/example** method of organization to clarify the meaning of key concepts. To aid in this clarification, they use analogies, provide direct definitions with examples, or offer descriptions. Table 8.5 provides examples of organizational words that signal an author's use of the definition/example method.

TABLE 8.5 DEFINITION/EXAMPLE OWCs		
defined as	means the same as	is
another meaning	also referred to as	synonymous with
translated as	interpret the meaning as	decipher

Read the following textbook excerpt and note the italicized words and phrases—the definition/example OWCs—that let you know the author is using this method of organization.

> **Just about anything can be used as money if it is accepted as a medium of exchange. Some curious items that have been used as money, *for example*, include fish hooks, whale's teeth, money rings, elephant tail hair, dog's teeth, tin money trees, stones, copper crosses, and gold images.**
>
> **Source:** R. Hodgetts and T. Smart, *Essentials of Economics and Free Enterprise* (Menlo Park, CA: Addison-Wesley, 1987), p. 196.

Here are some examples of the types of definition questions an instructor might ask based on the excerpt above, and therefore the kind you should ask yourself before a test:

- What is the definition of money?
- According to the author, what are some examples of curious things used for money?

After reading this textbook excerpt and identifying the author's method of organization as definition/example, you could visually represent the information it contains as shown in Figure 8.5.

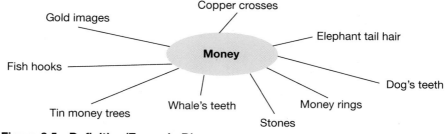

Figure 8.5   Definition/Example Diagram

Definition/Example   Topic/main idea

Read the following excerpt and underline the definition/example OWCs. Identify the topic and main idea of the reading passage. Predict one question a professor might ask using definition/example OWCs in the question stems. Create a visual representation of the excerpt, using Figure 8.5 as an example.

To solve this problem, psychologists typically use a procedure in which all participants receive a treatment, but those in the control group actually receive a placebo treatment. A placebo is a bogus treatment, such as a pill, "drug," or other substance without any significant chemical properties or active ingredient.

Source: R. Feldman, *Understanding Psychology* (New York: McGraw-Hill, 1999), p. 54.

Topic: _____

Main idea: _____

_____

Question #1: _____

Visual representation:

Take One Minute

Define *methods of organization*, list four of them, and provide at least three OWCs for each

Sequence

When authors use the **sequence** method of organization, they show the steps in a process or the chronological order of certain events. This organizational method is used not just to list ideas or events, but to highlight the fact that the order in which they occurred is important. Table 8.6 provides examples of organizational words that signal an author's use of the sequence method.

TABLE 8.6   SEQUENCE OWCs

first	second	then	next	following
first direction	order of events	stages	phases	process
steps	eras	events	cycles	sequence
procedures	treatments	rules	growth	

Read the following textbook excerpt and note that the italicized words and phrases are sequence OWCs:

> There were a *series of events* that shaped Goins's life. He went to the South *after first* taking a degree from Earlham College in his native Indiana and studying business administration in graduate school at Northwestern University. *Next,* he taught accounting and business courses at the Agricultural and Technical College in Greensboro before he was hired away by the Mutual to develop a statistical department in the home office. *Then,* over the years, he served in a variety of positions, including assistant manager and director of public relations. He enhanced his business skills with literary–philosophic interests, and unofficially he served as Company ideologue and speechwriter for C.C. Spaulding.
>
> **Source:** Adapted from W. Weare, *Black Business in the New South: A Social History of the North Carolina Mutual Life Insurance Company* (Durham: Duke University Press, 1993), pp. 110–111.

Here are some examples of the types of sequence questions an instructor might ask based on the previous excerpt, and therefore the kind you should ask yourself before a test:

- What happened after Goins earned a degree from Earlham?

- What were the events that led up to Goins becoming a speechwriter?

After reading the textbook excerpt and identifying the author's method of organization as sequence, you could visually represent the text information as shown in Figure 8.6.

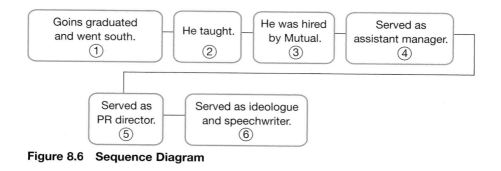

Figure 8.6   Sequence Diagram

Sequence

Read the following text excerpt and underline the OWCs. Identify the topic and main idea of the passage. Predict two questions a professor might ask if he or she used sequence OWCs in the question stems. Visually represent the excerpt, using Figure 8.6 as an example.

The basic steps of any digital computer system, regardless of its size or sophistication, are (1) input, (2) memory or storage, (3) control, (4) processing and (5) output. First, in order for a computer to follow instructions and perform calculations, the instructions and data must be entered into the computer. Various methods can be used to input such instruction and data.

Source: A. Antel and S. Porter, *A Survey of Mathematics with Applications,* 2nd ed. (Reading, MA: Addison–Wesley, 1985), pp. 610–611.

Topic: _____

Main idea: _____

_____

Question #1: _____

_____

Question #2: _____

Visual representation:

Identifying Methods of Organization

Based on what you have learned about methods of organization, see if you can identify which ones are used in the following excerpts. As you read, look for word clues that will indicate how the author is trying to convey his or her message. If you get stuck, go back to the lists of OWCs provided for each organizational method. While they do not include *all* the organizational word clues an author could possibly use, they do provide examples of the types of words authors use for each method, and can give you clues to the pattern an author is using.

Exercise 8g	## Identifying Methods of Organization

Read the following paragraphs and identify which organizational method the author uses in each. Underline all the OWCs. For each paragraph, develop a question that you would expect a professor to ask if you were to be tested on the information. Make sure you use the OWCs you find in your question stems. Finally, (when asked) create a visual representation of the information in each paragraph. The first one is modeled for you.

MODEL   **1.**   (Chemistry) The science of chemistry focuses on the chemical <u>properties</u> and chemical changes of matter. The <u>chemical properties</u> of matter are descriptions of how a substance interacts with other substances. Like physical properties, the <u>chemical properties</u> of matter are closely related to how materials are used.

One chemical <u>property</u> is reactivity. Some substances readily interact chemically with other substances. Many metals are highly reactive and tend to combine with other substances to form compounds. Corrosion is a common example of the reactivity of metals. Iron, copper, and most other metals tend to corrode when exposed to the atmosphere. Aluminum and some other metals do not readily corrode. They react with oxygen in the air to form a thin oxide film. This film protects the metal from further corrosion.

Source: C. Metcalfe and J. Williams, *Modern Chemistry* (New York: Holt, Rinehart and Winston, 1986), pp. 17–18.

Method of organization: <u>Analysis. Although the author uses examples</u> and provides definitions, the overall purpose of this paragraph is to analyze the chemical property, reactivity. You may have wanted to underline chemical changes in the first sentence, but they are not the focus or topic of this paragraph, although it is quite possible the author will discuss them in a later paragraph.

Question: <u>What is one of the many chemical properties of matter</u>

Visual representation:

Chemical properties of matter

One chemical property: reactivity (one property identified in paragraph)

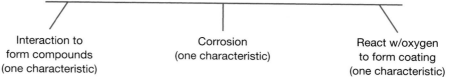

| Interaction to form compounds (one characteristic) | Corrosion (one characteristic) | React w/oxygen to form coating (one characteristic) |

2. (Geography) These facts have serious implications. They tell us a great deal about the impact geography and especially climate have on the people of an area and their economy. Much of Eurasia is subject to great ranges of temperature. Russia and the former Soviet Union have occupied a very extensive landmass with no large bodies of water to modify temperature extremes. Thus, much of Siberia can be blisteringly hot in the summer and frigidly cold in the winter.

Source: Richards and Vaillant, *From Russia to USSR and Beyond,* 2nd ed. (White Plains, NY: Longman, 1993), pp. 4–5.

Method of organization: _____

Question: _____

Visual representation:

3. (History) John Brown, a fanatical abolitionist, led a band of some twenty men in a raid against the federal arsenal at Harper's Ferry in Virginia. Brown hoped to secure guns, arm the nearby Blacks, and lead a slave rebellion. He was caught and tried for treason. In the North, Brown was honored for having sacrificed his life for human liberty. However, in the South, Brown was despised as a dangerous criminal.

Source: I. Gordon, *American History, Review Text* (New York: AMSCO School Publications, 1984), p. 163.

Method of organization: _____

Question: _____

_____

Visual representation:

4. (Physical science) For many solids, solubility increases as temperatures rise and solubility decreases as temperatures drop. With an increase in temperature, a solid's particles move faster and spread farther apart. This process allows more room in a liquid for dissolved particles.

On the other hand, an increase in temperature decreases the solubility of a gas in a liquid. When the solution's temperature increases, the speed of the dissolved gas particles increases. As the dissolved gas particles gain energy, they tend to leave the solution. (1990).

Source: *Physical Science,* Teacher's Annotated Edition (Glenview, IL: Scott Foresman, 1990), pp. 208–209.

Method of organization: _____

Question: _____

_____

Visual representation:

5. (Biology) Blood returning to the heart from the body tissues is low in oxygen and high in carbon dioxide. This blood first enters the right atrium and flows into the right ventricle. Next, the right ventricle pumps it through the pulmonary arteries to the lungs. The pulmonary arteries are the only arteries that carry oxygen-poor blood. All other arteries carry oxygen-rich blood. As the blood travels through the capillaries in the lungs, it gains oxygen and gets rid of carbon dioxide.

Source: Cebco, *Biology: The Study of Life*, Teacher's Edition (Newton, MA: Allyn and Bacon, 1987), p. 155.

Method of organization: _____

Question: _____

Visual representation:

6. (Mathematics) When solving mathematical "word problems,"... look for a goal: What do I want to find out? The value of identifying the goal is illustrated by a well-known English rhyme that poses a problem:

As I was going to Saint Ives
I met a man with seven wives;
Every wife had seven sacks;
Every sack had seven cats;
Every cat had seven kits.
Kits, cats, sacks and wives—
How many were going to Saint Ives?

Source: J. Growney, *Mathematics in Daily Life: Making Decisions and Solving Problems* (New York: McGraw-Hill, 1986), p. 12.

Method of organization: _____

Question: _____

7. (Law) Miranda vs. Arizona (1966)—Issue: Self-Incrimination and Right to Counsel. Ernesto Miranda was picked up by the police for questioning about kidnapping and assaulting a young woman. His confession was used in court and helped to convict him. This case was appealed on the ground that the police had denied the suspect his Constitutional protection against self-incrimination. As a result, there was a 5-to-4 decision overturning the conviction; the Supreme Court expanded the Escobedo case doctrine. The majority opinion held that, before questioning, the police must inform the suspect of his rights to remain silent and to legal counsel, and must warn him that his remarks may be used against him. The dissenting judges attacked the opinion for enabling criminals to gain freedom on technicalities. In a second trial Miranda was found guilty upon testimony of his common-law wife.

Source: I. Gordon, *American History* (New York: AMSCO School Publications, 1984), p. 94.

Method of organization: _____

Question: _____

_____

Visual representation:

8. (Literature/history) English literature is older than books. There was literature in England for hundreds of years before the first printed book. It was an oral literature, a literature sung, chanted, recited; and those who listened to it were never alone. They heard it in groups, sometimes as small as a family, sometimes as large as a band of warriors sitting in a hall with a chieftain at their head. The earliest English literature was social, communal—and noisy. It was close to the experience of daily life, not something one studied by oneself, but something one understood in experiencing it with others. There was no reading public. There was, rather, a live, expectant, sometimes vigorously participating audience.

The first English literature that we know much about was composed by professional poets called scops who sang to warrior bands of the deeds of their forefathers and kinsmen. The scop sometimes was assisted by a gleeman, a subordinate who memorized the scop's compositions and recited them, not letter-perfect, but "sound-perfect." Both must have had prodigious memories, for they could apparently recite for hours, even days, without stopping or forgetting. They could not depend on a book to get their stories right, for the story or the poem had nothing to do with writing. They spoke their poetry as they learned it or invented it, by heart, not by eye.

Source: R. Bennett, *English Literature: Ginn Literature Series* (New York: Ginn and Company, 1986), p. 4.

Method of organization: _____

Question: _____

Visual representation:

9. (Chemistry) There are several phases of matter. A block of ice is a solid. When it melts, it forms a liquid. When liquid water evaporates, it forms a gas. Iron is another familiar solid that melts and becomes a liquid if its temperature is high enough. At a temperature near that of the surface of the sun, liquid iron boils to form a gas, iron vapor. Materials exist either in the solid, liquid, or gas phase and may undergo changes of phase under suitable conditions.

Source: Cebco, *Biology: The Study of Life* (Newton, MA: Allyn and Bacon, 1987), pg. 8.

Method of organization: _____

Question: _____

Visual representation:

Team Up!

With two or three other students, discuss your responses to the previous exercise. Also, discuss the contrasts or differences between the various organizational methods. What distinguishes them from one another?

Organizational Methods in Longer Readings

Textbook assignments for classes will obviously be longer than one or two paragraphs. Look at the entire reading, whether it be 10 pages or a whole chapter, and come to a conclusion about the overall method of organization. Determining an author's overall method of organization requires you to look at how *all* of the paragraphs in a reading assignment are organized *with respect to each other*. Doing this will help you confirm what the main idea of the entire reading is, enabling you to develop effective practice test questions. For example, in a biology chapter on the characteristics of mammals, an author might use a listing organization to discuss the specific characteristics of certain mammals in the introductory paragraphs, but organize the chapter as a whole using the analysis method. The listing pattern would introduce and support the overall organizational pattern of analysis, characteristics of mammals. The phrase *characteristics of mammals* would be a significant clue to detecting the overall organizational pattern, and would probably figure in the title of the chapter.

Here's an example from a work of fiction titled *The Life and Times of the Last Kid Picked.* Word clues are underlined and followed by notes indicating which ones you would use to identify the author's overall method of organization, and which ones just signal how individual ideas are related.

Fat Vinny, who was one grade above mine, and therefore technically none of my responsibility, was so detested by everyone in school that his presence on the playground incited periodic riots. After *[word clue indicating time order but not the overall organization]* participating once in an anti–Fat Vinny demonstration, throwing sticks and rocks at him as he retreated toward school, cordoned off by his bodyguards—Fat Vinny was the only kid I ever knew who paid other kids to protect him from spontaneous assault by mobs of disgusted schoolmates—I was overcome with shame and remorse. Would Jesus have pitched pebbles at Fat Vinny and chanted, "Fat Vinny's full of greasy grimy gopher guts, greasy grimy gopher guts, greasy grimy gopher guts," over and over, in bad harmony with the apostles, 'til he was hoarse? This was a question that needed no answer.

A few weeks later *[word clue indicating time order but not the overall organization]*, I approached Fat Vinny in an aisle at the Red Owl store. He didn't recognize me as one of his tormentors. He had too many enemies to actually pick faces out of the ugly mob. So I had to introduce myself before I apologized, and then had to remind him of the particular riot for which I was sorry. Fat Vinny, intuiting that in me he had found a live one, forgave me on the spot and agreed to let me help him in his various downtown hustles. Fat Vinny was a twelve-year-old entrepreneur. He had the franchise on shoveling snow in front of most of the twenty or thirty bars in downtown Tomah, and the exclusive rights to distribute advertising flyers for the Coast-to-Coast Store, S&Q Hardware, both drugstores, and sundry other retail outlets. In getting to know Fat Vinny over the next year, I learned the main reason why *[word clue indicating cause and effect but not overall organization]* other kids hated him so passionately. He was—in kid terms—rich. Because *[word clue indicating cause and effect but not overall organization]* he had so many schemes working all the time, he always had pocket money that came in bills, not coins. In those days, the average kid's allowance topped off at fifty cents a week. The only known income source beyond that was a paper route, which earned your average kid about three bucks a week, maybe—except Freddy Foss, a workaholic geek who earned twice as much as anybody else, because *[word clue indicating cause and effect but not overall organization]* he had 120 customers on his *La Crosse Tribune* route, which ran literally from one end of the town to the other, and took three or four hours a day, except for collecting—which was literally a full-time job three days a week. Freddy Foss sacrificed his childhood to the *La Crosse Tribune*.

Another reason *[word clue indicating listing organization]* to hate Fat Vinny was that he was a piker. If he could find a sucker to help him do his chores on Superior Avenue, he'd let the sucker do all the work, collect five bucks from the bartender at the Hofbrau or old man Sorenson at the Tomah Hardware, and then Fat Vinny would turn around and give his helper—often me—a quarter. Fat Vinny knew a quarter was a fortune to a kid in those days. But *[word clue indicating contrast but not overall organization]* even I figured out eventually that a fifty-fifty split on five bucks was more than two bits.

Still, the main reason *[word clue indicating listing organization]* kids hated Fat Vinny—kids who didn't even go to the same school, kids who'd never met him, never talked to him, rarely even set eyes on Fat Vinny—was that Fat Vinny was the worst kind of fat. He was fat in that sloppy, droopy, voluptuous way that forty-year-old men are fat. Fat Vinny was adult-fat, and he was adult-ugly. Fat Vinny's ugly was sneery and vulgar and degenerate. You could see in Fat Vinny, at age twelve, the seeds of a sleazy adulthood, full of spilled booze, petty crime, mean swindles, and trailer park sex with underage girls. Kids sensed in Fat Vinny the worst possibilities of their own future, and they recoiled.

Source: David Benjamin, *The Life and Times of the Last Kid Picked* (New York: Random House, 2002), pp. 11–13.

Fat Vinny is the topic of the excerpt and *Kids hate Fat Vinny for many reasons* is the main idea. The author uses word clues that signal the sequence, or order of events, and the causes (reasons for) and effects of the kids' hatred. But the overall organizational method he uses is listing. Throughout the passage he lists the many reasons why kids hated Fat

Vinny and uses organizational word clues to draw your attention to the items on the list. See Figure 8.7 for a visual representation of this listing organization.

Reasons kids hate Fat Vinny (subject)

He was rich.	(detail 1)
He was a piker.	(detail 2)
He was the worst kind of fat.	(detail 3)

Figure 8.7 Hating Fat Vinny

Almost every word clue in this excerpt was noted in order to show, in an obvious, step-by-step way, the logical skeleton of the author's ideas. Use this model to heighten your awareness of the usefulness of word clues in signaling overall methods organization. As you practice the strategy of detecting OWCs it is handy to physically mark them as you find them. Once you become more proficient in locating word clues, you will find you do not have to mark each one. Instead, you will mentally note idea patterns as you read and become aware of the author's overall blueprint for presenting his or her main idea.

Exercise 8h

Internet Exercise

Journalists typically omit organizational word clues because they have a limited amount of space for their stories, and they want to reserve as much space as possible for content. Access the following Internet source: **www.ABCNEWS.com** and pick a story. Print it out, read it, and infer the overall organizational method. Add OWCs that you think would help others identify the overall organizational method, ones the writer might have used if space had not been a constraint.

Practice with Reading Passage

Answer all questions on a separate sheet of paper.

Reading Practice

Excerpt from *Wild Swans*
BY JUNG CHANG

PREPARE TO READ

1. Based on the title, what do you expect the reading to be about? What do you think the topic is?

2. What do you already know about the topic?

3. Below is a list of vocabulary words that might be unfamiliar to you. Look them up, if necessary, and refer to the definitions as you encounter these words in the reading.

   a. plait

   b. demure

   c. connoisseur

   d. demonstrative

   e. disdain

   f. concubine

4. Study-read the essay and circle all the OWCs. Identify the overall organizational method used by the author and explain how you determined what it was. Create a visual representation for one of the paragraphs, which is appropriate for the method of organization used in that paragraph. Discuss your visual with a classmate.

Wild Swans

My grandmother was a beauty. She had an oval face, with rosy cheeks and lustrous skin. Her long, shiny black hair was woven into a thick plait reaching down to her waist. She could be demure when the occasion demanded, which was most of the time, but underneath her composed exterior she was bursting with suppressed energy. She was petite, about five feet three inches, with a slender figure and sloping shoulders, which were considered the ideal.

But her greatest assets were her bound feet, called in Chinese "three-inch golden lilies" (san-tsun-gin-lian). This meant she walked "like a tender young willow shoot in a spring breeze," as a Chinese connoisseur of women traditionally put it. The sight of a woman teetering on bound feet was supposed to have an erotic effect on men, partly because her vulnerability induced a feeling of protectiveness in the onlooker.

My grandmother's feet had been bound when she was two years old. Her mother, who herself had bound feet, first wound a piece of white cloth about twenty feet long round her feet, bending all the toes except the big toe inward and under the sole. Then she placed a large stone on top to crush the arch. My grandmother screamed in agony and begged her to stop. Her mother had to stick a cloth into her mouth to gag her. My grandmother passed out repeatedly from the pain.

The process lasted several years. Even after the bones had been broken, the feet had to be bound day and night in thick cloth because the moment they were released they would try to recover. For years my grandmother lived in relentless, excruciating pain. When she pleaded with her mother to untie the bindings, her mother would weep and tell her that unbound feet would ruin her entire life, and that she was doing it for her own future happiness.

In those days, when a woman was married, the first thing the bride-groom's family did was to examine her feet. Large feet, meaning normal feet, were considered to bring shame on the husband's household. The mother-in-law would lift the hem of the bride's long skirt, and if the feet were more than about four inches long, she would throw down the skirt in a demonstrative gesture of contempt and stalk off, leaving the bride to the crit-ical gaze of the wedding guests, who would stare at her feet and insultingly mutter their disdain. Sometimes a mother would take pity on her daughter and remove the binding cloth; but when the child grew up and had to endure the contempt of her husband's family and the disapproval of society, she would blame her mother for having been too weak.

The practice of binding feet was originally introduced about a thousand years ago, allegedly by a concubine of the emperor. Not only was the sight of women hobbling on tiny feet considered erotic, men would also get excited playing with bound feet, which were always hidden in embroidered silk shoes. Women could not remove the binding cloths even when they were adults, as their feet would start growing again. The binding could only be loosened temporarily at night in bed, when they would put on soft-soled shoes. Men rarely saw naked bound feet, which were usually covered in rotting flesh and stank when the bindings were removed. As a child, I can remember my grandmother being in constant pain. When we came home from shopping, the first thing she would do was soak her feet in a bowl of hot water, sigh-ing with relief as she did so. Then she would set about cutting off pieces of dead skin. The pain came not only from the broken bones, but also from her toenails, which grew into the balls of her feet.

Source: Jung Chang, from *Wild Swans* (Simon & Schuster, 1991), pp. 23-25.

CHECK YOUR UNDERSTANDING

OBJECTIVE QUESTIONS

1. What was the author's grandmother's greatest asset?

   a. Her oval face.

   b. Her lustrous skin.

   c. Her bound feet.

   d. Her long, shiny black hair.

2. Why did the sight of bound feet have an erotic effect on men?

   a. Because women with bound feet walked like a tender young wil-low shoot in a spring breeze.

b. Because a woman's vulnerability brought out a feeling of protectiveness in others who looked at her.

c. Because a woman's vulnerability made her want to help people.

d. Because a woman's vulnerability was repugnant to Chinese society.

3. Why did the grandmother's mother stick a cloth in the grandmother's mouth?

   a. To give her something to bite down on in order to help her endure the pain.

   b. To complete the ritual of the foot binding process.

   c. To make her stop screaming.

   d. To wipe up the spit that came out when she screamed.

4. Based on the reading, the author seems:

   a. Happy that women had their feet bound.

   b. Jealous that she didn't have her feet bound.

   c. Regretful that she couldn't protect her grandmother.

   d. Empathetic toward her grandmother's family.

5. According to the author, how long did the process of foot binding last?

   a. Several years.

   b. Until a girl was two years old.

   c. Until a girl married.

   d. Until a woman objected.

SHORT-ANSWER QUESTIONS

6. According to the author, what would happen when a mother took pity on her daughter and removed the binding cloth?

7. How did the practice of binding feet first come about?

8. How would you describe the author's feelings about the practice of foot binding in her family?

9. What can you infer about the relationship between a husband and wife in China during the grandmother's youth?

10. What was the main idea of the reading selection?

Chapter Summary

Textbook authors usually organize information using certain classic methods or patterns. Being able to recognize organizational methods (listing, analysis, cause/effect, comparison/contrast, definition/example, and sequence) will help you understand the ideas in your textbooks and how they are connected to each other, because they will fit into logical patterns you are already familiar with. It will also help you to remember what you have read, because you are not memorizing facts in isolation, but relating them to each other to form patterns that hold and organize them in your memory. A useful way to identify an author's method of organization is to look for the organizational word clues (OWCs) that indicate which patterns he or she is using. It is also important to assess an author's overall method of organization. An author will frequently use more than one method from paragraph to paragraph, but have one overall method for each textbook chapter.

Post Test

Answer the following questions on a separate sheet of paper.

Part I

OBJECTIVE QUESTIONS

1. Match the vocabulary words in Column A to their correct definitions in Column B:

A	**B**
1. OWCs	a. Method author uses to show why something happened and the effects that occurred as a result.
2. Listing	b. Method that defines a concept to clarify meaning —may use examples and analogies.
3. Analysis	c. Organizational word clues.
4. Cause/Effect	d. Method that focuses on similarities and differences.
5. Comparison/Contrast	e. Method that lists a series of ideas or items, alphabetically, by category.

6.   Definition/Example

f.   Method that breaks apart a con-
     cept—presents basic elements.

7.   Sequence

g.   Method that shows steps or ideas
     the chronological order of
     events.

2.   An author's topic and his or her purpose will determine which organizational method
     he or she will use. True False

3.   Circle all the OWCs you would find in a passage organized using the compare/con-
     trast method of organization:

     a.   First.

     b.   On the other hand.

     c.   Because.

     d.   However.

4.   Read the following sentence and identify the organizational method used in it:
     There were three primary reasons for the fall of the G-Mart chain of stores.

     a.   Sequence.

     b.   Cause/Effect.

     c.   Definition.

     d.   Analysis.

5.   Read the following sentence and identify the organizational method used in it: Com-
     puters have often been compared to the human brain.

     a.   Sequence.

     b.   Compare/Contrast.

     c.   Analysis.

     d.   Listing.

Part II

Reading Passage

Why the Young Kill
BY SHARON BEGLEY

1.   Based on the title, what do you expect the article to be about? What do you think
     the topic is?

2.   What do you already know about the topic?

3.   Study-read the following excerpt. On separate index cards, write the main idea and the method of organization for each paragraph. (There are 12 paragraphs.)

4.   Organize the index cards into piles of organizational patterns.

5.   What is the overall organizational pattern?

6.   What is the overall main idea of the reading?

7.   Write three questions that an instructor might ask using the overall method of organization OWCs in your questions.

Why the Young Kill

1   Temptation, of course, is to seize on one cause, one single explanation for Littleton, and West Paducah, and Jonesboro, and all the other towns that have acquired iconic status the way "Dallas" or "Munich" did for earlier generations. Surely the cause is having access to guns. Or being a victim of abuse at the hands of parents or peers. Or being immersed in a culture that glorifies violence and revenge. But there isn't one cause. And while that makes stemming the tide of youth violence a lot harder, it also makes it less of an unfathomable mystery. Science has a new understanding of the roots of violence that promises to explain why not every child with access to guns becomes an Eric Harris or a Dylan Klebold, and why not every child who feels ostracized, or who embraces the Goth esthetic goes on a murderous rampage.

2   It should be said right off that attempts to trace violence to biology have long been tainted by racism, eugenics, and plain old poor science. The turbulence of the 1960s led some physicians to advocate psychosurgery to "treat those people with low violence thresholds," as one 1967 letter to a medical journal put it. In other words, lobotomize the civil rights and antiwar protesters. And if crimes are disproportionately committed by some ethnic groups, then finding genes or other traits common to that group risks tarring millions of innocent people. At the other end of the political spectrum, many conservatives view biological theories of violence as the mother of all insanity defenses, with biology not merely an explanation but an excuse. The conclusions emerging from interdisciplinary research in neuroscience and psychology, however, are not so simple-minded as to argue that violence is in the genes, or murder in the folds of the brain's frontal lobes. Instead, the picture is more nuanced, based as it is on the discovery that experience rewires the brain. The dawning realization of the constant back-and-forth between nature and nurture has resurrected the search for the biological roots of violence.

3   Early experiences seem to be especially powerful: a child's brain is more malleable than that of an adult. The dark side of the zero-to-3 movement, which emphasizes the huge potential for learning during this period, is that the young brain also is extra vulnerable to hurt in the first years of life. A child who suffers repeated "hits" of stress—abuse, neglect, terrorism—experiences physical changes in his brain, finds Dr. Bruce Perry of Baylor College of Medicine. The

incessant flood of stress chemicals tends to reset the brain's system of fight-or-flight hormones, putting them on hair-trigger alert. The result is the kid who shows impulsive aggression, the kid who pops the classmate who disses him. For the outcast, hostile confrontations—not necessarily an elbow to the stomach at recess, but merely kids vacating en masse when he sits down in the cafeteria—increase the level of stress hormones in his brain. And that can have dangerous consequences. "The early environment programs the nervous system to make an individual more or less reactive to stress," says biologist Michael Meaney of McGill University."If parental care is inadequate or unsupportive, the [brain] may decide that the world stinks—and it better be ready to meet the challenge." This, then, is how having an abusive parent raises the risk of youth violence: it can change a child's brain. Forever after, influences like the mean-spiritedness that schools condone or the humiliation that's standard fare in adolescence pummel the mind of the child whose brain has been made excruciatingly vulnerable to them.

4   In other children, constant exposure to pain and violence can make their brain's system of stress hormones unresponsive, like a keypad that has been pushed so often it just stops working. These are the kids with antisocial personalities. They typically have low heart rates and impaired emotional sensitivity. Their signature is a lack of empathy, and their sensitivity to the world around them is practically nonexistent. Often they abuse animals: Kip Kinkel, the 15-year-old who killed his parents and shot 24 schoolmates last May, had a history of this; Luke Woodham, who killed three schoolmates and wounded seven at his high school in Pearl, Miss., in 1997, had previously beaten his dog with a club, wrapped it in a bag, and set it on fire. These are also the adolescents who do not respond to punishment: nothing hurts. Their ability to feel, to react, has died, and so has their conscience. Hostile, impulsive aggressors usually feel sorry afterward. Antisocial aggressors don't feel at all. Paradoxically, though, they often have a keen sense of injustices aimed at themselves.

5   Inept parenting encompasses more than outright abuse, however. Parents who are withdrawn and remote, neglectful and passive, are at risk of shaping a child who (absent a compensating source of love and attention) shuts down emotionally. It's important to be clear about this: inadequate parenting short of Dickensian neglect generally has little ill effect on most children. But to a vulnerable baby, the result of neglect can be tragic. Perry finds that neglect impairs the development of the brain's cortex, which controls feelings of belonging and attachment. "When there are experiences in early life that result in an underdeveloped capacity [to form relationships]," says Perry , "kids have a hard time empathizing with people. They tend to be relatively passive and perceive themselves to be stomped on by the outside world."

Risk Factors

Having any of the following risk factors doubles a boy's chance of becoming a murderer:

- Coming from a family with a history of criminal violence.

- Being abused.
- Belonging to a gang.
- Abusing drugs or alcohol.
- Having any of these risk factors, in addition to the above, triples the risk of becoming a killer.
- Using a weapon.
- Having been arrested.
- Having a neurological problem that impairs thinking or feeling.
- Having had problems at school

6   These neglected kids are the ones who desperately seek a script, an ideology that fits their sense of being humiliated and ostracized. Today's pop culture offers all too many dangerous ones, from the music of Rammstein to the game of Doom. Historically, most of those scripts have featured males. That may explain, at least in part, why the murderers are Andrews and Dylans rather than Ashleys and Kaitlins, suggests Deborah Prothrow-Smith of the Harvard School of Public Health. "But girls are now 25 percent of the adolescents arrested for violent crime," she notes. "This follows the media portrayal of girl superheroes beating people up," from Power Rangers to Xena. Another reason that the schoolyard murderers are boys is that girls tend to internalize ostracism and shame rather than turning it into anger. And just as girls could be the next wave of killers, so could even younger children. "Increasingly, we're seeing the high-risk population for lethal violence as being the 10- to 14-year-olds," says Richard Lieberman, a school psychologist in Los Angeles. "Developmentally, their concept of death is still magical. They still think it's temporary, like little Kenny in 'South Park.'" Of course, there are loads of empty , emotionally unattached girls and boys. The large majority won't become violent. "But if they're in a violent environment," says Perry, "they're more likely to."

7   There seems to be a genetic component to the vulnerability that can turn into anti-social-personality disorder. It is only a tiny bend in the twig, but depending on how the child grows up, the bend will be exaggerated or straightened out. Such aspects of temperament as "irritability, impulsivity, hyperactivity, and a low sensitivity to emotions in others are all biologically based," says psychologist James Garbarino of Cornell University, author of the upcoming *Lost Boys: Why Our Sons Turn Violent and How We Can Save Them*. A baby who is unreactive to hugs and smiles can be left to go her natural, antisocial way if frustrated parents become exasperated, withdrawn, neglectful, or enraged. Or that child can be pushed back toward the land of the feeling by parents who never give up trying to engage and stimulate and form a loving bond with her. The different responses of parents produce different brains, and thus behaviors. "Behavior is the result of a dialogue between your brain and your experiences," concludes Debra Niehoff, author of the recent book *The Biology of Violence*. "Although people are born with some biological givens, the brain has many

blank pages. From the first moments of childhood the brain acts as a historian, recording our experiences in the language of neurochemistry ."

8   There are some out-and-out brain pathologies that lead to violence. Lesions of the frontal lobe can induce apathy and distort both judgment and emotion. In the brain scans he has done in his Fairfield, Calif., clinic of 50 murderers, psychiatrist Daniel Amen finds several shared patterns. The structure called the cingulate gyrus, curving through the center of the brain, is hyperactive in murderers. The CG acts like the brain's transmission, shifting from one thought to another. When it is impaired, people get stuck on one thought. Also, the prefrontal cortex, which seems to act as the brain's supervisor, is sluggish in the 50 murderers. "If you have violent thoughts that you're stuck on and no supervisor, that's a prescription for trouble," says Amen, author of *Change Your Brain/Change Your Life*. The sort of damage he finds can result from head trauma as well as exposure to toxic substances like alcohol during gestation.

9   Children who kill are not, with very few exceptions, amoral. But their morality is aberrant. "I killed because people like me are mistreated every day," said pudgy, bespectacled Luke Woodham, who murdered three students. "My whole life I felt outcasted, alone." So do a lot of adolescents. The difference is that at least some of the recent school killers felt emotionally or physically abandoned by those who should love them. Andrew Golden, who was 11 when he and Mitchell Johnson, 13, went on their killing spree in Jonesboro, Ark., was raised mainly by his grandparents while his parents worked. Mitchell mourned the loss of his father to divorce.

10   Unless they have another source of unconditional love, such boys fail to develop, or lose, the neural circuits that control the capacity to feel and to fond healthy relationships. That makes them hypersensitive to perceived injustice. A sense of injustice is often accompanied by a feeling of abject powerlessness. An adult can often see his way to restoring a sense of self-worth, says psychiatrist James Gilligan of Harvard Medical School, through success in work or love. A child usually lacks the emotional skills to do that. As one killer told Garbarino's colleague, "I'd rather be wanted for murder than not wanted at all."

11   That the Littleton massacre ended in suicide may not be a coincidence. As Michael Carneal was wrestled to the ground after killing three fellow students in Paducah in 1997, he cried out, "Kill me now!" Kip Kinkel pleaded with the schoolmates who stopped him, "Shoot me!" With suicide "you get immortality," says Michael Flynn of John Jay College of Criminal Justice. "That is a great feeling of power for an adolescent who has no sense that he matters."

12   The good news is that understanding the roots of violence offers clues on how to prevent it. The bad news is that ever more children are exposed to the influences that, in the already vulnerable, can produce a bent toward murder. Juvenile homicide is twice as common today as it was in the mid-1980s. It isn't the brains kids are born with that has changed in half a generation; what has changed is the ubiquity of violence, the easy access to guns, and the glorification of revenge in real life and in entertainment. To deny the role of these

influences is like denying that air pollution triggers childhood asthma. Yes, to develop asthma a child needs a specific, biological vulnerability. But as long as some children have this respiratory vulnerability—and some always will—then allowing pollution to fill our air will make some children wheeze, and cough, and die. And as long as some children have a neurological vulnerability—and some always will—then turning a blind eye to bad parenting, bullying, and the gun culture will make other children seethe, and withdraw, and kill.

Special thanks to Ms. Linda Talbert, reading instructor at Schoolcraft College, Livonia, Michigan, for her contributions regarding this exercise.

Source: From *Newsweek*, May 3, 1999, pp. 32–35. © 1999 by Newsweek, Inc. all rights reserved. Reprinted by permission.

Website Sources for Additional Practice

Textbook Methods of Organization

http://www.utexas.edu/student/lsc/handouts/553.html: nice chart—different ways to read for different subjects.

http://www.ucc.vt.edu/stdysk/skimming.html: skimming and scanning scientific materials.

Chapter 9

Using Preview, Study-Read, and Review (PSR) Strategies

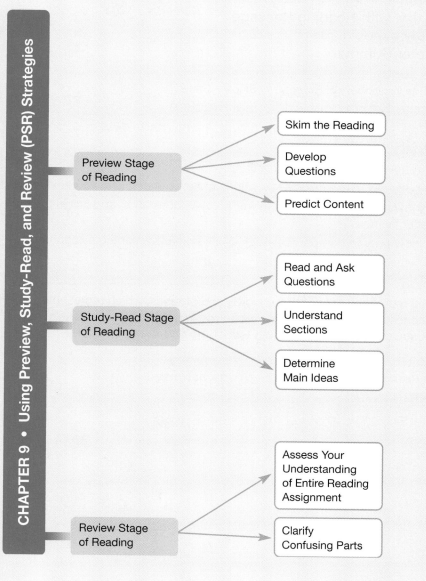

CHAPTER 9 • Using Preview, Study-Read, and Review (PSR) Strategies

Preview Stage of Reading
- Skim the Reading
- Develop Questions
- Predict Content

Study-Read Stage of Reading
- Read and Ask Questions
- Understand Sections
- Determine Main Ideas

Review Stage of Reading
- Assess Your Understanding of Entire Reading Assignment
- Clarify Confusing Parts

Chapter Contents

Chapter Goals

After reading this chapter, you will:

- Know how to use the PSR technique to better understand your textbooks.
- Know how to create and answer preview questions, and judge their effectiveness.
- Know how to paraphrase ideas and summarize reading assignments.

Chapter Vocabulary

As you read, take note of these words and phrases, which represent important concepts from the chapter; they will be in **boldface** print. Make sure you understand them before the post test at the end of the chapter.

preview
study-read
review

summary
paraphrase

Jackie's Journal Entry

I had heard about previewing before this class, but I had never done it. I don't have a lot of time and it just seemed like a lot of extra work. But once I tried it, I noticed it was easier to remember things we had read. I wish I had known about this during my first year in college! I think the thing that surprised me the most was that I was able to come up with really good questions to ask myself. Answering them was hard sometimes but it paid off big time on my exams!

id you know you can learn about casting spells, market economies, alternative lifestyles, and ethics all in the same day? You can even learn about the history of the toilet. Books make all kinds of information available. You just have to know how to get the most out of what you read. The best way to do this is to systematically question yourself before, while, and after you read.

Learning Journal

In your journal, explain how you currently prepare to read a textbook chapter or other reading materials.

Questioning Yourself: Preview, Study-Read, Review (PSR)

The key to **PSR: Preview, Study-Read, Review** is purposeful, direct questioning before, during, and after reading. Creating effective questions about your reading material, and then answering them, helps you confirm that you have correctly identified main ideas and details. *What* you should ask yourself depends on *when* in the reading process you are asking the questions. There are several benefits to questioning yourself at different stages during your reading:

- You establish a purpose for reading, which gets your brain ready to learn.

- You create a mental framework that holds new information in an organized way.

- You give yourself the opportunity to react to what you read and not just accept what an author is saying.

- You read more closely because you are looking for answers to your questions.

Source: J. Steiner 1999 *Look-Alikes, Jr.* Little, Brown, & Co. pp. 18–19.

Preview Stage of Reading

When you **preview** a chapter you develop a framework to fill in as you read. Previewing allows you to assess how difficult a chapter is so you can allot an appropriate amount of time for studying it. Previewing also encourages you to read actively. By asking questions, predicting textbook content, and hypothesizing about the main idea, you are participating in a conversation with the author. As an example of how questioning can enhance and direct your reading, complete the following exercise.

Previewing

Cover the questions below. Now look at the picture on page 286 and take one minute to remember as many details from it as you can. Then cover the picture and answer the following questions on a separate sheet of paper.

1. How many Rice Chex are pictured in the crane?

2. What are used for wheels on the truck?

3. How many vehicles are visible in the picture?

4. How many animals are visible in the scene?

5. How many items are used to make the mixing truck?

6. Where is the ice cream cone?

7. Is the stick of gum on the left or right side of the picture?

8. What items are used to make the plane?

9. How many trees are in the picture and what is used to make the trees?

10. How many dice are visible?

11. What object is next to the wheelbarrow?

12. List at least 12 food items that are visible in the picture.

This exercise demonstrates how the preview concept works. If you had known what the questions were before you looked at the picture, do you think you would have known more of the answers? You are probably thinking, "Of course!" By developing questions *before* you read, you focus better as you actively search for their answers; you create a purpose for reading. You will find that consistently developing questions, and answering them as you read, will help you understand and remember more of your reading assignments.

Steps for Previewing a Reading Assignment

Step 1: Skim the reading.

Step 2: Develop questions.

Step 3: Predict content.

Step 1: Skim the Reading

Skim the amount you plan to read in one episode of reading. Skimming means reading quickly, skipping details and focusing on the title of the chapter, the introduction, each subheading and the summary. For textbooks you should also read any questions at the end of the chapter.

Step 2: Develop Questions

Reread the title and subheadings and develop questions about them using these six words: *who, what, when, why, where,* and *how*. Although many of the questions you create during the preview stage will be very basic, they will help you pay closer attention as you read. As you become more proficient at preview questioning, you will probably be able to ask the questions in your head; but while you are learning this technique, write out your questions and predictions in your journal.

Here is a list containing the title and headings from a chapter in a book titled *An Underground Education,* which provides little-known facts from history. For step one of the preview process you would read the title and headings. The questions you might then develop from them, for step two, are modeled in italics.

Title: **EVERYDAY LIFE**

What historical facts are there about everyday life?

Headings: **The Toilet Training of the Human Race**

How was the human race toilet trained?

The Evolution of Underwear

How did underwear evolve?

The Underside of Breastfeeding

What is the underside of breastfeeding?

Missteps in Men's Fashion

What were some of the missteps in men's fashion?

Hair Strategies through the Ages

What were some hair strategies through the ages?

The Smell of History: Filthy Saints

Were saints filthy?

Etiquette Rules for Breaking Wind and Bread

What were the rules for breaking wind and bread?

When Men Were Men and Wives Were Chattel

What happened when men were men and wives were chattel?

Flogging Knowledge into Young Scholars

Why were young scholars flogged?

Curse Words before Today's Four-Letter Drudgery

What curse words were popular in the past?

Painfully Odd Entertainment

What was painful about the entertainment? Why was it considered entertainment if it was painful?

Step 3: Predict Content

Predict what you think a reading assignment will be about based on the information you have gathered and the questions you have developed. Then consider what else you know about the topic. New information is best remembered when purposely connected to information you already know about a subject. Write your predictions, and what you already know, in your journal. Here is an example from Gill's learning journal:

Predictions about the chapter contents of EVERYDAY LIFE:

This chapter is probably going to talk about small historical facts that are strange, maybe even gross (breaking wind?). All the headings seem to be related to the human body, things you put on (underwear) things you take off (hair, clothes,...hey, underwear too!) things we enjoy (painful entertainment?), relationships. Everyday things. Regular things that people back then just did and didn't really think about that seem strange to us today. Maybe the wig thing will be explained. George Washington and all those guys wearing wigs. What was up with that?

I know that hair was a big thing a long time ago. Men wore wigs. I don't know if women did too. I know people didn't bathe much back then so when women got ready for a party, they put waxy perfume chunks in their hair. As the party went along the room got hotter and the perfume chunks would begin to melt on the women's heads, making them, and the rest of the room, smell good. And I know someone named Crapper invented the toilet. What did they use before toilets?

The purpose of the chapter is probably to make people aware of some of the strange facts that make people from the past more real to us today. I think I'll be surprised by what I read.

Gill might find, after reading the chapter, that some of her initial predictions were inaccurate. For example, the "Painfully Odd Entertainment" heading actually refers to castrated singers, not audiences in pain. She might also find that some of her previous learning ("I know that someone named Crapper invented the toilet") has to be modified: "And if any reader had thought the honor (of inventing the first modern flush toilet) belonged to a Victorian named Sir Thomas Crapper, they've been hoaxed" (p.140). However, the answers to most of her questions will be found in the reading, including the "wig thing."

Exercise 9b

Previewing Practice

Preview the following reading passage. Develop questions, using the title and headings, and predict what information will be covered. Do not read the entire passage yet; you just want to get a general idea of what it's about.

The Microeconomic Players

In the marketplace, people buy and sell goods, services, and factors of production. Microeconomics examines the decisions to buy and sell, or alternatively, the decisions to refrain from buying and selling. Economists place those who participate in the market economy into one of four groups: consumers, firms, factory owners, and government. An individual may fall into two or more of these categories at different times even during a single day, since the categories describe economic functions rather than a person's role in life.

Consumers, firms, and factory owners share a few things in making economic decisions. They all have objectives, or goals, which they hope to promote in market transactions. They all face constraints on their actions, which make it necessary for them to sacrifice some things in order to obtain other things. Finally, they all make choices in ways they feel will promote their own interests.

Consumers

Consumers buy goods and services produced by firms. This advances their objective of maximizing their utility, or satisfaction. Yet very few people can buy all the goods they might like to consume. Consumers' purchases are constrained by their limited incomes and by the positive prices for each good. Each purchase subtracts from the consumer's available income, and eventually nothing remains. Given limited purchasing ability, the consumer will attempt to gain as much utility as possible from each dollar spent. In practice, this is done by choosing to use marginal analysis in making consumption decisions—by comparing the additional (marginal) benefits and additional (marginal) costs of each purchase. We examine how marginal analysis works in the next chapter.

Firms

Firms hire productive factors or resources, combine them in a certain way to produce a final good, then sell that good to consumers. In short, firms play two roles in the economy: They are the buyers of factors and the sellers of goods.

FIRMS AS BUYERS

When they hire workers and other productive factors, the objective of firm managers is to maximize profits. Among other things, this implies that they will hire a mix of factors that will minimize their costs of producing the desired amount of output. Their hiring decisions are constrained by the positive price of factors and by the need to cover opportunity costs. Firm managers achieve their objectives by choosing to hire only those factors that contribute more at the margin to the firm's output and sales receipts than the additional cost of employing them. The marginal analysis employed by firms as buyers is the subject of a later chapter.

FIRMS AS SELLERS

When they decide how many units of a good to produce or what price to charge for it, the objective of firm managers is to maximize profits. If they are successful in purchasing resources and managing the production process, the constraints on sellers are those imposed by consumers, who search for lower prices and higher quality, and competitors, who attempt to undercut prices charged by other sellers or produce a more desirable product.

Source: R. Arnold, *Microeconomics*, 2nd ed. (St. Paul, MN: West Publishing Co., 1992), p. 94.

Your question using the title:

_____

Your questions using the headings:

_____

_____

Your prediction of the passage's content:

_____

What do you already know about the topic?

_____

Learning Journal

Do you already preview your textbooks? In your own words, explain the procedure and the benefits of the previewing stage of reading as presented in this chapter. Then compare this process with what you already do before you read. Are there any parts of the previewing process presented here that you feel would not work for you? Why?

Study-Read Stage of Reading

Study-reading means asking and answering the questions you developed in the preview stage, and relating the text information to what you already know *as you are reading*. Once you think you understand an assignment, it is useful to share what you have learned with a classmate. If you can explain what you have just read and how it relates to what you already know so that someone else understands you, it means you have accurately comprehended the material. If he or she can't understand you, reread the textbook assignment or seek help from your instructor. Fellow classmates can also be wonderful resources as they can sometimes answer questions you may have by explaining passages you didn't understand.

Steps for Study-Reading an Assignment

Step 1: Read and ask questions.

Step 2: Understand sections.

Step 3: Monitor your reading.

Step 4: Determine main ideas.

Step 1: Read and Ask Questions

Start reading at the first heading or subheading, and ask the questions you developed during the preview stage. For example, when you previewed the passage "The Microeconomic Players" (Exercise 9b), you might have asked,

Who are the players? When you study-read the passage, you would be looking for the answer to that and any other questions you developed.

Step 2: Understand Sections

Read one complete part at a time. Read either from heading to heading or, for more challenging material, from paragraph to paragraph. Then pause to ask and answer your previewing questions. Don't read chapters from beginning to end without pausing for questions and answers. Textbook chapters contain too much information to remember all at one time.

Step 3: Monitor Your Reading

Monitor your understanding of what you have read in one section, before moving on to the next, using the following journal prompts:

A. What do I understand about what I have read so far?

B. Where in the text did I lose concentration or become confused?

C. What questions do I still have and how can I answer them?

The first journal prompt helps you separate what you do understand in an assignment from what is still unclear. Sometimes just writing down what you are having difficulty with helps you to clarify it. If you realize, after writing down what you *do* understand from an assignment, that there are still points that are confusing to you, use the second prompt to identify at what place in the text you lost concentration or started having difficulty following the author's train of thought. Sometimes, without careful thought, you can miss precisely where your confusion started, which can lead to your finishing a reading assignment without completely understanding it. Once you know exactly where you became confused, you can use the third prompt to develop questions about the material you don't understand and think about ways to find the answers you need in order to understand it.

Here is an example of how to monitor your reading using these journal prompts.

Journal Prompt A: What Do I Understand?

Michael is reading a chapter from his chemistry text and having difficulty understanding the content. He stops reading, takes out his learning journal, writes the date and the title of the reading assignment at the top right side of his page, and responds to the first prompt.

> Sept. 10
> Ch. 3, pp. 123–151
> The reading assignment begins with an explanation of the atomic theory of matter. Matter has small parts and can be in different combinations. An atom is the smallest part. An element is a

collection of atoms that are all of one type. A compound is a mixture of atoms of two or more elements. A chemical reaction is a rearrangement of atoms.

Journal Prompt B: Where Did I Lose Concentration or Become Confused?

Once he has written down what he does understand, he realizes he is still unclear about parts of the reading, and he continues on to the next reading prompt. After some careful thought, he writes this response:

I became confused when the discussion turned to the law of multiple proportion. (p. 149)

Journal Prompt C: What Questions Do I Have?

Because Michael knows exactly where he became confused in his reading, he is able to develop questions about the material he does not understand and make a plan to find the answers to them.

What is the law of multiple proportions? What is a concrete example of it? How is atomic theory related to the law? Ask study group for concrete examples. I know I'll get it if I can see it in an example. Note: office hours for instructor: Tues. 2—4 P.M.

Notice in this entry that Michael is aware that concrete examples will help him. He knows that if he can "see" the theory in practice, he will be able to understand the reading.

When you've finished reading a section of an assignment, ask yourself the following questions and record your answers in your journal:

- Am I able to answer my preview questions?
- Can I relate this section to what I've read so far in the chapter?
- Can I relate the material to what I already know?

Interrupting your reading to make a journal entry causes you to reflect on what you have just read and ensures that you understand it before you continue with the assignment. Use your study-reading journal entries to clear up any misunderstandings you have about the textbook content before moving on to new material. Comprehension is more important than speed. If you find you understand what you are reading, and stopping to write a journal entry is interrupting your concentration, skip this monitoring step in your journal and write an entry after you have read the entire assignment.

Step 4: Determine Main Ideas

As you finish reading each section, stop and determine what the main idea of that part is.

Team Up!

Find a classmate and explain the study-reading stage to each other. Work with your classmate to create a mnemonic to help you remember the four steps of study-reading. Make your mnemonic as unusual as you can: memory loves oddity.

Exercise 9c

Study-Reading

Study-read the economics passage in Exercise 9b, "The Microeconomic Players," using the four steps of study-reading just discussed. Then make a journal entry using the following prompts to help you assess your understanding. Because you don't have access to the rest of the chapter, you won't be able to answer prompt #2; however, this is an important prompt to use when reading textbook chapters.

1. Am I able to answer my preview questions?

2. Can I relate this section to what I've read so far in the chapter? (No need to answer at this time—but it is a strategy to use when reading an entire chapter.)

3. Can I relate the material to what I already know?

Exercise 9d

Main Idea

Is the main idea of the economics passage "The Microeconomic Players" that *microeconomics looks at the decisions to buy, sell, not to buy, and not to sell things*? Or is it *There are four categories of participants in the economic world: consumers, firms, factory owners, and government*? How do you know? Defend your answer with the tools you have learned.

_____

_____

_____

_____

_____

Review Stage of Reading

In the **review** stage, you ask yourself questions in order to understand what you have read in relation to what you already know about a subject. The purpose of these postreading journal prompts is to assess your overall understanding of the textbook material.

Steps in Reviewing a Reading Assignment

Step 1: Assess your understanding of entire reading assignment.

Step 2: Clarify confusing parts.

Step 1: Assess Your Understanding of Entire Reading Assignment

After study-reading your assignment, use the following prompts to make a final journal entry assessing how well you understand what you have read and pinpointing any areas of confusion:

A. Summarize what you have read.

B. What do you already know about the topic? (attach new information to old)

C. What parts of the reading do you still not understand? (comprehension check)

Review Journal Prompt A: Summarizing What You Read

In order to write your review journal entries, you need to be able to effectively summarize textbook information. When you write a **summary**, your goal is to capture the original meaning of someone else's writing in a brief statement, using your own words and omitting nonessential details. Therefore, your summary will be considerably shorter than the original version. Here are six steps for writing a good summary:

1.) Read your assignment in sections, using the preview and study-reading strategies discussed earlier.

2.) Identify the main idea of *each part* and *paraphrase it in your journal*. **Paraphrasing** means you unpack the meaning of something by explaining it in your own words, making implied ideas and making figurative language concrete. Aim for one or two sentences per main idea.

3.) Pick out the major supporting details from each section—those that explain, exemplify, or otherwise support the main idea of each part—and paraphrase them. Omit all details not essential to understanding the author's main ideas.

4.) Do not add anything to the author's ideas such as your personal opinions on the topic or other information you know about the subject.

5.) Use the same title for your summary as the author uses for the reading assignment. Begin your summary of the entire reading with your version of the author's first main idea. Then, using complete sentences, add the major details that support the first main idea. Repeat this process for all the main ideas and the details that support them using the same order as the author. Connect the ideas together by using words that show how they are related. If the author used a listing method of organization, for example, use organization word clues (OWCs) that indicate this.

6.) Double-check your summary against the author's original writing. Is yours shorter? (It should be.) Although the words are different, are the author's main points restated accurately? (They should be.)

When you write a summary, try not to quote whole sentences from a passage. If you quote the author, you will find that your summary becomes a copy rather than a concise restatement of the author's points. Copying what an author says doesn't help you in assessing whether you have understood what you read.

Read the following passage and the summary that follows it:

Formal Magic

There are five steps central to formal magic. Each plays a different role in guaranteeing the success of your magic working.

Intention

Your intention focuses your spell and channels your absolute will to succeed. I try to never do a spell unless I feel it well up inside of me beforehand. Spells don't work unless you are able to focus your will. Your intent must be clear, or your spell may have unintended results.

Preparation

The spell actually begins as you assemble your tools and materials, because your will starts to focus itself as you gather the herbs, select the candles, choose the incense, decorate the altar, and lay out your tools. Knowledge of correspondences is essential here, so that you select materials appropriate to the spell.

Incense, candles, music and ceremonial dress, and makeup or masks can all be used to make your space sacred and set the mood for a spell. You should have something to represent each element—earth, air, fire, water—on the altar or other working surface.

Cast the Circle, Raise the Power

- Call corners (also called calling quarters): Magic relates to both time and space. Ancient peoples divided space into the four quarters: North, South, East, and West. Sometimes, they further subdivided it, but the four basic directions are the crucial ones.

- Cast the circle, invoking the Lords of the Watchtowers: The ancients also assigned deities to guard each of the quarters, deities to whom the power of each quarter accrued. The Lords of the Watchtower can be male or female. By invoking them, we call upon their spatial powers to guard and inform our magic circles.

- Raise power: You should feel it between your hands, like the force of two magnets that repel each other, as you invoke the lords or ladies to cast the circle. The power, as the good witch told Dorothy, is in you. Or, to be more precise, the ability to *use* the power is in you. We are conduits for the natural power in the universe. We channel it though our bodies when we do magical work. You effect magic with your will. Spells, incantations, candles, herbs, and crystals are just props that help you channel it in the desired direction. There are eight ways to raise power:

    1. Meditation or concentration.
    2. Chants, spells, poetry, or invocations.
    3. Trance, or projection of the astral body.
    4. Incense, drugs, or alcohol.
    5. Rhythm (dancing or drumming).
    6. Binding, to control the flow of blood.
    7. Flagellation, light scourging (traditionally forty lashes).
    8. The Great Rite (ecstatic sexual union).

I usually use incense and psychic concentration, drawing power from wherever I can feel it: the jet stream, an approaching storm, trees, rain, the city, my love, my anger, my desire, the Sun or Moon, even the universe itself. You have to experiment with different methods in order to find the best way for you to raise the power. With practice, you will come to recognize the state of psychic readiness that tells you when you are prepared to make magic.

We all experience the sensation of magical power rising in different ways. For some, it is a tingling or warmth, while others may feel it vibrating or hear it whooshing around them. You'll know it when you feel it, whatever form the sensation takes for you. You will also come to know when someone with whom you have a strong connection is casting a spell, even if they are hundreds of miles away.

You can boost your power by invoking the Mighty Ones (the Old Gods), by working with spirits or elementals, by working with other witches, by practicing regular meditation, and by going barefoot, to draw on earth energy.

Power is connected to the Moon. It increases as the Moon waxes, decreases as it wanes. Witches are most powerful at the Full Moon. Many witches wear their hair long because cutting your hair can diminish your power. This is probably why Joan of Arc had her hair shorn before she was burned at the stake.

Cast the Spell

Close the circle and ground the power you have raised. Clean up. Carry out any after-spell actions required.

Source: Eileen Holland, *The Wicca Handbook* (York Beach, ME: Samuel Weiser, 2000), pp. 59–60.

Summary Example: Formal Magic

> There are five steps to formal magic. The first, intention, involves concentration and focus. The second, preparation, involves creating the right setting and gathering appropriate materials. The third, cast the circle, raise the power, requires that you recognize the four corners of the earth, invoke the Lords of the Watchtowers, and raise the power from nature. The fourth, cast the spell, is to say the spell out loud. The last, close the circle, is to clean up and ground the energy where the spell was cast.

Notice the summary is considerably shorter than the original but maintains its basic meaning. The main idea of the excerpt, *There are five steps central to formal magic,* is stated in the first sentence of the summary. The second sentence of the summary is derived from the first heading in the excerpt, *intention,* and the rest of the sentences from the other four headings. Considerable detail has been left out. In the original excerpt, the author presented a list of five steps for performing formal magic; the summary does the same, using listing OWCs.

Exercise 9e

Summary Writing Practice

In your journal write a summary of "The Microeconomic Players" on pages 290–291. Compare your summary with the original excerpt. Is your summary shorter? Does it include all of the major supporting ideas? Are they in the same order as in the original? Did you use your own words?

_____

_____

_____

_____

Team Up!

Find a classmate and exchange the summaries you wrote for Exercise 9e. Did you include the same information? Is there any unnecessary detail in either of the summaries? Are the summaries true to the original excerpt?

Take One Minute

In your own words, write directions for how to write a summary.

Review Journal Prompt B: Attaching New Information to Old

Review journal prompt B asks you to integrate prior knowledge with the new information you learn from your textbook. To do this, write about the old and the new together. The following journal entry, based on the previous reading excerpt "Formal Magic," demonstrates how to do this:

> I have heard of energy coming from nature. I believe some Eastern religions refer to it as ki, chi, or prana. Catholics might call it the Holy Spirit. Many would label it B.S. I thought Joan of Arc cut her own hair to disguise herself as a man, to be a warrior. The ritual with the altar and other materials is similar to religious rituals.

In these few sentences a connection is made between magic and religion; both rely on a higher power; both involve ritual. Whether magic is a legitimate religion is another issue, but the connection between new information (magic) and old (religion) will make it easier to recall what you have learned in the future.

Exercise 9f	# Connecting New Information to Old

Read the following excerpts. Write a short paragraph for each on a separate sheet of paper, relating what you already know about the topic to the information in the excerpt. The first one is modeled for you.

MODEL **1.** The researchers had to take another tack to understand how *Sesame Street* impacted children's learning. They decided to divide children into four groups, based on frequency of viewing. High viewers of *Sesame Street* learned more in the curriculum areas of letters, numbers, geometric forms, sorting, and classification than the low viewers did. Disadvantaged children learned just as much as advantaged children, and boys and girls learned equally well from the program.

Source: Sandra Calvert, *Children's Journeys through the Information Age* (New York: McGraw-Hill, 1999), p. 193.

I remember, when I was a kid, watching an educational cartoon on TV

that was repeated frequently during the week. It explained how a

bill became a law. It had a catchy song I liked. To this day, I remember

the words and the process for a bill becoming law, although I have to

sing the song to remember the process. ("I'm just a bill, yes I'm only a

bill. And I'm sitting here on Capitol Hill…")

2. I feel that we too often focus only on the negative aspect of life—on what is bad. If we were more willing to see the good and the beautiful things that surround us, we would be able to transform our families. From there, we would change our next-door neighbors and then others who live in our neighborhood or city. We would be able to bring peace and love to our world, which hungers so much for those things.

Source: Mother Theresa, *No Greater Love* (Novato, CA: New World Library, 1997), p. 26.

3. Sexual harassment guidelines, if overdone, will end by harming women morethan helping them. In the rough play of the arena, women must make their own way. If someone offends you by speech, you must learn to defend yourself by speech. The answer cannot be to beg for outside help to curtail your opponent's free movement. The message conveyed by such attitudes is that women are too weak to win by men's rules and must be awarded a procedural advantage before they even climb into the ring. Teasing and taunting have always been intrinsic to the hazing rituals of male bonding. The elaborate shouting matches and satirical putdowns of African tribal life can still be heard in American pop music ("You been whupped with the ugly stick!"—uproarious laughter) and among drag queens, where it's called "throwing shade." Middle-class white women have got to get over their superiority complex and learn to talk trash with the rest of the human race.

Source: Camille Paglia, *Vamps & Tramps* (New York: Vintage Books, 1994), p. 51.

4. Let me tell you a story. It's about two ants. In the early 1960s, when I was a young professor of zoology at Harvard University, one of the vexing mysteries of evolution was the origin of ants. That was far from a trivial problem in science. Ants are the most abundant of insects, the most effective predators of other insects, and the busiest scavengers of small dead animals. They transport the seeds of thousands of plant species, and they turn and enrich more soil than earthworms. In totality (they number roughly in the million billions and weigh about as much as all of humanity), they are among the key players of Earth's terrestrial environment. Of equal general interest, they have attained their dominion by means of the most advanced social organization known among animals.

Source: Edward Wilson, *The Best American Science and Nature Writing* (New York: Houghton Mifflin, 2001), p. xiii.

Review Journal Prompt C: Identifying Unclear Parts of a Reading

Review journal prompt C asks you to reflect on what you do not understand in a reading. It is similar to the study-reading prompt B, but instead of identifying the unclear parts of a section, you are asked to focus on the unclear parts of the entire reading assignment. The benefit of the two prompts is the same: when you focus on what you don't understand, you can either figure it out yourself by thinking about it, or work out exactly what is unclear to you so you can ask for help in clarifying it.

Take One Minute

Reflect on the excerpt "The Microeconomic Players" and pinpoint any area in the reading that is unclear to you.

Here is an example of how to review your reading using these journal prompts.

Andrea is a community college sophomore. She is using her journal to review a psychology reading assignment she has completed. Use the steps she takes as a model for how to respond to readings. Notice she has written the date and reading assignment at the top right corner of the paper to serve as a reference point when she has to go back to her journal to review for an exam.

Review Journal Prompt A: Summarize What You Read

Oct. 16
Ch. 6, pp. 167–210

Language and different derivatives of language are basic building blocks of everyday conversation for us as cognitive beings. The three major components of language are phonology, syntax and semantics. Although people of the world speak many different languages, some theorize that there is a universal grammar, a common underlying language structure. When all children are young, their attempts at the development of language include babble, telegraphic speech, and overgeneralization. These examples of communication lay the foundation on which a more developed and sophisticated language can be built. These young children might benefit from the learning-theory approach.

Other studies of language show that there may be a relationship between language and thought and that complex grammar usage might be an exclusively human characteristic. According to the linguistic-relativity hypothesis, the words people use may in fact shape how they think. This language—thought relationship informs the study of dialects, such as Ebonics and Spanglish, and bilingual education.

Andrea's summary begins with the main idea of the reading: *Language and different derivatives of language are the basic building blocks of everyday communication for us as cognitive beings.* The remainder of these two paragraphs contains the major supporting details from her reading assignment.

Review Journal Prompt B: What Do You Already Know about the Topic?

Because of my former employment at a local recording studio, I have had quite a lot of exposure to different American dialects, such as Ebonics. It comes as no surprise to me that this dialect is classified as separate from other forms of English. It is almost a "clique" lingo. Unless you are familiar with the phrases and terminology, you will not understand what is being said.

In this paragraph Andrea connects what she has read to what she already knows about the topic. Relating the newly learned information to her personal experience helps her to understand it better. It will also help her to store what she has learned with what she already knows, making it easier to access later.

Review Journal Prompt C: Identifying Unclear Parts of a Reading

There were no parts of this text excerpt that I did not understand.

In this sentence Andrea decides that she understood the reading pretty well and is ready to move on.

Responding to each of the review journal prompts may be too time-consuming given your particular study schedule. If you are doing well in a class you probably need to complete only review journal prompt C. Alternatively, you may choose to complete the review journal prompts after each chapter and not after every reading assignment.

Step 2: Clarify Confusing Parts

If you complete review step one and determine there are parts of a reading assignment you don't understand, you should make a concrete plan for getting help before moving on in your reading. Ask your instructor, a classmate, or a tutor for help or find out what other campus resources are available to you.

Exercise 9g	**Internet Practice**
	Access the following web site: **http://www.litrix.com/readroom.htm.** Read one chapter of any of the books available at this website using the PSR technique, and submit a summary of it to your instructor.

Practice with Reading Passage

Answer all questions on a separate sheet of paper.

Reading Practice	**"Gay"**
	BY ANNA QUINDLEN

PREPARE TO READ

1. Based on the title of the essay, what do you expect the reading to be about? What do you think the topic is?

2. What do you already know about the topic?

3. Here are some vocabulary words that might be unfamiliar to you. Look them up, if necessary, and refer to the definitions as you encounter these words in the essay.

a. Chasm

b. Subterfuge

c. Disapprobation

d. Ostracism

Gay

When he went home last year, he realized for the first time that he would be buried there, in the small, gritty industrial town he had loathed for as long as he could remember. He looked out the window of his bedroom and saw the siding on the house next door and knew that he was trapped, as surely as if he had never left for the city. Late one night, before he was to go back to his own apartment, his father tried to have a conversation with him, halting and slow, about drug use and the damage it could do to your body. At that moment he understood that it would be more soothing to his parents to think that he was a heroin addict than that he was a homosexual.

This is part of the story of a friend of a friend of mine. She went to his funeral not too long ago. The funeral home forced the family to pay extra to embalm him. Luckily, the local paper did not need to print the cause of death. His parents' friends did not ask what killed him, and his parents didn't talk about it. He had AIDS. His parents had figured out at the same time that he was dying and that he slept with men. He tried to talk to them about his illness; he didn't want to discuss his homosexuality. That would have been too hard for them all.

Never have the lines between sex and death been so close, the chasm between parent and child so wide. His parents hoped almost until the end that some nice girl would "cure" him. They even hinted broadly that my friend might be that nice girl. After the funeral, as she helped with the dishes in their small kitchen with the window onto the backyard, she lost her temper at the subterfuge and said to his mother, "He was gay. Why is that more terrible than that he is dead?" The mother did not speak, but raised her hands from the soapy water and held them up as though to ward off the words.

I suppose this is true of many parents. For some it is simply that they think homosexuality is against God, against nature, condemns their sons to hell. For others it is something else, more difficult to put into words. It makes their children too different from them. We do not want our children to be too different—so different that they face social disapprobation and ostracism, so different that they die before we do. His parents did not know any homosexuals, or at least they did not believe they did. His parents did not know what homosexuals were like.

They are like us. They are us. Isn't that true? And yet, there is a difference. Perhaps mothers sometimes have an easier time accepting this. After all, they must accept early on that there are profound sexual differences between them and their sons. Fathers think their boys will be basically like them. Sometimes they are. And sometimes, in a way that comes to mean so much, they are not.

I have thought of this a fair amount because I am the mother of sons. I have managed to convince myself that I love my children so much that nothing they could do would turn me against them, or away from them, that nothing would make me take their pictures off the bureau and hide them in a drawer. A friend says I am fooling myself, that I would at least be disappointed and perhaps distressed if, like his, my sons' sexual orientation was not hetero. Maybe he's right. There are some obvious reasons to feel that way. If the incidence of AIDS remains higher among homosexuals than among heterosexuals, it would be one less thing they could die of. If societal prejudices remain constant, it would be one less thing they could be ostracized for.

But this I think I know: I think I could live with having a son who was homosexual. But it would break my heart if he was homosexual and felt that he could not tell me so, felt that I was not the kind of mother who could hear that particular truth. That is a kind of death, too, and it kills both your life with your child and all you have left after the funeral: the relationship that can live on inside you, if you have nurtured it.

In the days following his death, the mother of my friend's friend mourned the fact that she had known little of his life, had not wanted to know. "I spent too much time worrying about what he was," she said. Not who. What. And it turned out that there was not enough time, not with almost daily obituaries of people barely three decades old, dead of a disease she had never heard of when she first wondered about the kind of friends her boy had and why he didn't date more.

It reminded me that often we take our sweet time dealing with the things that we do not like about our children: the marriage we could not accept, the profession we disapproved of, the sexual orientation we may hate and fear. Sometimes we vow that we will never, never accept those things. The stories my friend told me about the illness, the death, the funeral and, especially, about the parents reminded me that sometimes we do not have all the time we think to make our peace with who our children are. It reminded me that "never" can last a long, long time, perhaps much longer than we intended, deep in our hearts, when we first invoked its terrible endless power.

Source: Anna Quindlen, *Living Out Loud* (New York: Random House, 1987).

CHECK YOUR UNDERSTANDING

OBJECTIVE AND SHORT-ANSWER QUESTIONS

1. Study-read the article "Gay" and then write a summary of it. Give your summary to a classmate and have him or her critique your summary using these steps:

   - Read the summary and underline the main idea.

   - Put a checkmark at the beginning of each detail in the summary.

- Explain whether you think the details you identified in the summary are important enough to be included. Are they major supporting details?

2. What was the main idea of the reading passage?

  a. Certain lifestyles can cause irreparable damage to the body, and parents have the responsibility to guide their children away from such lifestyles.

  b. Parents should take the time today to deal with things they can't accept about their children, or they may never get the chance to develop nurturing and sustaining relationships with them.

  c. Parents should consider joining support organizations to help them cope and learn more about their children's lifestyles, such as the Parents of Gay Children (PGC).

  d. A young man came home to die.

3. When the author talks about never, what does she mean about its terrible endless power when she says, "Perhaps much longer than we intended, deep in our hearts, when we first invoked its terrible endless power."

  a. You don't know what you've got till it's gone.

  b. Don't invoke spirits you can't handle.

  c. Sometimes we think we will have time later to deal with problems we don't want to deal with today.

  d. We can never change who we are.

4. What was the problem no one wanted to discuss at the young man's home?

  a. He was gay.

  b. He dropped out of college.

  c. He died of cancer.

  d. He was a womanizer.

5. Why didn't anyone want to talk about his illness with his parents?

  a. They were too embarrassed to discuss AIDs, because it was a disease associated with homosexuals.

  b. His parents weren't close to anyone in the small town.

  c. The neighbors were very angry with the parents for not accepting the boy for who he was.

  d. His parents were very ill.

6. Why do you think the young man disliked his home town so much?

  a. It was boring.

  b. The author doesn't really say why the young man disliked his home town.

  c. He felt trapped and unable to be himself.

  d. He was unable to find a job of choice.

7. In addition to being gay, list three things for which people are sometimes ostracized in cultures:

Chapter Summary

The PSR technique (preview, study-read, and review) requires that you question yourself before, during, and after you read. It encourages you to participate in a reader–author conversation rather than to read passively. In this conversation, you assess what the author says and decide if it makes sense to you. You also add what you know to the conversation by recalling related information. This dialogue, this active participation, helps you understand and remember textbook material.

The PSR technique also requires you to respond to readings by writing in your journal. Commenting in writing helps you digest and understand an author's ideas and articulate your own. By identifying exactly where you become confused in a reading, you can return to that point and reread the relevant section of text. This will help you to understand the material on your own or alert you to the fact that you need to ask a classmate or your instructor for help.

Post Test

Answer all questions on a separate sheet of paper.

Part I

OBJECTIVE QUESTIONS

1. Match the vocabulary words in Column A to their definitions in Column B:

A	B
1. PSR	a. Explain the meaning of someone else's words, phrases, or sentences in your own words.

2.   Summary

b.   Restate the original meaning of someone else's writing, in fewer and different words.

3.   Paraphrase

c.   Preview, study-read, review method of reading.

2.   The most important time to question yourself is right before you begin to read. True False

3.   Study-reading means

a.   Reading at a convenient time, when you have time to read the chapter straight through, and then making time to question yourself.

b.   Asking and answering the questions you developed in the preview stage as you read.

c.   Stopping to take a break after reading every 15 paragraphs.

d.   A bad habit of stopping to think about what you have read before you finish reading the entire chapter.

4.   If you don't understand what you have just read, you should

a.   Focus on what you do know.

b.   Seek assistance immediately for clarification—tutor, instructor, or classmate.

c.   Write down what you don't understand in your journal, and return to it in one week.

d.   Do nothing; it was just one of many reading selections.

5.   An example of active reading is

a.   Reading and walking simultaneously—an active technique for tactile learners.

b.   Completing your reading during regularly scheduled time throughout the week.

c.   Creating questions so that you are reading with purpose.

d.   Playing music while you read to activate your right brain.

SHORT-ANSWER QUESTIONS

6.   Explain why it is a good idea to make a journal entry when you find a reading assignment confusing.

7.   What is (are) the benefit(s) of summarizing a reading?

8.   List the three steps of the preview stage.

Part II

Reading Passage

"The Insufficiency of Honesty"
BY STEPHEN CARTER

1.   Based on the title, what do you expect the reading to be about? What do you think the topic is?

2. What do you already know about the topic?

3. Create a question to ask yourself, using the title or topic of the reading.

4. Study-read "The Insufficiency of Honesty" and stop after the first four paragraphs to write a journal entry, using these study-reading journal prompts:

    a. What do I understand about what I have read so far?

    b. Where in the text did I lose concentration or become confused?

    c. What questions do I have?

5. If you understand everything that you have read in the first four paragraphs, then answer only study-reading journal prompt *a* here and finish reading the essay. If there are any points of confusion, respond to all three study-read journal prompts. Then write a review journal entry using these prompts:

    a. Summarize what you have read.

    b. Write down what other information you know about the same topic.

    c. Identify the parts of the reading you do not understand.

The Insuffiency of Honesty

A couple of years ago I began a university commencement address by telling the audience that I was going to talk about *integrity*. The crowd broke into applause. Applause! Just because they had heard the word "integrity": that's how starved for it they were. They had no idea how I was using the word, or what I was going to say about integrity, or, indeed, whether I was for it or against it. But they knew they liked the idea of talking about it.

Very well, let us consider this word "integrity." Integrity is like the weather: everybody talks about it but nobody knows what to do about it. Integrity is that stuff that we always want more of. Some say that we need to return to the good old days when we had a lot more of it. Others say that we as a nation have never really had enough of it. Hardly anybody stops to explain exactly what we mean by it, or how we know it is a good thing, or why everybody needs to have the same amount of it. Indeed, the only trouble with integrity is that everybody who uses the word seems to mean something slightly different.

For instance, when I refer to integrity, do I mean simply "honesty"? The answer is no; although honesty is a virtue of importance, it is a different virtue from integrity. Let us, for simplicity, think of honesty as not lying; and let us further accept Sissela Bok's definition of a lie: "any intentionally deceptive message which is *stated.*" Plainly, one cannot have integrity without being honest (although, as we shall see, the matter gets complicated), but one can certainly be honest and yet have little integrity.

When I refer to integrity, I have something very specific in mind. Integrity, as I will use the term, requires three steps: discerning what is right and what is wrong; acting on what you have discerned, even at personal cost; and saying openly that you are acting on your understanding of right and wrong. The first criterion captures the idea that integrity requires a degree of moral reflectiveness. The second brings in the ideal of a person of integrity as steadfast, a quality that includes keeping one's commitments. The third reminds us that a person of integrity can be trusted.

The first point to understand about the difference between honesty and integrity is that a person may be entirely honest without ever engaging in the hard work of discernment that integrity requires: she may tell us quite truthfully what she believes without ever taking the time to figure out whether what she believes is good and right and true. The problem may be as simple as someone's foolishly saying something that hurts a friend's feelings; a few moments of thought would have revealed the likelihood of the hurt and the lack of necessity for the comment. Or the problem may be more complex, as when a man who was raised from birth in a society that preaches racism states his belief in one race's inferiority as a fact, without ever really considering that perhaps this deeply held view is wrong. Certainly the racist is being honest—he is telling us what he actually thinks—but his honesty does not add up to integrity.

Telling Everything You Know

A wonderful epigram sometimes attributed to the filmmaker Sam Goldwyn goes like this: "The most important thing in acting is honesty; once you learn to fake that, you're in." The point is that honesty can be something one *seems* to have. Without integrity, what passes for honesty often is nothing of the kind; it is fake honesty—or it is honest but irrelevant and perhaps even immoral.

Consider an example. A man who has been married for fifty years confesses to his wife on his deathbed that he was unfaithful thirty-five years earlier. The dishonesty was killing his spirit, he says. Now he has cleared his conscience and is able to die in peace.

The husband has been honest—sort of. He has certainly unburdened himself. And he has probably made his wife (soon to be his widow) quite miserable in the process, because even if she forgives him, she will not be able to remember him with quite the vivid image of love and loyalty that she had hoped for. Arranging his own emotional affairs to ease his transition to death, he has shifted to his wife the burden of confusion and pain, perhaps for the rest of her life. Moreover, he has attempted his honesty at the one time in his life when it carries no risk; acting in accordance with what you think is right and risking no loss in the process is a rather thin and unadmirable form of honesty.

Besides, even though the husband has been honest in a sense, he has now twice been unfaithful to his wife: once thirty-five years ago, when he had his affair, and again when, nearing death, he decided that his own peace of mind was more important than hers. In trying to be honest he has violated his marriage vow by acting toward his wife not with love but with naked and perhaps even cruel self-interest.

As my mother used to say, you don't have to tell people everything you know. Lying and nondisclosure, as the law often recognizes, are not the same thing. Sometimes it is actually illegal to tell what you know, as, for example, in the disclosure of certain financial information by market insiders. Or it may be unethical, as when a lawyer reveals a confidence entrusted to her by a client. It may be simple bad manners, as in the case of a gratuitous comment to a colleague on his or her attire. And it may be subject to religious punishment, as when a Roman Catholic priest breaks the seal of the confessional—an offense that carries automatic excommunication.

In all the cases just mentioned, the problem with telling everything you know is that somebody else is harmed. Harm may not be the intention, but it is certainly the effect. Honesty is most laudable when we risk harm to ourselves; it becomes a good deal less so if we instead risk harm to others when there is no gain to anyone other than ourselves. Integrity may counsel keeping our secrets in order to spare the feelings of others. Sometimes, as in the example of the wayward husband, the reason we want to tell what we know is precisely to shift our pain onto somebody else—a course of action dictated less by integrity than by self-interest. Fortunately, integrity and self-interest often coincide, as when a politician of integrity is rewarded with our votes. But often they do not, and it is at those moments that our integrity is truly tested.

Error

Another reason that honesty alone is no substitute for integrity is that if forthrightness is not preceded by discernment, it may result in the expression of an incorrect moral judgment. In other words, I may be honest about what I believe, but if I have never tested my beliefs, I may be wrong. And here I mean "wrong" in a particular sense: the proposition in question is wrong if I would change my mind about it after hard moral reflection.

Consider this example. Having been taught all his life that women are not as smart as men, a manager gives the women on his staff less challenging assignments than he gives the men. He does this, he believes, for their own benefit: he does not want them to fail, and he believes that they will if he gives them tougher assignments. Moreover, when one of the women on his staff does poor work, he does not berate her as harshly as he would a man, because he expects nothing more. And he claims to be acting with integrity because he is acting according to his own deepest beliefs.

The manager fails the most basic test of integrity. The question is not whether his actions are consistent with what he most deeply believes but whether he has done the hard work of discerning whether what he most deeply believes is right. The manager has not taken this harder step.

Moreover, even within the universe that the manager has constructed for himself, he is not acting with integrity. Although he is obviously wrong to think that the women on his staff are not as good as the men, even were he right, that would not justify applying different standards to their work. By so doing he betrays both his obligation to the institution that employs him and his duty as a manager to evaluate his employees.

The problem that the manager faces is an enormous one in our practical politics, where having the dialogue that makes democracy work can seem impossible because of our tendency to cling to our views even when we have not examined them. As Jean Bethke Elshtain has said, borrowing from John Courtney Murray, our politics are so fractured and contentious that we often cannot even reach *disagreement*. Our refusal to look closely at our own most cherished principles is surely a large part of the reason. Socrates thought the unexamined life not worth living. But the unhappy truth is that few of us actually have the time for constant reflection on our views—on public or private morality. Examine them we must, however, or we will never know whether we might be wrong.

None of this should be taken to mean that integrity as I have described it presupposes a single correct truth. If, for example, your integrity-guided search tells you that affirmative action is wrong, and my integrity-guided search tells me that affirmative action is right, we need not conclude that one of us lacks integrity. As it happens, I believe—both as a Christian and as a secular citizen who struggles toward moral understanding—that we can find true and sound answers to our moral questions. But I do not pretend to have found very many of them, nor is an exposition of them my purpose here.

It is the case not that there aren't any right answers but that, given human fallibility, we need to be careful in assuming that we have found them. However, today's political talk about how it is wrong for the government to impose one person's morality on somebody else is just mindless chatter. Every law imposes one person's morality on somebody else, because law has only two functions: to tell people to do what they would rather not or to forbid them to do what they would.

And if the surveys can be believed, there is far more moral agreement in America than we sometimes allow ourselves to think. One of the reasons that character education for young people makes so much sense to so many people is precisely that there seems to be a core set of moral understandings—we might call them the American Core—that most of us accept. Some of the virtues in this American Core are, one hopes, relatively noncontroversial. About 500 American communities have signed on to Michael Josephson's program to emphasize the "six pillars" of good character: trustworthiness, respect, responsibility, caring, fairness, and citizenship. These virtues might lead to a similarly noncontroversial set of political values: having an honest regard for ourselves and others, protecting freedom of thought and religious belief, and refusing to steal or murder.

Honesty and Competing Responsibilities

A further problem with too great an exaltation of honesty is that it may allow us to escape responsibilities that morality bids us bear. If honesty is substituted for integrity, one might think that if I say I am not planning to fulfill a duty, I need not fulfill it. But it would be a peculiar morality indeed that granted us the right to avoid our moral responsibilities simply by stating our intention to ignore them. Integrity does not permit such an easy escape.

Consider an example. Before engaging in sex with a woman, her lover tells her that if she gets pregnant, it is her problem, not his. She says that she understands.

In due course she does wind up pregnant. If we believe, as I hope we do, that the man would ordinarily have a moral responsibility toward both the child he will have helped to bring into the world and the child's mother, then his honest statement of what he intends does not spare him that responsibility.

This vision of responsibility assumes that not all moral obligations stem from consent or from a stated intention. The linking of obligations to promises is a rather modern and perhaps uniquely Western way of looking at life, and perhaps a luxury that only the well-to-do can afford. As Fred and Shulamit Korn (a philosopher and an anthropologist) have pointed out, "If one looks at ethnographic accounts of other societies, one finds that, while obligations everywhere play a crucial role in social life, promising is not preeminent among the sources of obligation and is not even mentioned by most anthropologists." The Korns have made a study of Tonga, where promises are virtually unknown but the social order is remarkably stable. If life without any promises seems extreme, we Americans sometimes go too far the other way, parsing not only our contracts but even our marriage vows in order to discover the absolute minimum obligation that we have to others as a result of our promises.

That some societies in the world have worked out evidently functional structures of obligation without the need for promise or consent does not tell us what we should do. But it serves as a reminder of the basic proposition that our existence in civil society creates a set of mutual responsibilities that philosophers used to capture in the fiction of the social contract. Nowadays, here in America, people seem to spend their time thinking of even cleverer ways to avoid their obligations, instead of doing what integrity commands and fulfilling them. And all too often honesty is their excuse.

Source: Stephen L . Carter, "The Insufficiency of Honesty." In *Strategies for Successful Writing: A Rhetoric, Research Guide, Reader and Handbook,* ed. James A. Reinking (Upper Saddle River, NJ: Prentice Hall, 1996), pp. 547–551.

OBJECTIVE QUESTIONS

1. What is the main idea of the essay "The Insufficiency of Honesty"?

    a. Live an honest life and you'll live a life of integrity.

    b. Live a life of integrity and you'll live an honest life.

    c. Being honest is not enough; one must also have integrity.

    d. Integrity and honesty assume that all moral obligations stem from consent or from a stated intention.

2. What organizational method best describes the overall organization the author uses in this essay?

    a. Cause and effect.

    b. Sequence.

   c. Definition.

   d. Listing.

3. What three steps does the author say are required for a person to act with integrity?

   a.

   b.

   c.

4. The author believes that a person can be honest without having integrity. True False

5. The author believes that acting in accordance with what you think is right and risking no loss in the process is

   a. Admirable and a desirable way to behave.

   b. A rather thin and unadmirable form of honesty.

   c. Exactly what we should strive for when speaking and living the truth.

   d. Not only the honest thing to do, but your responsibility.

6. According to the author, the American Core is

   a. A set of moral understandings accepted by most Americans.

   b. A part of the military, designed to ensure honesty in politics.

   c. A youth group designed to teach ethics to other teenagers.

   d. A type of support group for liars.

7. The author believes that honesty is always the best practice...no matter what. True False

Website Sources for Additional Practice

Full Texts of Books Online
http://www.litrix.com/readroom.htm: an online reading room.

Newspapers Online
http://braindance.com/frambdi1.htm: find out how to "identify and understand useful ideas as efficiently as possible."

http://gator1.brazosport.cc.tx.us/~lac/inotes.htm: try the I-Note method.

Chapter 10

Textbook Marking

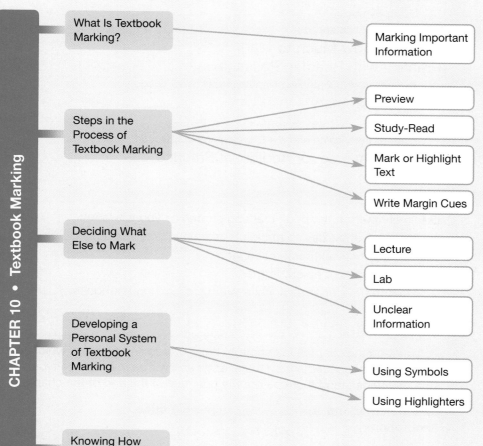

CHAPTER 10 • Textbook Marking

- What Is Textbook Marking?
  - Marking Important Information

- Steps in the Process of Textbook Marking
  - Preview
  - Study-Read
  - Mark or Highlight Text
  - Write Margin Cues

- Deciding What Else to Mark
  - Lecture
  - Lab
  - Unclear Information

- Developing a Personal System of Textbook Marking
  - Using Symbols
  - Using Highlighters

- Knowing How Much to Mark

Chapter Contents

Chapter Goals

In this chapter on textbook marking strategies you will learn:

- Why it is important to mark information in your textbooks.
- A system for textbook marking.
- What, and how much, to mark.
- How to develop a personal system for marking textbooks.

Chapter Vocabulary

As you read the chapter, take note of these words and phrases, which represent important concepts from the chapter and will be in **boldface** type. Make sure you understand them before the post test at the end of the chapter.

textbook marking   **margin cues**
annotations

Claudia has a brand new textbook for her History 108 class. She paid $85.00 for it and has decided not to write in it, so that when she sells it back to the bookstore she will receive at least $25.00. Stacia has the same history class this year. She also purchased a new book. However, she plans to write in her textbook, highlighting main ideas, underlining important details, and circling new vocabulary. Stacia knows the bookstore may not even buy her book back because of the markings. But unlike Claudia, Stacia regards the book as an investment; the return on her investment will be a deeper understanding of the textbook information and better grades.

Of these two students, Stacia has the advantage—a learning advantage. Claudia has a good reason for not wanting to write in her textbook: the book is expensive. But if she wants to learn as much as Stacia, she will have to take very detailed notes from her textbook, copy down new vocabulary, and write out the main ideas and important details from each chapter. Although note taking is a great reading and memory tool, it should not replace textbook marking. The advantages of writing in your textbook are worth the risk of not being able to sell it back to the bookstore, because textbook marking:

- Helps you remember what you read.
- Helps you to distinguish important from less important information.
- Is an efficient form of taking notes.
- Allows you to self-test before exams, using your margin cues to develop questions and your highlighted or marked text to check if your responses are correct.

Learning Journal

What do you already know about textbook marking? Do you apply what you know? Do you have a favorite strategy? If so, what is it?

What Is Textbook Marking?

Textbook marking is a systematic way of marking, highlighting, and labeling ideas to show how they are related to each other and which are most important. It involves marking or highlighting words, phrases, and sentences, and writing margin cues, or notes, in the space on either side of the text to explain why you have marked specific information. It should not replace taking notes from your textbook, but it will make the task more efficient. The following suggestions will help you prepare to mark your textbooks efficiently:

1. Try to purchase new books for your classes. You don't want to be distracted by another student's markings, which may be unclear to you or ineffective. If you can't, or don't want to, buy new books, pick used ones with as few markings as possible and use your own marking system.
2. Buy a fine-point pen in case the margins are narrow and there is limited space for your margin cues.
3. Buy some highlighters. This is optional. You can mark just as effectively with a pen alone, but it can be helpful to use different colors to differentiate between main ideas, vocabulary words, and major and minor supporting details.

Marking Important Information

When Stacia opens her new history book, she will need to know what to mark, and what kind of marking to use, to benefit from using this strategy. When students mark their textbooks without knowing how to do so effectively, they often make the following mistakes:

- They mark the wrong information.
- They mark too much.
- They do not mark enough.
- They cannot remember why they marked what they did because they did not label their markings.

At the end of the study-reading stage of textbook reading, you should look for and mark these items: main ideas, major supporting details, and new vocabulary. These are the three basic elements you need to learn from any reading assignment. Regardless of the class you are taking or the school you attend, your instructors will expect you to have recognized and understood at least these components.

The process of looking for, and highlighting or underlining, main ideas when study-reading should be familiar to you from Chapters 5 and 9. When deciding which details are important to mark, use word clues to guide you, and select only those primary details that clarify or further explain the main idea. Most good textbooks list specialized or technical vocabulary at the beginning of each chapter and use boldface or italicized print for key words and important phrases within the chapters making them easy to identify.

Read the following excerpt from a science textbook. The explanation that follows models how you would identify in it important information so you would know what to mark.

What Is Technology?

Technology is the creation of new products and processes that are supposed to improve our chances for survival, our comfort level, and our quality of life. In many cases technology develops from known scientific laws and theories. Scientists invented the laser, for example, by applying knowledge about the internal structure of atoms. Applied scientific knowledge about chemistry has given us nylon, pesticides, and countless other products.

Some technologies arose long before anyone understood the underlying scientific principles. Aspirin, originally extracted from the bark of a willow tree, relieved pain and fever long before anyone found out how it did so. Similarly, photography was invented by people who had no inkling of its chemistry. Farmers crossbred new strains of livestock and crops long before biologists understood the principles of genetics.

Science and technology differ in the ways the information and ideas they produce are shared. Many of the results of scientific research are published and passed around freely to be tested, challenged, verified, or modified, a process that strengthens the validity of scientific knowledge and helps expose cheaters. In contrast, technological discoveries are often kept secret until the new process or product is patented.

Source: G. Tyler Miller Jr., *Environmental Science: Working with the Earth* (Belmont, CA: Wadsworth, 1995), p. 42.

The main idea of the excerpt is contained in the first sentence: *Technology is the creation of new products and processes that are supposed to improve our chances for survival, our comfort level, and our quality of life.* You can identify this as the main idea sentence because it answers the question posed by the heading: *What is technology?* It is also the idea that drives the rest of the excerpt, the idea all the other paragraphs support.

The major supporting details in this excerpt are the ideas that further explain or clarify what technology is. There are three. The first one is in the first paragraph and comes right after the clue words *In many cases.* This detail explains how some technology develops. The second is in the second paragraph and follows the clue word *Some.* This detail explains how some technologies developed in the past. The third major detail is in the third paragraph and is presented after the clue words *In contrast.* This detail explains how new technologies currently emerge. Each of these major supporting details provides an explanation of what technology is.

Team Up!

Team up with another student and discuss the following questions about the excerpt "What Is Technology?"

1. Many examples of different technologies are given, but they are not considered major supporting details. Why not?

2. Why are the details about the results of scientific research in the third paragraph not considered major supporting details?

Learning Journal

Using the main idea of the "What Is Technology?" excerpt and its three major supporting details, write a one-paragraph summary of the excerpt.

Exercise 10a

Identifying What's Important

Read the following excerpt, and *highlight* the main ideas and underline the major supporting details. Circle the word clues that helped you identify the major supporting details.

What Do Scientists Do?

Scientists collect scientific data, or facts, by making observations and taking measurements, but this is not the main purpose of science. As French scientist Henri Poincaré put it, "Science is built up of facts, but a collection of facts is no more science than a heap of stones is a house."

Scientists try to describe what is happening in nature by organizing data into a generalization or scientific law. Thus, scientific data are stepping stones to a scientific law, a description of the orderly behavior observed in nature—a summary of what we find happening in nature over and over in the same way. For example, after making thousands of measurements involving changes in matter, chemists concluded that in any physical change (such as converting liquid water to water vapor) or any chemical change (such as burning coal) no matter is created or destroyed. This summary of what we always observe in nature is called the law of conservation of matter, as discussed in more detail later in this chapter.

Scientists then try to explain how or why things happen the way a scientific law describes them. For example, why does the law of conservation of matter work? To answer such questions, investigators develop a scientific hypothesis, an educated guess that explains a scientific law or certain scientific facts. More than 2,400 years ago Greek philosophers proposed that all matter is composed of tiny particles called atoms, but they had no experimental evidence to back up their atomic hypothesis. Scientists also develop and use various types of scientific models to simulate complex processes and systems. Many are mathematical models that are run and tested using computers.

Source: G. Tyler Miller Jr., *Environmental Science: Working with the Earth* (Belmont, CA: Wadsworth, 1995), pp. 41–42.

Team Up!

Compare your responses to Exercise 10a with one other classmate. Did both of you have the same main idea sentence highlighted? How many major supporting ideas did you each come up with?

Steps in the Process of Textbook Marking

Now that you know the three basic elements to mark in your textbook, main idea, important details, and vocabulary, follow these four basic steps.

Step 1: Preview

The first step in the textbook marking process is to preview or skim the reading material you have been assigned. As you skim, identify unfamiliar vocabulary words and write them down so you can look them up in your dictionary afterward. Then develop questions using the title and subheadings, and try to predict what the reading will be about. Although you can create questions and make predictions in your head, you might find it more effective to write them down in your journal. That way you can use them later when you are preparing for an exam.

Preview the following textbook excerpt and then read the model that follows.

Matter Exists in Various States

The things called matter exist in various states which include solids, liquids, and gases, the three common physical states of matter. Most matter can exist in each of these states if the temperature and pressure are changed.

You consider iron a solid because it exists in that state at ordinary temperatures, but you know iron can be melted. It can even be boiled away as a gas if it gets hot enough. Similarly, water is liquid, but you know it freezes to a solid in the freezer compartment of a refrigerator, and it changes into a gas when it boils on a stove or evaporates from your skin on a hot day.

A fourth state of matter, plasma, also should be included in discussions of the states of matter. A plasma has all of the properties of a gas except that it is composed of charged particles like electrons rather than uncharged atoms or molecules. Plasmas exist on stars like the sun, in nuclear explosions, and in neon signs.

Source: Herron, *Heath Chemistry* (Lexington, MA: D.C. Heath and Company, 1987), pp. 6–7.

We will follow Kelly's (a returning student) responses to Steps 1–4:

Previewing Model

Vocabulary words that I may need to review:

✓   *electrons*

✓   *molecules*

A question to ask from the title could be What are the various states of matter?

A prediction of the reading excerpt's content could be that the passage will be about the states of matter.

Step 2: Study-Read

In this stage of the textbook marking process you study-read your assigned reading selection or textbook chapter in sections (see Chapter 9). Make sure you read through each section *before you mark anything,* and pay close attention to any part of the passage that answers your preview question(s). It is important to think about each section as you read so you can check your comprehension and mentally piece the whole chapter together. Make sure you understand each section before continuing to read.

Study-Reading Model

After reading the passage, it is clear the answer to Step 1's previewing question is: The four states of matter are solids, liquids, gases, and plasma. As I predicted, the passage is about various states of matter.

Step 3: Mark or Highlight Text

After you have read your entire assignment, go back and mark (underline or highlight) the information that answered your questions—the main ideas (stated or implied) and the major supporting details. You should also circle the word clues that alerted you to the main idea and major supporting details, and mark any new vocabulary words.

Textmarking Model

Matter Exists in Various States

The things called matter exist in various states which include <u>solids, liquids, and gases, the</u> (three) <u>common physical states of matter.</u> Most matter can exist in each of these states if the temperature and pressure are changed.

You consider iron a solid because it exists in that state at ordinary temperatures, but you know iron can be melted. It can even be boiled away as a gas if it gets hot enough. Similarly, water is liquid, but you know it freezes to a solid in the freezer compartment of a refrigerator, and it changes into a gas when it boils on a stove or evaporates from your skin on a hot day.

A (fourth) <u>state of matter, plasma,</u> also should be included in discussions of the states of matter. A plasma has all of the properties of a gas except that it is composed of charged particles like electrons rather than uncharged atoms or molecules. Plasmas exist on stars like the sun, in nuclear explosions, and in neon signs.

Source: Herron, *Heath Chemistry* (D.C. Heath and Company, 1987), pp. 6–7.

Now that I have read and marked the excerpt, I realize that the main idea is that there are various states of matter. I underlined the parts of sentences that are major supporting details: <u>solids, liquids, and gases, the three common physical states of matter</u> and <u>A</u>(fourth)<u>state of matter, plasma</u>. I circled the word clues <u>three</u> and <u>fourth</u> because they signaled to me where the major supporting details were, and that the author is using a listing organization.

Step 4: Write Margin Cues

A **margin cue** is a symbol or notation you write in the margin of your text beside important information to indicate what you marked and why. For example, if you highlight or underline the main idea of a paragraph, you can put the letters MI in the margin beside the sentence containing the main idea to alert you to where it is the next time you review that section of your textbook. If you highlight or underline textbook material without labeling your markings, they will be almost meaningless as everything highlighted will seem to be of equal importance. The key to effective textbook marking is to show the relationships between ideas: you should be able to see, after quickly reviewing a page you have marked, the main idea, the major supporting details, and how they relate to each other.

Here is a list of common margin cues:

Textbook Information	Symbol
Vocabulary/Definitions	def
Main idea	MI
Important detail	ID

Other margin cues you can use to identify additional information, depending on what you think you need to clarify or remember or your instructor indicates is important, are these:

Textbook Information	Symbol
Examples	EX
Don't understand	?
Important information	*
Steps, sequence, ordering	1,2,3
Conclusion	Con
Author's opinion	Opin

The margin cues and markings you use will depend on you, your textbook, your instructor, and the course you are taking. Margin cues can also be in the form of short margin notes, called annotations. **Annotations** are shorthand messages—words, phrases, abbreviations—that alert you to particular areas of your textbook and briefly explain their importance. For example, in the Margin Cues Model below, the annotation *3 common states* marks the place in the reading where the writer lists common states of matter, and alerts you to how many states of matter to look for. Further down, the annotation *4th state* shows you where in the text the fourth state of matter is. Annotations work well when you need to know quickly why a piece of highlighted text is important. They usually provide more information than symbols but are almost as brief. How to develop your own personal textbook marking system will be discussed later in this chapter.

Margin Cues Model

The main idea of this excerpt is stated in the first sentence and is highlighted. The major supporting details are also marked, and from these it is clear the author is providing a list of the various states of matter.

MI
ID: 3 common
states

Matter Exists in Various States

The things called matter exist in various states which include [1]solids, [2]liquids, and [3]gases, the (three) common physical states of matter.

EX.

ID:
4th state

Most matter can exist in each of these states if the temperature and pressure are changed.

You consider iron a solid because it exists in that state at ordinary temperatures, but you know iron can be melted. It can even be boiled away as a gas if it gets hot enough. Similarly, water is liquid, but you know it freezes to a solid in the freezer compartment of a refrigerator, and it changes into a gas when it boils on a stove or evaporates from your skin on a hot day.

A (fourth) state of matter, °plasma, also should be included in discussions of the states of matter. A plasma has all of the properties of a gas except that it is composed of charged particles like electrons rather than uncharged atoms or molecules. Plasmas exist on stars like the sun, in nuclear explosions, and in neon signs.

Source: Herron, *Heath Chemistry* (Lexington, MA: D.C. Heath and Company, 1987), pp. 6–7.

Exercise

10b

Textbook Marking

Answer the prereading questions. Then read the article, "Lifting the Veil on Sex Slavery," and apply the four textbook marking steps that you have just learned.

1. Based on the title of the article, what do you expect it to be about?

_____

2. What do you already know about the Taliban's treatment of women?

_____

3. Are you familiar with the following vocabulary words? If not, look them up in a dictionary before you start reading:

 a. Burkas

 b. Tantamount

 c. Degradation

 d. Complicity

 e. Revering

4. What question might you expect this article to answer?

_____

_____

Lifting the Veil on Sex Slavery

Widow Shah Jan sits in an icy room with mud walls in a snowfield on the edge of Kabul. She wipes her tears with the edge of her grimy sweater as she recalls the day in August 1999 when the Taliban set fire to her home in the vineyards of the Shomali Plain and kidnapped her best friend, Nafiza. "The Taliban burst in with their guns and torches," says Shah Jan. "None of us even had time to put on our veils."

With the women stripped of their burkas, it was a simple task for Taliban invaders to cull the young beauties. Nafiza was one of them. Green-eyed, with raven-black hair that grazed her waist, Nafiza had rushed to help Shah Jan get her three kids out of the burning house. A Taliban fighter spotted the woman with the emerald eyes. She was his prize. With the butt of his AK-47 rifle, he slammed Nafiza into the dust and dragged her, crying and pleading, to the highway. There, Arabs and Pakistanis of al-Qaeda joined the Taliban to sort out the young women from the other villagers. One girl preferred suicide to slavery; she threw herself down a well. Nafiza and women from surrounding villages, numbering in the hundreds, were herded into trucks and buses. They were never seen again.

Only now, two months after the Taliban's fall, are the dirtiest secrets of their persecution of Afghan women coming to light. The Taliban often argued that the brutal restrictions they placed on women were actually a way of revering and protecting the opposite sex. The behavior of the Taliban during the six years they expanded their rule in Afghanistan made a mockery of that claim. The United Nations and relief agencies picked up warning signals of these abuses from women refugees fleeing the conquering Taliban. Now it is clear from the testimony of witnesses and officials of the new government that the ruling clerics systematically abducted women from the Tajik, Uzbek, Hazara, and other ethnic minorities they defeated. Stolen women were a reward for victorious battle. And in the cities of Kabul, Mazar-i-Sharif, Jalalabad and Khost, women victims tell of being forced to wed Taliban soldiers and Pakistani and Arab fighters of Osama bin Laden's al-Qaeda network, who later abandoned them. These marriages were tantamount to legalized rape. "They sold these girls," says Ahmad Jan, the Kabul police chief. "The girls were dishonored and then discarded."

In the mud-fortress villages above the Shomali vineyards, more than 600 women vanished in the 1999 Taliban offensive. Yet these abductions are considered such a great dishonor that the victims' families almost never mention them. Says Qadria Yasdon Parast, leader of Freedom Messengers, a Kabul women's rights group: "If you ask about the missing, they say, 'Our daughter's dead,' or that she's off married in Pakistan." Many of the women probably did end up in Pakistan—but were sold to brothels or kept as virtual slaves inside homes, say officials from relief agencies. None have come back. Even if they could escape, these women would probably calculate that their families would no longer welcome them.

The trail of the missing Shomali women leads to Jalalabad, not far from the Pakistan border. There, according to eyewitnesses, the women were penned up inside Sar Shahi camp in the desert. The more desirable among them were selected and taken away. Some were trucked to Peshawar with the apparent complicity of Pakistani border guards. Others were taken to Khost, where bin Laden had several training camps. The al-Qaeda Arabs had a hard time finding voluntary brides among the Afghan women, but they did have money. One Arab in Khost spent $10,000 on a teenage Afghan beauty, says Ahmad Jan, but abandoned her a week later, when the U.S. air strikes began.

Orders to abduct women came from the Taliban leaders, say the Kabul police, (but) not all commanders obeyed. In the Shomali Plain, Taliban commander Nuruludah says, he saw women being forced onto trucks by Pakistani members of al-Qaeda, so he gathered men, ambushed the trucks, and released the women. In Jalalabad too, a few local Taliban eventually stormed the camp and freed the women who remained there. These were the heroic exceptions. For others, apparently, the profound degradation of women seemed perfectly tolerable.

Source: Tim McGirk et al., "Lifting the Veil on Sex Slavery," *Time*, February 18, 2002.

Using your textbook marking, answer the following questions in the space provided.

1. What is the main idea of the article?

_____

_____

_____

2. What does "lifting the veil" in the title mean to you?

_____

3. Who is lifting the veil?

_____

_____

4. The author said that Afghanistan made a mockery of the claim that the brutal restrictions placed on women were actually a way of revering and protecting them. What did the author mean by this statement?

_____

_____

_____

_____

Learning Journal

What are the four steps of textbook marking? Which of these steps will be the biggest challenge for you? Why?

Deciding What Else to Mark

Knowing what else to mark, besides the main idea, major supporting details, and new vocabulary, or if more marking is even needed, depends on three factors: additional information provided in lectures, your own practical experience in lab assignments, and parts of a reading you find unclear.

Lecture

Your instructors will usually lecture on at least some of the content covered in your textbooks. When they do, pay close attention, as it is important to relate what they say to what you have read. You can judge the importance of specific information by their use of word clues such as *most important*, *in conclusion*, and *in summary*. You can also judge the relative importance of information from more subtle cues such as how much time an instructor spends on a topic. Once you decide a topic covered in a lecture is an important restatement of textbook material, you should mark it. Most textbook information that is restated in a lecture is information that your instructor considers significant and is therefore likely to be on an exam.

Lab

If your class has a lab component, you have another opportunity to identify what information is most important in your textbooks. Lab assignments are usually practical applications of the lessons being taught in your lectures and textbook. If you are learning about the digestive system, for example, you may well have a biology lab experiment that requires you to dissect an animal to examine its digestive system. By doing this, you gain firsthand experience of what you have been learning about, and a clearer sense of what is really important in the digestive process. If it becomes obvious to you from participating in a lab class that certain textbook information is important, you should label or mark it using a star symbol * or other appropriate notation.

Unclear Information

If a concept is not clear to you, mark that section in your textbook to remind yourself to ask a classmate or instructor to explain it. An easy symbol to indicate confusion is a question mark. Once you have obtained clarification, write an explanation of the concept in your journal, class notebook, or at the bottom of the relevant textbook page.

Team Up!

Pair up with another student, and explain to each other the criteria you can use to help decide what and how much to mark in your textbooks. Come to an agreement on your responses.

Developing a Personal System of Textbook Marking

Using Symbols

Developing a personal system of textbook marking means adopting and consistently using specific abbreviations and/or symbols to label your marked text. Earlier in this chapter, frequently used symbols and abbreviations were offered as examples. You may like and use some or all of these symbols, develop your own set of margin cues, or use a combination of both. It is important to *remember* what the symbols and abbreviations you use stand for. An easy way to do this is to develop a key by writing down the symbols you most often use, with their meanings, on 3 × 5 cards and taping the cards to the inside covers of your textbooks and journal.

Using Highlighters

Some students like highlighters and feel that using them is an incentive to read more. Others find that switching back and forth between highlighters and a pen while reading keeps them alert. Here are examples of how two students use them:

Sam uses two different colored highlighters. In his personal system the color yellow means main idea and the color green means important detail. He chooses not to write MI to indicate main idea or ID to indicate an important detail because he says the colors effectively communicate those messages to him. He still uses a pen to mark other types of information such as new terminology and examples emphasized in lectures.

Jason uses one highlighter. He highlights text, as opposed to underlining it, and uses a pen to write margin cues. He says that highlighted text catches his eye better when he is reviewing for tests. In the past, he found that when he underlined text but did not use a highlighter, he would sometimes miss the marked information.

Learning Journal

List the abbreviations you currently use to label your markings. List some problems you may have encountered with textbook marking. For example, do you overmark, undermark, or forget why you marked?

Knowing How Much to Mark

Knowing how much to mark is the key to the strategy's effectiveness. All main ideas, major supporting details, vocabulary words, and word clues should be marked.

Exercise 10c

How Much to Mark

Read the following excerpt and mark it using your personal system. Compare your marking with the three examples of marking provided and answer the questions that follow.

Case Study: The John Eli Miller Family

John Eli Miller was a farmer like many other farmers in the United States, except for one thing—when he died on his farm in Middlefield, Ohio, in the mid-twentieth century, he was the head of the largest family in the United States. He was survived by 5 children, 61 grandchildren, 338 great-grandchildren, and 6 great-great-grandchildren. Within his lifetime, John Miller witnessed a family population explosion. What was perhaps even more remarkable was that the explosion started with a family of just 7 children—not all that unusual for the nineteenth-century United States.

During most of John Miller's life, his family was not unusually large. It is just that he lived long enough to find out what simple multiplication can do, and he lived in a time when the death rate among infants, children, and young adults was very small compared with typical death rates during the history of most human populations. Of 7 children born to John Miller, 5 survived him; of 63 grandchildren, 61 survived him; and of 341 great-grandchildren (born to 55 married grandchildren—an average of slightly more than 6 children per parent), 338 survived him.

The history of John Eli Miller's family illustrates several important points about the human population. First, human beings, like almost all other species, have a great potential for rapid population increase. Second, from the viewpoint of an individual, that rapid increase can happen even if life seems to be proceeding in an ordinary fashion; John Eli Miller's life was not extraordinary except in the rate at which his family increased. Third, the rapid increase in the size of his family happened because modern civilization has increased survival rates and decreased death rates, especially among children. Thus, John Miller's family illustrates the importance of the question that faces us all: What individual actions will help limit the growth of the human population?

Now compare your marking with the following three examples:

Example #1: Undermarked Passage

Case Study: The John Eli Miller Family

John Eli Miller was a farmer like many other farmers in the United States, except for one thing—when he died on his farm in Middlefield, Ohio, in the mid-twentieth century, he was the head of the largest family in the United States. He was survived by 5 children, 61 grandchildren, 338 great-grandchildren, and 6 great-great-grandchildren. Within his lifetime, John Miller witnessed a family population explosion. What was perhaps even more remarkable was that the explosion started with a family of just 7 children—not all that unusual for the nineteenth-century United States.

During most of John Miller's life, his family was not unusually large. It is just that he lived long enough to find out what simple multiplication can do, and he lived in a time when the death rate among infants, children, and young adults was very small compared with typical death rates during the history of most human populations. Of 7 children born to John Miller, 5 survived him; of 63 grandchildren, 61 survived him; and of 341 great-grandchildren (born to 55 married grandchildren—an average of slightly more than 6 children per parent), 338 survived him.

The history of John Eli Miller's family illustrates several important points about the human population. First, human beings, like almost all other species, have a great <u>potential for rapid population increase</u>. Second, from the viewpoint of an individual, that rapid increase can happen even if life seems to be proceeding in an ordinary fashion; John Eli Miller's life was not extraordinary except in the rate at which his family increased. Third, the <u>rapid increase in the size of his family happened because modern civilization has increased survival rates and decreased death rates</u>, especially among children. Thus, John Miller's family illustrates the importance of the question that faces us all: What individual actions will help limit the growth of the human population?

Example #2: Overmarked Passage

Case Study: The John Eli Miller Family

<u>John Eli Miller was a farmer</u> (like) many other farmers in the United States, (except) for one thing—<u>when he died on his farm in Middlefield, Ohio, in the mid-twentieth century, he was the head of the largest family in the United States. He was survived by 5 children, 61 grandchildren, 338 great-grandchildren, and 6 great-great-grandchildren.</u> Within his lifetime, <u>John Miller witnessed a family population explosion.</u> What was perhaps even more remarkable was that the

explosion started with a family of just 7 children—not all that unusual for the nineteenth-century United States.

During most of John Miller's life, his family was not unusually large. It is just that he lived long enough to find out what simple multiplication can do, and he lived in a time when the death rate among infants, children, and young adults was very small (compared) with typical death rates during the history of most human populations. Of 7 children born to John Miller, 5 survived him; of 63 grandchildren, 61 survived him; and of 341 great-grandchildren (born to 55 married grandchildren—an average of slightly more than 6 children per parent), 338 survived him.

The history of John Eli Miller's family illustrates (several important points) about the human population. (First,) human beings, (like) almost all other species, have a great potential for rapid population increase. (Second,) from the viewpoint of an individual, that rapid increase can happen even if life seems to be proceeding in an ordinary fashion; John Eli Miller's life was not extraordinary (except) in the rate at which his family increased. (Third,) the rapid increase in the size of his family happened (because) modern civilization has increased survival rates and decreased death rates, especially among children. (Thus,) John Miller's family illustrates the importance of the question that faces us all: What individual actions will help limit the growth of the human population?

Example #3: Efficiently Marked Passage

Case Study: The John Eli Miller Family

John Eli Miller was a farmer like many other farmers in the United States, except for one thing—when he died on his farm in Middlefield, Ohio, in the mid-twentieth century, he was the head of the largest family in the United States. He was survived by 5 children, 61 grandchildren, 338 great-grandchildren, and 6 great-great-grandchildren. Within his lifetime, John Miller witnessed a family population explosion. What was perhaps even more remarkable was that the explosion started with a family of just 7 children—not all that unusual for the nineteenth-century United States.

During most of John Miller's life, his family was not unusually large. It is just that he lived long enough to find out what simple multiplication can do, and he lived in a time when the death rate among infants, children, and young adults was very small compared with typical death rates during the history of most human populations. Of 7 children born to John Miller, 5 survived him; of 63 grandchildren, 61 survived him; and of 341 great-grandchildren (born to 55 married grandchildren—an average of slightly more than 6 children per parent), 338 survived him.

The history of John Eli Miller's family illustrates several important points about the human population. (First,) human beings, like almost all other species, have a great potential for rapid population increase. (Second,) from the viewpoint of an individual, that rapid increase can happen even if life seems to be proceeding in an ordinary fashion; John Eli Miller's life was not extraordinary except in the rate at which his family increased. (Third,) the rapid increase in the size of his family happened because modern civilization has increased survival rates and decreased death rates, especially among children. (Thus,) John Miller's family illustrates the importance of the question that faces us all: **What individual actions will help limit the growth of the human population?**

1. Based on your review of the textbook marking examples, did you mark too little (Example 1), too much (Example 2), or just enough (Example 3)? Explain your answer.

_____

2. What changes could you make to increase the effectiveness of your textbook marking?

_____

Team Up!

With three or four other students, discuss the textbook marking strategies you applied to the "John Eli Miller" paragraphs. Focus on the differences and similarities between your textbook marking systems.

Take One Minute

Write down the key components of what you should mark in your textbooks on a separate sheet of paper.

Practice with Reading Passage

Answer all questions on a separate sheet of paper.

Reading Practice

"Controlling Nervousness"
BY H. GREGORY

Answer the questions under Prepare to Read. Then read the textbook excerpt, apply the four steps of textbook marking, and answer the questions that follow.

PREPARE TO READ

1. Based on the title and the headings, what do you expect this excerpt to be about?

2. What do you already know about the topic?

3. Here are some vocabulary words you should know before you read. If they are not familiar, look them up in your dictionary:

   a. Obliged

   b. Assailed

   c. Banish

   d. Inexplicably

   e. Eloquent

   f. Orate

   g. Unadulterated

   h. Pap

4. Using the title, headings, or topic, create three questions you think this selection should answer.

   a.

   b.

   c.

Controlling Nervousness
Reasons for Nervousness

Is it foolish to be afraid to give a speech? Is this fear as groundless as a child's fear of the boogeyman? I used to think so, back when I first began making speeches. I was a nervous wreck, and I would often chide myself by saying, "Come on, relax, it's just a little speech. There is no good reason to be scared." But I was wrong. There *is* good reason to be scared; in fact, there are *four* good reasons.

1. **Fear of being stared at.** In the animal world, a stare is a hostile act. Dogs, baboons, and other animals sometimes defend their territory by staring. Their hostile gaze alone is enough to turn away an intruder. We human beings have similar reactions; it is part of our biological makeup to be upset by stares. Imagine that you are riding in a crowded elevator with a group of strangers. Suddenly you realize that the other people are staring directly at you. Not just glancing. *Staring.* You probably would be unnerved and frightened because a stare can be as threatening as a clenched fist— especially if it comes from people you don't know. That is why public speaking can be so frightening. You have a pack of total strangers "attack-ing" you with unrelenting stares, while you are obliged to stand alone, exposed and vulnerable—a goldfish in a bowl, subject to constant scrutiny.

2. **Fear of failure.** "We're all afraid of looking stupid," says Jim Seymour, a columnist for *PC* magazine. "I give about 40 speeches a year....Yet every single time I get ready to walk out in front of an audience, I get that old, scary feeling: *What if I make a fool of myself?* That's as deeply embedded in our psyches as our DNA chains are embedded in our cells, I suspect; I don't know anyone who doesn't get the sweats at the prospect of looking dumb to someone else."

3. **Fear of rejection.** What if we do our best, what if we deliver a polished speech, but the audience still does not like us? It would be quite a blow to our ego because we want to be liked and, yes, even loved. We want people to admire us, to consider us wise and intelligent, and to accept our ideas and opinions. We don't want people to dislike us or reject us.

4. **Fear of the unknown.** Throughout our lives we are apprehensive about doing new things, such as going to school for the first time, riding a bus without our parents, or going out on our first date. We cannot put a finger on exactly what we are afraid of, because our fear is vague and diffused. What we really fear is the unknown; we worry that some unpredictable disaster will occur. When we stand up to give a speech, we are sometimes assailed by this same fear of the unknown because we cannot predict the outcome of our speech. Fortunately, this fear usually disappears as we become experienced in giving speeches. We develop enough confidence to know that nothing terrible will befall us, just as our childhood fear of riding in a bus by ourselves vanished after two or three trips.

All four of these fears are as understandable as the fear of lightning. There is no reason to be ashamed of having them.

The Value of Fear

In the first hour of my public speaking class, many students tell me that one of their goals is to completely eliminate all traces of nervousness. My response may surprise you as much as it surprises them: *You should not try to banish all your fear and nervousness. You need a certain amount of fear to give a good speech.*

You *need* fear? Yes. Fear energizes you; it makes you think more rapidly; it helps you speak with vitality and enthusiasm. Here is why: When you stand up to give a speech and fear hits you, your body goes on "red alert," the same biological mechanism that saved our cave-dwelling ancestors when they were faced with a hungry lion or a human foe and had to fight or flee in order to survive. Though not as crucial to us as it was to our ancestors, this system is still nice to have for emergencies: if you were walking down a deserted street one night and someone tried to attack you, your body would release a burst of **adrenaline** into your bloodstream, causing fresh blood and oxygen to rush to your muscles, and you would be able to fight ferociously or run faster than you have ever run in your life. The benefit of adrenaline can be seen in competitive sports: athletes *must* get their adrenaline flowing before a game begins. The great home-run slugger Reggie Jackson said during his heyday, "I have butterflies in my stomach almost every time I step up to the plate. When I don't have them, I get worried because it means I won't hit the ball very well."

Many public speakers have the same attitude. John Farmer, a criminal trial attorney in Norton, Virginia, who has argued high-profile murder cases before the Virginia Supreme Court as well as in local courts, was asked recently if he still gets nervous in the courtroom. "Oh, yes," he replied, "the day I stop being nervous is the day that I'll stop doing a good job for my clients."

In public speaking, adrenaline infuses you with energy; it causes extra blood and oxygen to rush not only to your muscles but to your brain as well, thus enabling you to think with greater clarity and quickness. It makes you come across to your audience as someone who is alive and vibrant. Elayne Snyder, a speech teacher, uses the term **positive nervousness,** which she describes in this way: "It's a zesty, enthusiastic, lively feeling with a slight edge to it. Positive nervousness is the state you'll achieve by converting your anxiety into constructive energy…. It's still nervousness, but you're no longer victimized by it; instead you're vitalized by it."

If you want proof that nervousness is beneficial, observe speakers who have absolutely no butterflies at all. Because they are 100 percent relaxed and cool, they give speeches that are dull and flat, with no energy, no zest. There is an old saying: "Speakers who say they are as cool as a cucumber usually give speeches about as interesting as a cucumber." Most good speakers report that if they don't have stage fright before a public appearance, their delivery is poor. One speaker, the novelist I. A. R. Wylie, said, "I rarely rise to my feet without a throat constricted with terror and a furiously thumping heart. When, for some reason, I *am* cool and self-assured, the speech is always a failure. I need fear to spur me on."

Another danger in being devoid of nervousness: you might get hit with a sudden bolt of panic. A hospital official told me that she gave an orientation speech to new employees every week for several years. "It became so routine that I lost all of my stage fright," she said. Then one day, while in the middle of her talk, she was suddenly and inexplicably struck with paralyzing fear. "I got all choked up and had to take a break to pull myself together."

Many other speakers have reported similar cases of sudden panic, which always hit on occasions when they were too relaxed. I once suffered such an attack, and the experience taught me that I must get myself "psyched up" for every speech. I remind myself that I need nervous energy in order to keep my listeners awake and interested. I encourage my butterflies to flutter around inside, so that I can be poised and alert.

Guidelines for Controlling Nervousness

We have just discussed how a complete lack of nervousness is undesirable. What about the other extreme? Is *too much* nervousness bad for you? Of course it is, especially if you are so frightened that you forget what you were planning to say, or if your breathing is so labored that you cannot get your words out. Your goal is to keep your nervousness under control, so that you have just the right amount—enough to energize you, but not enough to cripple you. How can you do this? By paying heed to the following tips for the three phases of speechmaking: the planning stage, the period immediately before the speech, and during the speech.

In the Planning Stage

By giving time and energy to planning your speech, you can bypass many anxieties.

Choose a Topic about Which You Know a Great Deal   Nothing will get you more rattled than speaking on a subject about which you know little. If you are asked to talk on a topic with which you're not comfortable, decline the invitation (unless, of course, it is an assignment from an instructor or a boss who gives you no choice). Choose a topic about which you know a lot (or about which you can learn by doing extensive research). This will give you enormous self-confidence; if something terrible happens (for example, you lose your notes), you can improvise because your head will be filled with information about the subject. Also, familiarity with the topic will allow you to handle yourself well in the question-and-answer period after the speech.

Prepare Yourself Thoroughly   Here is a piece of advice given by many experienced speakers: *The very best precaution against excessive stage fright is thorough, careful preparation.* You have heard the expression, "I came unglued." In public speaking, solid preparation is the "glue" that will hold you together. Joel Weldon of Scottsdale, Arizona (who quips that he used to be so frightened of audiences that he was "unable to lead a church group in silent prayer"), gives his personal formula for controlling fear: "I prepare and then prepare, and then when I think I'm ready, I prepare some more." Weldon recommends five to eight hours of preparation for each hour in front of an audience.

Start your preparation far in advance of the speech date, so that you have plenty of time to gather ideas, create an outline, and prepare speaking notes. Then practice, practice, practice. Don't just look over your notes—actually stand up and rehearse your talk in whatever way suits you: in front of a mirror, into a tape recorder, before a family member or friend. Don't rehearse just once—run through your entire speech at least four times. If you "give" your speech four times at home, you will find that your fifth delivery—before a live audience—will be smoother and more self-assured than if you had not practiced at all.

Never Memorize a Speech   Giving a speech from memory courts disaster. Winston Churchill, the British prime minister during World War II who is considered one of the greatest orators of modern times, learned this lesson as a young man. In the beginning of his career, he would write out and memorize his speeches. One day, while giving a memorized talk to Parliament, he suddenly stopped. His mind went blank. He began his last sentence all over. Again his mind went blank. He sat down in embarrassment and shame. Never again did Churchill try to memorize a speech. This same thing has happened to many others who have tried to commit a speech to memory. Everything goes smoothly until they get derailed, and then they are hopelessly off the track.

Even if you avoid derailment, there is another reason for not memorizing: you will probably sound mechanical, like a robot with a tape recorder in its mouth. In addition to considering you dull and boring, your audience will sense that you are speaking from your memory and not from your heart, and they will question your sincerity.

Imagine Yourself Giving an Effective Speech   Let yourself daydream a bit: picture yourself going up to the lectern, nervous but in control of yourself, then giving a forceful talk to an appreciative audience. This visualization technique may sound silly, but it has worked for many speakers and it might work for you. Whatever you do, don't let yourself imagine the opposite—a bad speech or poor delivery. Negative daydreams will add unnecessary fear to your life in the days before your speech, and sap you of creative energy—energy that you need for preparing and practicing. Actress Ali MacGraw says, "We have only so much energy, and the more we direct toward the project itself, the less is left to pour into wondering 'Will I fail?'"

Notice that the daydream I am suggesting includes nervousness. You need to have a realistic image in your mind: picture yourself as nervous, but nevertheless in command of the situation and capable of delivering a strong, effective speech.

This technique, often called **positive imagery,** has been used by athletes for years. Have you ever watched professional golf on TV? Before each stroke, golfers carefully study the distance from the ball to the hole, the rise and fall of the terrain, and so on. Many of them report that just before swinging, they imagine themselves hitting the ball with the right amount of force and watching it go straight into the cup. Then they try to execute the play just as they imagined it. The imagery, many pros say, improves their game.

Positive imagery works best when you can couple it with *believing* that you will give a successful speech. Is it absurd to hold such a belief? If you fail to prepare, yes, it is absurd. But if you spend time in solid preparation and rehearsal, you are justified in believing in success.

Know That Shyness is No Barrier   Some shy people think that their shyness blocks them from becoming good speakers, but this is erroneous. Many shy introverts have succeeded in show business: Gwyneth Paltrow, Halle Berry, Dana Carvey, Mariah Carey, Elizabeth Hurley, and David Letterman, to name just a few. Many less famous people also have succeeded. "I used to stammer," says Joe W. Boyd of Bellingham, Washington, "and I used to be petrified at the thought of speaking before a group of any size." Despite his shyness, Boyd joined a Toastmasters club to develop his speaking skills. Two years later, he won the Toastmasters International Public Speaking Contest by giving a superb speech to an audience of over 2,000 listeners.

Shift Focus from Self to Audience   Before a speech, some speakers cause their anxiety to mushroom because of excessive preoccupation with themselves, focusing on what listeners will think about them rather than concentrating on the audience.

"Here's how I get my jitters under control," says Carlos Jimenez, a member of a Toastmasters club in Northern California. "I try not to worry about whether I will be perceived as a brilliant, eloquent expert. Who am I to be so selfish? Who am I to think that the way I look and talk is more important than the people who are sitting in the audience? I look at public speaking as a way to help people, and I can't really help people if my mind is filled with 'me, me, me' instead of 'you, you, you."

One good way to shift the focus from self to audience is to change your "self-talk." Whenever you have a self-centered thought like "I will make a total fool out of myself," substitute an audience centered thought like "I will give my listeners information that will be very useful in their lives." This approach not only will liberate you from the grip of anxiety, but it will empower you to connect with your audience.

Plan Visual Aids   Research shows that using a visual aid helps reduce anxiety. Visual aids such as slides or overhead transparencies can help you in two ways: (1) you shift the audience's stares from you to your illustrations and (2) you walk about and move your hands and arms, thereby siphoning off some of your excess nervous energy. Whatever illustrations you decide to use, make sure they are understandable, appropriate, and clearly visible to everyone in the room.

Make Arrangements   Long before you give your speech, inspect the place where you will speak and anticipate any problems: Is there an extension cord for the slide projector? Do the windows have curtains so that the room can be darkened for your slide presentation? Is there a chalkboard? Some talks have been ruined and some speakers turned into nervous wrecks because at the last moment they discover that there isn't an extension cord in the entire building.

Devote Extra Practice to the Introduction   Because you are likely to suffer the greatest anxiety at the beginning of your speech, you should spend a lot of time practicing your introduction.

Most speakers, actors, and musicians report that after the first minute or two, their nervousness moves to the background and the rest of the event is relatively easy. Ernestine Schumann-Heink, the German opera singer, said, "I grow so nervous before a performance, I become sick. I want to go home. But after I have been on the stage for a few minutes, I am so happy that nobody can drag me off." Perhaps happiness is too strong a word for what you will feel, but if you are a typical speaker, the rest of your speech will be smooth sailing once you have weathered the turbulent waters of the first few minutes.

Source: H. Gregory, *Public Speaking for College and Career* (Boston: McGraw-Hill, 2002), pp. 29–34.

CHECK YOUR UNDERSTANDING

OBJECTIVE QUESTIONS

Read each question carefully and then circle the best possible answer from the choices given.

1. What is the topic of this excerpt?

   a. Eliminating nervousness during speechmaking.

   b. Making good speeches.

   c. Nervousness during speechmaking.

   d. Reasons for nervousness.

2. What is the main idea of this excerpt?

   a. Nervousness can be controlled during speechmaking.

   b. There are good reasons to be nervous while making speeches.

   c. Eliminating all nervousness is not a good idea when making a speech.

   d. Preparation is the key to controlling nervousness.

3. Which of the following statements is *not* a major supporting idea from the excerpt?

   a. There are good reasons for being nervous during a speech.

   b. Winston Churchill learned to never memorize a speech.

   c. Fear is valuable and necessary to good speechmaking.

   d. Nervousness can be controlled during all phases of speechmaking.

4. Which of the following statements is *not* a reason that the author gives for being afraid while making a speech?

   a. Fear of being stared at.

   b. Fear of failure.

   c. Fear of forgetting.

   d. Fear of the unknown.

5. How is fear valuable when giving a speech?

   a. Fear is a natural reaction when people are staring at you.

   b. Fear is necessary for proper visualization.

   c. Fear helps your memory.

   d. Fear energizes you.

6. According to the author, which of the following is *not* considered a guideline for controlling nervousness?

   a. Don't eat sugar the night before a speech.

   b. Choose a topic you know.

   c. Never memorize your speech.

   d. Don't let the audience upset you.

SHORT-ANSWER QUESTIONS.

7. The author gives many examples of famous people who are shy. Did you mark these examples in the excerpt? Why or why not?

8. Under the heading "Guidelines for Controlling Nervousness," did you highlight or mark each guideline? Why or why not?

9. Although you only read one, there are three main headings in this textbook chapter excerpt: "Reasons for Nervousness," "The Value of Fear," and "Guidelines for Controlling Nervousness." Which do you think is the most important? Why? Did the title of the chapter help you make your decision?

Chapter Summary

Textbook marking is a systematic mark-and-label reading tool that helps you distinguish important ideas from less important ones. At a minimum, you should aim to mark and label the main idea, important details, and new vocabulary in your textbook chapters. Beyond these three basic elements of textbook marking, you should use your experience in lecture and lab to decide if you need to mark more. Always mark information that is unclear, to remind yourself to find out what it means before you are tested on the material. Because every university, college, class, student, and textbook are different, you will develop your own system of textbook marking. A personalized system will work well as long as it is consistent, makes sense to you, and achieves the main goal of textbook marking: showing the relationships between ideas in what you read.

Post Test

Answer all questions following on a separate sheet of paper.

Part I

OBJECTIVE QUESTIONS

Read each of the following questions and decide if they are true or false.

1. Everyone's textbook markings should look the same.

2. There can be more than one main idea in a textbook chapter.

3. Sometimes marking minor supporting details may be wise.

4. Whenever I mark in a textbook, I should always write a margin cue.

5. Everyone should always get the same main idea from a reading.

SHORT-ANSWER QUESTIONS

6. What are the four steps of textbook marking presented in this chapter?

7. How do you know if you are marking effectively?

8. What is the danger of marking too much?

Part II

Reading Passage

Excerpt from *Aging and the Life Course*
BY J. QUADAGNO

Answer these questions. Then read the excerpt, apply the four steps of textbook marking, and answer the questions that follow.

1. Based on the title and the headings, what do you expect this excerpt to be about?

2. What do you already know about the topic?

3. Use the title, headings, or topic to create three questions you think this selection should answer.

Ageism and Stereotypes

Forms of Ageism

In 1969, the gerontologist Robert Butler coined the term **ageism** to refer to "a systematic stereotyping of and discrimination against people because they

are old, just as racism and sexism accomplish this with skin color and gender."
According to Butler (1969), "old people are categorized as senile, rigid in
thought and manner, old-fashioned in morality and skills. . . . Ageism allows
the younger generation to see older people as different from themselves; thus,
they subtly cease to identify with their elders as human beings" (p. 243). The
concept of ageism was subsequently popularized by Maggie Kuhn, a senior
citizen who founded the Gray Panthers to fight against age discrimination
after she was forced to retire from her job at the United Presbyterian Church
(Ferraro, 1992). Ageism is similar to sexism and racism in that it precludes looking at people as individuals and instead judges people by virtue of their membership in a social category. Presently, the most widely accepted definition
of ageism is "prejudice and discrimination against older people based on the
belief that aging makes people less attractive, intelligent and productive" (Ferraro,1992:296).

The term *ageism* actually encompasses two distinct concepts: stereotypes
and age discrimination. **Stereotypes** are composites of ideas and beliefs attributed to people as a group or social category. They may incorporate some characteristics or attributes that accurately describe some people who belong to
a group, but they always fail to capture the diverse qualities of the individuals
in that group. Some older people, for example, may be rigid in thought, but
many others are open-minded and interested in exploring new ideas. The second concept, **age discrimination,** refers to behavior, not just to beliefs about
someone because he or she is old. When people act on the basis of stereotypes, they are guilty of age discrimination.

Like discrimination on the basis of race or gender, age discrimination takes
many forms (Butler, 1989). Refusing to hire older workers is a common form
of age discrimination. Age discrimination may also occur in decisions about eli-
gibility for health care. For example, in the British National Health Service, the
elderly are excluded from certain health-screening programs and surgical procedures (Arber and Ginn, 1991). Age discrimination also occurs when younger
people with identical symptoms to older people receive more aggressive medical treatment (Riley, 1995).

How predominant are stereotypes about the aged today? One study con-
sisted of interviews with 240 men and women aged 18 to 85, who were divided
into three age groups: young adult, middle-aged, and elderly adults (Hummert
et al., 1994). Stereotypical views were quite common.

The subjects were asked to think about how they would describe the typical elderly adult and to consider what they typically think about or read about
the elderly. They were then asked to write down these characteristics. The traits
were sorted into two clusters, one negative, the other positive. The positive trait
clusters included "golden ager," someone who was active, adventurous, healthy,
and lively; the "perfect grandparent," who was intelligent, knowledgeable, wise,
and kind; and the "John Wayne conservative," an individual who was patriotic,
old-fashioned. and conservative. Among the negative trait clusters were the
"shrew/curmudgeon," someone who was seen as greedy, selfish, stubborn, and
ill-tempered; the "recluse," who was timid, dependent, and forgetful; and the
"elitist," who was demanding, snobbish, and prejudiced. Although the young,

middle-aged, and elderly held many of the same stereotypes, older people created more groupings of traits and held more complex ideas about the elderly than young adults. They did not view the old as simply being demanding or wise but rather saw them in more realistic terms, as having a composite of traits.

Ageism in Historical and Cross-Cultural Perspective.

Although the term *ageism* has been recently coined, ageist stereotypes have existed at least as long as the written word. In his *Rhetoric,* Aristotle accused the aged of being cowardly, selfish, timorous, fearful, small-minded, ill-humored, and avaricious (Scrutton, 1990). In Shakespeare's *As You Like It,* the melancholy character, Jacques, describes old age as "second childness and mere oblivion, sans teeth, sans eyes, sans taste, sans everything" (II, vii). Sigmund Freud (1905) wrote that "psychiatry (was) not possible near or above the age of 50; the elasticity of the mental processes on which the treatment depends is as a rule lacking—old people are not educable" (p. 149).

For much of the twentieth century, the predominant stereotype was that the aged were poor and frail, and that their children often deserted them. The poem "'Over the Hill to the Poorhouse," popular in the 1920s, told of upstanding elderly people who, abandoned by children and too infirm to work, sought final refuge in the poorhouse (Haber, 1994).

In the past few decades a new stereotype, which has replaced this older view, depicts the aged as a prosperous, selfish, and politically powerful group who are gobbling up scarce societal resources (Binstock, 1996). In 1992, for example, the cover story of *Fortune* proclaimed that "The tyranny of America's old … is one of the crucial issues facing U.S. society" (Smith, 1992). Similarly, an article in *New Republic* characterized older people as "an unproductive section of the population, one that does not even promise (as children do) one day to be productive" (Fairlie, 1988:19).

One of the reasons for these changing stereotypes is the dramatic improvements that have taken place in the economic status of the aged. Between 1960 and 1996, the proportion of people over 65 with incomes below the poverty level dropped from nearly 40 percent to just over 12 percent. Another factor has been the rise of what has been called *apocalyptic demography,* which provides foreboding scenarios about the fiscal implications of population aging (Binstock, 1996). Regardless of the cause, these stereotypes are as inaccurate as those that portrayed the elderly as poor, frail, and incompetent.

Gender and Ageism

The form ageism takes tends to differ by gender, because there is a double standard of aging. Women are more likely to be valued according to their sexual attractiveness, whereas men are more likely to be evaluated by their occupational success. Thus, for women, being positively judged depends on maintaining a youthful appearance. A man with gray hair and wrinkles may be considered distinguished looking, a woman simply old (Gerike, 1990).

One study of men and women between the ages of 18 to 80 asked whether they had used any techniques like dyeing their hair. using wrinkle cream, or having plastic surgery to conceal their age (Harris, 1994). On every measure, women were more likely than men to use such techniques, especially dyeing hair (34 percent of women compared to 6 percent of men) and using wrinkle cream (24 percent of women compared to 1 percent of men). Although men and women were equally likely to indicate that they used age-concealment techniques because of concerns about their appearance, women rated looking younger as more important to them personally and for their job than men. Further, all subjects found signs of aging to be significantly less attractive for women than for men.

In another study, 554 psychotherapists were asked to rate a "mature, healthy, socially competent" individual on the Bern Sex Role Inventory, a scale designed to measure gender stereotypes (Turner and Turner, 1991). Each therapist was assigned a different description (young, middle-aged, or old; male or female). Young and middle-aged men and women were viewed by the therapists as assertive and willing to take risks. In rating the old, however, these characteristics were only attributed to men. Older women were viewed as less assertive and less willing to take risks. These stereotypes could have consequences for the course of therapy, for assertive older women might be perceived as aberrant or abnormal (Turner and Turner, 1991).

Although the double standard of aging devalues older women, stereotypes of men as independent and self-reliant may also be harmful. One consequence is that aged widowers receive less help and emotional support from family and friends than widows (Moyers, 1993).

The New Ageism

In recent decades, ageism has taken on a new form. What is termed the **new ageism** refers to a tendency to patronize the elderly and be overly solicitous. It may involve attitudes that discourage the elderly from taking risks, dissuade them from exercising, and even deny their sexuality. Steve Scrutton (1990) described his own ageist attitude toward his widowed mother:

> My father died in 1979, aged 76. After a period of normal grieving, my mother, who was then 74, decided that she wanted to travel.... A journey of about 100 miles... alone. My first reaction was that she was to do no such thing. I would go to Norwich and bring her myself. My second reaction was to let her do as she wished....This form of patronizing ageism is common where there is genuine care for aging people. (p. 1)

Similarly, one study on adjustment to life in a nursing home found that the most vulnerable individuals were those who had lost all control of their own lives. One woman in her 80s described the devastating sense of loss she felt after her children sold her home and belongings without consulting her first—so she "wouldn't have to worry about it" (Rubin-Terrado, 1994:42). The point is that paternalistic ageism can be as harmful as neglect.

Source: J. Quadagno, *Aging and the Life Course: An Introduction to Social Gerontology* (New York: McGraw-Hill, 1999), pp. 4–7.

OBJECTIVE QUESTIONS

Read each question carefully and then circle the best possible answer from the choices given.

1. What is the topic of this excerpt?

   a. Ageism.

   b. Ageism and gender.

   c. The new ageism.

   d. Age discrimination.

2. What is the main idea of this excerpt?

   a. Women are discriminated against more than men.

   b. The elderly used to be thought of as poor and frail but now they are thought of as prosperous and selfish.

   c. Ageism, a systematic stereotyping of and discrimination against old people, exists.

   d. One woman in her 80s was upset because her children sold her home and her belongings without consulting her first.

3. Which of the following statements is *not* a major supporting idea?

   a. Ageism affects men and women differently.

   b. Sigmund Freud wrote that psychiatry was not possible with people 50 and older because they are not educable.

   c. There are different forms of ageism.

   d. Ageism has existed throughout history and across cultures.

4. Which of the following statements does *not* discriminate against the elderly?

   a. Older people are rigid in thought.

   b. When an elderly person fails his vision screening test at the Secretary of State office, he may be denied driving privileges.

   c. The elderly don't drive well.

   d. Men age better than women.

5. You may have marked the italicized example, where a man discusses his 74-year-old mother who wants to travel alone. Which of the following statements provides a good reason for having marked this example?

   a. Although it's not a main idea, major supporting detail, or new vocabulary, the example helps me remember what the new ageism is.

b. It's in italics, which makes it stand out in the text, which means the author wanted to show its importance.

c. Both *a* and *b* are good reasons.

d. It should never be highlighted.

SHORT-ANSWER QUESTIONS

6. How many major supporting details did you find in the excerpt? List two reasons why you feel you've accurately identified the major supporting details.

7. Write a one-paragraph summary of the passage.

8. What examples of ageism can you think of? How might your personal examples help you remember what you learned from this textbook excerpt?

Website Sources for Additional Practice

http://www.byu.edu/ccc/learning/text-mkg.shtml:
Guidelines for purposeful reading and highlighting.

http://www.lsus.edu/sdcc/textbook_marking.htm:
Self-help study guides.

http://www.ups.edu/CWL/textbook_marking.htm:
Textbook marking and annotating.

http://www.und.edu/dept/ULC/rf-textb.htm:
Textbook underlining and marking.

Part Three

Advanced Strategies
for Critical Reading

Chapter 11

Reading, Understanding, and Creating Visual Aids

There is nothing in the mind, which was not first in the senses.
—Aristotle

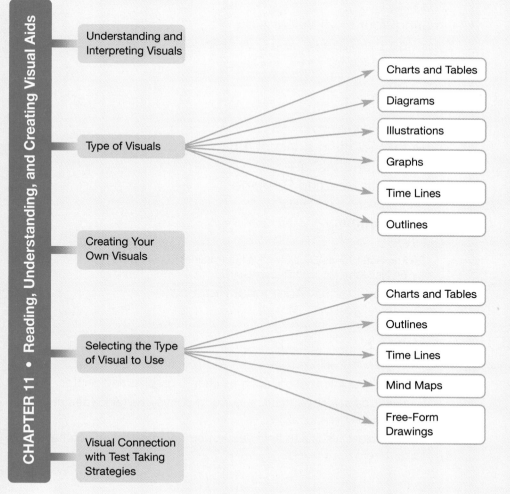

- Understanding and Interpreting Visuals

- Type of Visuals
  - Charts and Tables
  - Diagrams
  - Illustrations
  - Graphs
  - Time Lines
  - Outlines

- Creating Your Own Visuals

- Selecting the Type of Visual to Use
  - Charts and Tables
  - Outlines
  - Time Lines
  - Mind Maps
  - Free-Form Drawings

- Visual Connection with Test Taking Strategies

Chapter Contents

Chapter Goals

In this chapter you will learn:

- ■ To read visual information, such as charts, graphs, and photos.
- ■ Why authors select particular visuals to convey certain types of information to their readers.
- ■ How to create visuals to help you remember information you have learned from your texts.

Chapter Vocabulary

As you read, note these words and phrases, which represent important concepts from the chapter and will be in **boldface** type. Make sure you understand them before the post test at the end of the chapter.

charts	**photographs**	**tables**
diagrams	**free-form drawings**	**time lines**
outlines	**illustrations**	**mind maps/concept maps**
bar graphs	**line graphs**	**pictographs**
pie graphs		

Andy's Learning Journal

Sometimes when I'm reading, it gets way too boring. I mean, I can only take so many paragraphs of economics before I start to fall asleep. I've found myself paying more attention to the visuals in my textbooks since I learned how to read them properly. I always thought they were "extra" material put in the books to liven them up a bit. I didn't realize how important they were. Now, I study the visuals first, and use them as a guide to my reading. Econ still bores me, but at least the visuals help me learn the stuff. If I get stuck trying to remember a concept or detail, I think about one of the textbook pictures and then I can remember the information I need.

Understanding and Interpreting Visual Aids

A picture is worth a thousand words.

How many times have you said, "I see what you mean"? This statement is more powerful than you probably realize. When you can visualize what you have read, you have truly learned it. Many students don't recognize visual aids as important pieces of textbook information and skip over them because they have so much reading to do. But visual aids are a very important part of textbook reading. They are tools designed to help you learn and remember new concepts and key information.

Purpose of Visual Aids

Like Andy, many students are visual learners, so it is not surprising that college textbooks often use different types of visual aids to help readers better understand their content. Visual aids provide a quick, easily accessible format for information that *shows* you how ideas connect or relate to each other. They can bring a book to life and often do a better job than the written text of explaining difficult ideas. Visual aids are also mnemonic devices designed to help readers remember information.

It is important to know that each type of visual aid has a specific purpose, and there are reasons why authors choose certain visual techniques to illustrate particular pieces of information. For example, an author of a biology text who needs to explain the different parts of a flower could use a drawing or diagram, while a writer of an economics text could use charts, tables, flowcharts, or graphs to illustrate the relationship between the economy and the stock market.

Visual Aids and Main Idea

Authors use visuals as *learning aids*, as a way to illustrate and explain their main idea. Visuals enhance and clarify the written text. For example, when you are reading about the parts of the body in a biology book, it is much easier to understand the placement of the liver in relation to the stomach when you can actually see what the author is discussing. Visual aids, like major and minor details, support the main idea of a reading by *showing* the information an author is using to support the main point or argument.

Previewing Visual Information

When you are previewing a text or other reading assignment visual material, you will find it helpful to use the following steps to evaluate the information in the associated visuals:

1. Read the title and explanation so you know what idea in the text the visual illustrates.
2. Check the source of the material to see if the information provided is reliable.
3. Look for clues to the purpose of a visual in the headings and labels used. For example, in a graph, the horizontal axis could be marked in years and the vertical axis in the number of barrels of oil produced in Saudi Arabia, allowing you to see at a glance how oil production has fluctuated in that country over the years.
4. Circle key words in the title and associated text to help you remember what you have learned from reading the visual material.
5. When you encounter visuals in a text, get into the habit of asking yourself the following three questions and answering them in the margin of your text or in your learning journal:
   - What is the purpose of the visual?

- What information is being presented?
- What is the main point of the visual?

6. Highlight the main ideas and points expressed in the visual aids to remind yourself to review the material when preparing for exams.

Types of Visual Aids
Charts and Tables

Charts and **tables** condense large amounts of material into a format that makes it easy to see how different items of information relate to each other. They work especially well for information from history, economics, and psychology texts because many chapters in these books are organized using a comparison and contrast format. They are also used in biology, pharmacy, and nursing texts to show the hierarchy of certain information (such as the different classifications of the animal kingdom) or to demonstrate cause and effect (how different medications work to treat various diseases.)

Exercise 11a

Reading Charts and Tables

Read Table 11.1 and answer the following questions.

1. What is the purpose of this visual?

_____

_____

2. What are some details that are presented?

_____

_____

_____

3. What are two characteristics that have a positive impact on the organization, and what are their impacts?

_____

_____

Table 11.1 Characteristics of a Bureaucracy			
		NEGATIVE CONSEQUENCE	
CHARACTERISTIC	**POSITIVE CONSEQUENCE**	**FOR THE INDIVIDUAL**	**FOR THE ORGANIZATION**
Division of labor	Produces efficiency in large-scale corporation	Produces trained incapacity	Produces a narrow perspective
Hierarchy of authority	Clarifies who is in command	Deprives employees of voice in decision making	Permits concealment of mistakes
Written rules and regulations	Lets workers know what is expected of them	Stifles initiative and imagination	Leads to goal displacement
Impersonality	Reduces bias	Contributes to feelings of alienation	Discourages loyalty to company
Employment based on technical qualifications	Discourages favoritism and reduces petty rivalries	Discourages ambition to improve oneself elsewhere	Allows Peter principle to operate

Source: R. Schafer, *Sociology: A Brief Introduction* (Boston: McGraw-Hill, 2002), p. 141.

4. What is positive about "written rules and regulations?"

_____

5. According to the table, what characteristic reduces bias?

_____

Diagrams

A **diagram** illustrates the connections between related pieces of information using simple to complex drawings. Diagrams usually provide information about how items compare and contrast with each other, or demonstrate cause and effect. For example, a diagram might show the similarities and differences between different members of the primate family or demonstrate how levers and pulleys work.

<table>
<tr><td>

Exercise

11b
</td><td>

Reading Diagrams

Answer the following questions regarding Figure 11.1
</td></tr>
</table>

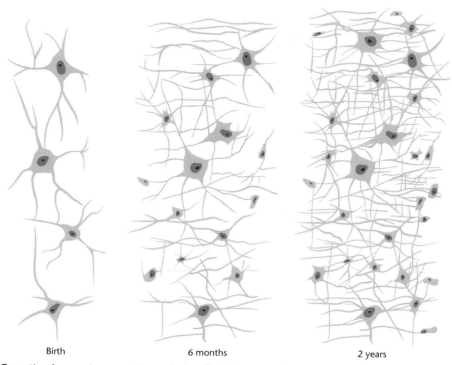

Birth   6 months   2 years

Growth of neural connections during first 2 years of life. The rapid increase in the brain's density and weight is due largely to the formation of dendrites, extensions of nerve cell bodies, and the synapses that link them. This mushrooming communications network sprouts in response to environmental stimulation and makes possible impressive growth in every domain of development.

Figure 11.1   Growth of Neural Connections
Source: D. Papalia, *A Child's World: Infancy Through Adolescence*, 9th ed. (Boston: McGraw-Hill, 2002), p. 124.

1.   What is the purpose of this visual?

_____

_____

2.   What is the difference in the neural connections at birth, compared to when a child is two years old?

_____

_____

3. According to this diagram, what causes neural connections to grow?

_____

_____

Illustrations

An **illustration** is a drawing that allows an author to show you the sections or parts of a machine, plant, or building, more clearly than a photograph could. Many science books use detailed, labeled illustrations of the topics they are discussing.

Exercise 11c

Reading Illustrations

Answer the following questions about Figure 11.2.

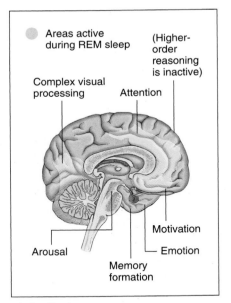

Figure 11.2   Sleep and the Brain
Source: R. Feldman, _Understanding Psychology_, 6th ed. (Boston: McGraw-Hill, 2002), p. 141.

1. What is the purpose of the visual?

_____

_____

2. What parts of the brain are active during sleep, according to Figure 11.2?

_____

3. According to Figure 11.2, which part(s) of the brain is inactive during sleep?

_____

Graphs

Graphs are used to make large amounts of information easily accessible so that you can see at a glance the similarities or differences between the items being discussed or recognize trends over time, such as consumer preferences for different brands of food or clothing. It is important to read the labels on the horizontal and vertical axes so that you can correctly interpret the information provided. There are several types of graphs, each of which is used for different purposes.

Bar graphs

Bar graphs illustrate information by using parallel rectangular bars of varying length to contrast information. They are an effective and comprehensive way to display data.

Reading Bar Graphs

Answer the following questions about Figure 11.3 on p. 362.

1. What is the purpose of the visual?

_____

_____

2. In what country were approximately half of the adult women employed in the 1960s and in the 1990s?

_____

3. What country employed the largest percentage of adult women in the 1990s?

_____

4. Which country's population of working adult women increased the most between 1960 and 1990?

_____

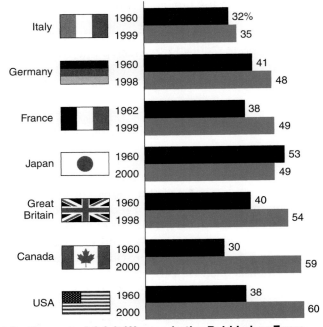

Figure 11.3   Percent of Adult Women in the Paid Labor Force by Country, 1960s and 1990s
Source: R. Schaefer, *Sociology: A Brief Introduction* (Boston: McGraw-Hill, 2002), p. 268.

Line Graphs

Line graphs are grids with vertical and horizontal axes. Each axis represents information, such as units of time or quantities of a product or numbers of people, and lines plotted on these graphs are used to illustrate trends such as the rate of deforestation in the United States and other countries between the 1950s and the present day. In order to understand a line graph, it's important to read what information is being presented on each axis.

Reading Line Graphs

Look at Figure 11.4 and answer the questions that follow.

1. What is the purpose of the visual?

_____

_____

2. What details are being illustrated?

_____

3. During what year(s) were approximately 50 percent of single women working in the paid labor force?

_____

4. From 1920 to 1998, what was the increase in the percentage of working married women?

_____

5. In 1970, what were the percentages of married working women and single working women?

_____

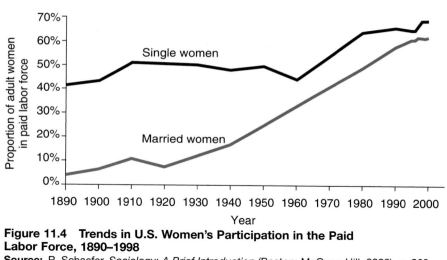

Figure 11.4   Trends in U.S. Women's Participation in the Paid Labor Force, 1890–1998
Source: R. Schaefer, _Sociology: A Brief Introduction_ (Boston: McGraw-Hill, 2002), p. 269.

Pie Graphs

Pie graphs represent data by using a circle to show the whole, and slices or wedges to show how that whole is divided up. They literally look like a pie, cut into slices.

Reading Pie Charts

Examine Figure 11.5 and answer the questions that follow.

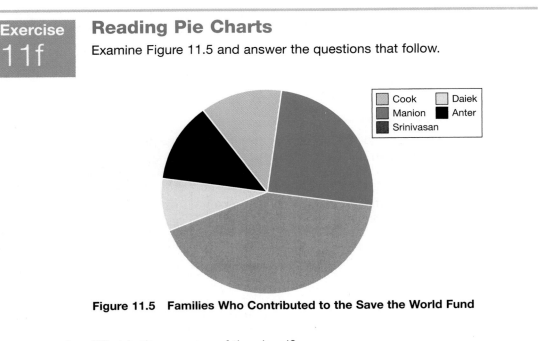

	Cook		Daiek
	Manion		Anter
	Srinivasan		

Figure 11.5   Families Who Contributed to the Save the World Fund

1. What is the purpose of the visual?

_____

_____

2. Which family made the smallest contribution?

_____

3. Which two families contributed the same amount?

_____

Pictographs

Pictographs represent data through the use of pictures. They rely on information in the text to explain the pictures presented in the graph.

Reading Pictographs

Read the pictograph presented in Figure 11.6 and answer the following questions.

One listener changed her eating habits after seeing a series of PowerPoint slides, including this one, which shows that the amount of fat in one ice cream cone equals the amount of fat in four cones of low-fat frozen yogurt.

Figure 11.6   Fat Gram
Source: H. Gregory, *Public Speaking for College and Career* (Boston: McGraw-Hill, 2002), p. 196.

1.   What is the purpose of the visual?

_____

_____

2.   What information is being presented?

_____

_____

3.   What is the main point of the pictograph?

_____

Photographs

Photographs help you make associations with information in the text. Pictures help you to "see" what is being discussed, which makes the information more real and memorable.

Exercise

11h

Reading Photographs

Look at Figure 11.7 and answer the questions that follow.

In wedding ceremonies in Sumatra, Indonesia, the bride's headdress indicates her village and her social status—the more elaborate the headdress, the higher her status. After she is married, the bride and her husband live with her maternal family, and all property passes from mother to daughter.

Figure 11.7   Indonesian Wedding
Source: © SAOLA/GAMMA.

1. What is the purpose of the visual?

_____

_____

_____

2. According to this visual, what is the status of the young woman getting married? Explain your answer.

_____

_____

_____

3. Do you think that this photo represents a culture that is dominated by the father or mother? Explain your response.

_____

_____

_____

Time Lines

Time lines are visual aids that use labeled marks on a straight line to show the time sequence or chronology of a series of events. They are often used in history books to provide summaries of events that occurred over a period of time.

Reading Time Lines

Inspect the example of a time line in Figure 11.8 and answer the questions that follow.

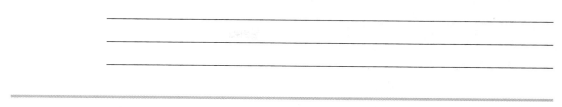

Figure 11.8   The Byzantine Empire
Source: Matthews and Platt, _The Western Humanities,_ 4th ed. (Boston: McGraw-Hill, 2002), p. 192.

1. What is the purpose of the visual?

_____

2. What detailed information is being presented?

_____

3. What events occurred between the Fall of Rome and the Schism between Orthodox and Roman Churches?

_____

4. Which period lasted the longest?

_____

5. When did the Golden Age begin and end?

_____

Outlines

Outlines provide an overview or summary of information. Tables of contents are outlines. They provide the chapter titles, headings, and subheadings as a guide to the framework of the text.

Exercise 11j

Outlines

Use this textbook's table of contents to answer the following questions.

1. What information is being presented in this outline?

_____

_____

2. Using the table of contents, list two topics covered in Chapter 4, "Managing Your Reading Time."

_____

_____

Team Up!

With three other students, compare and discuss your answers to Exercises 11a through 11j. Note the answers that are not the same. Be prepared to discuss them with the class.

Creating Your Own Visual Aids

Creating your own visuals is an effective study tool. The process of creating them increases your understanding of the information you are reading, and also serves as an intensive study session. Creating a visual engages you in deeper and more active thinking, allowing you to connect new information to what you already know, so that what you learn can be more easily retrieved when you need it. If you can draw a chart or picture of the ideas you are reading about, it means you truly understand them, are able to logically organize the information, and can identify the relationships between the different ideas and topics being discussed—connections you might otherwise overlook. Finally, creating visuals as you read will cut down on the amount of note taking you need to do.

If you find it difficult to organize information visually, it probably means you do not fully comprehend it and need to reread the relevant textbook material or ask your instructor or a tutor for assistance. You have to be able to literally see in your mind how the information is organized in order to create a useful outline, map, drawing, or chart to illustrate it.

When creating your visuals, don't be concerned about how artistic you are. Just draw a simple picture based on the information you are studying. Your primary goal is to capture the main idea of an assignment. Too much detail can make it difficult for you to see the main point clearly. It doesn't matter if your visual is meaningful to anyone else; it just has to work as a study aid for you. Always label your visuals—don't assume that you'll understand or remember what they mean two weeks later!

Exercise 11k

Creating a Visual

Read the following paragraph and then create your own drawing to represent the information in it on a separate piece of paper. Take no more than five minutes.

Can you curl your tongue? If so, you inherited this ability through dominant inheritance. If your parents can curl their tongues but you cannot, recessive inheritance occurred. How do these two types of inheritance work? Genes that can produce alternative expressions of a characteristic (such as an ability or inability to curl the tongue) are called alleles. Every person receives a pair of alleles for a given characteristic, one from each biological parent. When both alleles are the same, the person is homozygous for the characteristic; when they are different, the person is heterozygous.

Source: Papalia, Olds, and Feldman, *A Child's World: Infancy through Adolescence*, 9th ed. (Boston: McGraw-Hill, 2002), p. 55.

Team Up!

With one other student, share and compare your pictures. Now practice drawing from listening. One of you should read Passage A while the other draws a picture of what he or she is hearing. Then switch roles and have the person who drew first read Passage B while the other draws. Again, don't be concerned about how "artistic" your picture is. This is a comprehension exercise. After you have completed the exercise, explain your pictures to each other and see how accurately you heard what was read to you.

Passage A

On January 8, 1800, a naked boy, his face and neck heavily scarred, appeared on the outskirts of the village of Saint-Sernin in the sparsely populated province of Aveyron in south central France. The boy, who was only four and a half feet tall but looked about 12 years old, had been spotted several times during the previous two and a half years, climbing trees, running on all fours, drinking from streams, and foraging for acorns and roots.

Source: H. Lane, *The Wild Boy of Aveyron* (Cambridge, MA: Harvard University Press, 1976).

Passage B

Sit up straight in a chair, put your feet flat on the floor, and place your palms on your thighs. Breathe, very slowly, feeling the air spiral through your body. Focus on a spot on the floor. Feel each part of your body relax, starting with your feet. Take your time. Listen to the most distant sounds you can hear, the faintest sounds. Take several minutes or more being still, concentrating on your slow breathing. Then take a deep breath and begin to freewrite.

Source: Silverman, Hughes, and Wienbroer, "A Relaxation Technique to Clear Your Mind," *Rules of Thumb: A Guide for Writers* (Boston: McGraw-Hill, 1999), p. 63.

Selecting the Type of Visual to Use

The type of visual aid you choose to create will depend on the material you are trying to learn and remember. Most scientific information, for example, is related to processes, systems, and classification; free-form drawings, charts, or diagrams work well to illustrate these concepts. History texts, on the other hand, often list or compare and contrast significant events, so graphs, charts, time lines, or maps are effective tools for organizing and studying this type of material.

When creating visuals of new information, it is important to include what you already know about a topic in your chart or drawing. Attaching "new" information to "old" allows you to add what you have just learned to your memory where you can easily locate it. For example, if you draw a diagram to help you remember the details of the digestive system, it will help to include parts of the body you are already familiar with, such as the neck and head, as well as showing the esophagus, stomach, and large intestine.

Charts and Tables

Charts and tables are popular visual aids because they are effective and easy to use. The format lets you see, relatively easily, how different items compare with each other. For example, a chart would be a useful tool if you had to remember a chapter's worth of information about the human eye. Look at Table 11.2. Reading it, you can quickly ascertain that both

Table 11.2 The Eye				
COMPONENTS	**CHARACTERISTICS**			
EYE PARTS	**APPEARANCE**	**LOCATION**	**OPERATION**	**FUNCTION**
Iris	Curtain • Colored • Circular	Behind cornea	Opens and closes (compare to diaphragm of camera)	Regulates amount of light into eye
Cornea	Membrane • Tough • Transparent • Rounded	Front of eye	Bends light rays (compare to convex lens of camera)	Focuses light rays

Source: Adapted from M. Willey and B. Jarecky, *Analysis and Application of Information* (City: Publisher, 1976).

the iris and cornea are round, the iris is colored and the cornea is transparent, and the iris is located behind the cornea, which is in the front of the eye.

Exercise 11

Creating a Chart

Read the following excerpt and create a chart on a separate piece of paper representing the information contained in the excerpt.

The fifth stage of Erikson's theory is labeled the identity-versus-role-confusion stage and encompasses adolescence. This state is a time of major testing, as people try to determine what is unique and special about themselves. They attempt to discover who they are, what their strengths are, and what kinds of roles they are best suited to play for the rest of their lives—in short, their identity. Confusion over the most appropriate role to follow in life can lead to lack of a stable identity, adoption of socially unacceptable roles such as that of a social deviant, or difficulty in maintaining close personal relationships later in life.

During the identity-versus-role-confusion period, pressures to identify what one wants to do with one's life are acutely felt. Because these pressures come at a time of major physical changes as well as important changes in what society expects of them, adolescents can find the period particularly difficult. The identity-versus-role-confusion stage has another important characteristic: a decline in reliance on adults for information, with a shift toward using the peer group as a source of social judgments. The peer group becomes increasingly important, enabling adolescents to form close, adultlike relationships and helping them clarify their personal identities. According to Erikson, the identity-versus-role-confusion stage during adolescence marks a pivotal point in psychosocial development, paving the way for continued growth and future development of personal relationships.

Development continues during middle adulthood as people enter the generativity-versus-stagnation stage. Generativity is the ability to contribute to one's family, community, work, and society, assisting the development of the younger generation. Success in this stage results in positive feelings about the continuity of life; difficulties lead to feelings that one's activities are trivial, a sense of stagnation, or feeling that one has done nothing for upcoming generations. In fact, the person who has not successfully resolved the identity crisis of adolescence might still be floundering in middle adulthood to find an appropriate career.

Finally, the last stage of psychosocial development, the period of ego-integrity-versus-despair, comprises later adulthood and continues until death. Success in resolving the difficulties presented by this stage of life is signified by a sense of accomplishment; difficulties result in regret over what might have been achieved but was not.

Source: Adapted from R. Feldman, *Understanding Psychology*, 6th ed. (Boston; McGraw-Hill, 2002), pp. 392–393.

Outlines

To develop an outline, you must categorize the information in a reading assignment, noting the topic(s), the main ideas, and the supporting details. An effective way to do this, especially if the information is new to you, is to let your textbook be a guide and use the chapter title, headings, and subheadings as a framework for your outline. Once you understand the ideas and how they are organized, you can arrange the topics you have identified in order of their importance using Roman numerals. Beneath each topic heading, indent the related main ideas using capital letters. Supporting details are further indented and listed using numbers, while the most specific details are tabulated using lowercase letters.

Here is a general outline format:

Title
I. Topic (Roman numeral)
    A. Main idea (capital letter)
        1. Major supporting detail (number)
            a. More specific detail—usually vocabulary (letter)
            b. Additional information to provide support (letter)
        2. Major supporting detail (number)
    B. Main idea (capital letter)
II. Topic
    A. Main idea
    B. Main idea
        1. Major supporting detail
        2. Major supporting detail

Exercise 11m

Creating an Outline

Read the following excerpt and create an outline on a separate sheet of paper using the information contained in the excerpt.

Why Listen?

A person must listen to their body every day, and throughout the day. This is necessary in order to identify problems early, before they become serious imbalances. By listening, we can make necessary adjustments as soon as they occur. Such ongoing adjustments are very important because we are planting the seeds today for our health tomorrow. Most of the problems which appear today actually began long ago; perhaps as a result of an illness, an emotional upset, an injury, or some type of "invasion" of the body by an external pathogen (outside disease causing agent)...in Traditional Chinese Medicine (TCM) this pathogen could include wind, dryness, dampness, heat, or cold, which was not corrected, that is, cleared and/or rebalanced. By listening, watching, and balancing each day, we avoid problems accumulating and accelerating over time.

What Keeps Us from Listening?

What keeps us from listening? Many people are simply too busy to pause long enough to listen. During the day, a person feels dizzy, has a headache, feels an ache or pain, but because of the pressures and rush of life, the problem is ignored or a pill is quickly taken to relieve the "temporary" problem. A second reason people sometime do not listen is because they are afraid of what they hear. "Fear" can be debilitating. Whatever the message the individual simply decides that they are unable or unwilling to address the "message" being sent by the body. A third problem is that some people are not very sensitive—that is, they have not developed their ability to feel what is occurring in and around them. Finally, some people have a lack of understanding of what they are hearing. They assume that the sign being given by the body is unimportant or that it is temporary and has no long-term impact on their health.

Source: Yu-Cheng Huang, *Qi: The Journal of Traditional Eastern Health and Fitness*, 7 (4) (Anaheim Hills, CA: Insight Graphics, Inc., 1998), pp. 26–27.

Time Lines

When textbooks do not provide a time line but events are being discussed in chronological order, it can be useful to draw one to give yourself a framework for the information you are learning. It can also be helpful to add any other relevant information about historical events that you know occurred during the period described in your textbook. This will help you correlate the new details with what you already know and provide additional context for the topic you are studying. In Figure 11.9 a student has added the dates of the Gulf War to her timeline to help her understand and remember the sequence of other wars.

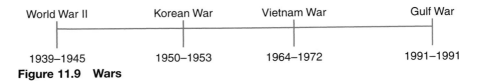

World War II   Korean War   Vietnam War   Gulf War

1939–1945   1950–1953   1964–1972   1991–1991

Figure 11.9 Wars

Learning Journal

In your journal, create a time line of the major events in your life. Start with your own birthday. Include at least 10 major events.

Mind Maps

Mind maps are visual aids that use shapes and lines to show the relative importance of ideas. Because they are in free-form style, you decide how to arrange the information. They are used in this textbook at the beginning of each chapter to give you an overview of what you will be studying. Unlike outlines, mind maps, also known as **concept maps**, do not present information linearly, although they do represent the organization and hierarchy of information.

You usually place your *topic* in the center or at the top of your mind map, where it serves as the "core" to which other ideas are attached. *Main points* or *main ideas* that directly relate to the topic are attached to it by lines. *Major supporting details* that relate to the main ideas are attached to them by lines, and *minor supporting details* are connected to the major details they support. See Figure 11.10 for an example.

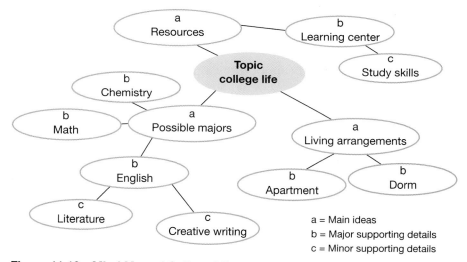

Figure 11.10   Mind Map of College Life

Exercise
11n

Creating a Mind Map

Use the information in the outline you created for Exercise 11m to create a mind map on a separate sheet of paper.

Free-Form Drawings

A **free-form drawing** is a useful way to illustrate and organize what you read so you can remember it. For example, if you were learning about the human eye, you could draw one and label its parts. Figure 11.11 (p. 376)

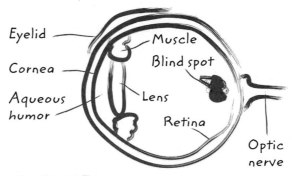

Figure 11.11   The Human Eye

is an example of a free-form drawing of the eye made by a nursing student. This is an alternative way to present information similar to that in Table 11.2.

If you cannot draw a picture to illustrate the material you are reading, stop and rethink. You can't learn and remember what you don't understand, as the following exercise demonstrates.

Using Free-Form Drawings as a Comprehension Check

Read the following paragraph, and draw a picture on a separate sheet of paper to explain what the passage means.

If the balloons popped, the sound wouldn't be able to carry since everything would be too far away from the correct floor. A closed window would also prevent the sound from carrying, since most buildings tend to be well insulated. Since the whole operation depends on the steady flow of electricity, a break in the middle of the wire would also cause problems. Of course, the fellow could shout, but the human voice is not loud enough to carry that far. An additional problem is that a string could break on the instrument. Then there would be no accompaniment to the message. It is clear that the best situation would involve less distance. Then there would be fewer potential problems. With face-to-face contact, the least number of things could go wrong.

Source: J. D Bransford and M. K. Johnson, "Contextual Prerequisites for Understanding: Some Investigations of Comprehension and Recall," *Journal of Verbal Learning and Verbal Behavior*, 11, 1972, p. 718.

Team Up!

With three other students, share your picture. Discuss whether you had difficulty with this exercise. Explain why or why not.

When you have completed the Team Up! exercise, your instructor will share an example of a free-form drawing that provides an interpretation of this paragraph.

Take One Minute

Explain the differences between mind maps and free-form drawings. When would it be appropriate to use each type of visual?

Guide for Selecting a Visual Aid

Table 11.3 is a chart you can use as a guide for matching specific kinds of information with the types of visual aids that best illustrate them. As you read through the table, look for the visual technique you would use to illustrate information learned in class and from a textbook about how the human digestive system works. You want to choose one that will allow you to include what you already know about the subject and let you connect that information to what you have just learned.

Table 11.3 Guide for Selecting a Visual Aid		
VISUAL AIDS	**TYPES OF INFORMATION THEY BEST ILLUSTRATE**	**EXAMPLES**
Photographs	• Used to show how actual events appeared as they occurred (such as bombing of oilfields during the Gulf War). • Used to show a person, place, or thing as it currently exists or previously existed (pictures before and after plastic surgery). • Useful in literature, history, drama, psychology, reading, English, hard sciences, newspaper articles, magazines and journals, and brochures.	Figure 11.7

(continued on next page)

Table 11.3 (continued)		
VISUAL AIDS	**TYPES OF INFORMATION THEY BEST ILLUSTRATE**	**EXAMPLES**
Charts or tables	• Used to depict many kinds of information, can be made using any list of facts. • Used to organize large amounts of information—listing different characteristics of a person, place, or thing, how something looks, where it's located, what function it serves, or the like—so that a number of items and their characteristics can be viewed simultaneously (for example, various properties of several different minerals). • Used to compare and contrast items easily (such as, mammals versus amphibians). • Used to demonstrate cause and effect (like the effect of gravity on objects). • Useful in history, psychology, biology, nursing, pharmacy, English, literature, and economics.	Table 11.1 Table 11.2 Table 11.3 Tables 8.1–8.6
Graphs	• Used to compare data on a specific topic over time (world population growth during the last 50 years). • Used to compare the growth or loss of an item over time (stocks and shares, wildlife populations). • Used to convey information about quantities of an item. • Useful in economics, math, and all sciences.	Figure 11.3 Figure 11.4 Figure 11.5 Figure 11.6
Diagrams	• Used to represent things and places (but parts, places, and processes are labeled). • Used to illustrate sequences and processes (photosynthesis, steps in the process of creating a commercial product). • Useful in all sciences.	Figure 11.13 Figure 11.11 Figures 8.1–8.6
Outlines	• Used to show linear organization of information (progression of historical events). • Used to demonstrate hierarchy of information (feudal relationship between monarch and subjects). • Useful in most disciplines.	Table of Contents of this book. Page 354 of this chapter.

(continued on next page)

Table 11.3 (continued)		
VISUAL AIDS	**TYPES OF INFORMATION THEY BEST ILLUSTRATE**	**EXAMPLES**
Mind maps	• Used to show organization of information in a nonlinear way. • Used to demonstrate relationships between topic, main ideas, and supporting details in written/oral material. • Useful in most disciplines.	Figure 11.9 Figure 5.1
Time lines	• Used to represent chronology of events that occurred over a specific period (events preceding World War I). • Used to summarize information that covers a long period (geological eras). • Useful in history, sciences, and social studies.	Figure 11.8 Figure 11.10
Free-form drawings	• Used to make concepts concrete by creating a visual representation of text information— and for interpretation, problem solving, and reading between the lines of written/oral material. • Used to visually represent your thinking process. • Used to symbolize text information. • Used to provide personal representation and understanding of written/oral material. • Useful in geology, biology, literature, and technology.	Figure 11.11

Based on the information in Table 11.3, you probably selected free-form drawing as the best visual aid for your purposes, particularly if you enjoy drawing and find it useful for organizing information. The reasons for choosing the free-form drawing technique would include the following:

- It helps makes the concept (the digestive process) concrete.
- It visually represents your thinking about and understanding of the concept.
- It symbolizes the information provided in the text or lecture.
- It is a useful technique for illustrating biology course information.

Selecting a Visual

1. Read the following geology textbook excerpt.

2. Use Table 11.3 to decide which visual technique to use.

3. On a separate sheet of paper, create a visual in a format that will help you understand and remember the information.

Contagious Diffusion

Let us suppose that a scientist develops a gasoline additive that noticeably improves the performance of his or her car. Assume further that the person shows friends and associates the invention and that they, in turn, tell others. This process is similar to the spread of a contagious disease. The innovation will continue to diffuse until barriers are met (that is, people will not be interested in adopting the new idea) or until the area is saturated (that is, all available people have adopted the innovation). This contagious diffusion process follows the rules of distance decay at each step. Short-distance contacts are more likely than long-distance contacts, but over time the idea may have spread far from the original site.

Source: Adapted from Getis, Getis, and Fellman, *Introduction to Geology*, 8th ed. (Boston: McGraw-Hill, 2002), p. 294.

Using the visual aid you developed, answer the following questions:

4. What is the purpose of your visual?

_____

5. Why did you select the particular visual aid you used for this passage?

_____

_____

_____

6. What is the main idea of the reading selection?

_____

_____

7. Was your visual aid useful? Why or why not?

_____

Test Taking and Visual Aids

1. **One excellent technique to help you prepare for exams is to use tracing paper to copy diagrams in your textbooks, and then see if you can label the parts on your own.** Students enrolled in medical fields find this technique especially useful. Research has shown that students who trace diagrams are focused and perform better on memory questions related to parts and processes.

2. **Creating an outline of a chapter is a great way to prepare for an exam.** If you are able to fill in supporting details for the major concepts, you know you have grasped the chapter information.

3. **Write and draw on your exam papers.** Often when you are taking an exam, drawing related pictures next to questions will help you remember concepts and supporting details.

Practice with Reading Passage

Answer all questions on a separate sheet of paper.

Reading Practice

"Drug Therapy"
BY R. FELDMAN

PREPARE TO READ

1. Based on the title, what do you expect this reading selection to be about?

2. What information do you already know about this topic?

3. You should know the following list of vocabulary words. Look up those you don't know in your dictionary.

   a. neurotransmitters

   b. neurons

   c. dopamine

   d. receptor

   e. synapse

   f. bipolar disorder

Drug Therapy

Drug therapy, the control of psychological disorders through drugs, works by altering the operation of neurotransmitters and neurons in the brain.

Some drugs operate by inhibiting neurotransmitters or receptor neurons, thus reducing activity at particular synapses, the sites where nerve impulses travel from one neuron to another. Other drugs do just the opposite: they increase the activity of certain neurotransmitters or neurons, allowing particular neurons to fire more frequently.

Antipsychotic Drugs

Probably no greater change has occurred in mental hospitals than the successful introduction in the mid 1950s of antipsychotic drugs—drugs used to reduce severe symptoms of disturbance, such as loss of touch with reality and agitation. Previously, the typical mental hospital fulfilled all the stereotypes of the insane asylum, with screaming, moaning, clawing patients displaying the most bizarre behaviors. Suddenly, in just a matter of days, the hospital wards became considerably calmer environments in which professionals could do more than just try to get the patients through the day without causing serious harm to themselves or others.

This dramatic change was brought about by the introduction of a drug called chlorpromazine. This drug, and others of a similar nature, rapidly became the most popular and successful treatment for schizophrenia. Today drug therapy is the preferred treatment for most cases of severely abnormal behavior and, as such, is used for most hospitalized patients with psychological disorders. For instance, the drug clozapine represents the current generation of antipsychotics. How do antipsychotic drugs work? Most operate by blocking the dopamine receptors at the brain's synapses. Some newer drugs, like clozapine, increase dopamine levels in certain parts of the brain, such as those related to planning and goal-directed activity.

Despite the effectiveness of antipsychotic drugs, they do not produce a "cure" in the same way that, say, penicillin cures an infection. As soon as the drug is withdrawn, the original symptoms tend to reappear. Futhermore, such drugs can have long-term side effects, such as dryness of the mouth and throat, dizziness, and sometimes tremors and loss of muscle control that might continue even after drug treatments are stopped (Figure 11.12).

Antidepressant Drugs

As you might guess from the name, antidepressant drugs are a class of medications used in cases of severe depression to improve patients' mood. They were discovered quite by accident: It was found that patients suffering from tuberculosis who were given the drug iproniazid suddenly became happier and more optimistic. When the same drug was tested on people suffering from depression, a similar result occurred, and drugs became an accepted form of treatment for depression. Most antidepressant drugs work by changing the concentration of particular neurotransmitters. For example, tricyclic drugs increase the availability of norepinephrine at the synapses of neurons, whereas MAO inhibitors prevent the enzyme monoamine oxidase (MAO) from breaking down neurotransmitters. Newer antidepressants, selective

Figure 11.12 Drug Treatments			
CLASS OF DRUG	**EFFECTS OF DRUG**	**PRIMARY ACTION OF DRUG**	**EXAMPLES**
Antipsychotic drugs	Reduction in loss of touch with reality, agitation	Block dopamine receptors	Chlorpromazine (Thorazine), Clozapine (Clozaril)
Antidepressant drugs			
Tricyclic antidepressants	Reduction in depression	Permit rise in neurotransmitters such as norephinephrine	Trazodone (Desyrel), Amitrittyline (Elavil), Desipramine (Norpamin), Phenelzine (Nardil)
MAO inhibitors	Reduction in depression	Prevent MAO from breaking down neurotransmitters	
Selective seratonin reuptake inhibitors	Reduction in depression	Inhibit reuptake of seratonin	Fluoxetine (Prozac), Luvox, Paxil, Celexa, Zoloft, Nefazodone (Serzone)
Mood stabilizers		Can alter transmission of impulses with neurons	Lithium (Lithonate), Depakote, Tegretol
Lithium	Mood stabilizer		
Antianxiety drugs	Reduction in anxiety	Increase activity of neurotransmitter GABA	Benzodiazepines (Valium, Xanax)

Figure 11.12   Drug Treatments
Source: R. Feldman, *Understanding Psychology,* 6th ed. (Boston: McGraw-Hill, 2002), p. 520.

serotonin reuptake inhibitors (SSRIs), target the neurotransmitter serotonin, permitting it to linger at the synapse. One of the latest antidepressants, Nefazodone, blocks serotonin at some receptor sites but not others. (See Figure 11.13.)

Although antidepressant drugs can produce side effects such as drowsiness and faintness, their overall success rate is quite good. Unlike antipsychotic drugs, antidepressants can produce lasting, long-term recoveries from depression. In many cases, even after patients stop taking the drugs, their depression does not return.

Antidepressant drugs have become some of the most heavily prescribed of all drugs. Billions of dollars are spent each year on antidepressants, and sales are increasing at a rate of more than 20 percent a year. In particular, the

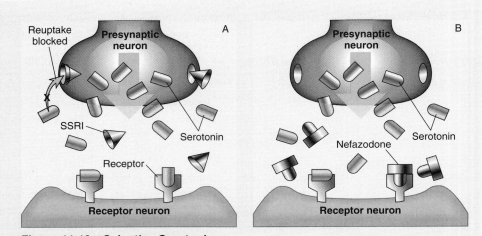

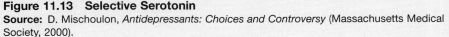

Figure 11.13   Selective Serotonin
Source: D. Mischoulon, *Antidepressants: Choices and Controversy* (Massachusetts Medical Society, 2000).

antidepressant Fluoxetine, sold under the trade name Prozac, has been high-lighted on magazine covers and been the topic of best-sellers.

Does Prozac deserve its acclaim? In some respects, yes. Despite its high cost—each daily dose costs more than $2—it has significantly improved the lives of thousands of depressed individuals. Compared to other antide-pressants, Prozac (along with its cousins Luvox, Paxil, Celexa, and Zoloft) has relatively few side effects. Furthermore, many people who do not respond to other types of antidepressants do well on Prozac. On the other hand, like all drugs, Prozac does not agree with everyone. For example, 20 to 30 percent of users report experiencing nausea and diarrhea, and a smaller per-centage report sexual dysfunction.

Another drug that has received a great deal of publicity is St. John's Wort, an herb that has been likened to a "natural" antidepressant. Widely used in Europe for the treatment of depression, the substance is considered a dietary supplement in the United States and therefore is available with-out a prescription. Despite popularity, the jury is still out on the effectiveness of St. John's Wort. Although the American College of Physicians has sup-ported the use of the herb in treating mild, short-term depression, the most recent and carefully designed study found the drug useless in treating depression, making its use problematic.

Lithium

Lithium, a mineral salt, is a drug that has been used very successfully to treat bipolar disorder. Although no one knows definitely why, it and other drugs such as Depakote and Tegretol are effective in reducing manic episodes. However, they are not effective in treating depressive phases of bipolar dis-order, and antidepressants are usually prescribed during these phases.

Lithium and drugs similar to it have a quality that sets them apart from other drug treatments: they can be a preventive treatment, blocking future episodes of bipolar disorder. Many people who have had episodes of bipolar disorder in the past can prevent a recurrence of their symptoms by taking a daily dose of lithium. In contrast, most other drugs are useful only after symptoms of psychological disturbance occur.

Antianxiety Drugs

As the name implies, antianxiety drugs reduce the level of anxiety a person experiences and increase feelings of well-being. They are used not only to reduce general tension in people who are experiencing temporary difficulties but also to aid in the treatment of more serious anxiety disorders.

Antianxiety drugs such as Xanax and Valium are among the medications most frequently prescribed by physicians. In fact, more than half of all U.S. families have someone who has taken such a drug at one time or another.

Although the popularity of antianxiety drugs suggests that they hold few risks, they can produce a number of potentially serious side effects. For instance, they can cause fatigue and long-term dependence. Moreover, taken in combination with alcohol, some antianxiety drugs can become lethal. But a more important issue concerns their use to suppress anxiety. Almost every therapeutic approach to psychological disturbance views continuing anxiety as a signal of some sort of problem. Thus, drugs that mask anxiety can simply be hiding difficulties. Consequently, people who use antianxiety drugs might simply be hiding from, rather than confronting, their underlying problems.

Source: R. Feldman, *Understanding Psychology*, 6th ed. (Boston: McGraw Hill, 2002), pp. 519–522.

CHECK YOUR UNDERSTANDING

OBJECTIVE QUESTIONS

1. According to this excerpt, drug therapy is defined as

  a. Taking drugs.

  b. The control of physical disorders through drugs.

  c. Drugs prescribed in conjunction with counseling sessions.

  d. The control of psychological disorders through the use of drugs.

2. Which of the following best describes synapses?

  a. Pieces of information.

  b. Sites where nerve impulses travel from one neuron to another.

  c. Breaks in memory; an inability to recall information.

  d. A process used to photograph nerve impulses in the brain.

3. Antipsychotic drugs are

    a. Used to reduce severe symptoms of mental disturbance.

    b. Used to destroy parts of a patient's frontal lobes.

    c. Used to produce a lasting cure for aberrant behavior.

    d. Used to produce long-lasting side effects.

4. Which of the following types of drugs are most frequently prescribed by physicians?

    a. Antianxiety drugs.

    b. Antipsychotic drugs.

    c. Antidepressant drugs.

    d. Antisocial drugs.

5. _____ is a drug used to treat bipolar disorder.

6. One of the biggest changes to occur in mental hospitals was due to the introduction of _____.

7. Antianxiety drugs eliminate the anxiety a person experiences. True or False?

8. St. John's Wort is a drug that has proved effective in treating depression. True or False?

9. Antidepressant drugs were discovered by accident. True or False?

10. Drug therapy works by altering the operation of the neurotransmitters and neurons in the brain. True or False?

SHORT-ANSWER QUESTIONS

11. What is the main idea of this reading selection?

12. Did vocabulary words prevent you from fully understanding this reading selection? If so, list them.

13. Using Figure 11.12,

    a. How many classes of drugs are listed?

    b. What characteristics are charted regarding the class of drugs?

    c. What is the primary action of benzodiazepines?

    d. What is the primary effect of chlorpromazine?

    e. Which drug(s) were given as examples of mood stabilizers?

14. Using the information regarding antidepressant drugs, create a visual that shows how each specific drug or herb is alike and different.

15. What is the purpose of Figure 11.13?

16. What methods of organization were primarily used to present the information in this reading selection?

Chapter Summary

Textbook authors often use visual aids to help their readers better understand the information they are presenting. Visual information reinforces and supplements reading material. Types of visual aids include mind maps, outlines, charts, diagrams, graphs, illustrations, photographs, and time lines. The type of information being conveyed determines what type of visual aid an author will use. Learning how to read visuals will help you to understand and remember the textual information they illustrate.

An effective reading and study strategy is to make your own visual aids. To create an effective visual aid, you have to recognize the important elements in what you are reading and be able to prioritize and organize them in a logical and useful format. It will quickly become obvious how well you know the material; you can't draw a diagram or devise a table if you don't understand what you have read or heard. In many instances, an effective visual will save you from taking as many notes from your texts or in lectures.

Post Test

Answer all questions on a separate sheet of paper.

Part I

OBJECTIVE QUESTIONS

1. Outlining can be used to (circle all correct answers)

   a. Show the relationship between ideas.

   b. Effectively show topics, but not the details.

   c. Demonstrate the main idea by representing information in a linear (top-down) way.

   d. Take notes using a free-form format.

2. Which of the following statements accurately describes charts?

   a. They can be used to organize large amounts of information.

   b. They are useful for comparing and contrasting information.

   c. Completing them lets you know how well you have learned new information.

   d. All of the above.

3. In order to design a successful visual you have to

   a. Become an accomplished artist.

   b. Fully understand the information you have read.

   c. Use different colors.

   d. Memorize all of the information in an assignment before you create one.

SHORT-ANSWER QUESTIONS

4. Why are visuals such an important part of the reading process?

5. Create a chart listing at least three examples of visual aids, and provide the following details for each:

   a. A definition.

   b. An explanation of when it would be appropriate or preferable to use this type of visual.

   c. A small drawing of the visual.

Part II

Reading Passage

"So Far, Steel Tariffs Do Little of What President Envisioned"
BY NEIL KING, JR., AND ROBERT GUY

1. Based on the title, what do you expect this reading selection to be about?

2. What information do you already know about this topic?

3. Study the two graphs (Figures 11.14 and 11.15. What do you think is the purpose of these two visual aids?

So Far, Steel Tariffs Do Little of What President Envisioned

The administration hoped they would give U.S. steelmakers time to modernize, bolster Republican candidates in vote-rich patches of the heartland, and give the U.S. a club to use in continuing efforts to cut global steel overcapacity and curtail foreign steel subsidies.

Steel Blues

President Bush's efforts to help the steel industry haven't reduced global overcapacity.

Supply booms . . .
World-wide steel consumption and production, in millions of tons

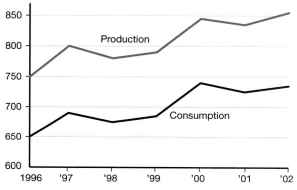

On the global stage
Share of estimated steel production in 2002

World total: **856 million tons**

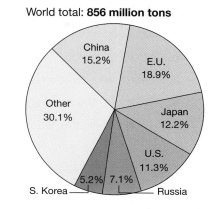

Figure 11.14 & Figure 11.15
Source: Organization for Economic Cooperation and Development, *The Wall Street Journal*, September 13, 2002, p. 1.

Six months later, the gambit has backfired on nearly every front. Steel prices are up more sharply than Bush advisers anticipated. Lured by the higher prices, mills around the world are producing more steel today than they were two years ago, worsening the global glut. Brazil produced 36% more steel in July 2002 than in July 2001. Production in Russia, the EU, and Japan is up about 3% in a year.

U.S. trade partners are angrier than Mr. Bush's foreign policy advisers expected. And users of steel are more vociferous than his business advisers anticipated, prompting the administration to carve exceptions to the tariffs. These, in turn, have angered the steel-state legislators and union members whom Mr. Bush's political advisers were courting.

So the industry appears doomed to the peak-and-valley cycle that has plagued it for decades. Prices are up now but could ease if production continues to increase. "What we could see is another pricing death-spiral that would bring more pain and suffering," says Peter Marcus, managing partner of World Steel Dynamics, a consulting firm.

The only long-term hope, he says, is for the industry to develop an iron-clad early-warning system. Then, when demand begins to slip, mills around the world would scale back production in unison. "And the chance for that happening," he adds, "is about nil."

Source: Adapted from Neil King, Jr., and Robert Guy, "So Far, Steel Tariffs Do Little of What President Envisioned," *The Wall Street Journal*, September 13, 2002, pp. 1, 12.

OBJECTIVE QUESTIONS

1.   The president's purpose for the steel tariffs was:

   a. To increase steel production.

   b. To cut global steel overcapacity.

   c. To bring about world peace.

   d. To raise the economic capacity of Brazil.

2.   Based on what you read, why do you think the president's plan backfired?

   a. There were exceptions made to the tariffs.

   b. All of the countries shut down their production of steel.

   c. Japan took the lead in production, causing the other countries to decrease production.

   d. Mills around the world just aren't producing as much steel today as they were two years ago.

SHORT-ANSWER QUESTIONS

3.   What are the two items being compared in Figure 11.14?

4.   Read the second graph, Figure 11.15, and answer the following questions:

   a. What is the purpose of this graph?

   b. What country produces the most steel?

   c. What country produces the least amount of steel?

   d. Not including "Other," where does the United States place, in relationship to the six other countries and areas, in its estimated steel production?

   e. Were you surprised by the data? Why or why not?

5.   What is the purpose of Figure 11.14?

6.   Were the visuals for the article effective? Why or why not?

7.   What was the main idea of the article you just read?

8.   Write a summary of the article.

9.   Use the article to create either an outline or a mind map.

Website Sources for Additional Practice

http://clem.mscd.edu/~leggettw/visuallit.htm

http://www.esd105.wednet.edu/ReadingCadre/BeforeOrganizers.html

Chapter 12

Identifying and Evaluating Arguments

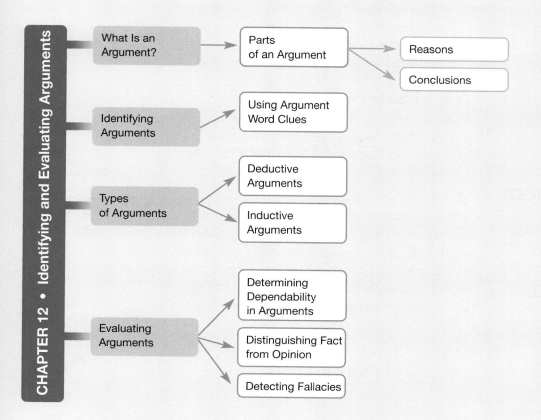

CHAPTER 12 • Identifying and Evaluating Arguments

- What Is an Argument?
  - Parts of an Argument
    - Reasons
    - Conclusions
- Identifying Arguments
  - Using Argument Word Clues
- Types of Arguments
  - Deductive Arguments
  - Inductive Arguments
- Evaluating Arguments
  - Determining Dependability in Arguments
  - Distinguishing Fact from Opinion
  - Detecting Fallacies

Chapter Contents

Chapter Goals

In this chapter on argumentation, you will learn:

- To identify arguments and their parts in textbook assignments.
- To distinguish between deductive and inductive arguments.
- To critically evaluate arguments in textbooks and other reading media.
- To differentiate between facts and opinions.
- To understand and identify basic fallacies.

Chapter Vocabulary

These vocabulary words and phrases represent important concepts from this chapter. As you read the chapter, take note of these words and phrases, which will be in **boldface** type. Make sure you understand them before the post test at the end of the chapter.

argument	**conclusion**	**fact/opinion**
reasons	**fallacies**	**deductive argument**
inductive argument	**either/or thinking**	**hasty generalization**
red herring	**false cause**	**slippery slope**
ad hominem	**circular reasoning**	

Gracie, a freshman at a four-year university, has just finished a book called A People's History of the United States, 1492–Present, *by Howard Zinn. In it, Zinn describes Christopher Columbus as an unscrupulous opportunist whose quest for gold and slaves drove his ambition for the New World and fueled his cruelty toward its occupants. Although Columbus' navigational skills were suspect, his ability to stretch the truth, gain financial support from European royalty, and commit heinously violent acts against native peoples to meet his own material goals were well practiced. Gracie wonders how Zinn's characterization of Columbus can differ so dramatically from the "hero" image she previously learned from other textbooks. Howard Zinn is, among other things, a historian and a prolific author. His arguments are well supported. Understandably, Gracie is puzzled and wonders whom to believe.*

What Is an Argument?

Many people think of arguments as heated discussions, sometimes involving shouting and fighting. They can be. However, arguments are also the logical structures that people use when they write and speak to present ideas and to persuade others to support those ideas. These logical structures consist of statements, some of which are conclusions and some of which are the reasons that support them. For example, if your friend tells you that *Jaws* is the best movie ever made, he is stating a conclusion. If he continues by saying that it is suspenseful, scary, and has great dialogue, he is providing reasons for his conclusion. You may not agree with his argument, but he has, in fact, developed one. If you, in turn, say "No! I hated *Jaws*!" then you are offering a conclusion. If your comments end there, however, you are not constructing an argument at all because you have not provided any reasons for your conclusion. You are just stating your opinion. Before you decide whether *Jaws* merits praise, it is useful to learn about the parts necessary for building an argument: the conclusion and the reasons that support it.

Learning Journal

Think about an argument you have constructed in the past. It can be an argument on any subject where you have drawn a conclusion about something and provided at least one reason to support it. Write it down in your journal.

Here is a sample response to the learning journal exercise from Serja, a business major at a four-year university.

> Marketing is the crux of profit making. In business, marketing is the tool used to communicate with consumers. How do they know what is out there? How do they know what toothpaste gets their teeth the whitest? Crest advertises a "whitening gel." Other manufacturers say that baking soda is the way to go. They know what is available from seeing TV commercials, and print ads. The language used to describe a product creates a specific image for a consumer. If the consumer perceives Crest Whitening Gel as being effective, he's likely to give it a try. Of course a product has to be good, but marketing creates that initial spark that gets people interested. Look how many people buy bottled water these days. It's just water but it's marketed with great skill and people pay for it!

Notice how Serja develops an argument about the value of marketing. Her first sentence is also the conclusion of her argument: "Marketing is the crux of profit making." The rest of her sentences contain reasons that support her conclusion.

Parts of an Argument

An **argument** consists of two or more statements that include one conclusion and at least one reason that supports it. A **conclusion** is the judgment, decision, or opinion you reach after thinking about or investigating an issue. For example, you could conclude that the Detroit Lions play poorly, or that Islam is a profound religion. Both of these conclusions require at least one reason to support them in order to qualify as valid arguments. A **reason** is a statement that explains, justifies, or otherwise supports a conclusion. For example, you could offer the fact that the

Detroit Lions have won only one game all season as a reason for your conclusion that the Lions are playing poorly. Or you could cite the Qu'ran and its rigorous requirements for daily prayer and financial support for the poor as reasons for your claim that Islam is a profound religion. The structure, a conclusion with at least one reason to support it, defines them as arguments. A statement that simply provides a conclusion *without* any reasons to support it is not an argument at all.

The following examples are all arguments because each has a conclusion and a reason, or reasons, that supports it:

1. *Reason:* Milk is rich in minerals and vitamins.
   Conclusion: Milk is an excellent food source.

2. *Reason:* If you study regularly every day, you will find it easier to remember what you learn.
   Reason: By studying carefully you will be alerted to when you do not understand a particular passage or chapter, and you will be able to get help before you take a test.
   Conclusion: There are several reasons why consistent study is more effective than cramming.

Exercise

12a

Engaging in Argument

Read the following version of the fairy tale *Cinderella* and decide whether the statements that follow it are *true*, *false*, or *questionable*. Provide a reason for each of your answers. For the purposes of this exercise, accept each sentence of the fairy tale as fact and forget about the common version of it. Think about what information each sentence conveys before making judgments about the statements that follow. Afterward you will share your responses with other members of your class. Some will agree with you and some will disagree, and you will see how a harmless fairy tale can turn into an argument.

Cinderella of the 21st Century

Cinderella's stepmother and stepsisters disliked her. They bought themselves beautiful clothes and gifts and went to all of the important social events, but Cinderella wore rags and had to stay at home. On the night of the Prince's Ball, the stepmother and stepsisters wore beautiful gowns and jewels, and they left Cinderella at home to clean the fireplace. But Cinderella's fairy godmother appeared and turned Cinderella's rags into a beautiful gown. Then the fairy godmother, whose powers were granted to her for all eternity, found a pumpkin and turned it into a gold-plated automobile; she turned a mouse into a chauffeur; and Cinderella rode to the Prince's Ball in grand style.

Now read each of the following statements and indicate in the space provided whether you think they are true (T), false (F), or questionable (?). Provide one reason for each of your judgments.

T, F, or ?

1. Cinderella had more than one stepsister. ＿＿＿＿＿＿

Reason: ＿＿＿＿＿＿＿＿＿＿＿＿＿＿＿＿＿＿＿＿＿＿＿＿＿＿

2. Cinderella's natural mother was dead. ＿＿＿＿＿＿

Reason: ＿＿＿＿＿＿＿＿＿＿＿＿＿＿＿＿＿＿＿＿＿＿＿＿＿＿

3. The stepmother and stepsisters went to many social events. ＿＿＿＿＿＿

Reason: ＿＿＿＿＿＿＿＿＿＿＿＿＿＿＿＿＿＿＿＿＿＿＿＿＿＿

＿＿＿＿＿＿＿＿＿＿＿＿＿＿＿＿＿＿＿＿＿＿＿＿＿＿＿＿＿＿

4. Cinderella's stepmother and stepsisters didn't buy any beautiful clothes for Cinderella. ＿＿＿＿＿＿

Reason: ＿＿＿＿＿＿＿＿＿＿＿＿＿＿＿＿＿＿＿＿＿＿＿＿＿＿

＿＿＿＿＿＿＿＿＿＿＿＿＿＿＿＿＿＿＿＿＿＿＿＿＿＿＿＿＿＿

5. A pumpkin can't be turned into a gold-plated automobile. ＿＿＿＿＿＿

Reason: ＿＿＿＿＿＿＿＿＿＿＿＿＿＿＿＿＿＿＿＿＿＿＿＿＿＿

＿＿＿＿＿＿＿＿＿＿＿＿＿＿＿＿＿＿＿＿＿＿＿＿＿＿＿＿＿＿

6. The stepmother and stepsisters disliked Cinderella. ＿＿＿＿＿＿

Reason: ＿＿＿＿＿＿＿＿＿＿＿＿＿＿＿＿＿＿＿＿＿＿＿＿＿＿

7. Cinderella's stepmother or stepsisters made Cinderella stay home when they went to the important social events. ＿＿＿＿＿＿

Reason: ＿＿＿＿＿＿＿＿＿＿＿＿＿＿＿＿＿＿＿＿＿＿＿＿＿＿

＿＿＿＿＿＿＿＿＿＿＿＿＿＿＿＿＿＿＿＿＿＿＿＿＿＿＿＿＿＿

8. The stepmother and stepsisters offered to take Cinderella to the Prince's Ball with them. ＿＿＿＿＿＿

Reason: ＿＿＿＿＿＿＿＿＿＿＿＿＿＿＿＿＿＿＿＿＿＿＿＿＿＿

＿＿＿＿＿＿＿＿＿＿＿＿＿＿＿＿＿＿＿＿＿＿＿＿＿＿＿＿＿＿

9. Cinderella walked to the Prince's Ball. ＿＿＿＿＿＿

Reason: ＿＿＿＿＿＿＿＿＿＿＿＿＿＿＿＿＿＿＿＿＿＿＿＿＿＿

10. Cinderella wanted to go to the Prince's Ball. ＿＿＿＿＿＿

Reason: ＿＿＿＿＿＿＿＿＿＿＿＿＿＿＿＿＿＿＿＿＿＿＿＿＿＿

＿＿＿＿＿＿＿＿＿＿＿＿＿＿＿＿＿＿＿＿＿＿＿＿＿＿＿＿＿＿

11. The stepmother and stepsisters left Cinderella home on the night of the Prince's Ball. _____

Reason: _____

_____

12. Cinderella rode to the Prince's Ball in a carriage drawn by six white horses. _____

Reason: _____

_____

13. Although the stepmother and stepsisters had beautiful clothes, they never bought any clothes for themselves. _____

Reason: _____

_____

14. The stepmother and stepsisters went only to social events that were important. _____

Reason: _____

_____

_____

15. Cinderella's fairy godmother was an evil witch in disguise. _____

Reason: _____

_____

Source: Adapted from A. Harnadek, *Critical Thinking Book 1* (Pacific Grove, CA: Midwest Publications, 1976).

Team Up!

With one or two of your classmates, discuss your responses to the Cinderella exercise. Are all of your responses the same? If not, discuss the reasoning behind your individual choices. Why might there be different answers? Now ask your instructor for the answers to the Cinderella exercise. How many did you answer correctly? If any of your answers or those of the classmates in your group were incorrect, do you understand why?

Whether or not you agreed with your classmates or your responses matched the answers provided by your instructor, you developed arguments about the fairy tale. You came to a conclusion about each statement and provided a reason for each of your conclusions. Your arguments might have been in the form of raised voices and differences of opinion about the various responses that you had; they could have been faulty or sound. Maybe you reconstructed them as the discussion with your classmates continued and they convinced you they were correct about certain questions. Regardless of your approach, you constructed arguments.

Exercise	**Parts of an Argument**

Exercise 12b

Parts of an Argument

Read the following statements, some of which are reasons and some of which are conclusions. Supply the missing parts for each argument. The first one is modeled for you.

MODEL
1. *Conclusion:* Education is the key to success (one of many possible conclusions).

   Reason 1: Education provides opportunities not otherwise available.

   Reason 2: Education, with perseverance, can effect positive change.

2. *Conclusion:* The government should spend more money on drug control in large cities such as New York, Detroit, Chicago, and Los Angeles.

   Reason 1: _____

   Reason 2: _____

3. *Conclusion: It takes a whole village to raise a child.*

   Reason 1: _____

   Reason 2: _____

4. *Conclusion:* _____

   Reason 1: People need to be more sensitive to the needs and suffering of the terminally ill.

   Reason 2: _____

5. *Conclusion:* _____

   Reason 1: Organized sports keep children and adolescents busy and off the streets.

   Reason 2: _____

Reasons and Conclusions

Read the following sentences and determine which ones in each group are conclusion statements and which are reasons. There is only one conclusion for each numbered group of sentences. The first one is modeled for you.

MODEL **1.** **a.** I need to study more effectively.   *Conclusion*

          b. I failed the last exam.   *Reason*

2. **a.** I feel much better lately.   _____

    b. I must be eating better.   _____

3. **a.** Therefore, legislation needs to address the AIDS issue.   _____

    b. It is estimated that 1 to 2 million Americans are infected with the virus that causes AIDS.   _____

    c. In 1996 more children and women continued to get AIDS.   _____

4. **a.** Jason is guilty.   _____

    b. Two eyewitnesses saw Jason commit the crime.   _____

    c. Jason had three pieces of the stolen jewelry in his pocket.   _____

    d. Jason's fingerprints matched those at the crime scene.   _____

5. **a.** The results of exercise include better, more restful sleep.   _____

    b. Exercise lowers the risk of heart attack.   _____

    c. Moderate exercise improves the immune system.   _____

    d. There are several benefits of exercising.   _____

Identifying Arguments

Recognizing *what,* and *where,* the main argument is in a textbook chapter allows you to understand the framework of a piece of writing and see how its ideas are connected to one another. You could read a 52 page chapter and consider all the words equally important, but it would be more useful to organize the material into the logical skeleton of an argument with a conclusion (main idea), three or four major reasons that support it (major supporting details), and a number of minor reasons that support them (minor supporting details). By doing this, the task of learning the information automatically becomes less intimidating and difficult because you have an organized group of ideas arranged in order of importance rather than a mass of unstructed material, to remember.

You can find arguments by looking for structures that have a conclusion and at least one supporting reason. Questioning yourself during all stages of the reading process will help you locate these structures more easily because the answers are often contained within them. An author usually makes one central point in a textbook chapter and provides several reasons that support it. This central point is the conclusion of the entire chapter. The reasons that support it are usually found in individual paragraphs and can also serve as smaller conclusions (main ideas) in their own right. They in turn are supported by reasons, also known as minor supporting details.

Argument Word Clues

Another way to detect the parts of arguments is to look for word clues within them. In Chapter 5 you learned that word clues help readers to follow authors' ideas; authors also use word clues to indicate the different parts of an argument. When authors do this it makes the task of locating the parts of an argument a little easier. Consider the following argument, for example:

Reason:	First of all, millions of innocent lives are wasted.
Reason:	Second, it takes years and billions of dollars to undo all of war's damage.
Reason:	Finally, war is getting more dangerous since the development of nuclear weapons and chemical warfare.
Conclusion:	It follows that no one ever really wins a war.

The phrases *first of all, second,* and *finally* are used to introduce and signal the reasons the author uses to support the conclusion that no one ever really wins a war; the phrase *it follows that* is used to introduce the conclusion.

Table 12.1 provides examples of some words and phrases commonly used to indicate that reasons are being discussed in an argument. Table 12.2 provides examples of words and phrases commonly used to identify that a conclusion to an argument is being stated.

TABLE 12.1   REASON WORD CLUES

may be inferred from/ may be deduced from	in view of the fact	as shown by
in the first place/ in the second place	because	first of all
for the reason that	as indicated by	first, second...
for example	finally	since

TABLE 12.2   CONCLUSION WORD CLUES

therefore	hence	shows that	it follows that
consequently	as a result	it should be	then
demonstrates that	points to	clear that	leads me to
implies that	proves that		believe that
in short	in my opinion		thereby showing
the point I'm making is	so		
the truth is	thus		

Identifying Arguments and Their Signal Words

For each of the following textbook excerpts you should:

- *Circle* any argument word clues.

- *Identify* the main argument or conclusion.

- *List* the reasons that support the argument.

The first one is modeled for you.

MODEL   **1.**   The idea that women and men think differently has traditionally been used to justify subjugating one to the other. Aristotle said that women are not as rational as men, and so women are naturally ruled by men. Kant agreed, adding that for this reason women "lack civil personality" and should have no voice in public life. Rousseau tried to put a good face on it by emphasizing that men and women merely possess different virtues, neither better than the other; but of course it turned out that men's virtues fit them for leadership, whereas women's virtues fit them for home and hearth.

Source: James Rachels, *The Elements of Moral Philosophy* (New York: McGraw-Hill, 1999), p. 162.

What is the main argument or conclusion?

The idea that women and men think differently has traditionally been

used to justify subjugating one to the other.

What are the reasons the author uses to support his argument?

a. Aristotle said that women are not as rational as men, so women

   are naturally ruled by men.

b. Kant added, that for this reason women "lack civil personality"

   and should have no voice in public life.

c. Rousseau emphasized that men and women merely possess different

   virtues, neither better than the other. Men's virtues fit them for

   leadership, whereas women's virtues fit them for home and hearth.

2. Certain taste preferences seem to be largely innate (Bartoshuk and Beauchamp, 1994). Newborns prefer sweet tastes to sour or bitter ones. The sweeter the fluid, the harder they suck and the more they drink (Haith, 1986). Sweetened water calms crying newborns, whether full-term or two to three weeks premature—evidence that not only the taste buds themselves (which seem to be fairly well developed by 20 weeks of gestation), but the mechanisms that produce this calming effect are functional before normal term (B. A. Smith and Blass, 1996). An inborn "sweet tooth" may help a baby adapt to life outside the womb, since breast milk is sweet. Newborns' rejection of bitter tastes is probably a survival mechanism, since many bitter substances are toxic (Bartoshuk and Beauchamp, 1994).

Source: Diane Papalia et al., *Human Development* (New York: McGraw-Hill, 2001), p. 139.

What is the main argument or conclusion?

_____

What are the reasons the author uses to support this argument?

_____

_____

_____

_____

3. This book takes a conceptual, nonmathematical approach to physics for nonscientists. There is a significant amount of educational research showing that all students, including science students, grasp the essential ideas of physics better if they conceptualize before they calculate. Furthermore, because the average nonscience student is deterred and discouraged by a mathematical presentation of physics, a conceptual, nonalgebraic approach is especially appropriate for the nonscientists.

Source: A. Hobson, *Physics: Concepts and Connections* (Englewood Cliffs, NJ: Prentice Hall, 1995).

What is the main argument or conclusion?

_____

_____

What are the reasons the author uses to support this argument?

_____

_____

_____

4. Proposals to solve problems are the workhorses of our society. Business, education, and government especially depend on proposals to decide where to direct resources and energy. Proposals enable us as individuals and as a society to make things better. We probably value this kind of thinking and writing because it makes us feel effective. It convinces us that difficulties can be overcome, that we can make practical, material changes that will improve our lives and the lives of others.

Source: R. Axelrod and C. Cooper, *The St. Martin's Guide to Writing*, 4th ed. (New York: St. Martins Press, 1994), p. 297.

What is the main argument or conclusion?

_____

_____

What are the reasons the author uses to support this argument?

_____

_____

_____

_____

_____

Team Up!

Compare your responses to Exercise 12d with one other classmate. Did you both identify the same arguments and signal words? Discuss possible reasons for any differences in your responses.

Exercise

12e

Arguments in an Essay

Read the following excerpt from the essay "No Disrespect" by Sister Souljah, and answer the questions that follow it.

The basic assumption of welfare was that since you were on it, you of course had time to stand in lines, wait in lobbies, and stay at home waiting for social workers, simply because you obviously had nothing else to do. Self-improvement in the welfare system at this time was unknown. For instance, if you were on welfare and you found a job, you had to immediately report it to the welfare department or risk prosecution as a welfare fraud. If you were foolish enough to go the honest route, the welfare agency would take away your rent subsidy and raise the rent to full market value. They would cancel your Medicaid so your children no longer qualified for subsidized health services. They would cut your food stamps in half and slash your monthly benefit check.

This strikes some people as fair, since you are now employed and ought to be able to pay your own way. Here's the catch. If you are on welfare and you get a job, usually it is minimum wage employment with no benefits. Therefore, when you report your new job to the agency and they cut and scale down your benefits, you now earn less money from your job than you would have if you had simply stayed home doing nothing. So, to make ends meet, you have to quit your job. Or, say you get a decent job with a decent wage above the minimum. You report it to welfare and one of your children gets a common illness like chicken pox. The private medical fees will still cost more than the decent wage you earn. So, in fear of medical bills and wanting to protect those services for your children, you quit your job to regain Medicaid.

Or say you decide you've met a good man. You would like to get married and try again at having a family. You must report it to welfare and they will cancel everything because you are not allowed to be married and receive welfare benefits. This policy perversely encourages single-mother households, as women are asked to choose between their man and the financial survival of their children. It destroys any impulse of self-improvement. It is a system designed to fail.

Source: Sister Souljah, *No Disrespect* (New York: Times Books, 1994), pp.13–14.

1. What reasons do you think the author could use to support the implied conclusion that welfare recipients do not have more time to stand in line and wait in lobbies than people who are working? In other words, what might occupy the time of welfare recipients?

_____

_____

_____

_____

2. According to the author, why is self-improvement difficult for those on welfare?

_____

_____

_____

3. What reasons does the writer provide to support her conclusion that welfare policy encourages single-mother households?

_____

_____

_____

Learning Journal

In her essay, Sister Souljah concludes that the welfare system is designed to fail. Do you agree or disagree? Write a journal entry where you argue your position. Provide three reasons that support your conclusion that are either from the excerpt or ones you provide yourself. Your entry should be at least one page in length.

Once you can detect argument structures in textbooks and create your own arguments using textbook information, you are less likely to accept everything you read as true. You will become more critical of what you read and hear and expect authors to provide logical reasons for their arguments. Knowing how arguments work allows you to question ideas and encourages you to draw your own conclusions about what an author is saying. This question-forming and answer-seeking activity makes you an active participant in the reading process.

Types of Arguments

There are two primary types of arguments, deductive and inductive. When you read textbooks or journal articles, you need to determine which kind of argument is being used as a preliminary step in judging their quality.

Deductive Arguments

A **deductive argument** begins with a general statement or a general law that is then supported by specific details, reasons, or examples that prove or explain it, which are called premises. Deductive arguments are judged as either being true or false. If the premises are true and logically lead to the conclusion, then the conclusion is true. Figure 12.1 (p. 406), is a visual example of this structure.

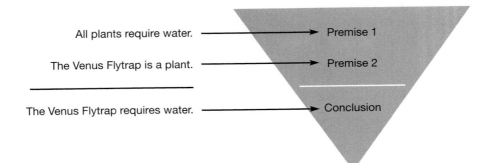

All plants require water. ⟶ Premise 1

The Venus Flytrap is a plant. ⟶ Premise 2

The Venus Flytrap requires water. ⟶ Conclusion

Figure 12.1   Deductive Reasoning

Here's another example of a deductive argument:

Premise 1:   All men attending this event wear ties.

Premise 2:   Jack is coming to this event and he is a man.

Conclusion: Jack will wear a tie to this event.

Many arguments you will encounter in your college science reading material are deductive arguments because they are based on facts and self-evident, verifiable truths that lead the reader to specific conclusions. Here is an example:

Premise: As warm air rises, it cools.

Premise: As it cools, the water vapor it contains condenses and clouds form.

Conclusion: If the water content of the air is greater than the air's capacity to retain moisture, some form of precipitation will occur.

Source: Adapted from Getis, Getis, and Fellmann, *Introduction to Geography*, 8th ed. (Boston: McGraw-Hill, 2002), p. 112.

Exercise 12f

Deductive Arguments

With a partner, try your hand at solving the following deductive argument problems. Remember that with deductive arguments there is only one correct answer based on the supporting statements.

1. On a certain day, I ate lunch at Penelope's Pocket Pitas, took out two magazines from the library (*Playgirl* and *Popular Mechanics*), visited the museum, and had a cavity filled. Penelope's Pocket Pitas is closed on Wednesday; the library is closed on weekends; the museum is open only on Monday, Wednesday, and Friday; and my dentist has office hours Tuesday, Friday, and Saturday.

Conclusion: There is only one day of the week that I could do all of these things and that is _____

2.   *Conclusion:* There are no lower bus fares from Detroit to New York than those of Hound Dog Bus Line. Which of the following is logically inconsistent with this advertising conclusion?

> *Premise 1:*   Peach Tree Airways has a Detroit to New York City fare that is only half that charged by Hound Dog Bus Line.
>
> *Premise 2:*   Rapid Transit Bus Company charges the same fare for a trip from Detroit to New York City as Hound Dog Bus Line charges.
>
> *Premise 3:*   Cherokee Bus Corporation has a lower fare from New York City to Boston than does Hound Dog Bus Line.

- **a.** 1 only.
- **b.** 2 only.
- **c.** 1 and 2 only.
- **d.** 1, 2, and 3.
- **e.** None of the premises is inconsistent.

3.   In another language *joe poppa* means "yellow corn," *poppa hat gab* means "little yellow car," and *sum gab* means "little cow." What is the word for car?

- **a.** poppa
- **b.** gab
- **c.** hat
- **d.** sum
- **e.** joe

Learning Journal

Construct three deductive arguments using facts from your own life.

Here is a sample journal entry written by Thomas, a university sophomore. Notice that he keeps writing until he comes up with three deductive arguments that are acceptable to him.

> *Deductive arguments. Hmm. Well, I know that if I cheat on an exam, I will be expelled from the university. That's the policy. I*

don't think they let you explain your way out of it. Okay. Two more. If I smoke, I will get cancer. No. There are people who smoke and they live forever. If I smoke, I might get cancer. No. That might be true but it's not a deductive argument. In a deductive argument, if the reason is true and logically leads to the conclusion, then the conclusion (cancer) must be true. Forget that one. Hey! If I get my hair cut, it will be shorter. One more. If I throw my book up in the air, it will come down.

Inductive Arguments

An **inductive argument** begins with a series of specific observations and concludes with a generalization that logically follows from it. Because an inductive argument is based on limited observations, the conclusion, in a good inductive argument, is probably, but not definitively true. An inductive argument is judged as being strong or weak. It is considered strong if the reasons are strong and lead to the conclusion in a logical fashion. Most arguments encountered in everyday life are inductive. Figure 12.2 shows how an inductive argument is structured.

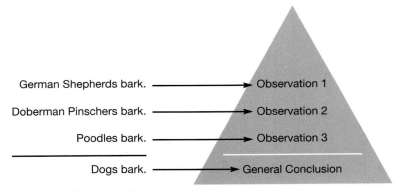

German Shepherds bark. ⟶ Observation 1

Doberman Pinschers bark. ⟶ Observation 2

Poodles bark. ⟶ Observation 3

Dogs bark. ⟶ General Conclusion

Figure 12.2   Inductive Reasoning

The following items are all examples of inductive arguments:

1. *Observation 1:*   The men and women of California were polled regarding the upcoming election.

   Observation 2:   Eighty-five percent of those polled said that they would vote for Arnold Schwarzeneger.

   Conclusion: So Arnold Schwarzeneger will most likely be the next governor.

2. *Observations 1 and 2:*   Most Republicans are conservative and Newt Gingrich is a Republican.

Conclusion: So it's safe to say that Newt Gingrich is
conservative.

3. Textbook example: "Even if there is no scriptural basis for it, the contemporary church's standing is strongly antiabortion (*observation 1*).
The typical churchgoer will hear ministers, priests, and bishops
denouncing abortion in the strongest terms, claiming all the while
to express the 'Christian' view (*observation 2*). It is no wonder, then,
that many people feel that their religious commitment binds them
to oppose abortion (*conclusion*)."

Source: James Rachels, *The Elements of Moral Philosophy* (New York: McGraw-Hill, 1999),
p. 68.

Learning Journal

Construct three inductive arguments using facts from your own life.

Team Up!

Find a classmate and discuss your answers to the following questions:

1. What is inductive reasoning?

2. An interpretation of a poem is a good example of what kind of reasoning?

3. What are the differences between deductive and inductive reasoning?

Exercise

12g

Inductive or Deductive Arguments?

Read the following statements and determine whether they are inductive (I)
or deductive (D) arguments. To help make your decisions, ask yourself if it
is *likely* that the conclusion follows from the statements (induction) or whether
the conclusion is logically supported by the statements or premises and
therefore is *absolutely* true (deduction).

1. All salespersons are extroverts. Lisa is a salesperson.
Therefore Lisa is an extrovert.   I D
_____

2. The Tigers have lost all of their home games for the last
two years; so they will lose their next home game.   I D
_____

3. We have interviewed thousands of students attending schools as diverse as the University of Michigan, Yale, Oakland Community College, University of Arizona, and Florida State. All of the students we interviewed liked rock and roll. Therefore, all the students at the University of Texas like rock and roll.

I   D
_____

4. The longer a pendulum is, the longer it takes to swing. Therefore, when the pendulum of a clock is lengthened, the clock will slow down.

I   D
_____

5. Reserves of coal in the United States have an energy equivalent 33 times that of oil and natural gas. On a worldwide basis the multiple is about 10. By shifting to a coal-based economy, we could satisfy our energy requirements for at least a century.

I   D
_____

6. Either the bumps on people's heads are indicators of personality characteristics or phrenology is a fraud. The bumps on people's heads are not indicators of personality characteristics. Therefore, phrenology is a fraud.

I   D
_____

(Special thanks to Keith Binkowski, a graduate student at Wayne State University, for this exercise.)

Exercise 12h

Deductive/Inductive Reasoning

Now read the following textbook excerpts and determine whether the reasoning used in them is deductive or inductive.

1. In the United States, aging is generally seen as undesirable. Stereotypes about aging reflect widespread misconceptions: that older people are usually tired, poorly coordinated, and prone to infections and accidents; that most of them live in institutions; that they can neither remember nor learn; that they have no interest in sexual activity; that they are isolated from others; that they do not use their time productively; and that they are grouchy, self-pitying, and cranky.

Source: Diane Papalia et al., *Human Development* (New York: McGraw-Hill, 2001), p. 635.

Is the passage deductive or inductive? _____

Explain your answer. _____

2. Judging from television, magazines, and books, no topic is more important to Americans than weight control. Dieting has become a national obsession, as people of all ages strive to be thinner and thus more "attractive."

Source: J.Greenberg and G. Dintiman, *Exploring Health: Expanding the Boundaries of Wellness* (Englewood Cliffs, NJ: Prentice Hall, 1992), p.192.

Is the passage inductive or deductive? _____

Explain your answer. _____

3. When you're navigating the Net, you can go from a Web page in Paris to one in Peru. What happens? When you click on a link, your computer sends out a request for information to another server. That server, which may be next door or across the planet, interprets your request, finds the information (text, graphics, or entire Web pages), and then breaks it up into packets. The server sends the packets to your computer, where your browser puts them back together and you see the Web page, all in the blink of an eye (or an eternity—they don't call it the World Wide Wait for nothing).

Source: William Nickels et al., *Understanding Business* (New York: McGraw-Hill, 2002), p. GR-21.

Is the passage inductive or deductive? _____

Explain your answer. _____

Evaluating Arguments

Gracie, the university student introduced at the beginning of this chapter, is having difficulty in her English class. Her assignment is to identify the arguments within two selected readings and to evaluate them, which she has done. However, she has also been asked to determine if the information contained in the articles is dependable. She has no idea what this means.

Learning Journal

Using your own words, explain how you currently evaluate arguments. What makes you change your mind about an opinion you hold? What do you look for when you read or listen to good arguments? How will learning about arguments help you in college and beyond?

Like many students, Gracie is not aware that arguments are tools authors use to support their opinions, claims, or beliefs. All arguments are not necessarily true. It's up to her to determine if the arguments she reads are supported by sound reasoning, and whether the author and reading source are reliable.

Knowing how to evaluate arguments is useful because it helps you to follow an author's line of reasoning and therefore understand his or her ideas more clearly. It is important to know how to differentiate between a good argument and a poor one. Although judging the quality of an argument is a complex task, you can use various strategies to help you decide if an argument in a textbook is sound:

- Determine dependability.
- Distinguish facts from opinions.
- Detect fallacies.

Determining Dependability in Arguments

As a critical reader, you must look beyond the words printed on the page to distinguish whether an argument is dependable or unreliable. Several key strategies can help you do this:

Check Date of Publication

Information changes rapidly and soon becomes outdated, especially in the fields of science and medicine. The amount of information students had access to 20 years ago doubled every 10 years; currently, the amount of available information is doubling every 20 months! So check the publication date of the article or textbook you are reading. If it was not published within the last five–10 years (possibly less if you are studying a rapidly changing field), you should question the reliability of the information it contains.

Check Source of Publication

Whether you are reading a textbook, journal article, or book of literary criticism, always consider its source of publication. Knowing that a publisher is reputable is important when you are trying to make decisions about the accuracy of information you are reading. Some questions you can ask to help guide you are:

- Who published the information?
- Is the source reliable? Reputable publishing companies invest time and money to authenticate the information they print.
- Was the text published by an unknown press or by one that is known for exaggerating the truth? If you are looking for factual

information regarding current medical research, for example, you would want to use the *American Journal of Medicine* as a source, rather than an article from the *Daily Sun*.

- Is the information self-published? If it is published by a source you aren't sure about, try to find out what other information has been published by this source and how reliable it has been.

Check Authorship

Another factor to consider is the author of the text and his or her qualifications and expertise in the field. Asking the following questions can help you determine how much you can rely on what an individual author has to say on a topic:

- Is the author considered an expert in the field? What credentials does he or she hold?
- Does the author have a reputation for accuracy?
- Is the author objective, or does the author tend to include his or her own opinions and biases about a topic?
- Is the author a firsthand source? Has the author personally researched the information you are reading? Or is he or she simply reporting what someone else has said?

Determining an author's dependability requires you to become an investigator. You can find out about an author's degrees, experience, previous publications, and professional associations by reading the information provided at the beginning of your textbook. Articles usually contain a brief statement about who wrote them. Your instructor or college librarian can also provide you with additional information regarding a specific author.

Distinguishing Fact from Opinion

In order to evaluate an argument, it is important to distinguish between facts and opinions.

Facts

Facts are statements that can be proved to be true. They can be verified through research, observation, experimentation, or direct experience. For example, you can research historical documents to find out when the first pioneers started moving out west, or set up a series of controlled experiments in a laboratory to determine how well a certain drug will treat a specific form of cancer. A fact does not reflect personal feelings or attitudes.

The following examples of factual information were selected from the book *2201 Fascinating Facts*. The authenticity of each item can be easily verified by using other sources, such as encyclopedias, historical trivia books, or textbooks. They are not statements of opinion, feelings, or beliefs. They are intended to inform you, not to persuade you to believe a certain point of view.

1. According to current research, the moon weighs 81 billion tons.
2. The yo-yo originated as a weapon in the Philippine Islands and was introduced to America in 1929.
3. In the United States in 1976, a pound of potato chips cost 200 times more than a pound of potatoes.
4. The Baby Ruth candy bar was named after the first baby girl ever born in the White House, Ruth Cleveland, daughter of President Grover Cleveland.
5. Crystals grow by reproducing themselves.

Source: David Louis, *2201 Fascinating Facts* (New York: Greenwich House, 1983).

These five facts are based either on scientific research (#1 and #5) or examination of historical documents (#2, #3, and #4).

Opinions

Opinions are the expression of personal perspectives or points of view regarding issues or topics, and cannot be proved or disproved. Though they can be based on factual information they should be questioned and treated with more caution than a statement of fact. For example, if a doctor who specializes in treating respiratory illnesses says she believes Brand X is effective for treating allergies, you might seriously consider using it. However, you may question whether a movie star promoting Brand X in television commercials, has the necessary expertise to support her opinion that it is a wonder drug.

When authors state their opinions, they sometimes use absolute words such as *worst, best, most, least,* or other emotive words that express strong feelings such as *exciting, annoying, delightful, horrible, beautiful,* or *ugly.* They also tend to use words such as *should* and *ought*. Although some authors will take a direct approach and state "this is my opinion," many will try to persuade you of their point of view by using emotive language and biased statements. So it is important to get as much background information on an author as possible when evaluating his or her arguments. Here are some examples of opinions:

1. George Bush should not have gone to war against Saddam Hussein.
2. The rapper 50 Cent is not a good performer.
3. Sammy Sosa is the best baseball player alive.

Recognizing Facts and Opinions

Read the following statements and determine if they are facts (F) or opinions (O). Remember that a fact is something that can be proved, whereas an opinion is a personal belief that cannot be proved.

1. Tibetans, Mongolians, and people in parts of western China put salt in their tea instead of sugar. (Can this be researched and verified?) _____

2. Salt tastes better in coffee than sugar does. (You may agree, but can this be proved? Could some people prefer sugar?) _____

3. In 1740 a cow was found guilty of sorcery in France and publicly hanged. _____

4. Cows thought to be guilty of sorcery should be hanged. _____

5. Ice hockey is the most exciting sport to view on television. _____

6. Progressive jazz is annoying and should not be played on the radio between 9 A.M. and 5 P.M. _____

7. According to a current study, it would take 27,000 spiders, each spinning a single web, to produce a pound of web. _____

8. A spider web is one of nature's more beautiful and fascinating phenomena. _____

9. At birth, baby kangaroos are only about an inch long—no bigger than a large waterbug or a queen bee. _____

10. A quarter has 119 grooves on its circumference; a dime has one fewer. _____

Facts and Opinions in Textbooks

Read the following textbook samples and identify which are based on opinions and which on facts. Provide reasons for your decisions.

1. A forager honeybee spends about three weeks becoming accustomed to the immediate surroundings of its hive, and then the rest of its life collecting pollen and nectar. A forager's flight muscles can last only about 500 miles—after that the bee dies. The total number of miles, T, a forager can fly in its lifetime, L (in days), can be modeled by $T = m(L - 21)$ where m is the number of miles it flies each day. A hardworking forager honeybee can fly about 55 miles each day.

Source: Larson, Kranold, and Stiff, *Algebra 2: An Integrated Approach* (Lexington, MA: D.C. Heath and Company, 1995), p. 35.

Is this passage based on fact or opinion? Explain your answer.

_____

_____

2. Dinosaur bones have been firing our imagination for hundreds of years. People in the Middle Ages found huge bones that were probably fossils of dinosaurs and large aquatic reptiles, which may have inspired the legends of dragons and giants.

Source: P. Dodson, _The Age of Dinosaurs_ (Lincolnwood, IL: Publications International, 1993).

Is this passage based on fact or opinion? Explain your answer.

_____

_____

3. When you edit and write at the same time, the result is often a disaster: a disaster for you as a writer and eventually for your reader. Purple patches come from the unrestricted pen. Go back and edit later. Later is when you invite the logical sequential strength side of you to come forward and apply all the techniques of good grammar and construction that have been drilled into you since the beginning of your school days.

Source: H. Klauser, _Writing on Both Sides of the Brain_ (San Francisco: HarperCollins, 1987), p. 15.

Is this passage based on fact or opinion? Explain your answer.

_____

_____

4. In the long swing of history, elections with broad mass participation are rather new. Such elections originated with democratic government, which means that they came along at the end of the eighteenth century and the beginning of the nineteenth. Today elections are widespread around the world, even though many of the world's states are not democracies. Many nondemocratic states, such as the pre-1989 Soviet Union, have held them regularly.

Source: W. Shively, _Power & Choice: An Introduction to Political Science_ (New York: McGraw-Hill, 1999), p. 204.

Is this passage based on fact or opinion? Explain your answer.

_____

_____

5. Marx argued that a free market system is exploitative because producers, through their control of production and markets, can compel workers to labor at a wage below the value they add to production and can force consumers to pay higher prices for goods than are justified by the cost of production. To end the exploitation of labor, Marx proposed a collective economy. When the workers owned the means of production, the economy would operate in the interest of all people.

Source: T. Patterson, *The American Democracy* (New York: McGraw-Hill, 1999), p. 498.

Is this passage based on fact or opinion? Explain your answer.

Detecting Fallacies

Fallacies are errors in reasoning. Recognizing whether an argument contains fallacies helps you evaluate its strength and validity and make your own decisions about what an author is saying. Authors may intentionally or unintentionally use fallacies to persuade their readers to agree with their point of view. Regardless of their motives, detecting errors in an author's reasoning can help you become a good judge of the soundness of arguments. Here are some common reasoning errors or fallacies you will encounter in your college reading, newspapers, and other sources.

Either/Or Thinking

The error in **either/or thinking** is that it allows for only two answers to a problem when in fact there may be more.

Example

Reason 1:	Either I can study all night, every night of this weekend for my history exam, get no sleep, and be too tired to do well.
Reason 2:	Or, I can go to the movies tonight with my friends, go to the football game on Saturday, and just relax on Sunday, and not study at all.
Conclusion:	I'm going to fail the exam.

This is not an either/or situation. There are many alternative possibilities. For example, you could study for several hours on each weekend day, but still sleep. Or you could study Friday night before the movie, attend the football game during the day on Saturday, and pursue a strict study schedule on Sunday.

Hasty Generalization/Overgeneralization

When using **hasty generalizations**, authors make the error of using too few or weak reasons to support a broad, sweeping conclusion.

Example

Reason 1:   My neighbor is a Republican and he never contributes to charity.

Reason 2:   Beth, a colleague of mine, is a Republican and she never pays for lunch.

Conclusion: All Republicans are closefisted.

Each reason may be true, but together they do not provide enough evidence to generalize that *all* Republicans are stingy or closefisted. In arguments, it is very difficult to be so absolutely sure of an opinion as to use the word "all." When you see words such as *every, never, always,* or *none* used, be careful when evaluating an argument.

Red Herring

Authors introduce **red herrings** (irrelevant material) into an argument when they want to distract their readers' attention away from important information that does not support their conclusion. An argument with this error leaves the original issue and moves to another one.

Example

Reason 1:   Men and women use the services of prostitutes.

Reason 2:   Prostitutes earn enough money to support themselves and pay taxes.

Conclusion: Prostitutes should not be punished.

Whether prostitution should be punished is a matter for the law to decide in each state. How well a business is doing is irrelevant. After all, drug dealers also make a lot of money and satisfy a need. The real issue here is lawfulness, not entrepreneurship.

False Cause

In a **false cause** arguments authors state a conclusion and gives reasons for it, but fails to explain how the conclusion and reasons are connected to each other, or provides unclear or provide faulty connections between them.

Example

Reason 1:   Dr. Jay's window is broken.

Reason 2:   My window is broken.

Conclusion: I'm positive Ben broke the windows; I saw him playing outside yesterday.

Although two windows are broken, and Ben was playing outside the previous day, there is no evidence presented in this argument to prove that Ben had anything to do with breaking them; there is no proof of cause and effect.

Slippery Slope

The error in **slippery slope** reasoning is that authors assume that one event will precipitously lead to another event, which will lead to another event, and so on. They provide a chain of improperly linked conclusions as reasons to support an unjustified main conclusion. Conclusions in this type of reasoning are often greatly exaggerated.

Example

Reason 1:	Voting for a Democrat will raise taxes.
Reason 2:	The taxes will become so intolerable, people will begin to riot.
Reason 3:	With the riots, anarchy will occur and the United States will divide into separate countries.
Conclusion:	Don't vote for Democrats or the country will be in ruins.

Although a government led by the Democratic Party could raise taxes, it is highly unlikely that doing so would cause riots so severe that states would secede to become independent countries.

Ad Hominem

When authors commit an **ad hominem** error of reasoning, they avoid the true issue of an argument by attacking the person they disagree with.

Example

Reason 1:	I studied for the multiple-choice exam.
Reason 2:	I read most of the assigned chapters.
Conclusion:	But I failed anyway because my professor is a woman who doesn't like me and is too emotional to grade objectively.

The fact that this student's professor is a woman has nothing to do with the fact the student failed the exam. The student failed because he or she didn't read all the assigned chapters and therefore couldn't answer all the questions on the exam.

Circular Reasoning

When authors use **circular reasoning**, instead of presenting an argument with a reason and a conclusion, they make two statements that essentially say the same thing.

Example

Reason: The Red Hawks won their baseball game today.

Conclusion: The Red Hawks won because they scored the most points.

Both the reason and the conclusion assert the same thing.

Exercise 12k

MODEL

Detecting Fallacies

Read the following arguments and determine if they contain a fallacy or error in reasoning; if so, identify what kind it is. The first one is modeled for you.

1. If you don't get good grades, you'll never get to college.

If you don't get into college, you'll never get a job.

Therefore, you'll end up a homeless person in some major city.

Error in reasoning? __Yes__

If so, which fallacy was committed?
Slippery slope

2. Flowers are so beautiful in the springtime.

The air seems cleaner and the grass seems greener.

In my opinion, there is something so rejuvenating about the onset of spring.

Error in reasoning? _____

If so, which fallacy was committed?

3. The doctor said that I could either stick to his diet plan, or accept being overweight.

Error in reasoning? _____

If so, which fallacy was committed?

4. Ima Geeke, mayoral candidate, suggests changing several local laws. She believes that the laws need to be more reflective of the times. She's just a generation X'er; what does she know?

Error in reasoning? _____

If so, which fallacy was committed?

5. Every student who earns a 3.0 grade point average or higher is eligible for the Lah D. Dah scholarship. I have a 3.2 GPA. If I apply, I could get the scholarship.

Error in reasoning? _____

If so, which fallacy was committed?

_____

6. If I go to the casino with Andy, I know that I'll win money.

The first time I went to the casino with Andy, I won $10.

The second time, I won $50.

Error in reasoning? _____

If so, which fallacy was committed?

_____

7. Judy gave an outstanding presentation in class today, and I admit that she seems like a good candidate for student council. But I am leery of someone whose parents support euthanasia.

Error in reasoning? _____

If so, which fallacy was committed?

_____

_____

8. It's easy to prove that Santa Claus exists. Most people do believe in Santa, even if they are not able to define exactly what they mean in the same way. To some it means a real person living in the North Pole. To some it's a spirit of giving, a supernatural force. And to others, he's a saint. But setting aside the differences in these interpretations, we can be confident that there is a Santa because Santa would not cause so many people to believe in him if he did not exist.

Error in reasoning? _____

If so, which fallacy was committed?

_____

9. I'm not bringing my brother to the Rangers' football games anymore. Every time I bring him, the team loses.

Error in reasoning? _____

If so, which fallacy was committed?

_____

10. Maya Aspirin will help relieve headaches because Maya Aspirin contains a secret new ingredient, which serves to increase the strength of relief it provides. What is the secret ingredient? It is an ingredient that has the ability to provide relief from headaches. So buy Maya Aspirin and get relief from your headaches.

Error in reasoning? _____

If so, which fallacy was committed?

_____

Team Up!

In groups of four, share your responses to Exercise 12K. Each person needs to explain his or her answers.

Practice with Reading Passages

Reading Practice 1

Answer all questions on a separate sheet of paper.

Arguments can also be expressed visually, as the following cartoon demonstrates.

"IMAGINE THAT CANOEIST CUSSING RIGHT IN FRONT OF A CHILD!"

Copyright © 2002 H. Payne, *Detroit News*.

CHECK YOUR UNDERSTANDING

SHORT-ANSWER QUESTIONS

1. What are the important details in the cartoon? (identify at least four).

2. What argument do you believe the cartoonist is making? Explain your answer using three reasons.

"Down and Dirtier"

BY N'GAI CROAL

PREPARE TO READ

1. Based on the title, what do you expect the reading to be about? What do you think the topic is?

2. What do you already know about the topic?

3. Here are some vocabulary words that might be unfamiliar to you. Look them up, if necessary, and refer to the definitions as you encounter these vocabulary words in the reading.

a. Apocalypse

b. Demographics

c. Pandora's box—In case you do not find this expression in the dictionary, here is a brief definition: The phrase "Pandora's box" refers to a Greek myth where a woman, faced with a box or jar, gives in to her curiosity and opens the box, only to find evil spilling out.

4. Create a question to ask yourself, using the title of the reading.

Down and Dirtier

Last year's best selling videogame wasn't Pokémon, Maden Football, Metal Gear Solid 2, or even The Sims. It was Grand Theft Auto 3, where players try to move up through the ranks of the Mafia by delivering mysterious packages, ferrying hookers to and from their dates, tailing suspected snitches, planting car bombs to take out rival bosses, and more. Like that Humvee? Just carjack it. Looking for some female companionship? Pick up a prostitute in the red-light district for a red-light special. But each of your actions has consequences. Start shooting pedestrians, and the cops will do their best to bring you in. Shoot a cop, and his buddies will call in the FBI; kill an FBI agent, and the military will pull out all the stops to take you down. With extreme prejudice.

To the folks at three-year-old Rockstar Games, whose other outlaw hits include Smuggler's Run, Midnight Club Street Racing, and the hard-boiled cop thriller Max Payne, the runaway success of GTA3 is proof that the 12-year-olds who grew up on Mario are looking for something very different now that they're in their 20s: games whose look, feel, and sound are drawn from the edgy movies, comic books, and music that reflect a twentysomething's interests. But fans aren't just responding to the game's racy trappings; they're also getting a kick out of the wide range of behavior it allows. "It's brilliant," says Steve Kent, the 41-year-old author of *The Ultimate History of Video Games*, and the parent of two young kids whom he lets nowhere near GTA3. "They put together a great game, then layered the offensive stuff on top of it. If Tarantino or Scorsese made a game, this would be it."

Rockstar's certainly on to something; since its October 2001 release, GTA3 has sold nearly 3 million copies at $50 a pop. And Hollywood is noticing. New Line and Miramax have bought film rights to games from Rockstar, and more deals are in the works.

To some parents and politicians, GTA3 may seem like just another sign that the apocalypse is upon us. In a statement Sen. Joe Lieberman said, "Games like Grand Theft Auto are particularly troubling because they go beyond just celebrating violence generally, and actually reward players for engaging in organized crime, murdering innocent people and other forms of perverse, antisocial behavior." Rockstar COO Terry Donovan stresses that the game is rated M (for Mature, suitable for people 17 and older) and that the company's marketing isn't aimed at children. But that doesn't stop enterprising youngsters from getting GTA3; 16-year-old Los Angeleno Mike Garakian scored a copy from the local Electronics Boutique, no questions asked. "At first I thought my parents would freak out, but they didn't mind," he says. "The media has talked a lot about the violence, but that's not what makes it great."

Demographics account for some of GTA3's success. Console-game owners are refusing to put away childish things as they get older. On the original PlayStation the sweet spot of the market was 8 to 17, and none of the 10 biggest hits was M-rated. But for PlayStation 2, the key demographic has become 18- to 34-year olds. Six of last year's top 20 PS2 games were M-rated—two from Rockstar alone. Some industry veterans believe that the growing popularity of M-rated games will affect the tastes of young gamers. Naughty Dog cofounder Jason Rubin, best known for his all-ages PlayStation hit franchise Crash Bandicoot, believes his latest all-ages game missed the mass market because of this demographic shift. "We've opened up Pandora's box with these games," says Rubin, citing informal surveys showing that some kids as young as 12 want to play GTA3, and that 7-year-olds aren't responding as strongly to the colorful mascot games that powered the original PlayStation. "Looking ahead, videogames may not return to the children's era." If Rubin is correct, Rockstar will have done a drive-by on Mario, Crash Bandicoot, and the videogame industry as we know it.

Source: N'Gai Croal, "Down and Dirtier," *Newsweek*, March 18, 2002, p. 50A.

SHORT-ANSWER QUESTIONS

1. How would you summarize the article?

2. In this article, what reasons are given to explain why this video game is popular?

3. Other than the reasons given in the article, why do you think this video game would be popular?

4. What are some of the objections to the video game mentioned in this article?

5. What are other objections to this video that you can think of that were not mentioned in the article?

6. Are the arguments for and against this video game inductive or deductive?

Chapter Summary

Recognizing arguments as you read lets you critically examine an author's line of reasoning. Arguments always have the structure of at least one reason and one conclusion. One way to detect them is to look for an author's conclusions and then track the reasons he or she used to reach them. Another way is to look for the argument word clues an author uses to indicate when reasons are being presented and conclusions stated. When you find an argument, you should break it down into its constituent parts so that you can determine whether it is well founded and logical. Arguments can be evaluated using specific criteria including determining dependability, distinguishing fact from opinion, and detecting fallacies.

The two primary types of arguments are deductive and inductive. Deductive arguments have at least one premise that logically leads to a conclusion. If the premise or premises of a deductive argument are true, then the conclusion is true. Inductive arguments begin with a series of specific observations and conclude with a generalization that logically flows from them. As they are based on limited observations, even well-constructed inductive arguments cannot be considered absolutely true.

An author's views should be actively questioned so that flaws in the presentation of information are not passively accepted. Being able to detect and evaluate arguments in textbooks, and to create arguments using your textbook reading material, forces you to analyze the logic of what you read and helps you present your own ideas in a logical fashion.

Post Test

Answer the following on a separate sheet of paper.

Part I

OBJECTIVE QUESTIONS

1. Match the following words in Column A with their correct definitions in Column B:

A		B	
1.	Argument	a.	Error in reasoning where one fails to explain how the reasons and conclusions are connected to each other.
2.	Reason	b.	A statement that justifies a conclusion.
3.	Conclusion	c.	A type of argument that makes a conclusion based on facts and verifiable truths—absolutes.
4.	Fallacy	d.	A conclusion with at least one reason to support it.
5.	Deductive argument	e.	Error in reasoning.
6.	Either/or fallacy	f.	Error in reasoning where issue is avoided by attacking the person who disagrees.
7.	Inductive argument	g.	Error in reasoning that allows for only two absolute answers to a problem.
8.	Fact	h.	An example of circular reasoning.
9.	Ad hominem	i.	A type of argument where the conclusion is based on a series of observations.
10.	Circular reasoning	j.	Can be proven as a true statement.
11.	False cause	k.	A statement of judgment.
12.	Opinion	l.	Error in reasoning that assumes one event will precipitously lead to another event, which will lead to another, and so on.

13. Slippery slope

m. Error in reasoning that avoids reasoning by stating the same thing twice.

14. The Tigers won because they scored more points.

n. Point or claim someone makes.

2. Read the following arguments and decide whether they are inductive or deductive.

a. The legal age to drink should be 18. If people are old enough to vote, then they are certainly old enough to drink. Eighteen-year-olds are old enough to vote.

b. Three thousand six hundred autoworkers were surveyed regarding the minimum age to drink alcoholic beverages. Three thousand two hundred of them favored 18 as the preferred minimum legal age. Therefore, 18 should be the legal age to drink alcoholic beverages.

c. Every April 14th since I've been born, it rains. Tomorrow is April 14. I'd better bring an umbrella, because it's probably going to rain.

d. The space program deserves increased expenditures in the years ahead. Not only does the national defense depend on it, but the program will more than pay for itself in terms of technological spin-offs. Furthermore, at current funding levels, the program cannot fulfill its anticipated potential.

Part II

Reading Passage

"Racial Paranoia"
BY DAVID HOROWITZ

"Racial Paranoia" is an essay from a book titled *Hating Whitey and Other Progressive Causes*. The author, David Horowitz, is a white man who, during the 1960s, was a confidante of the Black Panthers, a radical civil rights group. After many years of active participation in liberal politics, Horowitz lost faith in some political leaders and was disappointed by the results of radical action. By the 1980s, his political convictions had changed completely. Today he is a writer, editor, and political leader. He says that even in his extended family, which includes both whites and blacks, there are some who agree with him and others who do not. All of them, however, support his decision to act on his beliefs, which he argues are based on experience.

The essay you are about to read is emotional in tone, with a definite author bias. It also contains many facts and arguments. Carefully read the essay and evaluate the arguments within it.

1. Read the title of the excerpt following these questions. Based on the title, what do you expect the reading to be about? What do you think the topic is?

2. What do you already know about the topic.

3. Create a question to ask yourself, using the title or topic of the reading.

Racial Paranoia

When Bill and Camille Cosby's son, Ennis, was brutally murdered in 1997 during a robbery in Beverly Hills, the entire nation grieved with them. But a year later Camille Cosby unburdened herself in print with a diatribe against white Americans in a *USA Today* column entitled "America Taught My Son's Killer to Hate Blacks." The feelings expressed in this column could not be regarded simply as grief over her terrible loss. For such pain a mother could be forgiven almost any emotional excess. Written a year after the fact, however, the sentiments expressed in her *USA Today* column reflected long-held, carefully scrutinized, patiently edited sentiments of hostility and rage against her native country and its white citizenry that could not be so easily excused. It was a form of race hatred that has become all too common among educated and successful African Americans.

Unlike the mothers of Nicole Brown Simpson and Ronald Goldman, who were destined to be disappointed by racially motivated "jury nullification," Camille Cosby saw swift justice rendered by the American system to the murderer of her son. The mainly white jury was not swayed to acquit the killer of Ennis Cosby because of his skin color, nor was there a racial constituency outside the courtroom hoping that he would "beat the system" and go free. Instead, the white prosecutor, judge, and jurors worked to bring in a verdict of guilty with all deliberate speed. This was better justice than most Americans receive, white or black. Nonetheless, Camille Cosby was not satisfied; she believed that true justice had not been served. In her eyes, the killer himself was a victim—of America.

By then, most of the salient facts in the case had come to light. It was questionable that race had played any role at all in the killing of Ennis Cosby. The gunman, a Ukrainian immigrant, was high on drugs at the time of the shooting and told police shortly after his capture that he regretted what he had done and that he had pulled the trigger because the young man "took too long" to remove his wallet. But none of these facts impressed Camille Cosby: "Presumably [the killer] did not learn to hate black people in his native country, the Ukraine, where the black population was near zero," she wrote. "Nor was he likely to see America's intolerable, stereotypical movies and television programs about blacks, which were not shown in the Soviet Union before the killer and his family moved to America in the late 1980s." In Cosby's fevered view, America's "intolerable, stereotypical movies and television programs" were responsible for the death of her son.

It is a logic that is as familiar as it is paranoid. The charge that white Hollywood portrays blacks in a stereotypically negative fashion is a standard protest heard from black spokesmen ranging from Louis Farrakhan to Jesse Jackson. But it has little basis in fact. Going back to the 1940s, white Hollywood has produced and directed an entire library of features about black Americans and their struggle for equality (*Home of the Brave, Pinky, Sergeant Rutledge, To Kill a Mockingbird, The Defiant Ones*), not to mention many of the principal epics of black liberation and pride, *Roots* and *Malcolm X* (both produced by whites) and *Amistad* (written and directed by whites) to name three, and television sitcoms and series focusing on admirable black families (*Julia, The Jeffersons, Good Times, Sister Sister, I'll Fly Away*). At the same time, black artists have themselves produced many of the negative stereotypes, from "blaxploitation" films like *Super Fly* to gangsta rap videos, which are the targets of many complaints.

But it is the name Cosby that almost by itself represents a refutation of the paranoid claim that white America and Hollywood are hostile to blacks. Camille Cosby enjoys a fortune estimated in the hundreds of millions because of the success of a television show featuring her husband as the head of a model black family. For ten years, the *Cosby Show* was the top-rated television program in America (and Bill Cosby the top-earning entertainer) thanks to the loyalty of tens of millions of viewers who happened to be white. If America was the country of Camille Cosby's paranoid imagination, the success of both the real and fictional Cosbys would be inexplicable.

As if to demonstrate the irrationality of these complaints, the *Cosby Show* was actually attacked quite regularly in the years of its popularity, often by the same people. They accused the show of being "unrepresentative" and "unrealistic," in other words of being an attempt by white network executives to portray African Americans as *better* than they actually were, while hiding the poverty, oppression and other injuries of race that white America had inflicted on them.

Nor does the illogic stop there. On what basis does Camille Cosby make the claim that because there were no blacks in the Ukraine, the killer of her son must have learned racism by watching American television? Is she suggesting that the presence of a persecuted group is *necessary* to provoke the irrationality of bigots? Do racists need evidence to substantiate their racism? There are no Jews to speak of in countries like Poland and Japan, but Jew hatred is rife in both places. Has Cosby forgotten (or as a leftist has she merely blanked out the memory of) Russia's racist culture that led to the mass expulsion of African students from Moscow's Lumumba University and Moscow's official protest at the Olympics that the American team's inclusion of black athletes was an unfair advantage because of blacks' innately superior abilities?

Early press reports of the Cosby murder indicated that, as a youth, Ennis Cosby's killer was raped by blacks in prison. What would Camille Cosby's reaction be to the claim that black rapists were responsible for her son's death? Yet that is exactly the logic she employs in attacking America for the drug-induced act of one immigrant sociopath. "Yes," she writes, "racism and prejudice are omnipresent and eternalized in America's institutions, media, and myriad entities." *Eternalized?* Are white Americans born racists and destined to die as such? This is indeed the accusation made by black racists like law professor Derrick Bell, who in several popular books has claimed that America is irretrievably hostile to blacks. How are Cosby's and Bell's views that white Americans are inherently morally depraved different from the attitudes of southern crackers and KKK racists toward blacks?

Like Cosby, Bell is culturally a product of the communist left, which fifty years ago brought a petition to the United Nations, at the behest of the Kremlin, charging the United States with "genocide" in its treatment of blacks. Perhaps it is also appropriate to recall that the Cosbys were vocal supporters of the notorious Tawana Brawley, who falsely accused a group of whites of raping her. (Brawley, incidentally, has made an after-the-fact career out of touring campuses to repeat her lies at the invitation of black student associations who reward her with handsome fees for her testimony.) At the time, the Cosbys put up reward money for anyone who could prove Brawley's lies were true and appeared at rallies organized by Al Sharpton to incite hatred and violence against the innocent whites she smeared.

In her *USA Today* column, Cosby began her "proof" of what she believed to be America's ineluctable racism with the meaningless fact that the Voting Rights Act would technically expire in ten years. From this she concluded, preposterously, that "Congress once again will decide whether African-Americans will be allowed to vote" and commented "no other Americans are subjected to this oppressive nonsense." On what planet is Camille Cosby living? What could possibly have inspired the idea that whites are plotting to take away the voting rights of American blacks? What majority in this country would deny African-Americans the right to vote, a right guaranteed by the Fifteenth Amendment? To be sure, this right was once denied in the American South, but black Americans led by King and supported by the overwhelming majority of white Americans—including the government, the courts, and law enforcement agencies—restored it. The Voting Rights Act was passed by 90 percent majorities in Congress. The once segregated South is today a region whose major cities are run by African-American elected officials, while black legislators like congresswoman Cynthia McKinney are now regularly elected in majority white districts.

Camille Cosby is a woman whose country has showered her with privilege, making her family wealthy and famous beyond the wildest dreams of almost anyone alive, including all but a handful of the white targets of her wrath. Yet Camille Cosby's hatred of her country is so deep as to provoke the following preposterous observation: "African-Americans, as well as all Americans, are brainwashed every day to respect and revere slave-owners and people who clearly waffled about race....Several slave-owners' images are on America's paper currencies: George Washington ($1), Thomas Jefferson ($2), Alexander Hamilton ($10), Andrew Jackson ($20), Ulysses Grant ($50), and Benjamin Franklin ($100)." Forget that the characterizations of Hamilton, Grant, and Franklin (whose last act was to file an antislavery petition to Congress) are probably libelous. What American is taught to praise these men for having owned (or possibly having owned) slaves? America is probably unique among the nations of the world in teaching every one of its children from kindergarten on that slavery was wrong, that all people are created equal, and that tolerance of differences is a cardinal virtue. Perhaps Cosby should direct her concerns to black leaders like Jesse Jackson and Louis Farrakhan who *are* still waffling about slavery in Africa more than a hundred years after the spiritual heirs of Washington and Jefferson abolished the institution in the United States.

Source: David Horowitz, *Hating Whitey and Other Progressive Causes* (Dallas: Spence, 1999), pp. 17–22.

SHORT-ANSWER QUESTIONS

1. In the first paragraph of the excerpt, Horowitz indirectly states his main idea, which is also the conclusion for his main argument. Reread this first paragraph. What is the implied main idea?

2. Also in the first paragraph, Horowitz creates a smaller argument with this conclusion: "[Camille Cosby's sentiments] could not be so easily excused." What reason does he provide for this conclusion? According to Horowitz, why couldn't her comments be excused due to her grief over the loss of her son?

3. What reason does Horowitz give to support another smaller argument he makes, that concludes race probably didn't play a part in Ennis Cosby's killing?

4. What argument does the author make about black artists and negative stereotypes?

5. What argument does the writer make about voting rights? What reasons does he give? What fallacies are committed?

6. Give some examples of emotive language that the author uses.

7. Write a summary of the excerpt. Use your response to question 1 in the beginning of your summary because this is the main idea of the excerpt. Then create a question from the main idea and look for major supporting ideas in the excerpt that answer that question. Leave out the rest of the details.

8. Is Horowitz's overall argument inductive or deductive? Would you judge it to be strong or weak?

9. What other information would help you make an even better judgment about the strength of his argument?

Website Sources for Additional Practice

http://www.colostate.edu/Depts/WritingCenter/references/reading/ toulmin/page1.htm—great tutorial on the Toulmin method.

http://www.sjsu.edu/depts/itl/graphics/main.html: try "Mission Critical"—a full-scale tutorial for critical thinking.

Chapter 13

Reading beyond the Words

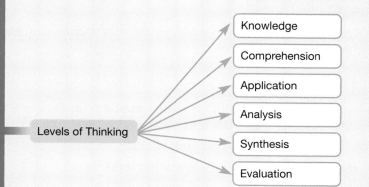

Levels of Thinking
- Knowledge
- Comprehension
- Application
- Analysis
- Synthesis
- Evaluation

Chapter Contents

Chapter Goals

In this chapter on critical reading comprehension, you will learn:

- What constitutes higher levels of thinking.
- How to use different levels of thinking to understand all types of reading material.
- How to create and answer questions based on your reading material in order to prepare for exams.

Chapter Vocabulary

As you read the chapter, take note of these words and phrases, which represent important concepts from this chapter and will be in **boldface** type. Make sure you understand them before the post test at the end of the chapter.

critical reading   **application level**
synthesis level   **knowledge level**
analysis level   **evaluation level**
comprehension level

Pam anxiously awaited the results of her sociology midterm. She watched carefully as the professor called out last names and dropped exams on other students' desks. She tried to predict the grades they had received by the expressions on their faces. If a student looked down at the exam and smiled, that meant at least a B⁺. If a student kept a straight face and slid the exam under a pile of books and papers, that meant a C⁻ or worse.

"Pam Moore?" the instructor called out, looking her way. She took the exam and looked at the grade. She kept a straight face but wanted to cry.

Although Pam had spent ample time studying for her exam, she did not do as well as she expected. She had read all the chapters, knew the definition of every vocabulary word, had marked the key issues in her textbook, and had memorized all the main ideas. What went wrong? Pam did not spend enough time thinking critically about the material. Reading is thinking. Critical reading is thinking about and understanding information on many intellectual levels. Comprehending an author's main idea is only one of them. Your instructors will test your ability to think on a number of different levels throughout the semester, so it is important to know what those levels are.

Levels of Thinking: Bloom's Taxonomy

Benjamin Bloom, an influential person in the field of education during the 1950s, developed a list of six levels of thinking for teachers to use as a curriculum guide and assessment tool. Teachers could target each level when developing their lesson plans, and use them when testing students to ensure they had mastered the material being taught. The list prompted teachers to start exploring different levels of thinking with their students. The idea gained popularity in the educational community and is still regarded as a helpful teaching tool today. Teaching assistants, instructors, and professors use Bloom's taxonomy, as it is called, to develop lesson plans and tests. Asking and answering questions about your reading material, at all levels of thinking, is **critical reading**.

Learning Journal

Based on what you have just read, what do you think the word *taxonomy* means? Write your definition in your journal.

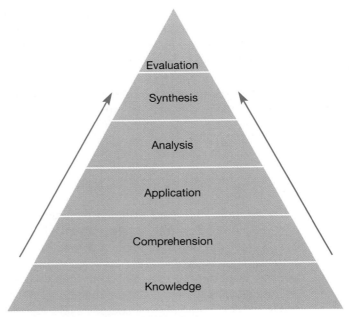

Figure 13.1   Bloom's Taxonomy of Knowledge

I: The Knowledge Level of Thinking

The **knowledge level** of thinking is the most literal one—the one you are operating on when you recall facts or recognize the correct answer from a list in a multiple-choice question. This is the level Pam was working at when she memorized the vocabulary terms for her test. Instructors question their students at the knowledge level when they want to be sure they know the common terms, specific facts, basic concepts, principles, and methods and procedures used in their discipline. Examples of words used in exam questions that require this level of knowledge include the following: *define, describe, label, list, match, reproduce, select,* and *state.*

Example

Read the following excerpt, taken from Roald Dahl's autobiography *Boy: Tales of Childhood,* in which he describes an experience he had at a British boarding school. The questions that follow are written at the knowledge level of thinking. Note that all of the answers to the questions are directly stated in the excerpt.

> **There was a boy in our dormitory during my first term called Tweedie, who one night started snoring soon after he had gone to sleep.**

"Who's that talking?" cried the Matron, bursting in. My own bed was close to the door, and I remember looking up at her from my pillow and seeing her standing there silhouetted against the light from the corridor and thinking how truly frightening she looked. I think it was her enormous bosom that scared me most of all. My eyes were riveted to it, and to me it was like a battering-ram or the bow of an icebreaker or maybe a couple of high-explosive bombs.

"Own up!" she cried. "Who was talking?"

We lay there in silence. Then Tweedie, who was lying fast asleep on his back with his mouth open, gave another snore.

The matron stared at Tweedie. "Snoring is a disgusting habit," she said. "Only the lower classes do it. We shall have to teach him a lesson."

She didn't switch on the light, but she advanced into the room and picked up a cake of soap from the nearest basin. The bare electric bulb in the corridor illuminated the whole dormitory in a pale creamy glow.

None of us dared to sit up in bed, but all eyes were on the Matron now, watching to see what she was going to do next. She always had a pair of scissors hanging by a white tape from her waist, and with this she began shaving thin slivers of soap into the palm of one hand. Then she went over to where the wretched Tweedie lay and very carefully she dropped these little soap-flakes into his open mouth. She had a whole handful of them and I thought she was never going to stop.

What on earth is going to happen? I wondered. Would Tweedie choke? Would he strangle? Might his throat get blocked up completely? Was she going to kill him?

The Matron stepped back a couple of paces and folded her arms across, or rather underneath, her massive chest.

Nothing happened. Tweedie kept right on snoring.

Then suddenly he began to gurgle and white bubbles appeared around his lips. The bubbles grew and grew until in the end his whole face seemed to be smothered in a bubbly foaming white soapy froth. It was a horrific sight. Then all at once, Tweedie gave a great cough and a splutter and he sat up very fast and began clawing at his face with his hands. "Oh!" he stuttered. "Oh! Oh! Oh! Oh no! Wh-wh-what's happening? Wh-wh-what's on my face? Somebody help me!"

The Matron threw him a face flannel and said, "Wipe it off, Tweedie. And don't ever let me hear you snoring again. Hasn't anyone ever taught you not to go to sleep on your back?"

With that she marched out of the dormitory and slammed the door.

Source: Roald Dahl, *Boy: Tales of Childhood* (New York: Puffin Books, 1984), pp. 91–92.

Knowledge Level Questions and Answers

1. What scared the narrator about the Matron?
Her appearance scared him, especially her bosom. (From the

   excerpt: "I think it was her enormous bosom . . . .")

2. What did the Matron want to know when she came into the dormitory room?
She wanted to know who was talking. (From the excerpt:

   "'Who's that talking?' cried the Matron, bursting in.")

3. What did the Matron do when she found out that Tweedie was snoring?
She put soap shavings into his mouth. (From the excerpt: "...she

   dropped these little soap flakes in his mouth.")

Answering questions at the knowledge level of thinking is a first step toward understanding what you read. Being able to recognize and remember facts does not constitute critical reading, but it does provide the necessary foundation of knowledge on which to exercise higher-level thinking.

Exercise 13a

Knowledge Level

Read this excerpt from the business textbook *Meeting the Challenges and Opportunities of the New Corporate Age*, and answer the knowledge level questions that follow it.

Conflict is constructive because it can lead to a win–win solution. There are at least five basic rules of proactive conflict management:

1. Every member of the group has the right to express his or her point of view on the problem.

2. Members may disagree with each other but are not permitted to attack each other personally, e.g., "I disagree with your solution, and I'd like to propose a different one" is okay, but "Your proposal is the work of a fool with one eye and half a brain" is not.

3. Asking questions of each other to further understanding is desirable.

4. Everyone present is a partner in making a decision that affects us all.

5. Every point of view expressed needs to be evaluated against the long-term welfare of the company and particularly the needs of its customers.

Source: G. Gardiner, *21st Century Manager: Meeting the Challenges and Opportunities of the New Corporate Age* (Princeton: Peterson's/Pacesetter Books, 1996), p. 159.

Knowledge Level Questions

Read each question and choose the best answer from the choices given.

1. What example is used to illustrate an inappropriate way of disagreeing with another group member?

   a. I disagree with your solution, and I'd like to propose a different one.

   b. Your proposal is the work of a fool with one eye and half a brain.

   c. I'm not sure the other members would agree.

   d. That proposal won't work due to budget constraints.

2. Which of the following is *not* a rule of proactive conflict management?

   a. Every member of the group has the right to express his or her point of view on the problem.

   b. Everyone present is a partner in making a decision that affects us all.

   c. Employees with the most seniority are best at making a decision that affects us all.

   d. Asking questions of each other to further understanding is desirable.

3. According to the excerpt, why is conflict constructive?

   a. Because every person has the right to disagree, if necessary.

   b. Because every person has the right to be heard.

   c. Because conflict allows people to blow off steam.

   d. Because it can lead to a win–win solution.

II: The Comprehension Level of Thinking

At the **comprehension level** of thinking you are able to paraphrase, draw conclusions from, and make predictions about your reading material. Professors question their students at this level to check whether they understand what facts and principles mean, can interpret charts and graphs, can estimate the future consequences implied by data, and are able to translate verbal language into mathematical formulas and vice versa. Pam was working at this level of thinking when she read the chapters from her sociology text and understood the main ideas discussed in them. Examples of words used in questions at the comprehension level include the following: *convert, defend, explain, infer, summarize, rewrite, distinguish,* and *predict.* You can use these same words, when you are preparing for an exam, to devise questions to test yourself on your basic comprehension of the textbook material.

Example

Read this excerpt, taken from a book titled *Actual Innocence: Five Days to Execution and Other Dispatches from the Wrongly Convicted,* by Jim Dwyer and his coauthors. The questions that follow are written at the comprehension level of thinking. Notice that the answers to these questions cannot be found word-for-word in the text but are instead conclusions *drawn from* the text.

> On the evening of December 19, 1974, a short documentary film was shown on the local NBC newscast in New York. In it, a young woman walks in a hallway. A man lurks in a doorway, wearing a hat, leather jacket, and sneakers. The man bursts from the doorway, grabs the woman's handbag, and runs straight toward the camera, full-faced. The entire incident lasts twelve seconds.
>
> After the film was shown, the show presented a lineup of suspects. The viewers were provided with a phone number and asked to choose the culprit from among those six, or to say that he wasn't in the lineup. "We were swamped with calls," Robert Buckhout, a professor at Brooklyn College who organized the experiment, would write later. They unplugged the phone after receiving 2,145 calls.
>
> The "thief" was seated in lineup position Number 2. He received a grand total of 302 votes from the callers, or 14.1 percent of the 2,145. "The results were the same as if the witnesses were merely guessing, since on the basis of chance (1 out of 7, including the "not in the lineup" choice), we would expect only 14.3 percent identification of any lineup participants, including Number 2," Buckhout wrote in an article with the charming headline NEARLY 2,000 WITNESSES CAN BE WRONG.
>
> **Source:** Jim Dwyer, Peter Neufeld, and Barry Scheck, *Actual Innocence: Five Days to Execution and Other Dispatches from the Wrongly Convicted* (New York: Doubleday, 2000), pp. 43–44.

Comprehension Level Questions and Answers

1. Using the title of the book and the excerpt itself, what do you infer is the main point of this passage?

   The main point is that eyewitness accounts are not very accurate
   and contribute to wrongly convicting innocent people.

2. Predict what the 2,000 callers would say if they were told that their responses were incorrect. What reason do you think they would give for wrongly identifying the thief in the lineup?

   Callers might say that they didn't get a good enough look at the
   man or that some people in the lineup strongly resembled others.

Exercise
13b

Comprehension Level

Read this excerpt from a philosophy textbook, *Friedrick Nietzsche* by H. L. Mencken, and answer the comprehension questions that follow it.

Nietzsche pointed out further that everything which makes for the preservation of the human race is diametrically opposed to the Christian ideal. Thus Christianity becomes the foe of science. The one argues that man should sit still and let God reign; the other that man should battle against the tortures which fate inflicts upon him, and try to overcome them and grow strong. Thus all science is unchristian, because, in the last analysis, the whole purpose and effort of science is to arm man against loss of energy and death, and thus make him self-reliant and unmindful of any duty of propitiating the deity. That this antagonism between Christianity and the search for truth really exists has been shown in a practical way time and again. Since the beginning of the Christian era the church has been the bitter and tireless enemy of all science, and this enmity has been due to the fact that every member of the priest class has realized that the more a man learned the more he came to depend upon his own efforts, and the less he was given to asking help from above. In the ages of faith men prayed to the saints when they were ill. Today they send for a doctor. In the ages of faith battles were begun with supplications, and it was often possible to witness the ridiculous spectacle of both sides praying to the same God. Today every sane person knows that the victory goes to the wisest generals and largest battalions.

Source: H. L. Mencken, *Friedrick Nietzsche* (New Brunswick: Transaction Publishers, 1993), pp. 143–144.

Comprehension Level Questions

1. Explain why, according to Nietzsche, Christianity and science are foes.

_____

_____

2. How does the author distinguish between the sources of power of science and Christianity?

_____

_____

3. Rewrite the following sentence in your own words: "Since the beginning of the Christian era the church has been the bitter and tireless enemy of all science, and this enmity has been due to the fact that every member of the priest class has realized that the more a man learned the more he came to depend upon his own efforts, and the less he was given to asking help from above."

_____

_____

Team Up!

Reread the passage excerpted from *Actual Innocence: Five Days to Execution and Other Dispatches from the Wrongly Convicted* and write three knowledge level questions based on it. Exchange questions with a classmate and answer his or her questions. Discuss your responses to each other's questions and discuss the difference(s) between the knowledge and comprehension levels of thinking.

III: The Application Level of Thinking

The **application level** of thinking requires you to solve problems by selecting and utilizing the appropriate concepts, principles, or theories. For example, if you have learned about the process through which a bill becomes law in your political science class, you could work out the status of a piece of legislation before Congress and what steps still need to occur for it to become a law. Professors ask students questions at this level to see if they are able to solve mathematical problems, demonstrate correct usage of procedures or methods, create charts and graphs, use familiar concepts to understand new information, or apply theories to real-life situations. Examples of words used in questions at the application level include the following: *change, compute, demonstrate, discover, manipulate, modify, prepare, show, solve, apply,* and *use*.

Pam did not use this level of thinking when studying for her test. Many students don't, believing that if they memorize formulas or key concepts they will be adequately prepared. However, instructors want to see you apply what you have learned. Practicing how to do this *before* a test will help you to be more successful on the day you take it.

Example

Read the following excerpt taken from a writing manual called *Writing Down the Bones*. In it, author Natalie Goldberg describes a procedure for creating figurative language, language that creates pictures in your mind, by playing with verbs in sentences. Her goal is to help writers

realize the power of verbs. Notice that here you are being given information you can *apply* in order to achieve the goal of using verbs in fresh,
new ways in your writing.

The Action of a Sentence

Verbs are very important. They are the action and energy of a sentence. Be aware of how you use them. Try this exercise. Fold a sheet
of paper in half the long way. On the left side of the page list ten
nouns. Any ten. Now turn the paper over to the right column. Think
of an occupation, for example, a carpenter, doctor, flight attendant.
List fifteen verbs on the right half of the page that go with that position. Open the page. You have nouns listed in a row down the left side
and verbs listed on the right. Try joining the nouns with the verbs to
see what new combinations you can get, and then finish the sentences, casting verbs in the past tense, if you need to.

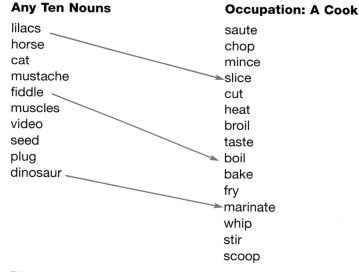

Any Ten Nouns	**Occupation: A Cook**
lilacs	saute
horse	chop
cat	mince
mustache	slice
fiddle	cut
muscles	heat
video	broil
seed	taste
plug	boil
dinosaur	bake
	fry
	marinate
	whip
	stir
	scoop

Dinosaurs marinate in the earth.

The fiddles boiled the air with their music.

The lilacs sliced the sky into purple.

Source: Natalie Goldberg, *Writing Down the Bones: Freeing the Writer within* (Boston:
Shambhala, 1986), pp. 87–88.

Learning Journal

Apply what you have just learned about how to use verbs in fresh, new ways.
Follow the directions in the excerpt and create five sentences.

Application Level

Read the following excerpt from an algebra textbook and solve the questions that follow.

If it is known that 5 times a certain number is 40, a simple process in arithmetic enables us to calculate that the number is 8. In algebraic form the problem could be expressed as follows:

Let n = the unknown number. Then the question can be put in this way: If $5n = 40$, what is the value of N?

The statement $5n = 40$ is called an *equation*. It is a statement of equality, but it also implies that a value of n is required which will make the left-hand side of the equation equal to the right, or as we say, "satisfies the equation." The process of finding the value of n which thus satisfies the equation is called "solving the equation." The solution of the above equation involves no more than the division of the right-hand side by the coefficient of n, and could be stated thus:

$5n = 40$
$n = 40/5$
$n = 8$

The solution of an equation is rarely as simple as this. Equations usually consist of more or less complicated expressions on both sides of the equation. By various operations we aim at reducing the equation to the simple form above. The value of the unknown letter is then easily found.

Example: If 8 times a number is decreased by 5, the result is 123. What is the number?

Let n = the number. Then $8n - 5$ is the expression which states algebraically "8 times the number decreases by 5." But this is equal to 123. Hence we form the equation: $8n - 5 = 123$

Source: *Algebra* (Chicago: NTC Publishing Group, 1991), pp. 60–61.

Application Level Questions

1. If 10 times a number is divided by 5, the result is 120. What is the number?

2. If a number is added to 76, the result is 1,102. What is the number?

3. If 98 times a number is divided by 7, the result is 14. What is the number?

Team Up!

Find a classmate and together define the application level of thinking and explain why it requires a higher level of thought than the knowledge and comprehension levels. Also, discuss what type of visuals might be useful when trying to remember the application level of information.

IV: The Analysis Level of Thinking

At the **analysis level** of thinking, you take a difficult or complex concept, such as democracy, mitosis, or phonics, from your textbook, and break it apart into the smaller ideas or parts it is made up of. Once you break a concept down into its constituent parts, you will have a much clearer understanding of what it means and how the different elements it consists of interact with each other. Mentally reassembling them back into the larger concept, using your own words and examples, further adds to your knowledge. You can then use and apply what you have learned. Consider the following example.

A 19-year-old student on a university swim team comes in second in an important 100-meter race. The concept he wants to analyze is *Why didn't I win?* The parts that make up this concept are the variables that contributed to his performance—what he ate that day, how much he practiced during the past week, his ability to concentrate, his level of nervousness, his sleeping habits, his mental attitude, and the strength of his competitor. After some thought, he realizes that the problem is not his competitor, who is not as strong a swimmer as he is, but his own behavior. Specifically, he has been staying up late and not practicing enough. He decides that from now on he will go to bed earlier, get a full eight hours of sleep each night, and stick to a strict practice schedule. Using this careful analysis of his performance and making the necessary changes to his routine, he now has a good chance of winning in the future.

Professors question students at the analysis level to see if they are able to recognize fallacies in an author's reasoning, distinguish between facts and opinions, or take apart the organizational structure of a work (for example, a painting, a concerto, or a novel) and recognize how the different parts interact together to form the whole. It is unlikely Pam studied at this level of critical thinking given her test results. Examples of words used in questions at the analysis level include the following: *break down, differentiate, discriminate, infer, outline, classify,* and *trace the growth of*.

Example

Read this excerpt from "Abortion and Brain Waves" by Edward Wilson. The questions that follow it are written at the analysis level of thinking.

Notice that the questions (and the modeled answers) break the excerpt down into its constituent parts.

> But new science shows that conception usually does not produce a baby. "The majority of cases in which there is a fertilized egg result in the nonrealization of a person," says Dr. Machelle Siebel, a reproductive endocrinologist at the Boston University School of Medicine. What exists just after conception is called a *zygote*. Research now suggests that only about half of all zygotes implant in the uterine wall and become *embryos*; the others fail to continue dividing and expire. Of those embryos that do trigger pregnancy, only around 65 percent lead to live births, even with the best prenatal care. The rest are lost to natural miscarriage. All told, only about one-third of sperm–egg unions result in babies, even when abortion is not a factor.
>
> This new knowledge bears particularly on such controversies as the availability of "morning after" birth control pills, which some pharmacy chains will not stock. "Morning after" pills prevent a zygote from implanting in the uterine wall. If half of all fertilized eggs naturally do not implant in the uterine wall, it is hard to see why a woman should not be allowed to produce the same effect using artificial means.
>
> More generally, the evidence that two-thirds of conceptions fail regardless of abortion provides a powerful new argument in favor of choice in the early trimesters. Perhaps it is possible that God ordains, for reasons we cannot know, that vast numbers of souls be created at conception and then naturally denied the chance to become babies. But science's new understanding of the tenuous link between conception and birth makes a strong case that what happens early in pregnancy is not yet life in the constitutional sense.
>
> **Source:** Gregg Easterbrook, "Abortion and Brain Waves" from *The Best American Science and Nature Writing,* ed. Edward Wilson (New York: Houghton Mifflin, 2001), p. 24.

Analysis Level Questions

1. What is the "powerful new argument" that the writer offers?
   If two-thirds of conceptions fail naturally, then women should be allowed to choose to end their pregnancies in the early trimesters, if they choose.

2. What type of argument structure does the writer use? Inductive or deductive?
   Inductive. The writer begins with a specific observation, continues with more observations, and finishes with a general claim or conclusion.

3. The first part of the writer's argument (the first observation) is presented in the first paragraph. What is it?
   Most sperm and egg unions don't result in a baby.

4. The second part of the writer's argument (the second observation) is presented in the second paragraph. What is it?

Because many sperm and egg unions fail naturally, a woman

should be able to simulate this situation artificially.

Note that the writer of the excerpt separated his argument into three paragraphs, the first two containing observations and the last the conclusion. Analysis of the excerpt helps you to see the parts of the argument more clearly, allowing you to decide whether you agree with it.

Learning Journal

In your own words, explain what the analysis level of thinking is. What makes it more challenging than the application level? Would you use the same types of visuals to help you remember analysis information? Explain your answer.

Exercise 13d

Analysis Level

Read this passage from *See, I Told You So* by Rush Limbaugh, and analyze the point the author is making. Then answer the questions that follow it.

We're reluctant as a society now to teach that certain things are wrong. We think the highest ideal is simply to teach people how to love one another and get along. That may have a nice ring to it, but what that means in practice is teaching kids about anal sex and using a textbook called *Heather Has Two Mommies*. Today, in our increasingly secular world, loving one another doesn't just mean "loving." It means being forced to accept as normal those behaviors and lifestyles that are absolutely abnormal. It's not enough to live and let live. You must chant their mantra as well; you must repent, renounce your own values, and pronounce those of the radical left as superior and adopt them. However, some things are strictly forbidden in this brave intellectual world. For instance, we can't teach the Ten Commandments. In fact, we can't even post them in the classroom. Why? Because their origin is religious, and that (God forbid!) might offend.

Source: Rush Limbaugh, *See, I Told You So* (New York: Pocket Books, 1993), p. 84.

Analysis Level Questions

1. What is the author's main point or conclusion in this passage?

2.   What examples does the author provide to support his conclusion?

_____

_____

3.   Based on your reading of the passage, do you detect any biases on the part of the author? Write down words or phrases from the reading passage that support your answer.

_____

_____

4.   Has the author committed any fallacies? Which one(s)?

_____

_____

Learning Journal

In your journal, respond to the following: As a society, are we reluctant to teach right from wrong? Are there specific actions or behaviors that schools should teach students are wrong?

V: The Synthesis Level of Thinking

The **synthesis level** of thinking requires you to arrive at an understanding of the "bigger picture" by combining the individual elements that contribute to it. For example, suppose you want to make a quilt for your bed that somehow reflects your life. You decide to use pieces of fabric that have special significance to you. You choose a piece of an old receiving blanket your mother used when you were a baby, a dress you wore for an elementary school picture, parts of a suede glove that belonged to an old boyfriend, a sheet that covered the armchair in your dorm room, and a faded corduroy shirt worn by your father, who died last year. You take all these pieces and arrange them to form one big rectangle, and border them with pieces of blue fabric, your favorite color. Although your quilt is made up of a combination of different fabrics, it is itself one bigger item. By undertaking this project, you have synthesized a number of important memories into one picture of your life.

Being able to synthesize information is important in college because professors will ask you to think about discrete items of information in order to arrive at a deeper, more comprehensive understanding of the larger topics they relate to. For example, you may be asked in a political science class to explain how Hitler gained power in pre–World War II Germany. By synthesizing information about the political situation, the economic state of the country, and the culture of the German people at the time, you could answer the larger question of how the combination of these factors set the stage for Hitler's rise to power. Pam did not think about the material in her textbook in this way and so had difficulty adequately answering the synthesis questions on her exam.

Professors question their students at the synthesis level of thinking to see if they are able to use different concepts and principles to arrive at a new understanding of complex issues; write a well-organized theme; present a well-organized speech; write a creative story or poem; create a scheme for classifying objects, events, or ideas; or propose a plan for research. Examples of words used in questions at the synthesis level include the following: *categorize, write, relate, reconstruct, design, create, compose,* and *tell.*

Example

Read the following excerpt from *Dave Barry Hits below the Beltway*. Even though the excerpt, the question, and the modeled answer are intended to be humorous, they all demonstrate the skill necessary to synthesize different items of information to create an explanation of a larger topic, in this case, government and how it works.

Why do we have government?

This is a hard question, and, like so many hard questions, the best way to answer it is to consider ants. When you see an ant on your kitchen floor, it appears to be an insignificant insect scurrying around randomly, so you stomp it into a little smear without a second thought.

But if, instead of stomping on the ant, you were to get down on your hands and knees and follow it, something fascinating would happen: Your head would bonk into the wall, because the ant has scurried into a hole. So I'll just tell you where the ant goes: It goes to a nest containing an ant colony that is every bit as complex and organized as a human society. In fact, it is more organized, because there are no teenagers.

Yes, even ants—tiny creatures with a primitive brain no larger than that of a psychic-hotline caller—have a government. The ant government operates on what political scientists call the "Smell System," whereby your role in society is based on what chemicals you secrete. At the top of the hierarchy is the queen, who is elected unanimously by the other ants after a very brief political campaign that consists of hatching.

"Hey!" the other ants say. "This smells like the queen!"

Most of the other ants smell like workers, so they spend their lives scurrying around looking for food and exchanging important chemical information with the other ants they bump into ("I'm an ant!" "Hey, me too!"). Also, there are a few winged ants, whose job is to scare you by flying around your house pretending to be termites. (This is the only form of entertainment that ants have.)

Ants are not the only animals that have government. Similar organizational structures can be found throughout nature: Monkeys form troops, birds form flocks, fish form schools, worms form bunches of worms, intestinal parasites form law firms, etc. In other words: Governments are natural. All animals form them, including humans. In a way, we are like the ants scurrying across our kitchen floor: We give our Cheez-It fragments (tax money) to the colony (government), and in return we enjoy the many benefits provided by the colony (the Federal Avocado Safety Administration).

Of course human beings are far more advanced than animals; we do not elect the president of the United States based on how he smells. As cerebral beings, we are much more interested in other qualities in our president, such as height. As a result, we here in the United States have developed a sophisticated, highly complex government structure involving three major branches. (Among other animal species, only woodpeckers have more.)

Source: Dave Barry, *Dave Barry Hits below the Beltway* (New York: Random House, 2001), pp. 5–6.

Synthesis Level Question

Design a fictitious government structure for an animal group not mentioned in the excerpt. Using the information provided by Dave Barry as a guide, include details on your criteria for selecting a leader, the role of followers, the types of taxes you would impose, and the various branches of government.

The government structure in a group of weasels consists of one

leader. This leader is chosen on the basis of bravery. The weasel who

sneaks out in the night and grabs the biggest chicken, without first

becoming chicken and running home, gets the job. The rest of the

weasels have the responsibility of standing around with their paws

in their pockets looking big-eyed and pathetic, waiting for a handout

from the leader. The chances of getting a handout are increased if

a weasel can appeal to the leader's weakness for bribes. Information

on the whereabouts of predators and comfortable sleeping areas

are often exchanged for food. There is only one branch of government
in a weasel group— the executive. Many times, the branch is
inoperative because few weasels ever muster the nerve to snare a
chicken in the night. It's a known fact that weasels are afraid of
the dark.

Unlike analysis questions, which ask you to break ideas down into
smaller units, synthesis questions ask you to bring ideas together to create a larger picture. In this example, the larger idea of *government* was
pieced together using people, ants, and even weasels to explain what government is and how it works.

Exercise 13e

Synthesis Level

Read this excerpt from the textbook *Mother Tongue* by J. Davis, and complete the exercise that follows it.

Linguists are also like modern-day biologists. Biologists work with living animals and plants, studying their shape, their behavior, and their life cycles. From
the data they compile, biologists begin to uncover the rules that govern the lives
and deaths of living creatures. Some species are endangered, at risk of becoming extinct and lost forever from the face of the earth. Many biologists struggle to learn as much as possible about these species before they are gone.
(Others, including biologists, work to prevent extinction from happening, a wor-
thy goal.) The more we learn about living beings—both healthy species and
those in danger of extinction—the more we can understand the underlying rules
that guide all life on earth. In the same way, linguists today focus on living languages. Some are huge and healthy: English, French, Chinese, Russian. Others are in danger of extinction: Amuesha in Peru, with about four thousand
speakers; Nanai in China, with perhaps seven thousand speakers; Tlingit in
Alaska and Canada, with only two thousand or so.

Source: J. Davis, *Mother Tongue* (New York: Carol Publishing Group, 1994), p. 92.

Synthesis Level Question

1. Categorize linguists and biologists based on their similarities.
Linguists:

Biologists: _____

_____

Team Up!

Find one classmate and together define the synthesis level of thinking using a specific topic. Decide what type of visual you would use to help you remember the synthesis level of thinking and explain why you would use it.

Exercise 13f

Synthesis Level Practice

Write a paragraph on a separate sheet of paper to show the connection between the first two chapters of this textbook.

VI: The Evaluation Level of Thinking

The **evaluation level** of thinking involves making a value judgment based on specific criteria rather than on one's own opinions. The process of asking questions, evaluating answers, and developing or acknowledging criteria to use in evaluating information involves thinking at a very high level. Consider the O. J. Simpson trial, for example. Individual jurors could not judge the defendant based on their own personal experiences with black or white people, domestic abuse, or football. They had to follow specific criteria outlined in the law and interpret that law based on the judge's directions.

Similarly, different academic disciplines have rules or guidelines for evaluating whether information is valid and therefore acceptable. Here are some general questions you can ask yourself as you begin to evaluate the quality of information and arguments in your textbooks:

- Are the author's arguments based on research?
- Does the author argue inductively or deductively? What reasons does the author use to support what he or she says? Do the reasons seem logical and relevant?
- Does the author appear to be biased? Does he or she use emotive language?
- Do I agree with what the author is saying? Why or why not? What do I base my opinion on?

Students typically fail to prepare at this level before an exam because the questions they have to ask are difficult and the "right" answers are not always obvious. But it is important to ask evaluation questions because they challenge you to think critically about what you read and not passively accept what you are being told. They also require you to analyze an author's arguments using the specific criteria relevant to his or her discipline, and to develop your own arguments using those same criteria.

There were probably evaluation level questions on Pam's sociology exam. Had she critically evaluated the material in her textbook prior to taking the exam, she may have found the questions easier to answer. One strategy she could have used to prepare herself would have been to share her evaluation questions and answers with members of her study group so they could challenge her arguments and vice versa. In the process, members of the group would uncover criteria for judging their arguments based either on discipline-specific theory or on a format chosen by the group.

Professors question students at the evaluation level to see if they can assess the validity of a conclusion; judge the artistic merit of a play, poem, or sculpture using widely accepted standards; or evaluate the logic of written or spoken material. Examples of words used in questions at the evaluation level include *justify, support, appraise, judge,* and *conclude.*

Example

Read this excerpt from *Human Development* by Dianne Papalia and the four general evaluation questions that follow it. Read Pam's answers to each question and think about how you would have responded to them.

Living with Gay or Lesbian Parents

The number of children of gay and lesbian parents is unknown; conservative estimates range from 6 to 14 million (C. J. Patterson, 1992; C. J. Patterson & Redding, 1996). There are an estimated 1 to 5 million lesbian mothers and 1 to 3 million gay fathers (Gottman, 1990). These numbers are probably low because many gay and lesbian parents do not openly acknowledge their sexual orientation. Some are raising children born of previous heterosexual relationships. Others conceive by artificial means..., become foster parents, or adopt children (C. J. Patterson, 1997).

Several studies have focused on the personal development of children of gays and lesbians, including sense of self, moral judgment, and intelligence, and on their social relationships. Although research is still sparse and studies vary in adequacy of methodology, none has indicated psychological concerns (C. J. Patterson, 1992, 1995a, 1995b, 1997). Contrary to popular belief, openly gay or lesbian parents usually have positive relationships with their children (P. H.

Turner et al., 1985) and the children are no more likely than children raised by heterosexual parents to have social or psychological problems (Chan, Raboy, & Patterson, 1998; E. J. Patterson, 1992, 1995a, 1997). Abuse by gay or lesbian parents is rare (R. L. Barrett & Robinson, 1990; Cramer, 1986).

Source: Diane Papalia et al., *Human Development* (New York: McGraw-Hill, 2001), p. 383.

Evaluation Level Questions

1. Are the author's arguments based on research?
   Yes. Almost every sentence is followed with a reference to an earlier study.

2. Does the author argue inductively or deductively? What reasons does the author use to support what she says?
   It appears to be an inductive argument. The author cites lots of research and synthesizes it into a picture of gay parenting that seems pretty positive.

3. Does the author seem biased? Does she use emotive language?
   I didn't detect bias, but every writer has it. Maybe the bias is not in what is said in the textbook but in what is not said. It might help to look at the research the author cites. How large are the samples in the studies? If the number of gay and lesbian parents is unknown, how does the researcher know he or she has a big enough sample? If the research results are unclear, how can a study be judged as good? And what does "rare" mean when the author mentions abuse by gay parents?

4. Do I agree personally with what the author is saying? Why or why not? What do I base my opinion on?
   I agree because the author cites lots of research to support almost everything she says. The author may only be citing studies that support a positive view of gay parenting and omitting those that don't, but I don't know of any research that would challenge the textbook information.

Pam mentions the amount of research referred to in the excerpt and uses it as a criterion for judging the validity of the author's argument. This is appropriate considering that the excerpt came from a psychology text-book and citing research in arguments is expected within that field. She also mentions her concern about accepting the research because the number of gay parents in the studies quoted is unknown. If the number is unknown, how can she determine if the sample size was representative? This is a good question. In psychology, as in many other fields, sample size should be both proportional in number and representative (having similar characteristics) of the larger group being studied. In answering Question #3, Pam asks herself more questions. She does not answer them all, but her questioning helps her resist the habit of passively accepting what she reads and may have helped her answer Question #4 more critically. Her point that the author might have omitted research that conflicted with her conclusion is excellent.

Exercise
13g

Evaluation Level

Read this excerpt from *American Democracy* by T. Patterson:

America's poor include individuals of all ages, races, religions, and regions, but poverty is substantially more prevalent among some groups. Children are one of the largest groups of poor Americans. They constitute nearly 40 percent of the total, and one in every five children lives in poverty. Most poor children live in single-parent families, usually with the mother....a high proportion of Americans residing in families headed by divorced, separated, or unmarried women live below the poverty line. These families are at a disadvantage because most women earn less than men for comparable work, especially in nonprofessional fields. Women without higher education or a special skill often cannot find a job that pays enough to justify the child care expenses they incur due to their work. In recent years, single-parent, female-headed families have been three times as likely as single-parent, male-headed families and seven times as likely as two-income families to fall below the poverty line. Poverty in America has increasingly become a woman's problem, a situation referred to as "the feminization of poverty."

Source: T. Patterson, *The American Democracy* (New York: McGraw-Hill, 1999), p. 534.

Evaluation Level Questions

1. Is the main argument deductive or inductive? How do you know?

_____

_____

_____

2. Do you agree that poverty is becoming a woman's problem? Why or why not? What sentences from the excerpt helped you make your decision?

_____

_____

_____

_____

_____

_____

_____

Team Up!

With one other student, define the evaluation level of thinking. Reread the excerpt from the last exercise and develop one question at each of the following levels of thinking: knowledge, comprehension, application, analysis, and synthesis.

If Pam had questioned herself on the material in her sociology text using the six levels of thinking listed in Bloom's taxonomy, she would probably have done better on her exam. She read the chapters and memorized the new vocabulary, but that is only at the knowledge or factual level of thinking. She remembered all the main ideas from the chapters, but that required her to think only at the second level of thinking, the comprehension level. In order to succeed on future exams, she should also create and answer questions using the four more difficult levels of thinking—application, analysis, synthesis, and evaluation.

Practice with Reading Passages

Answer all questions on a separate sheet of paper.

Reading Practice
1

"The Chemistry of Love"
BY SANJAY GUPTA

PREPARE TO READ

1. Based on the title and headings, what do you expect the passage to be about?

2. What do you already know about the topic?

3. Here are some vocabulary words that might be unfamiliar to you. Look them up, if necessary, and refer to the definition as you encounter these vocabulary words in the reading.

a. Pheromones

b. Synchronized

c. Provocative

d. Aphrodisiacs

e. Colleagues

f. Camaraderie

g. Purported

4. Create a question, using the title or topic of the reading selection, and look for the answer to it as you read the following essay.

"The Chemistry of Love"

Do pheromones and smelly T-shirts really have the power to trigger sexual attraction? Here's a primer.

You can't make someone love you, even on Valentine's Day, no matter what Hallmark, Godiva, and FTD may say. But how much do we really know about how love works? What is it that attracts a particular man to a particular woman and (with any luck) vice versa? To see what light science could shed on the subject, I called Professor Martha McClintock at the University of Chicago. McClintock is an expert on odor and behavior who published a famous study in the early 1970s that showed that the menstrual cycles of college women living in dorms became synchronized through exposure to one another's pheromones, those faint chemical signals released from the skin that control the mating rituals of much of the animal kingdom. McClintock has a new study, published in the February issue of *Nature Genetics*, that makes an even more provocative link between sex and odor—specifically, the odor of a T-shirt worn by a man on two consecutive days.

The experiment was simple. The T-shirts were carefully prepared (no cologne, no cigarettes, no sex) and then placed in boxes where they could be smelled but not seen. Forty-nine unmarried women were asked to sniff the boxes and choose which box they would prefer "if they had to smell it all the time."

The results would have made Sigmund Freud proud. The women were attracted to the smell of a man who was genetically similar—but not too similar—to their dads. McClintock thinks there's an evolutionary explanation. "Mating with someone too similar might lead to inbreeding," she says.

Mating with someone too different "leads to the loss of desirable gene combinations."

McClintock isn't suggesting you can attract a mate by smell alone, but that hasn't discouraged companies like Erox from bottling pheromones and stopping just short of calling them aphrodisiacs. Marketing websites feature links to scientific papers on the power of pheromones. I spoke to Dr. David Berliner, CEO of Pherin Pharmaceuticals, who did some of the initial research. While working at the University of Utah with natural compounds produced by human skin, he noticed a surprising change in the behavior of his male and female colleagues. "They developed an increased level of camaraderie that was hard to explain," he says. There were smiles, eye contact, and increased approachability until the skin extracts were removed, at which point the group reverted to normal behavior.

But even Berliner balks at categorizing pheromones as aphrodisiacs. "I've been looking for an aphrodisiac for 11 years, and I'm convinced that there is no such thing," he says. The Food and Drug Administration agrees. It surveyed purported love potions—from oysters to rhino horn—and determined that none of them work. This Valentine's Day, I think I'll stick with flowers, a card, and some chocolate.

Dr. Gupta is a neurosurgeon and CNN medical correspondent.

Source: *Time,* February 18, 2002; with reporting by Jonathan D. Lynch/Atlanta.

CHECK YOUR UNDERSTANDING

OBJECTIVE QUESTIONS

Read each of the following multiple-choice questions and select the best possible answer from the four choices given.

1. What was the famous study in the early 1970s that Professor Martha McClintock published?

    a. One that showed that the menstrual cycles of college women living in dorms became synchronized through exposure to one another's pheromones.

    b. One that showed that the menstrual cycles of college women living in dorms lasted longer when the women were exposed to one another's pheromones.

    c. One that showed that college women want to find mates at different times.

    d. One that showed that the menstrual cycles of college women living in dorms stopped when they were exposed to one another's pheromones.

2. What new experiment did Professor McClintock conduct?

   a. She conducted a study that shows a link between wearing T-shirts and cigarette smoking.

   b. She conducted a study on sex and married adults.

   c. She conducted a study that shows a link between sexual attraction and odor.

   d. She conducted a study that shows a link between alcohol and chocolate consumption.

3. What were the results from the T-shirt study?

   a. Men who didn't bathe for two days had fewer dates.

   b. Women were attracted to the smell of a man who was genetically like their dads.

   c. Women were attracted to the smell of a man who was genetically similar to, but not too similar to, their dads.

   d. Women did not cooperate in the experiment because of the smell.

4. What happened during another research project at the University of Utah with men and women colleagues?

   a. The colleagues behaved exactly as they had before the experiment was conducted.

   b. The colleagues developed an increased level of camaraderie that was hard to explain.

   c. The colleagues developed a decreased level of camaraderie that was hard to explain.

   d. The colleagues developed adversarial relationships.

5. According to the article, is there such a thing as an aphrodisiac?

   a. The Food and Drug Administration says there is.

   b. The Food and Drug Administration say no, and so does Dr. David Berliner, of the University of Utah experiment.

   c. Yes, oysters and rhino horns are.

   d. Yes, chocolate and flowers are.

SHORT-ANSWER QUESTIONS

6. Did Dr. Professor Martha McClintock believe that she had discovered an aphrodisiac?

7. At what level of thinking are questions 1 – 6 targeted?

8. What is the main idea or main argument of this reading?

9. Is the main argument inductive or deductive? List the reasons for your answer.

10. What else do you think attracts a mate other than chemistry (smell)? Question #8 is asked at what level of thinking?

Reading Practice 2

"Call Me Crazy, but I Have to Be Myself"

I want to be part of the 'normal' world, but I also need to be open about being bipolar.

BY MARY SEYMOUR

PREPARE TO READ

1. Read the title of the excerpt following these questions.

2. Based on the title, what do you expect the reading to be about? What do you think the topic is?

3. What do you already know about the topic?

4. Here are some words that might be unfamiliar to you. Look them up, if necessary, and refer to the definitions as you encounter these vocabulary words in the reading.

   a. Calibration

   b. Vigilance

   c. Schisms

5. Create a question to ask yourself, using the title or topic of the reading.

Nearly every day, without thinking, I say things like "So-and-so is driving me crazy" or "That's nuts!" Sometimes I catch myself and realize that I'm not being sensitive toward people with mental illness. Then I remember I'm one of the mentally ill. If I can't throw those words around, who can?

Being a functional member of society and having a mental disorder is an intricate balancing act. Every morning I send my son to junior high school, put on professional garb, and drive off to my job as alumni magazine editor at a prep school, where I've worked for six years. Only a few people at work know I'm manic-depressive, or bipolar, as it's sometimes called.

Sometimes I'm not sure myself what I am. I blend in easily with "normal" people. You'd never know that seven years ago, fueled by the stress of a failing marriage and fanned by the genetic inheritance of a manic-depressive grandfather, I had a psychotic break. To look at me, you'd never guess I once ran naked through my yard or shuffled down the hallways of a psychiatric ward. To hear me, you'd never guess God channeled messages to me through my computer. After my breakdown at 36, I was diagnosed as bipolar, a condition marked by moods that swing between elation and despair.

It took a second, less severe psychotic episode in 1997, followed by a period of deep depression, to convince me I truly was bipolar. Admitting I had a disorder that I'd have to manage for life was the hardest thing I've ever done. Since then, a combination of therapy, visits to a psychiatrist, medication, and inner calibration have helped me find an even keel. Now I manage my moods with the vigilance of a mother hen, nudging them back to center whenever they wander too far. Eating wisely, sleeping well, and exercising regularly keep me balanced from day to day. Ironically, my disorder has taught me to be healthier and happier than I was before.

Most of the time, I feel lucky to blend in with the crowd. Things that most people grumble about—paying bills, maintaining a car, working 9 to 5—strike me as incredible privileges. I never forget gazing through the barred windows of the psychiatric ward into the parking lot, watching people come and go effortlessly, wondering if I'd ever be like them again. There's nothing like a stint in a locked ward to make one grateful for the freedoms and burdens of full citizenship.

Yet sometimes I feel like an imposter. Sometimes I wish I could sit at the lunch table and talk about lithium and Celexa instead of *Will & Grace*. While everyone talks about her fitness routine, I want to brag about how it took five orderlies to hold me down and shoot me full of sedatives when I was admitted to the hospital, and how for a brief moment I knew the answers to every infinite mystery of the blazingly bright universe. I yearn for people to know me—the real me—in all my complexity, but I'm afraid it would scare the bejesus out of them.

Every now and then, I feel like I'm truly being myself. Like the time the school chaplain, in whom I'd confided my past, asked me to help counsel a severely bipolar student. This young woman had tried to commit suicide, had been hospitalized many times, and sometimes locked herself in her dorm room to keep the "voices" from overwhelming her. I walked and talked with her, sharing stories about medication and psychosis. I hoped to show by example that manic-depression did not necessarily mean a diminished life. At commencement, I watched her proudly accept her diploma; despite ongoing struggles with her illness, she's continuing her education.

I'm able to be fully myself with my closest friends, all of whom have similar schisms between private and public selves. We didn't set out to befriend each other—we just all speak the same language, of hardship and spiritual discovery and psychological awareness.

What I yearn for most is to integrate both sides of myself. I want to be part of the normal world but I also want to own my identity as bipolar. I want people to know what I've been through so I can help those traveling a similar path. Fear has kept me from telling my story: fear of being stigmatized, of making people uncomfortable, or being reduced to a label. But hiding the truth has become more uncomfortable than letting it out. It's time for me to own up to who I am, complicated psychiatric history and all. Call me crazy, but I think it's the right thing to do.

Source: Mary Seymour, "Call Me Crazy, But I have to Be Myself," *Newsweek*, July 29, 2002.

CHECK YOUR UNDERSTANDING

OBJECTIVE QUESTIONS

Read the following multiple-choice questions and select the best possible answer from the choices given.

1. What does the term "bipolar" mean?

   a. Dementia.

   b. A condition marked by moods that swing between elation and despair.

   c. A condition marked by depression and severe fatigue.

   d. Schizophrenia.

2. Why does the author say she feels like an imposter?

   a. She would like to share her bipolar experience but doesn't want to scare people.

   b. She would like to share her bipolar experience but doesn't want people to discriminate against her.

   c. She would like to share her bipolar experience, but her close friends advised against it.

   d. She would like to share her bipolar experience, but she doesn't want to embarrass her parents.

3. What is the main idea of the essay?

   a. She wants people to feel sorry for those with bipolar disorder.

   b. She wants to stop her bipolar condition but she can't.

   c. She feels she can really help students when they come to see her because she has bipolar disorder.

   d. The author feels the need to be honest with people about her condition.

4. What organizational pattern did the author use?

    a. Analysis.

    b. Sequence.

    c. Cause and effect.

    d. Definition.

5. What does the author yearn for most of all?

    a. To blend in with the crowd.

    b. To be herself with her closest friends.

    c. To manage life better.

    d. To integrate both sides of herself.

SHORT-ANSWER QUESTIONS

6. If you were bipolar, how could you integrate both sides of yourself into society? Would you tell people of your condition?

7. What do you think is the greatest challenge for people with mental illness? Why?

8. Do you think the author is wise to write this article in a national magazine? What could be some consequences of her honesty?

9. What are some of the reasons why the author has kept her psychiatric history quiet all this time?

10. How does reading the title and the heading of this essay, before reading the entire essay, help you discover the essay's main idea?

Chapter Summary

Critical reading comprehension involves challenging yourself to understand what you read in your textbooks at different levels of complexity. Bloom's taxonomy lists six levels of critical thinking —knowledge, comprehension, application, analysis, synthesis, and evaluation—that you can use to deepen your understanding of textbook material. By creating and answering questions at each of these levels, you will be better able to predict the kinds of questions your instructor will ask on an exam and better prepared to answer them.

Post Test

Answer all questions on a separate sheet of paper.

Part I

OBJECTIVE QUESTIONS

1. Match the words in Column 1 to their definitions in Column 2:

Column 1		Column 2
1. Critical reading	a.	Ability to create a bigger picture after combining individual elements.
2. Knowledge level	b.	Ability to make a judgment based on specific criteria.
3. Comprehension level	c.	Literal level of thinking.
4. Application level	d.	Thinking and understanding on many levels.
5. Analysis level	e.	Ability to break an idea down into parts.
6. Synthesis level	f.	Ability to apply what you have learned.
7. Evaluation level	g.	Ability to paraphrase, make inferences, draw conclusions, or make predictions.

2. Which of the following is an example of critical reading on multiple levels?

   a. Developing mnemonics to recall important dates from a book on World War II.

   b. Understanding the main ideas of a large biology chapter.

   c. Understanding the concept of area in geometry, working out the problems at the end of the chapter, and figuring out the areas of shapes outside the Student Union.

   d. Remembering physics formulas, remembering trigonometry formulas, and recalling the stages of human development in your psychology book.

SHORT-ANSWER QUESTIONS

3. Read the following scenarios, determine what level(s) of thinking is (are) involved and explain your answers.

   a. Toni was assigned a psychology chapter to read. She was asked to

   i. Explain, in her own words, the definitions of selected words.

    ii. Identify the chapter's main idea.

    iii. Construct a chart to visually represent the bell curve theory.

  b. Julia reads several books on early American history. After thoroughly reviewing all the available literature, she writes a report for her History 103 course.

  c. Mark is currently taking Biology 342. During the first few weeks of class he is told to learn the name and location of every bone in a human skeleton because he will need to identify all of them on the first exam.

  d. In Economics 101 Crystal is assigned to read Chapter 5, which contains several graphs. At the end of the chapter she is asked two questions: What do the graphs demonstrate? Based on current trends in economics, what do you think will happen?

  e. In the morning section of an English class, students are given essays written by students in the afternoon section. They are asked to select the best essay, using criteria discussed during the semester, for placement in the student newspaper.

4. Answer the following questions about this book, and think about why the level of the question makes some easier to answer than others. The level of difficulty is listed for each question or set of questions.

  a. *Knowledge:* List the goals of this chapter.

  b. *Comprehension:* What is the main idea of this chapter?

  c. *Application:* Demonstrate your understanding of concentration by explaining how to create an effective study environment in your home.

  d. *Analysis:* Differentiate between the knowledge level and the comprehension level of Bloom's taxonomy.

  e. *Synthesis:* Write an explanation of why it is important to know textbook reading skills in college.

  f. *Evaluation:* Jerome studies five hours per day, the week before a major exam, so that he will not have to study much throughout the semester. Is this an effective study strategy? Why or why not?

5. Which questions in Post test question #4 were the easiest to answer?

6. Which questions in Post test question #4 made you think and apply yourself the most?

7. How do you think your understanding of Bloom's taxonomy could help you in all your college reading assignments, not just textbooks?

8. What levels of learning are Questions, #5, #6, and #7 examples of?

Part II

"Fighting the Failure Syndrome"
BY SUSAN TIFFT, WITH BRUCE HENDERSON AND JULIE JOHNSON

1.   Based on the title, what do you expect the reading to be about?

2.   What do you think the topic is?

3.   What do you already know about the topic?

4.   Create a question to ask yourself, using the title of the essay.

5.   Study-read the essay and answer the questions that follow it.

Fighting the Failure Syndrome
—SUSAN TIFFT, WITH BRUCE HENDERSON AND JULIE JOHNSON

Young black men in the United States today are more likely to die violent deaths than were soldiers who fought in World War II. Many argue that the root of this troubling statistic is a breakdown of the support services that should help these young men. In this recent article from a popular magazine, we learn of a controversial plan to change the way education deals with young African-American males before it is too late.

The signs of crises are everywhere. Nearly 1 in 4 black men, ages 20 to 29, is in jail, on probation, or on parole. Black men are less likely to attend college than black females or whites of either gender, and when they do go, they often drop out. Homicide, including fatalities resulting from clashes with police, is the leading cause of death among black males, ages 15 through 34. Says Secretary of Health and Human Services Louis Sullivan: "When you look at a long list of social pathologies, you find black men No. 1."

To reverse this downward spiral, a vocal minority of black educators are pushing a radical idea: putting elementary-school-age black boys in separate classrooms, without girls or whites, under the tutelage of black male teachers. Critics of the proposal say segregating classrooms by race and gender flies in the face of more than 25 years of civil rights gains. But supporters argue that such concerns are less important than the urgent need to rescue African-American males from a future of despair and self-destruction. "The boys need more attention," says Spencer Holland, a Washington educational psychologist and champion of the black-male classroom concept. "The girls are not killing each other."

Advocates of this approach believe low expectations and low self-esteem are largely responsible for the poor academic performance of African-American boys. A recent study of the New Orleans public schools, for example, showed that black males accounted for 80% of the expulsions, 65% of the suspensions, and 58% of the nonpromotions, even though they made up just 43% of the students. "Black boys are viewed by their teachers as hyperactive and aggressive," says Jewelle Taylor Gibbs, a clinical psychologist at the University of California, Berkeley. "Very early on, they get labeled."

The absence of positive male role models may also cripple black boys' development. Nationally, 55.3% of black families with children under 18 are maintained by the mother, many of them living in inner cities. Moreover, most elementary school teachers are female, leading black boys to view academic success as "feminine."

Bill Cosby, Jesse Jackson, and other black celebrities are too remote to offer realistic models of responsible manhood. The adult males whom many black boys try to emulate come from their own neighborhoods, and in tough urban areas, these "models" are all too often involved in drugs and crime. One lesson boys learn from such men is that doing well in school is for sissies or, worse yet, for blacks who are trying to "act white."

Three years ago, in an attempt to overcome these problems, a school in Florida's Dade County opened two classrooms for black boys with no fathers at home, one in kindergarten and one in first grade. The results were encouraging. Daily attendance rates increased 6%, test scores jumped 6% to 9%, and there was a noticeable decrease in hostility. But after only a year, the U.S. Education Department brought an abrupt halt to the experiment because it violated civil rights laws.

Since then, the closest thing to a black-males-only class is an effort in Washington run by a group called Concerned Black Men. Launched two years ago at Stanton Elementary School, in the city's drug-infested southeast section, the program brings some three dozen black male lawyers, architects, and other professionals into second-grade classrooms each week as teachers and mentors.

Although the classes include both genders, the main goal is to lift the sights and spirits of black boys, most of whom live only with their mothers or grandmothers. "The whole concept is to get the kids to look at themselves," says Albert Pearsall III, a computer security programs manager at the U.S. Department of Justice who teaches black history, along with a traditional second grade curriculum. "If I can work effectively in a professional career, why can't these kids?"

Some critics of the all-black, all-male classroom idea are concerned that separating students by sex and race could intensify black boy's feelings of anger and inferiority. Others argue that the notion's underlying assumptions do not hold up. If poor, female-headed families are bad for black boys, they say, then they must be equally disastrous for black girls and whites of both sexes.

Detractors also contend that there is no clear link between self-esteem and academic performance and that a variety of people—not just black men—can effectively teach African-American boys. "It's helpful to have role models from one's own group," says child psychiatrist James Comer, director of the Child Study Center at Yale. "But there's probably no need to have role models exclusively from that group."

Supporters counter that black males are more frequently tracked into special education classes than black girls or their white peers and would be no worse off segregated for normal instruction. "Black boys are already in classes by themselves," points out Jawanza Kunjufu, author of *Countering the Conspiracy to Destroy Black Boys.*

Such passionate debate makes it unlikely that primary grade classrooms for black boys will become the norm anytime soon. Still, unless something else is done to make single-parent black homes more supportive of these children, or to help reduce their soaring dropout and suspension rates, the idea could attract more disciples—ironically hastening the day when "separate but equal" may actually help black youths rather than hurt them.

Source: Reprinted with permission, copyright © 1996. Time Life Syndication.

OBJECTIVE QUESTIONS

Read each of the following multiple-choice questions and choose the best answer from the four choices provided.

1. What is the main idea of the essay?

    a. Blacks and whites should not be in the same classroom.

    b. Providing separate elementary school classrooms for black boys, with black male teachers, may help solve the problem of black male violence.

    c. Black boys are viewed by their teachers as hyperactive and aggressive.

    d. Black boys are more frequently tracked into special education classes than black girls.

2. According to the essay, why is Bill Cosby not a good role model for black boys?

    a. He is too old.

    b. He is rich, and many inner-city black boys do not identify with him.

    c. He is too remote to offer a realistic model of responsible manhood.

    d. He is too unlike the men in the tough urban areas where some black boys live.

3. What happened to the program in Dade County, Florida?

    a. It violated civil rights laws and was aborted.

    b. It was not popular with the citizens and was aborted.

    c. It was ineffective and was aborted.

    d. It was aborted due to lack of funds.

4. What did the group called Concerned Black Men do in Washington?

    a. They taught and mentored students in second grade classroom.

    b. They volunteered to give speeches against violence.

    c. They taught and mentored kindergarten children.

    d. They taught and mentored first grade children.

5.   What did child psychologist James Comer say about role models?

   a.   He said that children need role models from their own race group.

   b.   He said that male children need male role models.

   c.   He said that it is helpful to have role models from one's own group, but not necessary to have role models exclusively from one's group.

   d.   He said that it is not only helpful to have role models from one's group, but necessary that role models come exclusively from one's own group.

SHORT-ANSWER QUESTIONS

6.   Use the following guidelines to devise a chart:

   a.   List three reasons, from the essay, that supporters of the plan offer.

   b.   List three reasons, from the essay, that critics of the plan offer.

   c.   Add your own two reasons, one for and one against the plan.

7.   How do you think the authors of the essay feel about the plan? Do you detect any biases? What is the tone of the essay?

8.   Do you think this plan would work at the college level? Provide one reason for your answer.

9.   Do you think the plan, as described in the essay, is a good one? Provide two reasons for your opinion.

10.   At what levels of thinking are Questions #8 and #9? Explain how you know.

Website Sources for Additional Practice

http://gator1.brazosport.cc.tx.us/~lac/mindmap.htm: Click here for an example of a mind map.

http://braindance.com/frambdi1.htm: More on mind mapping.

http://www.to.utwente.nl/user/ism/lanzing/cm_home.htm: The Concept Mapping homepage.

Chapter 14

Evaluating Internet Resources

The central work of life is interpretation.
-Proverb

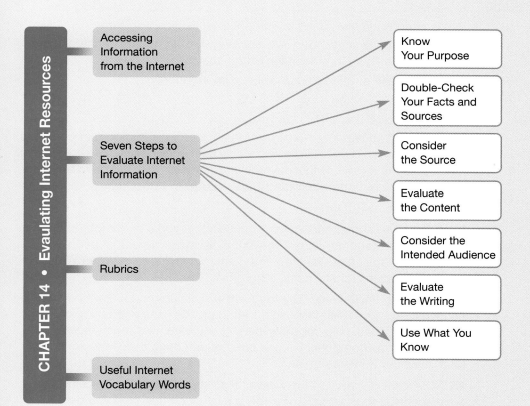

CHAPTER 14 • Evaluating Internet Resources

- Accessing Information from the Internet
- Seven Steps to Evaluate Internet Information
  - Know Your Purpose
  - Double-Check Your Facts and Sources
  - Consider the Source
  - Evaluate the Content
  - Consider the Intended Audience
  - Evaluate the Writing
  - Use What You Know
- Rubrics
- Useful Internet Vocabulary Words

Chapter Contents

Chapter Goals

In this chapter on evaluating Internet resources, you will learn:

- How to use a seven-step evaluation system to determine the accuracy and reliability of Internet information sources.
- How to use a rubric to rate website information.

Chapter Vocabulary

The following vocabulary words and phrases represent important concepts from this chapter. They are listed here along with their definitions. As you read the chapter, take note of these words and phrases; they will be in **boldface** type. Make sure you understand them before the post test at the end of this chapter.

Internet: The Internet consists of countless networks of computers that are connected together across the world, allowing millions of people to share information. Components of the Internet include the World Wide Web, newsgroups, chat rooms, and e-mail.

WWW (World Wide Web): The Web is the visual component of the Internet. Created with HTML language, Web pages can include text, pictures, sound clips, video, links for downloading software, and much more. The Web is only one component of the Internet, although the terms are often (and mistakenly) interchanged.

2RCA: An abbreviation of the words reliability, relevance, credibility, and accuracy—the four aspects of website evaluation that help you determine whether a site is valuable to you.

Key word: A word or phrase used by a search engine as a reference point for locating information related to a specific topic.

Rubric: A type of chart used that lists the characteristics necessary to consider when evaluating a product or process.

Ben's Journal Entry

I like using the Internet, but there is so much out there. Sometimes I'm not sure which source to use or even where to start looking when my search results in "250 sites found." Usually I start with the first site and keep going until I find the information I need.

Knowledge is power, but only if it is accurate. It's important to apply your critical thinking skills to everything you read, including information you find on the Internet. The **Internet** allows millions of people to share information. More and more instructors are requiring students to use the **World Wide Web**, the component of the Internet where information is stored online, and many students *choose* to access information this way because it's so convenient. Using a computer was once considered a luxury. Now, at most colleges and universities, it's become an expectation or even a course requirement; many schools include computer literacy as a general education goal requirement. This means that you can't graduate without learning how to effectively use a computer as a learning resource.

Learning Journal

Write about whether you enjoy working on the Internet, and how much time you currently spend searching for information.

Accessing Information from the Internet

Accessing information from the Web is a skill you need to learn not only for college, but also for the world of work. Therefore, we feel it is essential to include a chapter devoted to evaluating Internet sources of information in this book. The format of this chapter is slightly different from that of the previous ones. The information is more condensed; much of it employs the same textbook strategies and skills you have already learned because the same skills apply to assessing online information. This chapter requires you to have access to the Internet. If your class does not include computer time, you will have to access the Internet from a computer in your home, college library, local library, or college computer lab.

The amount of information available to you on the Internet is staggering and continues to double every few months. You can actually spend hours on the Web searching for information that you might have looked up more easily in printed textbooks or reference books. But many students find searching on the Internet both convenient and compelling. Although the Internet can be a valuable source of information, it is important to question everything you read, using all the critical reading skills you have learned in this book. This chapter will help you to consider the Internet in terms of the quality of available sources, their credibility, and accuracy. It will also encourage you to think critically about online information and demonstrate how to use a seven-step evaluation tool that focuses on a source's relevancy, reliability, credibility, and accuracy.

This chapter is not intended to assist you with the computer skills needed to use your computer or the skills you will need to access the Internet effectively. For that assistance it is recommended that you check with your librarian for sources, both online and offline.

Exercise 14a

Evaluating Internet Sources

Are you a critical observer? Learning how to evaluate Internet information sources quickly is a valuable skill. Take 10 minutes to skim **two** of the following sites. Begin timing yourself as soon as you access each site; be honest—you have 10 minutes altogether! See how well you can evaluate the sites within the time limit, and answer the following questions for each on a separate sheet paper:

- **http://more.abcnews.go.com/sections/scitech/cuttingedge/ cuttingedge020118.html**

- **http://www.pediatrics.org/cgi/content/full/103/3/e36**

- **http://www.media-awareness.ca/eng/issues/minrep/default.html**

- **http://www.jamalx.com/wbt/weird.html**

1. What is the focus, or point, of the site?

2. What evidence did you find to support the claims made by the author(s)?

3. How could you tell, by quickly looking over the website, whether it was accurate and reliable? What were the reasons for your decision?

Learning Journal

In your journal, explain how you currently select sites to use for your course-work. How do you decide whether the information is reliable?

Seven-Step Internet Source Evaluation System

When you search the Internet, you will find huge amounts of seemingly "accurate" information available. However, just because material is published on the Internet doesn't make it either true or accurate. *Don't confuse Internet sources with library material.* Anyone can post anything on the Web, with little or no screening of the content. Accuracy is not always easy to determine. The seven steps discussed here will help you to critically analyze Internet content in terms of reliability, relevance, credibility, and accuracy. These four aspects of analyzing a site help you decide whether it will be valuable to you. To remember the point of the seven-step website evaluation, use this abbreviation as a mnemonic: **2RCA—R**elevance, **R**eliability, **C**redibility, and **A**ccuracy.

Team Up!

With two other students, discuss the following scenario: You have to research how to make a movie. What steps should you take before you actually begin your search for information? Discuss the steps as a group. Have someone take notes, and be prepared to share your list with the rest of the class. *After* you have brainstormed together and created your list, read Step 1: Know Your Purpose.

Step 1: Know Your Purpose (Relevance)

Before you begin surfing (searching) for information, you need to know exactly what you are looking for; you need a plan. The following questions and statements will help you to prepare one:

- *Define your topic.* Write down the topic you are researching and the type of information you want to find out about it.

- *What is your purpose in gathering information?*
  - Are you writing a research paper that requires factual information, including well-argued opinions or statistics?
  - Is your purpose to explore popular opinions?
  - Do you need to locate firsthand sources of information?

Knowing exactly what you are looking for will help you identify the best key words for your search and save you time. **A key word** is used by a search engine as a reference point for locating information related to a specific topic. For example, suppose you wanted to know more about kung fu. When you enter a search program like Google or Altavista, you will be asked to provide a *key word* or *words*. You could enter "kung fu" alone or with related terms (key words) such as martial arts, Chinese martial arts, Shaolin, dojo, Sifu, Uchia, or Wu Shu. Knowing *exactly* what you are looking for allows you to generate a larger number of key words. The more key words you use, the better the computer can search for the information you want. The good news is that you will find hundreds of additional sites; the bad news is that you'll find hundreds of additional sites you'll have to evaluate for accuracy. To use the Internet efficiently, you have to know how to narrow your search and distinguish between useful, credible sites and inaccurate ones.

Team Up!

Now that you have read Step 1, is there anything you need to add to the list that your team developed? Or did your team come up with something that was not identified in Step 1?

Step 2: Double-Check Your Facts and Sources (Reliability, Credibility, and Accuracy)

Sifu Robert Brown, an outstanding teacher in Berkley, Michigan, consistently reminds his students to question everything. He tells them to be "open-minded skeptics." Being an open-minded skeptic means never assuming that information is accurate or true simply because it's in print. Consider the articles published in tabloids like the *Mirror* or the *Enquirer*, for example, and compare them to the articles you might read in the *Review of Educational Research*, a journal devoted to current theory and practice in higher education. What type of information would you expect to find in each? Which one would you expect to present unbiased, research-based information? If you said the professional journal, you would probably be correct. On the other hand, don't reject information simply because it sounds unbelievable. Double-check and continue to research material that sounds "off" until you can find additional information that proves or disproves it. If information is accurate, other sources will usually back it up. The bottom line, however, is that it saves time and energy to use reliable sites that do not require you to verify everything they report.

Exercise
14b

Fact or Fiction

Access the website **http://www.angelfire.com/wv/lucyb8/coolfacts.html**. Select five of the "weird statements" and research them to see if they are true. List the five you have selected, provide a reference source that confirms or disproves the authenticity of each, and then answer the following questions:

1. What does this exercise tell you about appearances?

_____

_____

2. If you have to double-check all the information on a site, how reliable is it as a source?

_____

3. In your opinion, was this site more like the *Journal of Modern Medicine* or more like the *National Enquirer*?

_____

Websites Designed to Help You Evaluate Online Information

There are sites available that you can use to help you assess the accuracy and reliability of online articles. One such resource for students is **http://www.argusclearinghouse.com.** This site does searches to determine the credibility of various websites. Two other useful sources of this type of information are **http://www.clearinghouse.net** and **http://www.bestwebsites.com**. Although such sites are useful, they can never replace your own ability to review a site. These programs are generic and cannot determine exactly what you are looking for or the kind of information you need.

Step 3: Consider the Source (Reliability and Credibility)

Everything that you learned in Chapter 12 regarding validity and reliability applies to Internet information. You need to evaluate Internet material the same way you evaluate information in your textbooks. The first step is to consider the source, the author of the material. Most credible sites tell you the author's credentials and contact information. Links on the site should also connect you to related material. When you review these, it should quickly become obvious if the information is reliable. For example, a site that links to a university is probably more credibl than one linked to a hate group's website. The questions you should ask yourself about a website's source will sound familiar:

- Who is the author of the information you are reading?
  - What, if any, credentials are listed for the author?
  - What is his or her educational background?
  - Is he or she experienced in that field?
  - What are his or her institutional affiliations?
  - Is contact information for the author or producer included in the document?
  - Does the author have something to gain if you take what he or she says as fact?
- When was the Web item produced?
- Are the ideas presented drawn from primary source material?
- When was the website last revised?
- How up-to-date are the links?
- What is the URL for the source? Knowing what the URL codes mean provides you with clues to the type of information you can expect to find on a site:
  .com (commercial)   .net (network)   .edu (education)
  .gov (government)   .org (non-profit organization)

Usually URLs that end with .gov or .edu present the most factual, research-based information.

Exercise 14c

Good Sources or Not

Access and read the following two websites. Use the criteria presented in Step 3 to evaluate whether they are good sources of information. Write your opinions of each on a separate sheet of paper, listing your answers to the Step 3 questions, and noting when you are unable to find the answers you are looking for.

1. http://www.nade.net

2. http://www.hate.org

Evaluate the Look and Content of a Site
'ity and Accuracy)

Websites whose creators have invested time in choosing what material post and how to present it are usually more reliable. This is not always true, but it tends to be a good indicator of the credibility of a site. It's also important to ask yourself what the *purpose* of a specific website is. Is it to sell you something? Is it to provide information? Is it a platform for someone to spout off about a pet cause? Once you know the true purpose of a site, it becomes clearer how reliable it is. Use the following set of questions to guide you in evaluating the look and purpose of a site:

- Is the website clearly identified and easy to find?
- How is content presented? Is it clear and easily accessible?
- What is the purpose of the information presented?
  - To advertise a product?
  - To provide information?
  - To make a public service announcement?
  - To invoke an emotional response—anger, sympathy, humor?
  - To provide personal opinions?
- Is the information presented accurately?

You will not always know the answer to this last question because you may not have enough background knowledge on the topic (that's why you're researching it). So don't settle for just one source; access several sites and see if the information on them is consistent with the site you are evaluating. Also consider whether the information matches what your professor has said about the topic. If necessary, look up unfamiliar terms and information in sources you know to be reliable. If the information is consistent and accurate across sources, you have probably found a good site. However, if the information is only partially correct, is missing supporting documentation, contradicts what you know to be true, or is at odds with what you have learned from other sources of information, *don't use it!* The following questions will guide you in evaluating a website's content:

- Does the site clearly state which topics it intends to address?
- Does the author provide evidence to support her/his conclusions?
- How is the evidence documented?
  - Does the author cite other sources to verify his or her points? Is credit given to other authors?
  - Do other links verify what is being stated?
  - If the information involves research, is the place the research was conducted credited?
  - Does the author provide a bibliography?
- Are the conclusions well researched?
- Is the information biased?
  - Is emotive language used as a means of persuasion?
  - Does the author make broad, unsubstantiated statements?
  - Does the site offer more than one viewpoint?
  - Are there links to sites that provide other points of view?

- What is the scope of the site?
  - Are links provided to other relevant sites?
  - How does the information provided compare with that from other sources on the topic?
  - What is the copyright status? Most quality information will be copyrighted.
- Is the information current?

Evaluating Website Content

Evaluate the website **http://www.d-b.net/dti/.**

1. What is its title?

   _____

2. What is the main idea of the article?

   _____

3. What do you already know about the topic?

   _____

   _____

   _____

4. Using the criteria presented in Step 4, explain why it would or would not be a good site to use as a source. Provide examples to support your conclusion.

   _____

   _____

   _____

   _____

Step 5: Consider the Intended Audience (Relevance and Reliability)

Knowing a website's intended audience can save time when you're surfing for information. Ask yourself the following questions to help determine the intended audience for a specific site:

- Is the information in the article appropriate to the topic you are researching, but written at a level that is:

- Too elementary?
- Too technical?
- Too advanced?
- Is the article aimed at a specialized or general audience?

Does the language used require a certain amount of background knowledge? For example, if you are researching the topic of AIDS and the language in an article consists of highly technical medical terminology, then it is probably intended for physicians. If the language consists of common terms and familiar comparisons, and is lacking a lot of details and statistics, then it was probably written for a general audience. As a student you are somewhere in the middle. You need accessible language but you also need specific facts and in-depth exploration of a topic in order to satisfy your research requirements. Skim sites to determine if you are the intended audience before you study-read them.

| Exercise 14e | **Intended Audience** |

Read the article at this website: **http://www.coai.org** (click on history). Then answer the following questions in the space provided.

1. What is the title?

_____

2. What is the main idea?

_____

3. Who is the intended audience? How do you know?

_____

4. Would you consider the information from this source reliable enough to use in a research paper? Why or why not?

_____

_____

Step 6: Evaluate the Writing (Accuracy, Credibility, and Reliability)

When you read information on the Internet, bad grammar, misspelled words, and other typographical errors can indicate that a source is unreliable. The following questions are designed to guide you in evaluating websites in terms of their tone, organization, and use of language:

- Check the author's tone. (Refer to Chapter 7 for additional information on tone.)
  - Is the writing manipulative or self-serving?
  - Is it politically slanted or distorted?
  - Is there evidence of exaggeration?
- Is the text easy to read, or is it choppy and disconnected?
- Does each page begin with a clear transition?
- Does the writing seem organized and flow logically, or is it disconnected and confusing?
- Do the writer's conclusions logically follow from the facts given?
- Is the information comprehensive enough?
  - Does it give the reader enough supporting details?
  - Does the author deliberately leave out important facts or qualifications so the information is misleading?
  - Are there inconsistencies within the information?
- Does the author use vague or sweeping generalizations?
- What is the purpose of the writing?
  - To point out a problem?
  - To teach or explain?
  - To criticize or tear something down?
  - To make you laugh or cry?
  - To persuade?
  - To call you to action?
- Are most of the author's statements supported by hard evidence—verifiable facts?

Learning Journal

In your journal, explain why a site that is easy to read—not choppy and disconnected—is perhaps more reliable. What does writing style have to do with the authenticity of content?

Exercise

14f

Evaluate the Writing

Read this Web article: **http://www.resist.com/positions/military.html**. Answer the following questions and provide examples (evidence) to support your conclusions.

1. Are spelling and grammar used correctly?

   _____

   _____

2. Is the text easy to read?

   _____

3. Is the information biased? Explain your answer.

   _____

   _____

   _____

4. Is the information emotionally charged? Provide examples, if your answer is yes.

   _____

   _____

   _____

   _____

5. Does the author use vague, sweeping generalizations? If yes, provide examples.

   _____

   _____

6. What is the purpose of the article?

   _____

   _____

   _____

Step 7: Compare Content with What You Already Know (Relevance, Reliability, Credibility, and Accuracy)

If the information on a site seems reasonable, based on what you already know, it is probably a reliable source. If the information seems outrageous, don't accept it as factual, but don't completely discount it either. Do a little more research, and if the information is indeed true, you should be able to find corroboration from a different source. The following questions are designed to guide you in determining when you can trust your instincts in evaluating a site:

- Is the information generally accepted? By whom?
- Where and when did you learn about the information?
- Do you have ideas or opinions about the topic that might prevent you from reading it critically?
- Are you interested enough in the topic to spend the time and energy necessary to read and research it critically?

Exercise 14g

Using What You Already Know

Read this Web article: **http://www.counseling.uci.edu/counsel/testanx.html**. Then answer the following questions:

1. What is the main idea?

_____

2. How much do you already know about this topic?

_____

_____

3. Is it easy for you to judge the accuracy of the information presented?

_____

_____

_____

Team Up!

With one other student, review the seven-step evaluation system. Provide a brief overview of each step. Make a note of any step that one of you can't explain. Also, note areas of disagreement.

Rubrics

A rubric can be an effective tool for evaluating Internet information. A **rubric** is a chart that contains criteria designed to evaluate specific information. For example, you can design one to help you assess whether a website is an outstanding, average, or unacceptable source of information.

A rubric for evaluating Internet information is provided here in Table 14.1. If you evaluate an Internet source, and it fits all the criteria listed in column 2, you can assume it is an excellent source of information. On the other hand, if your Internet source fits the criteria listed in column 3, you should seriously consider not using it.

Table 14.1	Rubric to Evaluate Internet Information	
	CRITERIA	
ELEMENTS TO EVALUATE	**ACCEPTABLE SITE**	**QUESTIONABLE SITE**
Source	• Site easy to navigate. • Links work well. • Credentials are listed for the author(s). • Contact information provided. • Site states date when it was posted. • Site fairly current–within last three years. • Most links are up-to-date.	• Site difficult to navigate. • Links don't work properly. • No credentials are listed for author(s). • No contact information provided. • Site has no date posted. • Site is not current or has not been updated within the last three years. • Source is selling a product to user.
Writing	• Text easy to read. • Writing is well organized. • No grammar or spelling errors. • Emotion, if present, is appropriate. • Most statements and opinions are supported with evidence.	• Text difficult to read. • Writing is not well organized. • Grammar and/or spelling errors. • Emotional writing/exaggerated claims. • Very biased information. • No evidence to support statements. • Fallacies are present.
Audience	• Intended audience is clear. • Level of writing is acceptable. • Writing style is appropriate.	• Intended audience is unclear. • Level of writing not appropriate for audience–too technical, too elementary, or too advanced. • Writing style seems arrogant and/or superior.
Content	• Purpose is clear. • Information is accurate. • Information has sources listed for verification. • Author's argument is logical. • Title is appropriate and useful.	• Purpose is unclear. • Information is not accurate. • Information has no sources listed–no way to check validity of information. • Author's argument is not logical. • Title misleading–does not fit with article content.

Team Up!

With three other students, complete this exercise. Examine the Internet rubric together. Discuss the differences between the two levels (acceptable and questionable), and as a group, answer the following questions:

- Is information missing?
- If so, what criteria would you add?
- Why is a rubric an effective tool?
- In what other ways could you use this kind of guide? Explain possible uses in the following areas: business class, English paper, history project.

Keep track of your individual responses in your journals.

Exercise 14h

Evaluate an Internet Source

Rate each of the following sites as *acceptable* or *questionable* using the Internet rubric as a guide. Then explain your reasons. Write your responses on a separate sheet of paper.

Source This exercise was adapted from a lesson created by Keith Mack, Webmaster for the Meridian School District.

http://eserver.org/philosophy/chicken.txt.

http://eserver.org/philosophy/hegel-summary.html

www.aryabhatt.com

Exercise 14i

Evaluating Websites

Select one of the following websites and use the rubric to evaluate it. Then answer the questions that follow.

- Halloween **http://www.jeremiahproject.com/halloween.html**
- Genochoice Institute **http://www.genochoice.com/**

Check Your Understanding

1. What is the point or main idea of the website you selected?

_____

_____

_____

2. Is the main argument persuasive to you? Why or why not?

_____

_____

3. List one strong and one weak aspect of the website.

_____

_____

_____

_____

_____

Team Up!

With two other students, use the Internet rubric to evaluate one of your favorite websites. (As a team, you will need to vote for one.) Evaluate the site, and see if you agree on your conclusions. In your journal, note the areas about which your group disagreed. Explain why you disagreed. Be prepared to share with the class.

Useful Internet Vocabulary Words

The Internet is its own land with its own language. To travel there you have to not only know where to go but also understand the language used. The chart here discusses more Internet vocabulary words that will make your travels on the Web a little easier.

A Directory of Useful Internet Vocabulary Words

Bookmarks: A personal list of interesting websites. Bookmarks make it quick and easy to get to your favorite places on the World Wide Web—just like putting a marker into a book.

Browser: A browser is the software that lets you "surf" around and view pages on the Web. Netscape and Microsoft Explorer are two commonly used browsers.

Directory: A website that organizes and offers a collection of links to other sites. Directories can be specific or general in topic; www.yahoo.com is an example of a general directory.

Download:	The process of transferring computer files from the Internet to your computer.
HTML (hypertext markup language):	HTML is the computer language of the World Wide Web. All the Web pages you view with your browser have been created using HTML. When you are looking at a Web page, click on "View" in your browser then "View Source"—and you'll see what the HTML code looks like on the page.
Search engine:	An Internet site that allows users to search for specific information or websites. Two popular search engines are **www.altavista.com**. and **www. google.com**.
URL (uniform resource locator):	An address on the Internet, the URL shows the specific path that locates a site or document online. The URL for a Web page looks like this: http://www.domain name/folder name/filename.

Source: 2000 www.media-awareness.ca/english/resources/special_initiatives/wa_resources/ wa_shared/backgrounders/internet_glossary.cfm.

Chapter Summary

Evaluating Internet sources of information helps you determine if they are reliable and useful. Knowing how to critically evaluate Internet material not only helps you become a better student, but will help you in your work life beyond college. Use the Internet source evaluation system described in this chapter as a tool for assessing websites. As a reader and thinker, become an *"open minded skeptic"* by considering each website's **R**elevancy, **R**eliability, **C**redibility and **A**ccuracy using the following seven steps: 1. Know your purpose. 2. Double-check facts and sources. 3. Consider the source. 4. Evaluate content. 5. Determine intended audience. 6. Evaluate the writing. 7. Use what you already know.

Post Test

Answer questions on a separate sheet of paper.

Part I

OBJECTIVE QUESTIONS

1. Match the words in Column A to their definitions in Column B

Column A	**Column B**
1. Rubric	a. A visual component of the Internet, which can include pictures, sound, video clips, and more.

2. HTML b. A type of chart used to evaluate a product or process.

3. 2RCA c. Countless networks of computers that are connected.

4. WWW d. The computer language of the WWW.

5. Internet e. A mnemonic used to remember the seven-step website evaluation.

2. An "open-minded skeptic" refers to someone

a. Who does not accept everything read as truth but is willing to consider and research questionable information.

b. Who does accept everything he or she reads as truth, and does not consider any information questionable.

c. Who does not accept any new information as truth.

d. Who is open-minded.

3. Which of the seven steps of the Internet source evaluation system is missing from this list: know your purpose; evaluate the look and content; know the intended audience; evaluate the writing; compare content to what you already know; double-check your facts and sources.

a. Consider how comprehensive the site is.

b. Consider the way colors and images are presented.

c. Consider the source.

d. Know your purpose.

4. Which of the following is *not* a reason to use a rubric?

a. To evaluate the intended audience of a website.

b. To help you evaluate the writing on a website.

c. To judge the quality of the information on the website.

d. To determine if you will receive a good grade on your research paper.

5. If information is *relevant*, it is

a. Interesting and you would enjoy reading about it.

b. Related to the topic you are researching.

c. Part of a current trend.

d. Up-to-date.

Part II

SHORT-ANSWER QUESTIONS

1. Using the rubric on page 485, evaluate and rate one of the following websites as acceptable or questionable as a source.

    a. Feline reactions to bearded men: **http://www.improb.com/archives/classical/cat/cat.html**.

    b. The first male pregnancy: **http://www.malepregnancy.com**.

2. What is the main idea of the site?

3. Was the source reliable? Provide evidence for your conclusion.

4. Based on the information on the site you selected, are you able to list the author's credentials?

5. Is emotive language used? If yes, provide an example.

6. In your opinion, who is the intended audience? Explain your answer.

7. Now that you have had an opportunity to view the websites, do you think the titles are effective? Why?

8. What questions would you like to ask the author?

9. How could you use the information at this website?

Website Sources for Additional Practice

Beck, Susan. "The Good, the Bad, and the Ugly: Why It's a Good Idea to Evaluate Web Sources." New Mexico State University Libraries. http://lib.nmsu.edu/instruction/eval.html July 29, 1997).

Brandt, D. Scott. "Evaluating Information on the Internet." http://thor-plus.lib.purdue.edu/~techman/evaluate.htm (January 28, 1998).

Richmond, Betsy. "Ten C's for Evaluating Internet Resources" http://uwec.edu/Admin/Libray/Guides/tencs.html University of Wisconsin.

Shuirman, J. "Evaluating Internet Sites." http://libwww.cabrillo.cc.ca.us/html/about/jsworksheet-3.html (December 2, 1999).

Winter, Kevin. "Evaluating Internet Research." http://www.vmi.edu/library/kw/evaluate.htm August 13, 1998).

Part Four
Application Selections

Application Selection #1: Sociology

This selection provides you an opportunity to practice your critical reading strategies on a longer textbook excerpt. Your instructor will provide directions and feedback.

Courtship

Courtship is the process whereby two people agree to commit themselves to marriage. While finding a mate is only one of the functions of dating, dating is obviously a part of courtship. In this section, we will look at factors that make it likely that a relationship will move into courtship, the importance of courtship, and some differing patterns of courtship.

Moving into Courtship

What makes it likely that dating will turn into courtship? Actually, the same factors that sustain and enhance an intimate relationship are operative among those couples who move into courtship. For example, equity, the growth of trust, an increasing amount of self-disclosure, and the development of shared attitudes and values characterize courtship. In a longitudinal study, Stephen (1985) reported that as couples move into and through courtship, they become more alike in a variety of attitudes, beliefs, and values. They seem to be constructing a shared and unique world of their own. Couples who fail to do this are more likely to break up.

Thus, courtship means that the process of building an intimate relationship is continuing. The couple that moves from casual dating into courtship is constructing a more intense intimacy than is otherwise possible.

As a relationship becomes permanent, a couple constructs a unique, shared world of their own. © **W. Hill/The Image Works**

The Length of Courtship

To say that courtship is a process means that it takes place over a period of time. How much time? And does the amount make any difference? The authors personally know of couples who met and were married in as few as twenty-eight days and had satisfying marriages for the rest of their lives. We know of others who courted for years before marriage and eventually divorced, but they are the exceptions. Generally, a marriage is less likely to succeed if there is a very short courtship.

A study of fifty-one middle-aged, married women investigated marital satisfaction and length of courtship (Grover et al. 1985). All of the women were in their first marriage. Their ages ranged from thirty-two to seventy-one, and they had been married an average of twenty-three years. The researchers divided the women into four groups according to the amount of time spent in courtship (dating prior to engagement or marriage): five months or less, six to eleven months, one to two years, and more than two years. The amount of satisfaction with the marriage went up in each group; those who courted more than two years were the happiest with their marriages.

Of course, some of those who had dated for less than six months were also happy in their marriages. But they also were more likely to admit regret over having married, to say that their spouses got on their nerves, and to acknowledge some degree of dissatisfaction with the marriage. It seems then that the longer a couple goes together, the less likely they are to discover hidden incompatibilities after marriage.

Patterns of Courtship

Although people may move through courtship in very different ways, a number of typical steps are associated with the process (King and Christensen 1983):

1. Mutual attraction leads to an increase in interaction and communication.

2. The two partners are defined as a couple by themselves and by relatives, friends, and acquaintances.

3. The partners declare their love to each other and agree to an exclusive relationship.

4. The couple discusses the future of their relationship and joke or dream about the possibility of marriage.

5. The two people coordinate their activities, financial resources, and schedules so that they can function as a couple in important matters.

6. The two people make a final commitment to each other and may begin to cohabit and/or plan a wedding.

Even among those who go through this typical pattern, there may be differences. Surra (1985) examined the courtship patterns of thirty couples who had been married ten months or less. She asked about their perceptions of the likelihood of marriage and their activities at various stages of their relationships. She found four patterns of courtship: the accelerated, the accelerated–arrested, the intermediate, and the prolonged type.

In the accelerated type, the couple moved quickly and smoothly to marriage. Such couples tended increasingly to share tasks (shopping, housework, etc.) and leisure activities and to isolate themselves to some extent from other people. The accelerated–arrested pattern also involved sharing of tasks and leisure activities, but couples in this pattern had some doubts at the point of engagement. At that point, they tended to revert back somewhat to more individual activities. As a result, the engagement period was longer, amounting to nearly 60 percent of the overall courtship process.

In the intermediate courtship pattern, the partners tended to stay more involved with their individual activities and shared fewer tasks. Their courtship lasted a bit longer than the first two types. Finally, the prolonged pattern involved a very long courtship, as much as six to seven years. About 65 percent of that time was spent in serious dating, however, and 22 percent in engagement. Those in the prolonged pattern increased their sharing of tasks, though not as much as those in the first two groups. Those in the prolonged pattern also maintained more of their individual activities than did the others.

Engagement

The final phase of courtship is generally the engagement period. At one time, we could have considered engagement as a postcourtship period, because once people were engaged the commitment to marriage was nearly irreversible. But by the time of Burgess and Wallin's (1953) study of one thousand engaged couples, the researchers found that between a third and a half of the couples had more than one engagement before they were married. Engagement, in other words, is a kind of last testing period before the commitment to marry is finalized.

During the engagement period, a couple has an opportunity to closely examine their relationship. They can get a better picture of how each behaves in a variety of situations, including the somewhat stressful task of planning and executing a wedding. They have an opportunity to interact more closely with future in-laws and to get a sense of the expectations of the fiancé(e) about relationships with future in-laws.

Some couples use the engagement period to enhance the chances of a successful marriage. They may undergo premarital counseling or attend an "engaged couple encounter" seminar. They may read books on typical problems of marriage. Such experiences can help them to more thoroughly and reasonably discuss important topics, such as how they feel and think about their communication with each other, their methods of conflict resolution, their plans for handling their finances, their attitudes about having and rearing children, and so on.

In a sense, then, an engagement is a final countdown period in which potential problem areas can be detected before the union is finalized. This

Perspective: Bundling

In eighteenth-century colonial America, **bundling**—two people sleeping without undressing on the same bed—was a common practice. Bundling provided a place to sleep for travelers (for whom there was a scarcity of available beds) and for young people who were courting. For example, a young man who visited a young woman during a severe New England winter needed a place to sleep the night. It would hardly be possible for him, if he traveled any distance at all, to return over the rough, snow-covered road at night. He would, therefore, bundle with the young woman. This would also give the couple the opportunity to talk and get to know each other better.

Any sexual activity, of course, was forbidden. The couple was not even supposed to embrace. The records of premarital pregnancy and the tirades of preachers testify to the fact that the rules were frequently broken. Eventually, moral opposition led to the demise of the practice. The following is a commentary by an early historian (Stiles 1871:50–53) on the practice and its consequences for the Connecticut colonists, who, pointed out the historian, had multiplied to an "incredible" degree:

> This amazing increase may, indeed, be partly ascribed to a singular custom prevalent among them, commonly known by the name of bundling—a superstitious rite observed by the young people of both sexes, with which they usually terminated their festivities, and which was kept up with religious strictness by the more bigoted and vulgar part of the community. This ceremony was likewise, in those primitive times, considered as an indispensable preliminary to matrimony....To this sagacious custom do I chiefly attribute the unparalleled increase of the Yankee tribe; for it is a certain fact, well authenticated by court records and parish registers, that wherever the practice of bundling prevailed, there was an amazing number of sturdy brats annually born unto the state.
>
> Hear also that learned divine, the Rev. Samuel Peters, who thus discourseth at length upon the custom of bundling: Notwithstanding the modesty of the females is such that it would be accounted the greatest rudeness for a gentleman to speak before a lady of a garter, knee, or leg, yet it is thought but a piece of civility to ask her to bundle, a custom as old as the first settlement in 1634. It is certainly innocent, virtuous and prudent, or the puritans would not have permitted it to prevail among their offspring....People who are influenced more by lust, than a serious faith in God, ought never to bundle....I am no advocate for temptation; yet must say, that bundling has prevailed 160 years in New England, and, I verily believe, with ten times more chastity than the sitting on a sofa.

Clearly, the historian was appalled by the practice and by the minister's defense of it. Most ministers, however, did not defend the practice. In fact, they took steps to eliminate it. A Massachusetts minister, the Rev. Jason Haven, pastored a church in which bundling and, consequently, premarital pregnancy, was very common. He finally acted:

> Mr. Haven, in a long and memorable discourse, sought out the cause of the growing sin, and suggested the proper remedy. He attributed the frequent recurrence of the fault to the custom then prevalent, of females admitting young men to their beds, who sought their company with intentions of marriage. And he exhorted all to abandon that

custom, and no longer expose themselves to temptations which so many were found unable to resist....The females blushed and hung down their heads. The men, too, hung down their heads, and now and then looked out from under their fallen eyebrows, to observe how others supported the attack. If the outward appearance of the assembly was somewhat composed, there was a violent internal agitation in many minds....The custom was abandoned. The sexes learned to cultivate the proper degree of delicacy in their intercourse, and instances of unlawful cohabitation in this town since that time have been extremely rare (Stiles 1871:78–79).

is not to say that every couple uses the engagement period in such a productive way. But judging from the number of people who have more than one engagement, a considerable number of couples use the time for a more intensive examination of their potential for a happy union.

Cohabitation

Technically, cohabitation is also a part of courtship for many couples. We will examine it separately because it has become a common method of establishing an intimate relationship, increasing rapidly since 1970 (Table 6.1). In fact, cohabitation may now be the most typical path to marriage. (However, we should note that for some people, cohabitation has become an alternative to marriage.) Examination of marriages in an Oregon county found an increase from 13 percent in 1970 to 53 percent in the early 1980s of cohabitation prior to marriage (Gwartney-Gibbs 1986). Thus, the increasing proportion of young people who are unmarried does not necessarily mean an increased number of singles. Rather, young people tend to set up a household at about the same age as they did before marriage rates started to decline, but the household comprises an unmarried couple (although about 40 percent have children in the home) (Bumpass, Sweet, and Cherlin 1991).

Who Cohabits?

Not everyone is equally likely to cohabit. Compared with noncohabitors, cohabitors are likely to have earlier and more sexual experience (Newcomb

Table 6.1   Number of Unmarried Couples Living Together: 1970 to 1993 (in Thousands)

	1970	1980	1985	1993
Number of couples	523	1589	1983	3510
Number with children under 15	196	431	603	1236

Source: U.S. Bureau of the Census 1994:56.

1986) and to come from homes broken by divorce (Thornton 1991). They tend to come from less religious families than those who do not cohabit (Thornton, Axinn, and Hill 1992). The most systematic comparison is provided by Tanfer (1987). Using data from a national survey of twenty- to twenty-nine-year-old never-married women, she found that cohabitors, compared to non-cohabitors, tend to:

Have less education (45.9 percent of those with less than twelve years and 22.2 percent of those with more than twelve years of education cohabited)

Have no religion (48 percent, compared with a little over 28 percent of Protestants and Catholics who cohabited)

Not be working (48.4 percent; 27.1 percent worked and 25.3 percent were in school)

Live in large, urban areas (38 percent live in cities of 100,000 or more)

She also noted that rates of cohabitation are much higher in the West (43.6 percent) than in other regions of the country (between 25 and 29 percent).

Tanfer also looked for attitudinal differences between cohabitors and noncohabitors. She found very few. Cohabitors, as we would expect, have less conventional attitudes about marriage. Interestingly enough, however, 31.7 percent of those who had ever cohabited, 34.7 percent of those currently cohabiting, but only 26.9 percent of those who had never cohabited said that they wish they were married.

Patterns of Cohabitation

A little over half of those who cohabit say that one important reason for doing so is that it permits a couple to be sure they are compatible before they marry (Bumpass, Sweet, and Cherlin 1991:920). And about 60 percent of first cohabitations end in marriage (Bumpass and Sweet 1989). In some cases, the relationship leads to marriage when the woman gets pregnant. Racial differences exist in this tendency, however. White cohabiting women are more likely than are African American women to marry if they get pregnant (Manning 1993). For African American and poorer white women, childbearing is as likely in cohabitation as it is in marriage (Loomis and Landale 1994).

People cohabit for reasons other than as a check on their compatibility. In their attempt to clarify the purpose of cohabitation, Ridley, Peterman, and Avery (1978) identify four types. The *"Linus blanket"* type (based on the popular *Peanuts* cartoon) is a relationship in which one of the partners is highly dependent and/or insecure. Such a person may prefer any kind of relationship to being alone. This relationship is unlikely to endure, because the nondependent partner will probably weary of the endless needs of the other.

In a relationship of *emancipation*, one or both partners use the cohabitation to gain independence from parental values and influence. They may, for instance, come from a sexually repressive home and use cohabitation in order to establish their own sexual values. In any case, the focus tends to be on the relationship with the parents rather than with the partner. The partner tends to be an instrument used for other purposes. A genuine intimate relationship is difficult to develop under such circumstances.

A relationship of *convenience* is the third type. The man generally wants a sexual relationship and someone to care for his home. The woman acquires a sexual relationship, a place to live, and financial care—the same things she would get in a traditional marriage, but without as much security. In this kind of relationship, it is usually the man who is opposed to the idea of marriage.

Finally, there is the *testing* relationship, cohabitation that is a trial marriage. The two partners are committed to each other and may be contemplating marriage. They decide to cohabit as a final testing of their relationship. If it works, they will marry.

These four types are a useful way to categorize cohabiting relationships. But they do not capture the full variety of patterns. They focus on motives, purposes, and styles of relating. We could also categorize relationships according to whether they include children or not. As Table 6.1 shows, there were 1,236,000 couples cohabiting in 1993 who had children under the age of fifteen in their home. What difference does having children make in the cohabiting relationship? We don't have research on the relationship between the cohabiting adults, but a five-year study of one hundred families found that divorced mothers who were cohabiting had more maladjusted children than those who had remarried, those who were seriously involved but not living with a new partner, and those who were not involved with a new partner (Isaacs and Leon 1988). It may be that such children know how fragile relationships are and the lack of marital commitment intensifies their sense of insecurity.

Finally, we could discuss differing patterns of relationships among heterosexual and homosexual partners. Some research has been conducted that examines the differences between cohabiting heterosexual, gay, and lesbian couples. In terms of the quality of the relationship, as measured by a scale of marital satisfaction, there is little overall difference among the three types of couples (Kurdek and Schmitt 1986). Rather, all three types of couples seem to go through similar stages of their relationship. In the first year, the *blending stage*, the partners tend to be "head over heels" in love and there is a good deal of sexual activity. In the *nesting stage*, the second and third years, there is a decline in the intensity of their passion, the emergence of some doubts about the relationship, and an emphasis on homemaking and finding compatibility in the relationship. Finally, the *maintaining stage* occurs during the fourth and fifth years. The couple now establishes certain traditions and typical patterns (such as ways of dealing with conflict).

In the research by Kurdek and Schmitt (1986), the stage was more important than the type of couple in determining relationship quality. This does not mean, however, that there were no differences among the couples. In their large-scale study of American couples, Blumstein and Schwartz (1983) looked at the areas of money, work, and sex. They found numerous differences among cohabiting heterosexual, gay, and lesbian couples (as well as married couples). We will give a few examples. With respect to money, they asked couples how often they fought over money management. Lesbians fought less than either gay or heterosexual couples. When asked about the extent to which the couples were relationship-centered or work-centered, 30 percent of the heterosexuals, 27 percent of the gays, and 41 percent of the lesbians said that both partners were relationship-centered. Finally, regarding the frequency of sexual relations, results varied depending on the number of years the couple had been together. But the lesbians had far less sex than gays or heterosexuals. In fact, 47 percent of lesbians who had been together for ten years or more reported having sex once a month or less (compared to 33 percent of gay couples; data were not available for cohabiting heterosexuals who were together more than ten years).

In sum, cohabitation is not the same experience for everyone. The nature of any individual's experience depends on such things as the motives and purposes of the two partners, the length of time the two have been together, and whether the relationship is heterosexual or homosexual.

Cohabitation Compared with Marriage

For many couples, cohabitation is a testing ground for marriage. How accurate is the test? How much is marriage like cohabitation? Married and cohabiting couples face the same kinds of problems—money, sex, division of labor in the home, and so forth. Nevertheless, just as there are differences among varying kinds of cohabitors, there are differences between the experiences of marriage and cohabitation.

Interestingly, Kurdek and Schmitt (1986) found that the married couples in their sample reported less tension than any of the three kinds of cohabiting couples. A study of communication patterns in married and in cohabiting couples reported that the younger married couples were more communicative and more satisfied than the younger cohabiting couples (Yelsma 1986). Analyses of national surveys find that, compared to those cohabiting, the married report greater happiness, less depression, higher levels of commitment to the relationship, and better relationships with parents (Kurdek 1991; Nock 1995).

On the other hand, Rotkin (1983) studied twenty married and twenty cohabiting graduate student couples and found that the married couples tended to give higher priority than the cohabiting couples to the male's career. This involved the woman's willingness to make her own aspirations and plans secondary in the case of any decisions that affected the male's career. Cohabiting couples who were not planning to marry were more egalitarian, giving equal weight to the career aspirations of both the male and the female.

Finally, the experience of marriage differs in some ways from that of cohabitation in the areas of money, work, and sex. As far as household work is concerned, married women spend significantly more time on housework than do cohabiting women (Shelton and John 1993). Cohabiting women and single, noncohabiting women spend equal amounts of time, suggesting that it is not merely the presence of a man but of a husband that makes a difference in the woman's household responsibilities.

Other differences were noted in the research of Blumstein and Schwartz (1983). With regard to conflict over money management, the researchers found that married couples fight more than the cohabiting couples. Only 23 percent said that they never fight about money management, compared with 31 percent of heterosexual cohabitors, 26 percent of gays, and 31 percent of lesbians. On the question about work, the married couples tended to be more work-centered (rather than relationship-centered) than any of the cohabiting groups. And in the matter of frequency of sex, married couples reported a lower frequency than the heterosexual cohabitors and gays but higher than the lesbians.

The differences noted above are not generally dramatic ones. One could argue, therefore, that cohabitation provides a reasonably good testing ground for marriage. People face the same kinds of problems. They have many of the same kinds of experiences, though with differing degrees of intensity. How well, then, has cohabitation prepared those couples who eventually marry?

Cohabitation as a Preparation for Marriage

One way to test the extent to which cohabitation helps people to have a more satisfying marriage is to compare the experiences of those who cohabited with those who did not. National surveys show that those who cohabit before marriage have a marriage of lesser quality and are more likely to perceive the possibility of divorce than those who do not cohabit (Thomson and Colella 1992; Stets 1993). And the actual divorce rates, both among Americans and Canadians, are higher among those who cohabit before marriage than among those who do not (White 1987/1989; Bumpass and Sweet 1989; DeMaris and Rao 1992).

We can't be sure that these consequences of cohabitation hold for all races. At least among Puerto Ricans who live on the U.S. mainland, cohabitation is more like marriage than two single people living together, in the sense that the women are likely to have children and function as a traditional wife and mother (Landale and Fennelly 1992). At best, then, cohabitation brings no advantage to those who desire marriage. At worst, cohabitors are at some disadvantage for entering marriage or even having a stable and satisfying intimate relationship. Most cohabitations end fairly quickly in either marriage or disruption (Bumpass and Sweet 1989). If the couple marry, they face the prospect of a greater likelihood of breakup than those who did not cohabit. Finally, rates of aggression and abuse are higher among cohabitors (Stets 1991). In spite of the logic of the arrangement, there is little to suggest that cohabitation yields the benefits that people expect from it.

Breaking Up

Most people experience a number of serious relationships rather than a single one. That means that most will have the painful experience of breaking up. *Painful* is the appropriate word, because most people grieve over the loss of an intimate relationship (Kaczmarek, Backlund, and Biemer 1990). Under

Most people have the painful experience
of breaking an intimate relationship.
© **Michael Siluk**

what conditions is a breakup likely, and how do people react to a deterio-
rating relationship?

Who Breaks Up?

On the basis of factors we have discussed that keep a relationship going, we
could make some reasonable inferences about when a relationship is likely to
break up. If, for instance, there is perceived inequity, the lack of self-disclosure,
or the absence of other factors that enhance intimacy, we would expect a
relationship not to last.

But there may be other factors as well. Simpson (1987) surveyed 222
undergraduate students about people they were dating. He gathered data
about such things as satisfaction with the relationship, closeness, sexual relationships, and perceived ease of finding a different partner. Three months
later, he again surveyed the students to see if they were still dating the same
person. Those who were still together differed from those who had broken
up on five measures. At the time of the first survey, those who stayed together
indicated greater satisfaction with the relationship. They had been dating their
partner a longer period of time. They had sexual relations with the partner.
They had a more difficult time conceiving of a desirable alternative partner.
Finally, they tended to have an exclusive relationship. In addition to these factors, couples are less likely to break up when they spend more time together,
are of the same race, and perceive social support for their relationship from
family and friends (Felmlee, Sprecher, and Bassin 1990).

Responding to Deterioration

People can react in a variety of ways when the quality of a relationship dete-
riorates. Rusbult (1987) has identified four kinds of responses: exit, voice,

loyalty, and neglect. *Exit* refers to a response of withdrawal or threatened withdrawal from the relationship. Those who decide to stop going or living together, to try being "just friends" instead of lovers, or to stop seeing each other altogether have chosen the response of exit. Breaking an intimate relationship, even for the person wanting out of it, is painful. Women tend to cope by confiding in a close friend, while men may try to cope by quickly starting to go out with others (Sorenson et al. 1993).

Voice is the response of facing up to, and trying to talk through, the problems. Discussion, compromise, counseling, and efforts to change oneself or one's partner are ways of dealing with the problems by voice. *Loyalty* is the response of staying with the partner in spite of the problems. Those who opt for loyalty do not try to resolve the problems; they simply try to endure them. They may believe that the situation will improve in time. They may insist that they must have faith in the relationship and the partner.

Finally, *neglect* is a refusal to face the problems and a willingness to let the relationship die. Some examples of behavior that fit the category of neglect are

> ignoring the partner or spending less time together, refusing to discuss problems, treating the partner badly emotionally or physically, criticizing the partner for things unrelated to the real problem, "just letting things fall apart," chronically complaining without offering solutions to problems….(Rusbult 1987:213).

As Rusbult notes, the terms used may be a little misleading. Voice does not refer only to talking. Rather, voice represents active and constructive reactions. Exit refers to active and destructive behavior. Loyalty is passive, constructive behavior. And neglect is passive, destructive behavior.

Differing personalities will prefer different responses, but there are also other reasons for selecting a response (Rusbult 1987:227–28). Research has shown that people exit when they believe that they have nothing to lose by doing so and that the relationship is not worth saving. A combination of dissatisfaction with the relationship, a sense of minimal investment in the relationship, and a belief that there are good alternatives will make exit a likely response. Exit tends to be used more by younger people in relationships that have been going on for only a short time.

Voice is a response that is appropriate when the relationship is valued but in danger. People who have been satisfied with the relationship and invested themselves in it are more likely to try the response of voice. Females are more likely than males to use voice.

Loyalty is an effort to maintain the status quo. People who have been satisfied with the relationship, feel invested in it, perceive few or no better alternatives, and believe the problems are relatively minor may opt for loyalty. Loyalty tends to be used more by older people who have been in a relationship for a longer period of time. Females are also more likely than males to use loyalty.

Application Selection #2: Biology

This selection provides you an opportunity to practice your critical reading strategies on a longer textbook excerpt. Your instructor will provide directions and feedback.

1.2 The Process of Science

Science helps human beings understand the natural world. Science aims to be objective rather than subjective even though it is very difficult to make objective observations and to come to objective conclusions because we are often influenced by our own particular prejudices. Still, scientists strive for objective observations and conclusions. We also keep in mind that scientific conclusions are subject to change whenever new findings so dictate. Quite often in science, new studies, which might utilize new techniques and equipment, tell us when previous conclusions need to be modified or changed entirely.

Scientific Theories in Biology

The ultimate goal of science is to understand the natural world in terms of **scientific theories**, concepts based on the conclusions of observations and experiments. In a movie, a detective might claim to have a theory about the crime, or you might say that you have a theory about the win–loss record of your favorite baseball team; but in science, the word theory is reserved for a conceptual scheme supported by a large number of observations and not yet found lacking. Some of the basic theories of biology are as follows:

NAME OF THEORY	EXPLANATION
Cell	All organisms are composed of cells.
Biogenesis	Life comes only from life.
Evolution	All living things have a common ancestor, but each is adapted to a particular way of life.
Gene	Organisms contain coded information that dictates their form, function, and behavior.

Evolution is the unifying concept of biology because it pertains to various aspects of living things. For example, the theory of evolution enables scientists to understand the history of life, the variety of living things, and the anatomy, physiology, and development of organisms—even their behavior. Because the theory of evolution has been supported by so many observations and experiments for over a hundred years, some biologists refer to the **principle** of evolution. They believe this is the appropriate terminology for theories that are generally accepted as valid by an overwhelming number of scientists.

The Scientific Method Has Steps

Scientists, including biologists, employ an approach to gathering information that is known as the **scientific method**. The approach of individual scientists to their work is as varied as they themselves; still, for the sake of discussion, it is possible to speak of the scientific method as consisting of certain steps (Fig. 1.5). After making initial observations, a scientist will most likely study any previous **data**, which are facts pertinent to the matter at hand. Imagination and creative thinking also help a scientist formulate a **hypothesis** that becomes the basis for more observation and/or experimentation. The new data help a scientist come to a **conclusion** that either supports or does not support the hypothesis. Because hypotheses are always subject to modification, they can never be proven true; however, they can be proven untrue—that is, hypotheses are falsifiable. When the hypothesis is not supported by the data, it must be rejected; therefore, some think of the body of science as what is left after alternative hypotheses have been rejected.

Figure 1.5 Flow diagram for the scientific method.
On the basis of observations and previous data, a scientist formulates a hypothesis. The hypothesis is tested by further observations or a controlled experiment, and new data either support or falsify the hypothesis. The return arrow indicates that a scientist often chooses to retest the same hypothesis or to test a related hypothesis. Conclusions from many different but related experiments may lead to the development of a scientific theory. For example, studies in biology of development, anatomy, and fossil remains all support the theory of evolution.

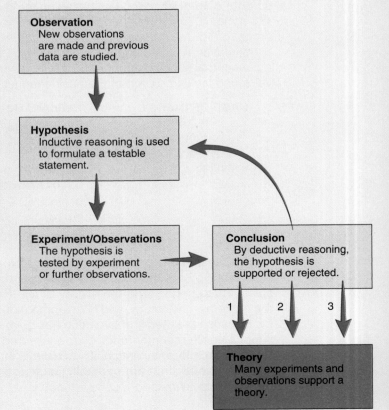

Observation
New observations are made and previous data are studied.

Hypothesis
Inductive reasoning is used to formulate a testable statement.

Experiment/Observations
The hypothesis is tested by experiment or further observations.

Conclusion
By deductive reasoning, the hypothesis is supported or rejected.

1 2 3

Theory
Many experiments and observations support a theory.

The Discovery of Lyme Disease

In order to examine the scientific method in more detail, we will relate how scientists discovered the cause of Lyme disease, a debilitating illness that affects the whole body.

Observation

When Allen C. Steere began his work on Lyme disease in 1975, a number of adults and children in the city of Lyme, Connecticut, had been diagnosed as having rheumatoid arthritis. Steere knew that children rarely get rheumatoid arthritis, so this made him suspicious and he began to make observations. He found that (1) most victims lived in heavily wooded areas, (2) the disease was not contagious—that is, whole groups of people did not come down with Lyme disease, (3) symptoms first appeared in the summer, and (4) several victims remembered a strange bull's-eye rash occurring several weeks before the onset of symptoms.

Hypothesis

Inductive reasoning occurs when you generalize from assorted facts. Steere used inductive reasoning; that is, he put the pieces together to formulate the hypothesis that Lyme disease was caused by a pathogen most likely transmitted by the bite of an insect or a tick (Fig. 1.6).

Deductive reasoning helps scientists decide what further observations and experimentations they will make to test the hypothesis. Deductive reasoning utilizes an "if...then" statement: If Lyme disease is caused by the bite of a tick, then it should be possible to show that a tick carries the pathogen and that the pathogen is in the blood of those who have the disease. However, when Steere tested the blood of Lyme disease victims for the presence of infectious microbes, not a single test was positive. Finally, in 1977, one victim saved the tick that bit him, and it was identified as *Ixodes dammini*, the deer tick. Then Willy Burgdorfer, an authority on tick-borne diseases, was able to isolate a spirochete (spiral bacterium) from deer ticks, and he also found this microbe in the blood of Lyme disease victims. The new spirochete was named *Borrelia burgdorferi*, after Burgdorfer.

Conclusion

The new data collected when Burgdorfer applied deductive reasoning supported the hypothesis and allowed scientists to conclude that Lyme disease is caused by the bacterium *Borrelia burgdorferi* transmitted by the bite of a deer tick.

Even though the scientific method is quite variable, it is possible to point out certain steps that characterize it: making observations, formulating a hypothesis, testing it, and coming to a conclusion.

Figure 1.6   Flow diagram for Lyme disease study.

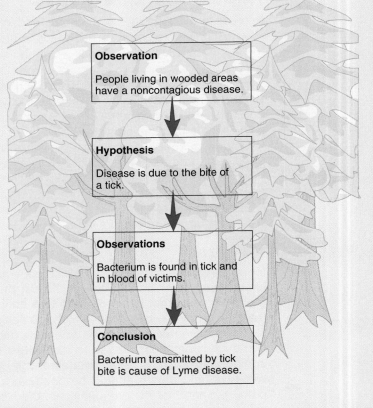

Observation

People living in wooded areas have a noncontagious disease.

Hypothesis

Disease is due to the bite of a tick.

Observations

Bacterium is found in tick and in blood of victims.

Conclusion

Bacterium transmitted by tick bite is cause of Lyme disease.

Reporting the Findings

It is customary to report findings in a scientific journal so that the design and the results of the experiment are available to all. For example, data about tick-borne diseases are often reported in the journal *Clinical Microbiology Review.* It is necessary to give other researchers details on how experiments were conducted because results must be repeatable; that is, other scientists using the same procedures must get the same results. Otherwise, the hypothesis is no longer supported.

Often authors of a report suggest what other types of experiments might clarify or broaden the understanding of the matter under study. People reading the report think of other experiments to do, also. In our example, the bull's-eye rash was later found to be due to the Lyme disease spirochete.

Observations and the results of experiments are published in a journal, where they can be examined. These results are expected to be repeatable; that is, they will be obtained by anyone following the same procedure.

Scientists Use Controlled Experiments

When scientists are studying a phenomenon, they often perform **experiments** in a laboratory where extraneous variables can be eliminated. A **variable** is a factor that can cause an observable change during the progress of an experiment. Experiments are considered more rigorous when they include a control group. A **control group** goes through all the steps of an experiment but lacks the factor or is not exposed to the factor being tested.

Designing the Experiment

Suppose, for example, physiologists want to determine if sweetener S is a safe food additive. On the basis of available information, they formulate a hypothesis that sweetener S is a safe food additive even when it composes up to 50% of dietary intake. Next, they design the experiment described in Figure 1.7 to test the hypothesis.

Test group: 50% of diet is sweetener S

Control group: diet contains no sweetener S

The researchers first place a certain number of randomly chosen inbred (genetically identical) mice into the various groups—say, 100 mice per group. If any of the mice are different from the others, it is hoped random selection

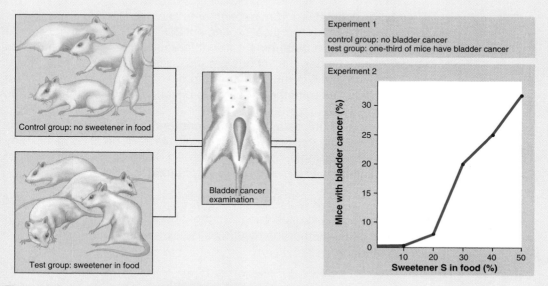

Figure 1.7   Design of a controlled experiment.
Genetically similar mice are randomly divided into a control group and one or more test groups that contain 100 mice each. All groups are exposed to the same conditions, such as cage setup, temperature, and water supply. The control group is not subjected to sweetener S in the food. At the end of the experiment, all mice are examined for bladder cancer. The results of experiment 1 and experiment 2 are shown on the far right.

has distributed them evenly among the groups. The researchers also make sure that all conditions, such as availability of water, cage setup, and temperature of the surroundings, are the same for both groups. The food for each group is exactly the same except for the amount of sweetener S.

At the end of Experiment 1 in Figure 1.7, both groups of mice are to be examined for bladder cancer. Let's suppose that one-third of the mice in the test group are found to have bladder cancer, while none in the control group have bladder cancer. The results of this experiment do not support the hypothesis that sweetener S is a safe food additive when it composes up to 50% of dietary intake.

Continuing the Experiment

Science is ongoing, and one experiment leads to another. Physiologists might now wish to hypothesize that sweetener S is safe if the diet contains a limited amount of sweetener S. They feed sweetener S to groups of mice at ever greater concentrations:

Group 1: diet contains no sweetener S (the control)

Group 2: 5% of diet is sweetener S

Group 3: 10% of diet is sweetener S

↓

Group 11: 50% of diet is sweetener S

Usually, data obtained from experiments such as this are presented in the form of a table or a graph (see Experiment 2, Fig. 1.7). Researchers might run a statistical test to determine if the difference in the number of cases of bladder cancer among the various groups is significant. After all, if a significant number of mice in the control group develop cancer, the results are invalid. Scientists prefer mathematical data because such information lends itself to objectivity.

On the basis of the data, the experimenters try to develop a recommendation concerning the safety of sweetener S in the food of humans. They might caution, for example, that the intake of sweetener S beyond 10% of the diet is associated with too great a risk of bladder cancer.

Scientists often do controlled experiments in the laboratory. The use of a control sample gives assurance that the results of the experiment are due to the variable being tested.

We have seen that scientists often use the scientific method to study the natural world. A particular observation backed up by data collected previously helps them formulate a hypothesis that is then tested. Testing consists of carrying out an experiment or simply making further observations. Particularly, if the experiment is performed in the laboratory, it should contain a control sample. The control sample goes through all the steps of the experiment but lacks the factor or is not exposed to the factor being tested. In this way scientists know that their results are not due to a chance event that has nothing to do with the variable being tested. Finally, scientists come to a conclusion that either supports or rejects the hypothesis. Scientists report their findings in journals that are read by other scientists who also make similar observations or carry on the same experiment. If experiments and observations are not repeatable, the hypothesis is subject to rejection. If use of the scientific method results in conclusions that repeatedly support the same hypothesis, a theory may result.

As time goes by, it is possible that a hypothesis/theory previously accepted by the scientific community will be modified in the light of new investigations. Still, there are certain theories, such as the theory of evolution, that have stood the test of time and are generally accepted as valid.

Scientists ask questions and carry on investigations that pertain to the natural world. The conclusions of these investigations are tentative and subject to change. Eventually, it may be possible to arrive at a theory that is generally accepted by all.

1.3 Science and Social Responsibility

Science is objective and not subjective. Scientists assume that each person is capable of collecting data and seeing natural events in the same objective way. They also assume the same theories and principles are applicable to past, present, and future events. Therefore, science seeks a natural cause for the origin and history of life. Doctrines of creation that have a mythical, philosophical, or theological basis are not a part of science because they are not subject to objective observations and experimentation by all. Many cultures have their own particular set of supernatural beliefs, and various religions within a culture differ as to the application of these beliefs. Such approaches to understanding the world are not within the province of science. Similarly, scientific creationism, which states that God created all species as they are today, cannot be considered science because explanations based on supernatural rather than natural causes involve faith rather than data from experiments.

There are many ways in which science has improved our lives. The discovery of antibiotics, such as penicillin, and of the polio, measles, and mumps vaccines has increased our life span by decades. Cell biology research is helping us understand the causes of cancer. Genetic research has produced new strains of agricultural plants that have eased the burden of feeding our burgeoning world population.

Science also has effects we may find disturbing. For example, it sometimes fosters technologies that can be ecologically disastrous if not controlled properly. Too often we blame science for these developments and think that scientists are duty bound to pursue only those avenues of research that are consistent with our present system of values. But making value judgments is not a part of science. Ethical and moral decisions must be made by all people. The responsibility for how we use the fruits of science, including a given technology, must rest with people from all walks of life, not with scientists alone.

Scientists should provide the public with as much information as possible when such issues as the use of atomic energy, fetal research, and genetic engineering are being debated. Then they, along with other citizens, can help make decisions about the future role of these technologies in our society. This text, while covering all aspects of biology, focuses on human biology. It is hoped that your study of biology will enable you to make wise decisions regarding your own individual well-being and the well-being of all species, including our own.

It is the task of all persons to use scientific information as they make value judgments about their own lives and about the environment.

Credits

Chapter 1

Fig. 1.1 NTL Institute for Applied Behavioral Science, 300 N. Lee Street, Suite 300, Alexandria, VA 2234. 1-800-777-5227. Reprinted with permission.

p. 21 Alison Kafer, "Letting Justice Flow" from *That Takes Ovaries!* Edited by Rivka Solomon. Copyright © 2002 by Rivka Solomon. Used by permission of Three Rivers Press, a division of Random House, Inc.

p. 27 James Alexander Thom, "The Perfect Picture," *Reader's Digest*, August 1976. Copyright © 1976 Reader's Digest Association, Inc. Reprinted with permission.

Chapter 2

pp. 37, 38 J. Halonen & J. Santrock, *Psychology: Contexts and Applications*. Copyright © 1999 The McGraw-Hill Companies, Inc. Used with permission of The McGraw-Hill Companies.

p. 38 R. Nichols, *The American Indian*. Copyright © 1999 The McGraw-Hill Companies, Inc. Used with permission of The McGraw-Hill Companies.

p. 49 Conrad Kottak, *Cultural Anthropology*, p. 225. Copyright © 2002 The McGraw-Hill Companies, Inc. Used with permission of The McGraw-Hill Companies.

p. 55 Richard Lederer, Introduction (pp. xxi-xxiii) from *The Highly Selective Dictionary for the Extraordinarily Literate* by Eugene Ehrlich. Copyright © 1997 by Eugene Ehrlich. Reprinted by permission of HarperCollins Publishers, Inc.

p. 60 Gillian Silverman, "It's a Bird, It's a Plane, It's Plagiarism Buster!" *Newsweek*, 7/15/02. Copyright © 2002 Newsweek, Inc. All rights reserved. Reprinted by permission.

p. 65 Patricia O'Connor, from "Verbal Abuse" in *Woe is I: The Grammarphobe's Guide in Plain English*. Copyright © 1996 by Patricia O'Connor. Used by permission of Grosset & Dunlap, Inc., a division of Penguin Group (USA) Inc.

Chapter 3

p. 88 Memory Process Letter Grid by J. Zadina. Copyright © J. Zadina. Used by permission of the author.

p. 88 A. Getis et al., *Introduction to Geography, 8th Edition*, p. 60. Copyright © 2002 The McGraw-Hill Companies, Inc. Used with permission of The McGraw-Hill Companies.

p. 96 D. Gumpert, *How to Really Start Your Own Business*. Copyright © 1994 Business Innovator Group Resources. Used with permission.

p. 104 Dave Barry, *Dave Barry Hits Below the Beltway*. Copyright © 2001 by Dave Barry. Used by permission of Random House, Inc.

Chapter 4

T 4.1, 4.4 J. Kollaritsch, *Reading & Study Organization Methods for Higher Learning, Fourth Edition*. Copyright © 1990 Wadsworth Publishing. Reprinted with permission from Thomson Learning.

p. 119 R. DiYanni & P. Hoy, *The Scribner Handbook for Writers*, Allyn & Bacon, 1995, pp. 147-148. Reprinted by permission of Pearson Education, Inc.

p 120 D. Zill, *Calculus, Third Edition*, PWS Publishing, 1992, pp. 15-16. © 1992 Dennis Zill.

p. 120 Reprinted with the permission of Scribner, an imprint of Simon & Schuster Adult Publishing Group from *Everything's Eventual: 14 Dark Tales* by Stephen King. Copyright © 2002 by Stephen King.

p. 125 Alexa Albert, *Brothel: Mustang Ranch and Its Women*. Copyright © 2001 by Alexa Albert. Used by permission of Random House, Inc.

p. 131 Reprinted with the permission of Scribner, an imprint of Simon & Schuster Adult Publishing Group from *Angela's Ashes* by Frank McCourt. Copyright © 1996 by Frank McCourt.

Chapter 5

p. 143 William Nickels, *Understanding Business*, p. 493. Copyright © 2002 The McGraw-Hill Companies, Inc. Used with permission of The McGraw-Hill Companies.

pp. 144, 150, 153 Sylvia Mader, *Human Biology*, p. 215. Copyright © 2002 The McGraw-Hill Companies, Inc. Used with permission of the McGraw-Hill Companies.

p. 388 Neil King, Jr. & Robert Guy, "So Far, Steel Tariffs Do Little of What President Envisioned," *Wall Street Journal*, 9/13/02, pp. 1 and 12. Copyright © 2002 Dow Jones & Co., Inc. Used with permission.

T 11.16 and p. 381 from R. Feldman, "Biomedical Therapy" from *Understanding Psychology, Sixth Edition*, pp. 520, 519-522. Copyright © 1990 The McGraw-Hill Companies, Inc. Used with permission of The McGraw-Hill Companies.

Fig. 11.17 Figure from "Antidepressants: Choices and Controversy," *Health News*, June 2000. Content © 1999 Massachusetts Medical Society. Published by Englander Communications LLC, an affiliate of Belvoir Publications, Inc. Reprinted with permission.

Chapter 12

p. 395 A. Harnadek, *Critical Thinking Book*. Copyright © 1976 Midwest Publishing Co.

pp. 402, 410 Diane Papalia, *Human Development*, pp. 139, 635. Copyright © 2001 The McGraw-Hill Companies, Inc. Used with permission of The McGraw-Hill Companies.

p. 403 Sister Souljah, *No Disrespect*. Copyright © 1994 by Sister Souljah. Used by permission of Times Books, a division of Random House, Inc.

p. 416 W. Shively, *Power & Choice: An Introduction to Political Science*, p. 204. Copyright © 1999 The McGraw-Hill Companies, Inc. Used with permission of The McGraw-Hill Companies.

p. 416 T. Patterson, *The American Democracy*, p. 498. Copyright © 1999 The McGraw-Hill Companies, Inc. Used with permission of The McGraw-Hill Companies.

p. 423 N'Gai Croal, "Down and Dirtier," *Newsweek*, 3/18/02. Copyright © 2002 Newsweek, Inc. All rights reserved. Reprinted by permission.

p. 427 David Horowitz, "Racial Paranoia" from *Hating Whitey and Other Progressive Causes*, pp. 17-22, Dallas: Spence Publishing, 1999. Used with permission.

Chapter 13

p. 436 Roald Dahl, *Boy: Tales of Childhood*, pp. 91-92. Copyright © 1984 by Roald Dahl. Reprinted by permission of Farrar, Straus and Giroux, LLC.

p. 443 Natalie Goldberg, *Writing Down the Bones: Freeing the Writer Within*, pp. 87-88. Copyright © 1986 Shambhala Publications, Inc. Used with permission.

p. 446 Gregg Easterbrook, "Abortion and Brain Waves," *Best American Science and Nature Writing*, Edward Wilson ed., p. 24. Copyright © 2001 Gregg Easterbrook. Used with permission from the author.

p. 447 Reprinted with permission of Atria Books, an imprint of Simon & Schuster Adult Publishing Group, from *See, I Told You So* by Rush Limbaugh. Copyright © 1993 by Rush H. Limbaugh III.

p. 449 Dave Barry, *Dave Barry Hits Below the Beltway*, pp. 5-6. Copyright © 2001 by Dave Barry. Used by permission of Random House, Inc.

p. 453 Diane Papalia, *Human Development*, p. 383. Copyright © 2001 The McGraw-Hill Companies, Inc. Used with permission of The McGraw-Hill Companies.

p. 455 T. Patterson, *The American Democracy*, p. 534. Copyright © 1999 The McGraw-Hill Companies, Inc. Used with permission of The McGraw-Hill Companies.

p. 456 Sanjay Gupta, "The Chemistry of Love" *Time*, February 18, 2002. Copyright © 2002 Time Inc. Reprinted by permission.

p. 460 Mary Seymour, "Call Me Crazy, But I Have to be Myself," *Newsweek*, 7/29/02. Copyright © 2002 Newsweek, Inc. All rights reserved. Reprinted by permission.

p. 466 Susan Tifft with Bruce Henderson and Julie Johnson, "Fighting the Failure Syndrome," *Time*, 5/21/90. Copyright © 1990 Time, Inc. Reprinted by permission.

Chapter 14

p. 487 © 2003 Media Awareness Network Canada, www.media-awareness.ca. Reprinted with permission.

p. 492 Jeannett Lauer & Robert Lauer, *Marriage and the Family: The Quest for Intimacy, Third Edition*, Chapter 6, pp. 124, 127, 130, 134, 135, 140, 141. Copyright © 1997 The McGraw-Hill Companies, Inc. Reprinted with permission from The McGraw-Hill Companies.

p. 503 Sylvia Mader, *Human Biology, Seventh Edition*, Chapter 1, pp. 1-10. Copyright © 2002 The McGraw-Hill Companies, Inc. Reprinted with permission from The McGraw-Hill Companies.

Index